THE POMP AND POLITICS
OF PATRIOTISM

CENTRAL EUROPEAN STUDIES

Series Editors

Gary B. Cohen

Charles W. Ingrao

THE POMP AND POLITICS
OF PATRIOTISM

Imperial Celebrations in Habsburg Austria,
1848–1916

Daniel L. Unowsky

Purdue University Press
West Lafayette, Indiana

Printed in the United States of America

Library of Congress Cataloging-in-Publication Data
Unowsky, Daniel L., 1966-
The pomp and politics of patriotism : imperial celebrations in Habsburg
Austria, 1848-1916 / Daniel L. Unowsky.
    p. cm. -- (Central European studies)
Includes bibliographical references and index.
ISBN 1-55753-400-4 (pbk.)
    1. Franz Joseph I, Emperor of Austria, 1830-1916--Portraits. 2. National
characteristics, Austrian--History. 3. Austria--History--1848-1867.
4. Austria--History--1867-1918. I. Title. II. Series.
DB87.U64 2005
943.6'044--dc22
                                                                                2005005570

C O N T E N T S

List of Illustrations   vii

Acknowledgments   ix

Foreword   xi

INTRODUCTION   1
Nationalism and Imperial Celebration   3
The Imperial Image   7

CHAPTER 1   Reasserting Empire: Court and Dynasty
            after the Revolutions of 1848–1849   11
The Expression of Herrschaft   12
Neoabsolutism and the Revival of the Imperial Court   19
Catholic Rituals   26

CHAPTER 2   Nasz Pan Kajzer: Imperial Inspection Tours
            of Galicia 1851, 1868   33
Habsburg Galicia   34
1851—Supporting the Monarchical Principle   37
1851—The Triumphant Procession   40
Evaluating the 1851 Kaiserreise   42
1868   46

CHAPTER 3   The Ideal Monarchy: Galicia, 1880 and 1894   52
Setting the Stage   53
Orchestrating Patriotism   55
Interpreting the Kaiserreise   58
Presenting the Emperor/Representing Galicia–Cracow   60
Franz Joseph in Lemberg: Conservative Hegemony Challenged   64
The Stańczyk Achievement   70
Franz Joseph and the 1894 Galician Provincial Exhibition   72

CHAPTER 4   Imagining Austria: The Cult of the
            Emperor during the Great Jubilee Year of 1898   77
Spectacular Imperial Celebrations, 1854–1888   79
Parliamentary Paralysis   81
Staging Patriotism: The Court and the 1898 Jubilee   82
The Death of the Empress   88

Jubilee Message from the Catholic Hierarchy   94
The Pillar of the Regime: The Armed Forces and the Jubilee   97
Pushing Patriotism: The Cisleithanian Government
and the 1898 Jubilee   101
The Imperial Family and Dynastic Patriotism   105

CHAPTER 5   Consuming the Emperor: Charity, Jubilee Kitsch,
            Popular Celebration, and Provincial Festivities   113
Giving in the Name of the Emperor   115
Buying and Selling the Emperor   120
Reading about the Emperor   127
Local Jubilee Celebrations   138

CHAPTER 6   Monopolizing Patriotism: Vienna,
            Karl Lueger, and the 1898 Jubilee   145
The Liberal City and Imperial Celebrations   146
Sharpening the Christian Social Message   149
The Christian Social Jubilee   152
Christian Social Lessons in Patriotism   155
Completing the Program   161
The 1898 Kaiser Jubilee Exhibition in Vienna   164

CONCLUSION   175
Notes   185
Abbreviations   241
Bibliography   243
Index   263

LIST OF ILLUSTRATIONS

Figure 1:   Marzipan Kaiser from Demel   1
Figure 2:   Trinity Monument in Vienna's Graben   14
Figure 3:   Baroque Altar in Karlskirche   14
Figure 4:   Sarcophagus of Maria Theresa and Franz Stephan   18
Figure 5:   Sarcophagus of Joseph II   18
Figure 6:   The Foot-washing Ceremony in the
            Ceremonial Hall of the Hofburg   30
Figure 7:   Corpus Christi Procession in Vienna, 1894   31
Figure 8:   Entrance of Franz Joseph into Lemberg   42
Figure 9:   *Entrance of His Majesty the Emperor into Cracow*   62
Figure 10: *Harvest Procession before His Majesty
            the Emperor on the Market Square in Cracow*   63
Figure 11: *His Majesty the Emperor in the Building
            of the Provincial Diet*   66
Figure 12: *The Welcoming of His Majesty the Emperor
            in the Greek Catholic Cathedral St. George*   69
Figure 13: Adam Sapieha Greets Franz Joseph
            at the Galician Exhibition   74
Figure 14: Unveiling of the Maria Theresa Monument   80
Figure 15: Maria Theresa Monument   80
Figure 16: Kaiser Jubilee Church   92
Figure 17: Elisabeth Frieze on the Jubilee Church   93
Figure 18: Jubilee Commemorative Medal
            for the Armed Forces, 1898   100
Figure 19: Kaiser Jubilee Fest-Blatt   104
Figure 20: The Kaiser and His Grandchildren   107
Figure 21: The Emperor at His Desk   107
Figure 22: *The Prince of Peace*   108
Figure 23: Title Page, *Viribus Unitis*   109
Figure 24: Hymn, *Viribus Unitis*   109
Figure 25: Illustration, *Viribus Unitis*   109
Figure 26: Cover of Luxury Edition, *Viribus Unitis*   110
Figure 27: Title Page, *Franz Joseph und seine Zeit*   110
Figure 28: Illustration, *Franz Joseph und seine Zeit*   110
Figure 29: Franz Joseph Portrait Bust, Postsparkasse, Vienna   111
Figure 30: Flyer for the Savings Association
            and Smoking Club "Nicotine"   120
Figure 31: 1854 Ceramic Portrait Busts of
            Franz Joseph and Elisabeth   122

Figure 32:   1879 Bronze Portrait Bust of Franz Joseph   123
Figure 33:   1879 Bronze Portrait Bust of Elisabeth   123
Figure 34:   Advertisement for Kaiser-Jubilee-Bitter   125
Figure 35:   1908 Jubilee Postcard   126
Figure 36:   1898 Jubilee Stamps   126
Figure 37:   Window of a Vienna Antique Shop, 1997   127
Figure 38:   Elisabeth Arrives at Nußdorf   128
Figure 39:   Archduke Franz Joseph Plays with Toy Soldiers:
              Portrait as a Small Child   130
Figure 40:   *The Constitutional Emperor of Austria, etc. 1848*   130
Figure 41:   Title Page, *Unser Kaiser*   132
Figure 42:   Title Page, *Nasz Cesarz*   132
Figure 43:   Cover Page, *Kaiserblatt*   136
Figure 44:   Cover Page, *Unsere Monarchie*   138
Figure 45:   Cover, Address of Congratulations from Nadworna   139
Figure 46:   Address of Congratulations from Nadworna   139
Figure 47:   "Train Group," 1879 Festzug   148
Figure 48:   1898 Procession of the Children   159
Figure 49:   1898 Kaiser Jubilee Exhibition, Prater Park   165
Figure 50:   Pavilion of the City of Vienna   168
Figure 51:   Opening of the Kaiser Jubilee Exhibition   169
Figure 52:   Karl Lueger and the Vienna
              Christian Women's Association Greet Franz Joseph   169
Figure 53:   Hubert Frankel Raises the Jubilee Banner   170
Figure 54:   Jubilee Giant Barrel   171
Figure 55:   Main Street of the Jubilee Exhibition with
              Bosnian Pavilion   171
Figure 56:   Franz Joseph's Funeral Procession Leaving the Hofburg   176
Figure 57:   1908 Address from Confectioner Julius Hava   178
Figure 58:   Harvest in Podolia, 1908 Kaiser-Huldigungs-Festzug   178

ACKNOWLEDGMENTS

It is a true pleasure to thank those who contributed in various ways to this project. Without them this book would not exist in its present form.

I am very grateful to the following institutions for providing funding during various stages of this project: the Department of History of the University of Memphis, the University of Memphis Faculty Research Grant Fund, Columbia University, the Joint Committee on Eastern Europe of the American Council of Learned Societies and the Social Science Research Council, the International Research and Exchange Board, and the Austrian Exchange Service (ÖAD).

Many librarians and archivists helped with photographs, archival guides, German handwriting, and many other matters. In Austria, I thank the staffs of the House, Court, and State Archives, the General Administrative Archives, the Vienna City and Provincial Archives, the Vienna City and Provincial Library, the Austrian National Library (from the reading room staff to the curators of the Bildarchiv), and the Lower Austrian Provincial Archives. I am also grateful to the Jagiellonian University Library, the State Archive and the National Museum in Cracow, the Ossolineum in Wrocław, Poland, as well as the Central State Archive, the Stefanyk Library, and the Scientific Library of the Iv. Franko State University in L'viv for their professional and friendly assistance. At Columbia University, I wish to thank the department of history, the Institute on East Central Europe, and the Butler Library.

Colleagues in Austria, Poland, and Ukraine were generous with their time and hospitality. I am grateful to Ernst Aichinger of the Austrian Exchange Service for his advice and encouragement. Professor Horst Haselsteiner graciously invited me to present my work and to participate in his Ph.D. seminar. I thank him for his introduction to Vienna. I deeply regret that I cannot share my work with the late Zbigniew Fras, professor of history at the University of Wrocław, who shared friendship and his work on Franz Joseph's inspection tours of Galicia with me.

Innumerable discussions, letters, and e-mails about history, research, scholarship, academics, and life with colleagues and friends transformed what might have been a lonely process into a rewarding experience. I thank Hugh Agnew, Ian Beilin, the late Stanislaw Blejwas, Marek Chodakiewicz, Gary Cohen, Patrice Dabrowski, Alice Freifeld, William D. Godsey, Jr., Atina Grossmann, Mark von Hagen, John-Paul Himka, Charles Ingrao, Jeremy King, Victor Hugo Lane IV, Peter Lindseth, Olga Litvak, Joe Meisel, Cynthia Paces, Alon Rachamimov, Ostap

Sereda, Viktoria Sereda, Nancy Sinkoff, Michael Stanislawski, Keely Stauter-Halsted, Philipp Ther, Claire Venghiatis, and Anna Veronika Wendland. Pieter Judson, Marsha Rozenblit, Nancy Wingfield, and Richard Wortman commented on sections and chapters, leading to numerous improvements and corrections. I am especially grateful for their support.

I owe a special thanks to Harald Binder and Laurence Cole. Their own work greatly influenced the writing of this book, and their support for and critiques of the manuscript proved invaluable. More importantly, the friendship of the Binders and the Perfahl-Coles helped make memorable the years of research in Vienna, Poland, and Ukraine as well as visits to France, Germany, Great Britain, and Italy.

István Deák, my teacher at Columbia University, inspired my interest in East Central Europe, the Habsburg Monarchy, nationalism, and dynastic patriotism. The subject of this book owes its genesis to a conversation we had at a small diner in Morningside Heights. Even before that moment and many times in the following years, he offered insights into history, research, and writing that have shaped my approach as a historian. His unwavering confidence in this project and his critical guidance informs every page of this book.

Finally, I dedicate this book to Keri and to our beloved children, Sarah and Micah, for love, patience, and everything.

FOREWORD

Scholars in other fields have often complained of the heavy emphasis on politics and the state in Central European historiography, but the strong focus on the decline and eventual collapse of the Habsburg Monarchy at the end of the nineteenth century has resulted, in fact, in serious neglect of the state's actual role in society and everyday life and the significance of its symbols in popular culture. This book makes an important contribution to a body of new scholarship that has begun to re-examine the functioning of the Habsburg state during the last decades before World War I and the place of its institutions, laws, and symbols in popular loyalties. Recently historians have found that the Habsburg Monarchy was able to function in many ways as an active, dynamic force in politics and society and to continue to command popular assent.

Conventional older historical accounts focused on the inexorable rise of nationalist movements and contending mass parties in late nineteenth-century Austria which seemingly sapped loyalties to an antiquated dynastic state. The decades before 1914 were, in this view, a period of growing national and class conflicts which could not be accommodated, let alone resolved, by a rigid state structure whose core traditions were those of dynastic loyalty and bureaucratic absolutism. In this narrative, epitomized in the English-language literature by A. J. P. Taylor's classic *The Habsburg Monarchy, 1809–1918: A History of the Austrian Empire and Austria-Hungary* (London, 1948), the confrontation between the seemingly irresistible forces of contending national and class-based parties and the immovable object of the dynastic state resulted in growing tendencies toward political anarchy. Political stalemate left the state bureaucracy to govern by administrative fiat in the name of the emperor.

In the last quarter century, scholars such as John W. Boyer, Lothar Höbelt, T. Mills Kelly, Jeremy King, and Jiří Malíř, among others, have begun to present a different, more complex picture in which the politics of the competing nationalist forces and the rising mass-based parties in imperial Austria played out within the dynamic framework of a developing civil society and evolving modern representative and administrative structures. The developing modern forms of political engagement and the state structures which dealt with them reflected, in turn, the needs of an increasingly urbanized, industrialized, and literate society. While the political parties and interest groups of the late nineteenth century brought their deep conflicts into the representative bodies and their dealings with the state bureaucracy, they directed much of their real political energy, in fact, to advancing their respective causes within existing structures. In the Austrian crown lands, the autonomous communal and provincial representative bodies and even the oft-maligned parliament developed roots in the popular political culture and strongly engaged the concerns and efforts of the parties and interest groups. Within institutional frameworks created or sanctioned by the Habsburg state, the political forces based in society participated in complex webs of negotiation with their erstwhile political rivals and with the state bureaucracy for the prizes of legislation, appointments and office holding, and benefits to their constituents from the provision of modern public services. Although the political arena saw intense contestation, the socially based political forces, autonomous communal and provincial authorities, state officials, and the emperor all engaged in a complex of negotiated political processes that were by no means always fruitless.

Daniel L. Unowsky's book offers us new insights into the significance for popular loyalties and political culture of the figure of the emperor and the state that he symbolized. Older historical narratives typically acknowledged popular loyalties to the emperor and the efforts of the central state authorities to use imperial visits and celebrations to affirm and strengthen popular support for the state. Nonetheless, historians commonly presented public respect for Emperor Francis Joseph as a traditional residue, which attached ever more narrowly to the person of an aged, old-fashioned monarch and after the 1890s had declining political valence for assuring popular loyalty to the state. Examining ceremonial visits of the emperor and celebrations of imperial jubilees both in the imperial capital and in a remote crown land such as Galicia, Unowsky depicts just how important and meaningful such events were and remained for both the Habsburg state and local political interests. The state, of course, wanted to maximize opportunities for mass public displays of affection for the emperor and the state which he headed; and in the 1860s, 1870s, 1880s, and into the 1890s the state authorities often proved highly resourceful and effective in staging such events. As Unowsky shows, however, the local political forces also proved highly adept in using the same celebrations to express, along with loyalty to the emperor, those forces' own political strength, interests, and aspirations. The efforts at staging and political representation thus came from both the state authorities and from the political forces based in society at large. The imperial visits and celebrations were very much part of a negotiated political theater of the everyday, and, as Unowsky shows, demonstrations of support for nationalist and other divisive political causes often accompanied the expressions of loyalty to the emperor and the Habsburg state as part of the normal order of public life.

The vigor and vitality of imperial rituals may have declined in the last years before 1914, and partisan political contention showed through the huge, elaborate festivities for the emperor's jubilee in 1908. Nonetheless, participation and belief in the value—or better, the usefulness—of such celebrations remained high, both on the part of the state officialdom and among popularly based political forces.

This book offers us new vistas of the processes for constructing modern civil society, its relationship to state institutions, and the modes of political discourse and representation in late imperial Austria, which involved organized political forces, the populace, and the state as well.

Gary B. Cohen
Series Editor

Introduction

In late December 1908, the governor of Galicia authorized the police in Lemberg/Lwów/L'viv,[1] the administrative capital of this Habsburg province, to convey an important message from the imperial-royal court in Vienna to Lemberg confectioner Władysław Podhalicz. The grand chamberlain wrote in reference to a creation produced by Podhalicz's first assistant in honor of the imperial jubilee. The candy-making apprentice had requested that the court chancellery accept in the name of the emperor "an ardent homage from a worker": a half-meter-tall portrait bust of Franz Joseph "according to the judgment of experts, very artistically successful," carved from a "chocolate mass." The grand chamberlain advised, however, that Podhalicz not send the chocolate Kaiser to Vienna, perhaps fearing the effects of the long journey on the edible imperial effigy. Podhalicz and his assistant had to be satisfied with an imperial acknowledgment and thanks for their "patriotic intentions."[2] (Figure 1 shows the marzipan Franz Joseph displayed in 1997 in the window of the venerable Vienna *Konditorei* Demel, no doubt almost as "artistically successful" as the chocolate Kaiser formed in Podhalicz's shop in Lemberg in 1908.)

Podhalicz's was only one of hundreds of requests to have goods, publications, and artistic creations accepted by the Habsburg court as patriotic gifts to the emperor on the occasion of imperial celebrations, an honor often emphasized in subsequent advertisements for the sale of such products to the general public.[3]

Figure 1: Marzipan Kaiser from Demel, photograph by author.

1

Millions of citizens expressed their loyalty to dynasty and fatherland in other ways. Every year on Franz Joseph's 18 August birthday and on other great imperial occasions, army bands paraded through the streets of towns and villages, awakening the population (as early as 4:30 A.M.) with the sounds of military marches. Emperor Franz Joseph's subjects packed churches, mosques, and synagogues to capacity for special ceremonies during which clergy praised the qualities of the ruler and the ruling house, tying patriotism and dynastic loyalty to religious duty. Huge crowds prayed for the emperor's health and sang the *Gott erhalte,* the state hymn, in Czech, Polish, German, Ukrainian and other languages. Habsburg subjects attended local festivities and read newspaper editorials narrating the heroic history of the dynasty and calling for an increase in devotion to the ruling house. By the late nineteenth century, portraits of the emperor, often purchased during imperial jubilee or birthday festivities, had become ubiquitous features in mansions, middle-class homes, and peasant huts, reminders of the benevolent imperial personage, the father-figure who aimed to satisfy the needs of all of his faithful subjects.

During Franz Joseph's reign as emperor (1848–1916), political leaders, parties, and notables throughout the monarchy sought to define themselves as the true voices of their respective national communities and to claim exclusive status as guardians of the national interest. Self-designated leaders endeavored to mark physical space as national—districts, cities, squares, cemeteries, dance floors—through public celebration and political ritual. The opening of new museums, unveiling of statues, and organizing of parades, picnics, banquets, and gatherings were intended to root the idea of the nation in the topography of the nation's supposed territorial home.[4] The seemingly coherent national narratives presented at such celebrations elided the messy, confusing, and jumbled past of multiple identities and alienated social orders.[5]

The Habsburg dynasty, however, did not leave the field of public symbolic action to the newcomers on the stage. Nationalist celebrations of events and heroes significant to the development of particular "nations" took place in the context of ongoing and expanding monarchical self-representation. The same decades that witnessed an increase in national conflict were also marked by an outpouring of public expressions of dynastic loyalty.

This study of Habsburg imperial celebration looks at the creation, dissemination, and reception of the image of Emperor Franz Joseph as a symbol of common identity within the Austrian half of the Habsburg Monarchy (Cisleithania). In the second half of the nineteenth century and the first decades of the twentieth century, usually characterized as a period of national conflict and political paralysis, the promotion of the cult of the emperor by central authorities and regional political groupings reinforced and deepened a Cisleithania-wide culture of imperial celebration. This book concentrates on the official presentation of the imperial cult, as well as on the use or rejection of the image of the emperor by regional social and ethnic factions. By looking at both the production of the cult of the emperor and its reception, I analyze the tension between national and supra-national identity in an age of expanding political participation.

The anthropologist Clifford Geertz asserts that monarchical celebrations were intended to display and define "the inherent sacredness of sovereign power." Geertz argues that "coronations, limousines and conferences mark the center as center and give what goes on there its aura of being not merely important but in some odd fashion connected with the way the world is built."[6] Under Franz Joseph, Habsburg imperial celebrations marked the center as center. Organizers of official imperial festivities adapted traditional Habsburg symbols and ceremonial forms to present the emperor as a binding force in this multinational state. Imperial celebrations did not seek to efface national identity; instead, official festivities defined national identity as a constituent element of a broader identification with the emperor-father and, through him, with "Austria." Dynastic patriotism and national belonging were presented as mutually reinforcing rather than mutually exclusive. The ability of the center to control the meaning of Habsburg patriotism was limited, however. Constitutional rule, increasing ethnic tensions, economic development, and the political mobilization of ever-larger sections of society did open the image of the good emperor to widely varying interpretations.

Nationalism and Imperial Celebration

Until recently, scholarship on the Habsburg Monarchy has largely focused on what historians Gary Cohen, James Shedel, and others have dubbed the Habsburg *Sonderweg*.[7] Surveys of the last two centuries of the monarchy's existence, as well as numerous more specialized studies, catalogue the moments when key institutions or social groups—state/government/dynasty/middle classes—strayed from the path leading toward modernization and instead traveled the road to inevitable self-destruction: the loss of Silesia to Frederick the Great; the incomplete state-building program of Maria Theresa and Joseph II; the failure of the "bourgeois" revolutions of 1848–49; the refusal of the dynasty to cut its losses in Italy; the attempt to play a dominant role in the German lands out of touch with the true strength of the state; the dynasty's suspicion of constitutional rule; and the 1867 *Ausgleich* (Compromise) which enabled the Hungarian gentry to oppress national minorities. More than any other single factor, historians have blamed the decline and dissolution of the monarchy on the failure of the Habsburg state to ameliorate nationality conflicts. For these historians, the greater the success of the so-called national awakeners among the many "historic" and "unhistoric" nations inhabiting this multinational conglomerate, the weaker the cohesion of the monarchy itself.[8]

Studies of national identity and nationalism by Miroslav Hroch, Ernest Gellner, Benedict Anderson, Eric Hobsbawm, and others bolster this "inevitability" thesis of Habsburg decay and eventual dissolution by naturalizing nations.[9] Nationalists themselves always argue for historical continuity and claim to speak on behalf of eternally existing national communities; scholars are almost as unanimous in emphasizing the essential novelty of nationalism in European history. These theorists of nations and nationalism, though differing in many key respects, concur that nationalism and national identity are phenomena closely related to the "modernization" process. They argue that print capitalism, the growth of state school systems, rising literacy rates, urbanization, and the increasing need for standardization in capitalist society forged "enduring collectivities," spurring on national consciousness and nationalism.[10] The Habsburg state, experiencing economic growth and associated social dislocation in the second half of the nineteenth century, could not escape this trajectory. Nor could the Habsburgs easily create a new, all-Habsburg national identity. Anthony Smith, a critic of "social constructivist" theories of nations, argues that nations can only be formed "within a pre-existing framework of collective loyalties and identities."[11]

Theorists of imperial decline also emphasize the role of nationalism in the demise of the Habsburg Monarchy. They posit that all territorially contiguous empires, like the Habsburg Monarchy, sow the seeds of their own destruction and are destined for the dustbin of history. Imperial overextension weakens the ability of the center to extract sufficient information and resources from the periphery. The imperial center has few choices aside from devolving some of its power and functions to the provinces. Agents of the imperial government and local elites often turn to nationalism as an ideology of struggle for local rights and privileges against the imperial occupier. Eventually, the balance of power shifts away from the central government, which is no longer able to exert control over the provinces. In a time of crisis, the brittle imperial bonds shatter.[12]

Yet late Habsburg history is not simply the history of inevitable decline. The monarchy did in fact survive and by many indications flourish until dismantled after four years of the most devastating war that had up to then ever been experienced. John Boyer, historian of Austria's Christian Social movement, has suggested that

> Rather than emphasizing the themes of decline and disintegration in the monarchy's (and Vienna's) final decades, it may be just as appropriate to explore those features of the imperial political system, which contributed to its stability and functionality, however marginal.[13]

Recent studies have highlighted trends and events that bolstered state cohesion and imperial loyalties and facilitated the formation of more advanced economic, educational, and even governmental structures that addressed the problems of a society experiencing industrialization, migration, and agricultural change.[14] Economic transformations did lead to peasants' and workers' movements and a radicalization of politics; yet the very diversity of the monarchy's regional political structures allowed for alternative routes to the definition of national identity, some compatible with imperial loyalty.[15] Non-national identities (religious, local, imperial) also persisted and often proved resistant to nationalization.[16]

Boyer's point is of particular relevance to the figure of Franz Joseph, given that his place in an ongoing political theater promoting loyalty to dynasty and fatherland was more than a "marginal" factor in the political culture of the monarchy. The Habsburg state came into being as the *Hausmacht* of the dynasty, and, in response to the revolutions of 1848–49 and to the later transformations of society wrought by agricultural and industrial advance, the dynasty and its supporters—government, nobility, church, army—took steps to publicly demonstrate the continued relevance of the dynasty to the lives of all its subjects.

The Habsburgs and their supporters were, of course, not alone in redefining and expanding the role of royalty in the creation of state-oriented political identities in the second half of the nineteenth century. The four or five decades preceding World War I witnessed what Eric Hobsbawm termed the "invention of tradition" on a massive scale.[17] Many European states introduced public holidays and built monuments venerating the ruling house and cultivating state and dynastic loyalty. Sponsors of dynastic celebrations often competed with national movements that commemorated events of allegedly crucial significance in the development of the nation and extolled national rather than dynastic heroes. During dynastic celebrations, government figures, aristocrats, and members of the ruling houses themselves equated national and state interests in order to counter and to harness popular nationalism.

The public presentation of the Habsburg dynasty contrasted sharply with that of its dynastic peers. Imperial celebrations portrayed Franz Joseph as the embodiment of the state. However, unlike Great Britain's Queen Victoria, Franz Joseph retained significant power within the constitutional system; he was not merely a "media monarch," important as a symbolic representation of the state but removed from all responsibility for everyday politics.[18] At the same time, the Habsburgs could not claim to embody the spirit of any single dominant nation within the state—as did the Hohenzollern emperors of the new German nation-state after 1871 and, in very different ways, Russia's Romanov tsars after the assassination of Alexander II—without alienating the non-German majority in the monarchy.[19] In any case, such an association of the dynasty with the interests of a "nation" would have been an admission that sovereignty arises from the people independently of the historic rights of the dynasty, an unlikely concession from this most traditional of ruling families.

Despite this inherent conservatism, the Habsburgs and their supporters presented the emperor as a living symbol of a "traditional" (in comparison with newfangled nationalism) patriotism that could exist above national identity. In his classic account of the centripetal and centrifugal forces acting on the monarchy, Oscar Jaszi charged that the dynasty and government did little to counter forces of separatism:

> The real outstanding and fundamental question of the monarchy, how to satisfy the different national and cultural claims of the various nationalities in such a way as to give them ample possibilities to develop their historical individuality and consciousness but at the same time to build up a super-national consciousness of a state solidarity among them, this question . . . with very few exceptions, was not even perceived or formulated.[20]

Oscar Jaszi may have been correct that the monarchy never developed a systematic civic education in constitutional and state patriotism. Yet the imperial court and the Cisleithanian government did find ways to drill the population in devotion to emperor and fatherland—a fatherland defined by its association with the long-ruling Habsburg dynasty. The emperor's birthday, the Corpus Christi procession, imperial inspection tours, jubilee celebrations, and other imperial festivities became opportunities for reminding the multinational population of the common bond to the emperor and "Austria."

Historians, sociologists, and anthropologists continue to write extensively on various aspects of Europe's late-medieval, renaissance, and baroque courts.[21] The persistence of court ritual and ceremony, the presentation of the royal house as a symbol of state unity, and the use of royal imagery by competing political groupings in the nineteenth and twentieth centuries have received less scholarly attention.[22] This gap is all the more glaring in the case of the Habsburg Monarchy, a heterogeneous patchwork of territories acquired largely through the ambitious marriage politics of the ruling house. Studies of the late Habsburg court tend to concentrate on the history of the court administration and the development of the imperial museums and theaters.[23] The handful of works that consider Franz Joseph's imperial progresses as well as spectacular imperial celebrations like the 1879 historical procession in honor of the imperial couple's silver wedding anniversary and the ethnographic-historical procession marking Franz Joseph's 1908 sixtieth jubilee focus on the artistic creation of the festivals and the aesthetic quality of the presentations.[24] These works rarely extend their inquiry beyond Vienna or consider partisan manipulation of the symbols of Habsburg patriotism. Biographies of Franz Joseph touch only briefly on imperial celebrations and make few references to the role of the court in asserting the centrality of the dynasty in the life of the state and its citizens.[25]

Habsburg historiography does repeatedly refer to the Catholic Church and the dynasty as bulwarks defending the old order against the rising forces of socialism and nationalism in the nineteenth century; in addition, recent work suggests the potential role of the army, its officer corps, and military veteran associations as schools of patriotism and dynastic loyalty.[26] Few scholars, however, treat the dynasty and its supporters as actors in the public sphere or look at the use of dynastic symbols to justify various political programs.

In the last decade, a number of scholars have considered the interplay between imperial celebrations and national conflicts within specific regions of the monarchy. Laurence Cole has looked at the diversity of national meanings in the German-speaking part of Tyrol, emphasizing how loyalty to the monarchy was a consensual position, if promoted for different reasons by different sectors of society. Nancy Wingfield and T. Mills Kelly have researched Czech-German street violence and nationalist conflicts around public space in Bohemia during Franz Joseph's reign. Historians have turned their attention to Franz Joseph's imperial visits to Croatia, to his failure to be crowned Bohemian King in 1871, and to the presentation of Franz Joseph as Hungarian King and Elisabeth as Hungarian Queen in the Hungarian half of the monarchy.[27] Other scholars have explored the legitimizing myths of the Habsburg dynasty, which sought, as Peter Urbanitsch has written, to "unify the entire population and make subjects immune to centrifugal forces (of which nationalism was the most vigorous among many)."[28] The present work is intended as a contribution to this growing body of scholarship, linking the study of nationalism, the invention of tradition, and public memory to an exploration of the Habsburg imperial cult and "Austrian" supranational patriotism under Franz Joseph.

The Imperial Image

This book concentrates on imperial celebrations in Habsburg Austria. After the 1867 reorganization of the state into the Dual Monarchy of Austria-Hungary, the "Austrian" half of the monarchy—including Galicia, Bukovina, Bohemia, Moravia, Austrian Silesia, a slice of northern Italy, and the mainly German-speaking provinces that form today's Austria—was designated officially "The Lands and Kingdoms Represented in the *Reichsrat*" and known less formally as Cisleithania or, simply, Austria. Dualism complicated efforts to define the emperor as a symbol of Austro-Hungarian unity. Imperial celebrations in Cisleithania presented Franz Joseph as father of all his peoples (including those of Hungary) and as the supranational symbol binding together the monarchy as a whole. However, the Hungarian noble elites viewed celebrations of Franz Joseph as *emperor* as holidays in a neighboring country. Hungary officially recognized only anniversaries of Franz Joseph's 1867 crowning as Hungarian king.[29]

The chapters explore both the official promotion of the imperial cult as well as the redefinition of imperial patriotism at the local level. A narrow study of one town or a single province within Cisleithania cannot hope to illuminate the variety of imperial celebration or provide a sense of the penetration of the imperial cult to the broader population. Franz Joseph was, after all, emperor over all provinces in Cisleithania (though his lengthy official title revealed the historical reality that the monarchy had been united only by personal union with the Habsburg ruler for most of its existence), and a study of Habsburg imperial celebration must consider both center and periphery. The presentation of the emperor was political, and a study of Habsburg imperial celebration must, therefore, consider regional politics in some detail in order to understand imperial celebrations within their specific historical contexts.

I concentrate on Vienna, the imperial capital, and Galicia, the Habsburg slice of the eighteenth-century partitions of Poland. Vienna was the residence of the emperor and the focus of Cisleithanian politics. The city's modern boulevards, medieval squares, and baroque architecture provided the settings for the most grandiose of all Habsburg imperial celebrations. Galicia, a northeastern border province, offers a fascinating location for the study of imperial celebration far from the imperial center. On the occasion of imperial celebrations, Polish commentators contrasted the development of Polish culture in Habsburg Galicia with what they saw as the repressive Germanization and Russification policies of the Hohenzollern and Romanov rulers of the other Polish partitions.

Chapter 1 introduces Habsburg ceremony and celebrations. In the wake of the revolutions of 1848–49, the neoabsolutist regime sought to revitalize the imperial court, the chief apparatus of imperial self-representation. Franz Joseph's participation in Catholic rituals like the Holy Thursday foot-washing and the Corpus Christi procession in Vienna reaffirmed the sacred nature of the political authority wielded by the pious monarch. This chapter describes the mechanisms behind what Richard Wortman has termed "elevation." Habsburg imperial etiquette "established a crucial symbolic distance" between the emperor and other mortals, "making the exercise of power and the possession of privilege appear rooted in the natural order of things."[30] The ceremonial rules (re)established in this period and the revival of traditional Habsburg symbols and myths in public Catholic celebrations lent the institution of the monarchy and the modernizing neoabsolutist state the legitimacy of tradition.

Chapters 2 and 3 analyze the 1851, 1880, and 1894 imperial visits to Galicia as well as the aborted 1868 *Kaiserreise*. The emperor's tours of the provinces brought the theater of court ritual to the masses outside of Vienna. Imperial visitations in the nineteenth century, though less lavish, retained some aspects of great medieval and renaissance royal progresses while representing the emperor as the face of the modernizing state.[31] Chapter 2 centers on the presentation of the emperor by the court and central government in 1851 and on the planned 1868 imperial visit to Galicia. By 1880, the devolution of power to provincial elites checked the ability of the dynasty to monopolize public discussion about the meaning of Austrian patriotism. Chapter 3, therefore, emphasizes the manipulation of the imperial cult by the dominant Polish conservatives during the

1880 inspection tour of Galicia. This chapter also considers the reaction of Polish democrats and Ruthenian factions to the monolithic vision of unity presented by the Polish conservatives, the imperial court, and the central government. The final section of the chapter looks briefly at the emperor's visit to the 1894 Galician Provincial Exhibition.

Chapters 4–6 examine the contested meaning of Habsburg patriotism during Franz Joseph's 1898 jubilee year. Chapter 4 looks at the official and semi-official presentation of the emperor in 1898. Facing divisive political strife, the court, government, army, Catholic Church, and imperial family appealed for a renewal of patriotism by focusing on the figure of the emperor. Official and semi-official celebrations distanced Franz Joseph from controversial government policies and decisions; at the same time, imperial celebrations presented the emperor as the symbol of the good intentions of an idealized, if unrealized, state that labored to fulfill the benevolent will of the good emperor. Imperial loyalty was not to supersede but to coexist with ethnic loyalties. The emperor, the living embodiment of the state, would assure that all legitimate ethnic and social interests were fulfilled.

Chapter 5 provides an overview of charitable donations, building programs, provincial festivities, jubilee products, popular publications, and local celebrations. More than the others, this chapter ranges across provinces, from center to periphery and back. Though the court and the Cisleithanian government sought to "channel" popular commemoration of the imperial jubilee to counter problems facing the monarchy, the successful marketing of the imperial image complicated attempts by the center to present the emperor as the source of progress, unity, and peace.

Chapter 6 examines efforts by Karl Lueger and the city of Vienna to use the jubilee for partisan advantage. Lueger's Christian Social Party turned dynastic patriotism into a weapon against political rivals. Imperial celebrations became opportunities to denounce opponents as anti-Christian, anti-Habsburg, and pro-Jewish enemies of Austro-German values. The final section of this chapter considers the Kaiser Jubilee Exhibition in Vienna and brings together many aspects of imperial celebration discussed in chapters 4 through 6. The exhibition, the single most significant jubilee event not organized or planned by the Cisleithanian government, Habsburg court, or Vienna's city council, provided Lueger with more opportunities to pose as the Habsburg-loyal defender of German and Christian Vienna. The epilogue briefly touches on the 1908 sixtieth jubilee, imperial celebrations during World War I, and the burial of Franz Joseph.

This study of the court, the presentation of the emperor, and the use, manipulation, and rejection of the mythic narratives of Habsburg power, which were created and bolstered during imperial celebrations, reveals much about Habsburg political culture. This book focuses on the presentation of the emperor to the population, the layers of meaning associated with this symbol of unity, the changing definitions of the community he was alleged to represent, and how these images of the emperor and of "Austria" were received by the intended audiences. The institution of the dynasty was considerably more flexible and adaptable to the times than is often assumed. Organizers of official imperial festivities tailored traditional Habsburg symbols and ceremonial forms to portray the emperor as the binding force in an Austria fractured by social and ethnic divisions. During imperial celebrations, the dynasty and its supporters called for an all-Austrian patriotism, based on an idealized image of the benevolent state as symbolized by the figure of the ruler. Official and semi-official celebrations posited national identity as a constituent part of a broader identification with the imperial house and with "Austria."

This study of imperial celebration also reveals effective limits to the ability of the court and Cisleithanian government to control the meaning of Habsburg patriotism. In later decades, regional political elites harnessed dynastic loyalties to legitimize their leadership of their respective national communities. Polish conservative elites in Galicia and Karl Lueger's Christian Socials in Vienna, for example, encouraged imperial patriotism even as they conveyed messages that, at times, conflicted with the official vision of ethnic and social harmony presented by central authorities.

CHAPTER 1

Reasserting Empire

Court and Dynasty after the Revolutions of 1848–49

In 1848–49, revolutions challenged Europe's social and political order defined at the Congress of Vienna in the wake of the French Revolution and the Napoleonic era. The Habsburg Monarchy, home of Klemens von Metternich, minister of state and the much reviled living symbol of conservative reaction, was not immune to the wave of insurrection. Uprisings in Bohemia, Galicia, Lombardy, Vienna, and Hungary threatened the integrity of the conglomeration of provinces acquired by the ambitious Habsburg dynasty over several hundred years through marriage politics, diplomacy, and war. The Habsburg army eventually proved capable of suppressing the revolutions; however, it was clear to the ruling family and its inner circle of advisors that the *Vormärz* (pre-March or prerevolutionary) system could not simply be reinstated.[1] From the moment Emperor Ferdinand abdicated and eighteen-year-old Archduke Franz succeeded to the Habsburg throne as Emperor Franz Joseph on 2 December 1848, the new regime sought to strengthen central authority through a program of modernization from above. As part of this neoabsolutist program, Franz Joseph's regime reasserted Habsburg legitimacy in Central Europe by revitalizing Habsburg imperial celebrations.

Guided in his first years as emperor by Prime Minister Felix von Schwarzenberg, Franz Joseph reluctantly agreed to make some constitutional concessions. The young emperor's education, however, had preconditioned him to favor personal monarchical rule.[2] When the liberal Kremsier parliament prepared to approve a constitution based on the principle of popular sovereignty in March 1849, Franz Joseph's government dismissed the parliament and promulgated a constitution authored by Schwarzenberg and Interior Minister Franz Stadion. The new constitution reserved power for the emperor and made no mention of popular sovereignty or ministerial responsibility. However, Franz Joseph never put even this constitution into force. He undermined many of its provisions by August 1851 and rescinded it in December.[3]

In the neoabsolutist system, brought to full fruition by Interior Minister Alexander Bach (Stadion's successor), General Adjutant Carl Graf Grünne, President of the Advisory Council Karl Friedrich von Kübeck, and others after the death of Schwarzenberg, the centralized bureaucracy and armed forces existed only to execute the will of the ruler. The emperor resided (for the most part) in Vienna, but the organs of the state acted in his name in every corner of the monarchy.[4] The imperial court and Habsburg ceremonial practice became tools for rebuilding confidence in the restored Habsburg dynasty and, by extension, in the reorganized and centralized Habsburg state.

This chapter considers the revival of Habsburg monarchical ritual in the first years of Franz Joseph's reign. Following a brief history of Habsburg imperial celebration and representation, I look at the reorganization of the imperial court after the revolutions and the renewal of public displays of the Catholic piety of the imperial house under Franz Joseph.

The Expression of *Herrschaft*

For centuries, the Habsburgs and other European dynasties had presented themselves as superior beings who possessed a natural and heaven-sanctioned right to rule. The tsars of Russia emphasized their descent from the Varangians and declared themselves heirs to the Byzantine emperors and, therefore, guardians of Christian Orthodoxy.[5] French and English dynasties demonstrated their God-approved right to rule by practicing forms of magic healing.[6] The crown of the Holy Roman Empire served the Habsburgs as a source of legitimacy. The Habsburg dynasty bribed and coerced the imperial electors (*Kurfürsten*) to vote Habsburg virtually without exception from the mid-fifteenth century until the demise of the empire in 1806.[7] The Habsburg court presented the Habsburg Holy Roman emperor to the population as the font of sacred political authority in Central Europe through ceremonies and rituals, magnificent buildings, colorful imperial guards, and the imperial court etiquette, a system of elaborate ceremonial rules that regulated all contact between the Habsburg monarch and lesser mortals.[8]

Pietas Austriaca, "piety as a quality of the ruler from the Domus Austriae," was central to Habsburg representation from the sixteenth century through the early eighteenth century.[9] Already during the reign of Charles V (Holy Roman emperor, 1519–55), the Habsburg court and imperial celebrations evoked the special Habsburg relationship with the Catholic Church and the self-defined Habsburg mission to defend Catholicism against Protestant heretics and Christian Europe from the advance of the Turk. Emperors Ferdinand II (Holy Roman emperor, 1619–37), Ferdinand III (emperor, 1637–57), and Leopold I (emperor, 1658–1705) raised Habsburg political ritual and theater to new heights. In alliance with the Jesuits, Capuchins, Carmelites, and other Catholic religious orders, these emperors intensified efforts to return the population to the Catholic fold.

The legend of Rudolf I's encounter with the Eucharist was the focus of the baroque Habsburg narrative of dynastic legitimacy. Jesuit and Capuchin theater productions propagated this story, disseminating the vision of Habsburg devotion to the Host as part of an ultimately successful bid to win back Protestants to Roman Catholicism. According to embellished versions of the tale, while out hunting in 1264, Rudolf, who would become the first Habsburg Holy Roman emperor in 1283, met an exhausted priest bearing the Eucharist to comfort a dying person. Pious Rudolf dismounted and offered the weary priest his horse. Following this selfless and humble gesture, a priest at a nearby monastery predicted that Rudolf, and thus the Habsburg family, would rise to world monarchy. In the seventeenth century, the legend of Rudolf served as religiously sanctioned proof of the Habsburg right to rule and to hold the title of Holy Roman emperor. The religious devotion of Rudolf, evidenced by his respect for the Host and his alleged veneration of the Virgin and the Holy Cross, became part of dynastic history as portrayed during imperial festivals and in court-commissioned paintings, sculptures, plays, and publications. The ritualized display of Habsburg self-sacrifice, humility, piety, and concern for others was central to Habsburg self-presentation.

Masses attended by the emperor accompanied by the court, pilgrimages to holy sights, and the erection of Marian and Trinity Pillars (figure 2), all manifesting the Habsburg claim to God-anointed status, multiplied under Leopold I. Leopold endeavored to rival the splendor of Louis XIV's court in France; more successfully, Leopold's armies confronted the Turkish siege of Vienna and pushed the Ottomans out of Hungary and much of the Balkans.[10] Leopold and Charles VI (emperor, 1711–40) initiated massive building projects to assert the power and prestige of the imperial house more forcefully than even their immediate predecessors. Both of these monarchs used religious imagery to stake their claims to the Spanish Habsburg inheritance.[11] In the midst of a plague outbreak, Charles VI contracted Johann Bernhard Fischer von Erlach to construct the late baroque Karlskirche in Vienna (figure 3). He also designed his partially realized plan for the monastery at Klosterneuburg, just upriver from Vienna, to rival the Escorial, the combination royal palace and ascetic religious sanctum built by Philip II, son of Charles V and king of Spain from 1555 to 1598. As historian T. C. W. Blanning has written, even in its uncompleted state Klosterneuburg "can still evoke a culture which was visual, aural, plastic, tactile and olfactory—in a word: sensual."[12]

These emperors participated with enthusiasm in the annual Corpus Christi procession, a reminder of the Habsburg veneration of the Eucharist, as well as the Easter week foot-washing, a ritual displaying at once the Catholic humility of the Habsburg ruler and the emperor's claim to be the temporal hand of Christ on earth. According to the Austrian historian Anna Coreth, Leopold I and Charles

Figure 2: Trinity Monument in Vienna's Graben, photograph by author.

Figure 3: Baroque Altar in the Karlskirche, Vienna, photograph by author.

VI, like their predecessors, publicly displayed their "conviction that the House of Austria had been assigned a specific mission for Empire and Church due to the religious merits of its great forefathers, or even better said, of its great forefather Rudolf von Habsburg."[13]

The absolutist courts of the seventeenth and early eighteenth centuries displayed the sacred nature of the Habsburg emperors and, at the same time, served to bind the upper aristocracy to the throne. The attractions of the court—theater, opera, entertainments, luxurious palaces, gala dinners—could be enjoyed only by the few recognized by the court as worthy of approaching the emperor.[14] The so-called Spanish etiquette, brought to Vienna by Ferdinand I, brother of Charles V, governed every movement of the emperor throughout the day and regulated every contact between the emperor and lesser mortals. Court ceremonial displayed the dependence of court society on the monarch for social prestige. Proximity to the ruler elevated the court elite above the rest of society.[15] In turn, the presence of court society riding with the emperor in costly carriages and wearing court uniforms manifested the exalted status of the ruler to the wider population. Court etiquette "embodied the idea of hierarchy that required a meaningful demonstration in order to be realized."[16]

Maria Theresa inherited the Habsburg lands when her father, Charles VI, expired without a male heir in 1740. Although Charles VI had negotiated the agreement of the European powers to the Pragmatic Sanction, first drafted in 1703 and which designated that a single Habsburg male or female heir would inherit all Habsburg lands, the new Habsburg ruler had to defend her inheritance against invasion by the armies of Prussian King Frederick II and his allies. After the death of Charles Albert of Bavaria (Emperor Charles VII) in 1745, Maria Theresa was able to win back the crown of the Holy Roman Empire for her husband, Franz Stephen of Lorraine, and for her house (now officially the House of Habsburg-Lorraine).

The Habsburg court had portrayed Charles VI, the last of the Habsburgs to actively seek the Spanish inheritance and the empire of Charles V, as heir to world monarchy and as the defender of the Catholic faith. The new imperial couple, Maria Theresa and Franz Stephen, introduced a much different style of imperial self-presentation. They sought to reserve for themselves a relaxed private life existing outside of court strictures. Maria Theresa continued to see the House of Habsburg as the agent of God on earth. At the same time, she concentrated her attention on her growing family. The imperial couple commissioned portraits of themselves surrounded by their sixteen children[17]: Maria Theresa and Franz Stephan had ensured that the genetic failure of the Spanish Habsburgs would never plague the new House of Habsburg-Lorraine.[18] The connection with the Habsburg past was not ignored, but the emphasis on the future and the depiction of Maria Theresa as the mother of her peoples constituted a break with the mode of Habsburg self-presentation dominant from Charles V to Charles VI.

The new informality in Habsburg court life stemmed from several sources. Franz Stephen's distaste for the Spanish ceremonial and his import of French fashion, language, and culture to Vienna played a role, as did the increasing spread of rationalist ideas associated with the Age of Reason. Although personally devoted to Catholicism and attracted to baroque display, Maria Theresa was greatly influenced by Jansenism. This Catholic reform movement opposed the cults of saints, veneration of relics, grandiose religious processions, and exaggerated public expressions of religious devotion. Jansenists wanted to return the Bible and moral teachings to the center of Catholic religious life.[19] Maria Theresa limited the number of imperial religious pilgrimages and moderated imperial participation in many religious celebrations.

War and the terrible condition of state finances prompted Maria Theresa to embark on a reorganization of the state administration, the army, the legal system, and the economy to compete with Prussia and the other great powers. Maria Theresa's wide-ranging reforms affected the position of the Catholic Church within the monarchy. Her advisors, including Jansenists, Protestants, converts to Catholicism from Protestantism and Judaism, and Catholics educated in northern German (Protestant) universities, pushed for a cessation of Jesuit control over education even before Pope Clement XIV dismantled the Society of Jesus in 1773. Maria Theresa's government transferred the wealth of the Jesuits to the state treasury to offset the costs of a new system of compulsory education directed toward the moral education of the population. The state now communicated more directly with the population, no longer relying on the church and the Catholic orders to teach their subjects duty and loyalty to the imperial family.[20]

Maria Theresa's more radical son, Joseph II, based his right to absolute rule on his function as first servant of the state. The baroque cult of the ruler and the emphasis on the sacrality of the Holy Roman emperor did not correspond to Joseph's dedication to reason and his program to rationalize state institutions and modernize society from above. Joseph II moderated court etiquette, replacing, for example, the black Spanish garb of court officials with uniforms based on military models. Joseph himself, like many of his royal contemporaries, appeared in public almost exclusively in military garb.[21] Joseph II forbade the practice of kneeling in the presence of the emperor, "because," as Joseph wrote, "this is not a fitting form of behavior from one human being to another and should be reserved for God alone."[22]

Pietas Austriaca fell prey to the reforming zeal of this ruler. A devotee of the rationalism of the Enlightenment and, like his mother, influenced by Jansenism, Joseph II viewed public manifestations of faith as poor substitutes for religious devotion based on morals and the teachings of the New Testament. Joseph II sharply reduced the number of public feast days and Catholic ceremonies in which the imperial family appeared in public surrounded by the imperial court. Dynastic festivals with religious overtones, like births, baptisms, weddings, and funerals were increasingly conducted in the privacy of the imperial palace.[23] Promotions within the Habsburg house orders were no longer accompanied by church services. Joseph II discontinued the imperial pilgrimages to Mariazell and other religious sites frequented by his predecessors and only rarely took the Eucharist at public mass. His predecessors often knelt in the street when meeting a priest carrying the Eucharist; Leopold I even proclaimed Mary empress, queen, and commander of the Habsburg armies. Joseph II rejected such dramatic expressions of personal piety as part of the irrational world he sought to transform through his wide-ranging reform efforts. Joseph II believed that a Habsburg emperor should be presented as a role model of sober morality and rationality, not as a pseudo-humble demi-god cloaked in baroque splendor (the sarcophagi in figures 4 and 5 illustrate the very different self-conceptions held by Maria Theresa and Joseph II).

Joseph II aimed at completely restructuring the church-state relationship. Joseph's reforms required bishops to swear loyalty to the ruler, decreased the influence of the papacy over the Austrian clergy, closed many monasteries, and redrew parish lines to conform to the monarchy's territorial borders. Catholic clergy became state employees and studied theology and secular subjects at new seminaries. In the early 1780s, Joseph II further eroded the privileged position of the Catholic Church by granting rights and privileges to non-Catholic Christians and issuing a series of Edicts of Toleration, removing some centuries-old restrictions on the Jews. These edicts, though far from offering true religious emancipation and freedom, made the Habsburg Monarchy arguably the most religiously tolerant state in Europe.[24] Though his successors moderated many of Joseph's more radical reforms, state controls over the Catholic Church remained in force until Franz Joseph began the negotiations that led to the signing of the 1855 Concordat with Rome.[25]

Confronted by the territorial and institutional changes made by Napoleon's armies and bureaucrats, Franz II/I (Habsburg ruler from 1792 to 1835; Franz II as Holy Roman emperor, and Franz I as emperor of Austria) invented the "Austrian Empire" in 1804, enabling his family to retain an imperial title after the by then foreseeable dissolution of the Holy Roman Empire. Franz's Austrian court preserved the Habsburg ceremonial calendar as modified by his predecessors and continued to use the Holy Roman Empire's double-headed eagle as the symbol of the Habsburgs even after the final dismantling of the empire in 1806. Franz had himself depicted wearing the crown of "Austria" and surrounded by the crowns of his inherited lands, reminiscent of earlier portrayals of Charles VI.

Although demonstrations of continuity with the imperial past differentiated the Habsburg Monarchy from the upstart empire of Napoleon, the Austrian Empire was in fact hardly less illegitimate than the empire of the French.[26] The costly festivities surrounding the Congress of Vienna in 1814–15 did not usher in

Figure 4: Sarcophagus of Maria Theresa and Franz Stephan, photograph by author.

Figure 5: Sarcophagus of Joseph II, photograph by author.

a revival of Habsburg celebration. Rather, Franz regularly appeared in public and in portraits dressed in white shirt and black coat, reflective of his sober style of rule, his self-conception as the leading bureaucrat of the state, and the separation of his private life from the grandeur of his office.[27]

Klemens von Metternich and the State Council did not pursue an expansion of imperial ceremonial forms after Franz's death in 1835. Franz's eldest son and heir, Ferdinand, physically weak and suffering from epilepsy, participated only intermittently in public ceremonies. During the *Vormärz,* Ferdinand "the Good" did not and could not project a majestic aura to his subjects. By the eve of the revolutions of 1848, Habsburg imperial etiquette had been relaxed and imperial celebrations limited to a handful of unenthusiastically performed public ceremonies.

Neoabsolutism and the Revival of the Imperial Court

In the first days of his reign, Franz Joseph, who eschewed luxury and pomp in his personal life, revitalized the imperial court, broke with the recent past and returned much of the formality, if not most of the public self-presentation, associated with the Habsburg courts of the seventeenth century.[28] The Habsburg imperial court, an administrative apparatus derived from medieval Germanic courts, was given new purpose and energy. Franz Joseph's court would continue to uphold and display the majesty of the Habsburg emperor through imperial celebrations and the maintenance and construction of Habsburg palaces and properties.[29]

In the first week of December 1848, Franz Joseph named Carl Graf Grünne acting grand court master. Franz Joseph assigned the task of reorganizing the court to Grünne, who also served as general-adjutant and chief of the new Military Chancellery. Financial crisis lent urgency to Grünne's efforts.[30] Quelling the revolutions had put a strain on already unstable state finances. In addition, ex-emperor Ferdinand retained the bulk of the wealth of the imperial family after his abdication.[31] Faced with these difficulties, Grünne was to revive the apparatus of imperial celebration and display to be more "fitting to the times."[32]

At Franz Joseph's direction, Grünne retained the basic structure of the court. The four most important officials, the *Obersthofchargen,* continued to direct the four major divisions, or *Hofstäbe,* of the court. In addition to their administrative duties, the *Obersthofchargen,* always aristocrats, appeared at important court ceremonies. The number of officials and servants in each of the *Hofstäbe* varied from decade to decade. When Franz Joseph ascended the throne, the court employed more than four thousand people.[33]

The grand court master (*Obersthofmeister*) headed the largest division of the court administration. The grand court master oversaw the production of imperial celebrations and enforced court ceremonial (etiquette), which, as legal scholar Ivan Żolger argued, aimed "to protect and secure the holiness and majesty of the princely person, to document the ruler's position of honor and power and to manifest the awe and devotion that is owed to the monarch and the members of his House."[34] The grand court master enforced and updated the court rankings (*Hofrangordnung*), which determined precedence at court. An exalted court ranking was a vulnerable and cherished attribute tenaciously defended by princely and aristocratic families even in the last decades of the monarchy's existence.[35]

The grand court master also presided over the various imperial guards that flanked the emperor on most ceremonial occasions, serving as visual reminders of the superior status of the ruler. In the mid-eighteenth century, Maria Theresa created the First Arciere Body-Guard. The Arciere Body-Guard, initially open only to young aristocrats from Austria and Bohemia, accepted commoners after the fall of the Holy Roman Empire in 1806. Its two highest officers were chosen from the ranks of the Habsburg generals. The Arciere Body-Guard "embodied . . . like no other institution the splendor of the imperial court" during the reign of Franz Joseph.[36] Hungarian nobles filled the ranks of the Hungarian Body-Guard (*Ungarische Leibgarde*), also founded by Maria Theresa. Hungarian nobles accepted into the Guard served in Vienna for three or four years.[37]

The second of the *Obersthofchargen,* the *Oberstkämmerer* (grand chamberlain), at times a rival to the grand court master for influence in the court administration, curated the imperial art and historical collections and directed the emperor's personal body-servants. The *Ahnenprobenexaminator* (examiner of pedigrees), an official in the Office of the Grand Chamberlain, examined the purity of the upper aristocracy. The *Obersthofmarschall* (grand marshal) directed the smallest of the four administrative divisions of the court and acted as the court judge. Finally, the *Oberststallmeister* (grand master of the stables) managed the imperial stables.

Though the structure of the court was retained, Grünne acted to increase the professionalism of the court administration. Grünne pensioned off many inefficient and aging officials, some of whom had served more than thirty years in the courts of Franz and Ferdinand.[38] In a sixty-four-page memorandum to Franz Joseph, Grünne argued that the employment of less than competent court officials at the behest of influential patrons had created a financial drag on the system and threatened to undermine all efforts at serious reform of the court administration. He was determined to staff the court administration with "talented and trustworthy" people who could provide proof of academic success and practical experience. In the new system, employees at every level would face dismissal should they not perform their duties satisfactorily.[39]

Grünne's reform efforts were centered on the largest of the court divisions, the Office of the Grand Court Master. Traditionally, the *Hofdienste,* always aristocrats, headed eight departments within the Office of the Grand Court Master and, like the *Hofchargen,* performed ceremonial duties.[40] Grünne wrote that the

Hofdienste "as men of high birth and position claimed special considerations . . . were often not very fundamentally experienced in their fields." He proposed separating a small number of ceremonial positions from the practical administrative tasks needed to run the court.[41] Grünne then directed all eight departments to utilize personnel and funds more efficiently. Seeking further savings and improvements, Grünne reassigned those responsible for the upkeep of imperial properties, for arranging housing during imperial travels, and for the medical needs of the emperor and members of the court, as well as a host of servants and lower officials to the Office of the Grand Court Master from the other three court divisions. The grand court master would now also oversee the imperial palace guards (*Hofburgwache*).[42]

Grünne's plan created a new imperial court within the framework of the four traditional court divisions. The position of grand court master had always imparted to its holder the highest ceremonial status at court. In 1772, Maria Theresa had confirmed that the *Obersthofmeister* held "first position before all princes at the imperial court, even if only ranked as a Count."[43] With Grünne's reorganization of court in mid-1849, however, the Office of the Grand Court Master became virtually synonymous with the imperial court as a whole. The grand court master was administrator, cultivator of imperial traditions, and defender of imperial prestige.[44] Franz Joseph's grand court masters were educated aristocrats who could boast of many years of experience in the imperial court or in the service of members of the imperial family or the high aristocracy. Well-trained and educated bureaucrats possessing university degrees and rewarded and promoted on the basis of merit assisted the grand court master.[45] The other three *Hofchargen* retained their official ceremonial roles, but were diminished in responsibility. The Habsburg court apparatus remained essentially under the control of the grand court master until the breakup of the monarchy in 1918.[46]

The reorganized and revitalized professional administration of the court oversaw a tightening of court ceremonial rules. Grünne and Karl Fürst von und zu Liechtenstein, grand court master from 1849 until 1864, replaced the weakened adherence to court etiquette that had characterized Ferdinand's court with a new commitment to court-defined standards. Every detail of dress and behavior within the Hofburg was once again specified by exacting regulations. Grand court master Liechtenstein reserved access to the inner chambers of the imperial palace to those with high court rankings, and court officials were even forbidden to wear hats inside the imperial palace, emphasizing the sacredness of the abode of the emperor.[47]

Liechtenstein and his officials probed the ceremonial protocol for precedents as they worked out the organization and performance of recurring and one-time imperial celebrations. The ceremonial protocol was a running calendar of imperial celebrations updated meticulously over the centuries by the keeper of the ceremonial protocol (*Zeremonial Protocol-Führer*). As he would throughout his reign, Franz Joseph read the grand court master's detailed descriptions of ceremonies with great care, making his own suggestions and deciding between variations. Utilizing the ceremonial protocol and conforming to Franz Joseph's wishes, the Office of the Grand Court Master orchestrated every aspect of imperial celebrations in which the emperor personally appeared before the public. The ceremonial decisions made in these first years set the stage for what observers in the late nineteenth century viewed as magnificent performances of unchanging Habsburg rituals.

Franz Joseph's neoabsolutist court assigned roles in imperial ceremonies according to court ranking, privileging those in possession of certain exclusive imperial titles. In this way, the appearance of the emperor with his *Hofstaat,* literally court-state, made manifest the superiority of the monarch and the dependence of court society on the emperor for social prestige. Even after the establishment of constitutional rule in the 1860s, the rules governing precedence at court were not altered significantly to accommodate the increasingly prominent role of the middle classes in the economic, political, and cultural life of the monarchy; however, in later decades the court did prove flexible enough to draw the commoner-elite into the court universe.

The four *Hofchargen* occupied the highest positions in the *Hofstaat.* The annual court calendar (*Hof-Kalendar* or *Hof-Schematismus*) also listed many who held imperial titles and were not employed in the court administration as members of Franz Joseph's *Hofstaat.* Those with the highest imperial titles, which had originally obligated their holders to attend the emperor when called upon, constituted the inner court.

The *Geheime Räte* (privy councilors) took pride of place in imperial processions (as opposed to church ceremonies and celebrations of the Habsburg house orders). There was no requirement of aristocratic heritage for this title. Franz Joseph granted this title to favorite non-noble government ministers, thus avoiding embarrassment to high government officials otherwise ignored or offered inferior seating and position by the court during imperial celebrations.[48] The emperor also bestowed this title on some important aristocrats who could not satisfy the rigorous conditions for the title of chamberlain (*Kämmerer*).

Only aristocrats of "pure" noble lineage could gain the ceremonial key of the chamber, the symbol of the chamberlain. Successful applicants for this title had to pass the pedigree examination (*Ahnenprobe*) administered by the Office of the Grand Chamberlain. Candidates produced marriage contracts and other materials documenting descent from twelve (and after 1898, sixteen) *"altadelige"* great-great-grandparents.[49] The grand chamberlain reminded even those with the proper family tree that the exclusive chamberlain title came only at the "Most High mercy of His Majesty." Aristocratic women who could document their descent from twelve noble great-great-grandparents could aspire to membership in the Order of the Star-Cross (*Sternkreuz-Orden*), the female equivalent of chamberlain. Women in the Star-Cross Order formed part of the *Hofstaat* of the empress.[50] The chamberlain title and membership in the *Sternkreuz-Orden,* awarded solely on the basis of descent, remained unattainable for bankers, merchants, and noble families married into the middle classes.[51]

Beginning in the 1860s, non-nobles of high civil service or military rank could attain the lesser court title of *Truchseß,* originally reserved for those of noble origin. However, never more than a few dozen people held this relatively unattractive title. Each *Truchseß,* considered only a member of the outer court, could be required to assist the emperor during the annual foot-washing ceremony.

Hoffähigkeit, the quality of court presentability, defined court society and automatically conferred court access (*Hofzutritt*), the right to appear at "announced" (*angesagt*) court ceremonies and festivities. Those who could document their descent from twelve noble-born ancestors (eight on the father's side, four on the mother's) to the satisfaction of the grand chamberlain were deemed *hoffähig.*[52] *Kämmerer* were, by definition, *hoffähig,* as were women holding rank in the Order of the Star-Cross. By the early twentieth century some members of the nobility complained that the standards for court presentability, which had effectively banned many important aristocratic families from court, no longer seemed appropriate for the times.[53]

In the early years of Franz Joseph's reign, few enjoyed the privilege of court access aside from the *Geheime Räte,* the *Kämmerer,* and the *hoffähig.* Franz Joseph never appointed large numbers of new privy councilors. He also dismissed pleas to ease the rules governing *Hoffähigkeit* and consideration for the key of the chamberlain or the Star-Cross. After the institution of constitutional rule, however, many non-nobles rose to the high positions in the state and court bureaucracies that conferred on the officeholder the title *Hofrat,* and therefore court access. Franz Joseph also extended this title and court access to prominent political and cultural figures. A number of nobles who could not meet the standards for *Hoffähigkeit* received this "act of Most High benevolence" as well. Franz Joseph's court bestowed court access on government ministers, the officer corps, and the wives of those with high titles and orders.[54]

Franz Joseph presided over a significant expansion of the Habsburg house orders, admitting many commoners to their ranks in the late nineteenth century. The Habsburg house orders included the Order of the Golden Fleece; the Order of St. Stephen; the Maria Theresa Order; the Leopold Order; the Order of the Iron Cross; the Order of Franz Joseph; and, after the death of Empress Elisabeth in 1898, the Order of Elisabeth. With the exception of the Golden Fleece, founded in the fifteenth century, these orders were products of the eighteenth and nineteenth centuries and were granted to individuals for outstanding state service.[55]

The constitutional governments after 1867 often favored political figures who had advanced the government agenda, long-serving bureaucrats, ministers, and army officers with these honors. Those holding the highest rankings within the house orders received access to the court.

In the early modern period, admission to the court bound nobles and aristocrats to the service of the monarch. In the constitutional era, the granting of honors and titles enabled the emperor and the state to recognize and share in the achievements of the commoner-elite. The guarantee of equality before the law, rooted in the constitutional reforms of the 1860s, all but eliminated the formal benefits enjoyed by recipients of titles and orders. Yet many Habsburg citizens apparently placed great value on the social prestige attached to such honors. Nationalist, socialist, and liberal critics lampooned the awarding of thousands of imperial decorations during the jubilee years of 1898 and 1908 as a "rain of orders."[56] Such comments did little to dampen the enthusiasm of those who scrambled for titles and memberships in the Habsburg house orders in order to distance themselves from the anonymous masses.[57]

Continued adherence to strict court procedures neither barred non-nobles from imperial titles and decorations nor resulted in the revival of most long-abandoned imperial festivities. Many court-controlled celebrations were retained only in modest form. The celebration of the emperor's birthday provides an example of the altered and changing nature of imperial celebration. Before 1824, official festivities commemorating the birthday of the emperor included a public procession; a series of formal receptions; an imperial dinner; and a special court mass in the Cathedral of St. Stephen, located in the heart of Vienna's First District and the seat of the Archbishop of Vienna. The rarefied circles of the inner court accompanied the emperor on his way to and from these events, heightening the significance of the imperial personage.

After 1824 the official festivities marking the imperial birthday were much more modest, and Franz Joseph did not allow the reinstitution of the pre-1824 practice. In 1849, he limited official court celebration of his 18 August birthday to services in the chapel of the imperial palace followed by military parades and artillery salvos. He wrote in the margins of Liechtenstein's 1849 report concerning the celebration of the imperial birthday that "nothing should be undertaken against the holding of freely undertaken festivities" commemorating the imperial birthday. Franz Joseph instructed his government to publicize his wish that the population demonstrate imperial loyalty by organizing and contributing to charitable actions.[58]

Franz Joseph's directives freed this imperial celebration from the absolute control of the court and opened it up to local initiative and popular participation. The birthday of the ruler was once an exclusive celebration limited geographically to the location of the emperor and entirely controlled by the dictates of court etiquette. In the early years of the restored dynasty, the emperor's birthday did not inspire many spontaneous expressions of joy. In contrast, by the late nineteenth century, Habsburg citizens contributed to charities founded on the emperor's birthdays; millions more attended popular festivals (*Volksfeste*) in provincial towns and small-scale celebrations sponsored by thousands of voluntary associations.[59] Habsburg subjects in every province attended special religious ceremonies during which priests, ministers, and rabbis exhorted their flocks to associate religious devotion with imperial loyalty. Mass literacy and improved transportation between center and province created a large readership for publications that disseminated information about patriotic festivities. Pamphlets and editorials from government and unofficial sources highlighted the achievements of the monarchy under the benevolent rule of the emperor. Newspapers reported on the imperial family's private gathering in Bad Ischl, Franz Joseph's summer home, and informed the reading public of events in the provinces.

Under Franz Joseph, the Office of the Grand Court Master applied court etiquette and approved ceremonial forms to every public contact between the emperor and his subjects. Court rankings governed the order and composition of imperial processions, and the complex rules of court access and court present-ability dictated the guest lists for celebrations like the annual *Hofball* and *Ball bei Hof*.[60] Court ceremonial rules did not only affect the behavior of the titled. Commoners holding high positions in the state bureaucracy enjoyed access to the court and, therefore, were subject to court etiquette. Until the demise of the monarchy, awed subjects who received imperial audiences (an estimated 100,000 people during Franz Joseph's reign) awkwardly backed out of the emperor's chambers bowing to their ruler.

Franz Joseph's personal adherence to ceremonial rules defined his public persona. Always in military garb, critical of any officer or soldier less exacting in following regulations governing appearance, Franz Joseph seems today an almost comic figure, a robot that played predetermined roles and was evidently incapable of spontaneous expression.[61] In the words of Joseph Redlich, a historian and biographer of Franz Joseph, the emperor's "human individuality so completely merged with his activity as ruler, as can be said of no other European monarch of the previous century."[62]

The revival of the imperial court and the standardization of court ceremonial forms not only provided Franz Joseph with scripted means to interact with his subjects, but also created an image of stability at the center of the state. Franz Joseph, who, as countless school textbooks, newspapers articles, and commemo-rative pamphlets in every major language of the monarchy informed the popula-tion, rose at 4 A.M. (in the summer) to work for his people's welfare, retained his commitment to uphold the honor of his house and displayed this commitment in the public arena at all times. The renewal of imperial celebration under Franz

Joseph mirrored the neoabsolutist program of the new regime. After the defeat of revolution, Habsburg ceremony and celebration presented Franz Joseph as a superior being whose right to rule had been confirmed by history, tradition, and military victory.

Catholic Rituals

When he came to power in 1848, Franz Joseph did not desire a return to the baroque splendor already under siege in the eighteenth century. At the same time, the neoabsolutist regime viewed the Catholic Church, along with the army and bureaucracy, as a pillar of the new order. Franz Joseph participated almost every year of his sixty-eight-year reign in the two most important expressions of the Catholic piety of the head of the House of Habsburg: the Corpus Christi procession and the foot-washing ceremony on Holy Thursday. These rituals, repeated with little variation, entered into the public consciousness as normal and natural parts of the yearly cycle of events and reminded the population of the stabilizing influence of religion and of monarchy.

From the sixteenth through the early eighteenth centuries, these rituals had underscored the special Habsburg role as the defender of the Catholic Church against Protestant heresy and Christian Europe against the Ottoman threat. Even after the reforms of enlightened absolutism, the imperial court continued to mark the passage of time with recurring rituals and public presentations of the emperor within a specifically Catholic context. Joseph II extended state control over the internal affairs of the Catholic Church and dispensed with what he viewed as empty ritual and exaggerated public professions of faith that had marked Habsburg imperial celebrations until the reign of Maria Theresa. Yet, whenever in Vienna during Corpus Christi, Joseph II, this self-styled student of philosophy, walked in the procession, a role performed regularly by Habsburg emperors since the mid-seventeenth century and intermittently since the thirteenth century.[63]

After the deaths of Joseph II (1790) and Joseph's equally enlightened if more moderate brother Leopold II (emperor, 1790–92), Franz did not reverse the Josephinian church reforms—despite his growing conservatism and his hatred and suspicion of the Enlightenment ideas that had given rise to the French Revolution. Franz made no moves to restore the religious feasts, pilgrimages, and public masses characteristic of seventeenth-century Habsburg court splendor. Yet Franz continued to perform those religious ceremonies that survived the reforms of Joseph II. During his son Ferdinand's thirteen-year reign, however, court participation was occasionally canceled; at other times an archduke performed the ceremonial role designated for the emperor.

The revolutions of 1848–49 threatened Habsburg authority and subverted the Habsburg calendar of imperial ceremonies and celebrations. After the court fled revolutionary Vienna for the safety of Innsbruck in May 1848, the 22 June Corpus

Christi procession in the imperial capital became an opportunity for celebrating the gains of the revolution. Described as the "first great resurrection celebration of freedom," the 1848 Corpus Christi procession retained some elements of the traditional ceremony.[64] As in previous years, the archbishop bore the Host, and a grenadier battalion fired a salvo. But the differences between the pre-1848 Corpus Christi processions and this revolutionary festival were profound. Middle-class revolutionaries usurped the central roles in the festival previously reserved for the dynasty, the court, the house orders, and the army. The Habsburg family and the court were absent from the city, and few units of the regular army remained in the city to line the streets during the procession. Instead, as reported in the popular *Allgemeine Theaterzeitung*, the cavalry of the national guard and the citizen's cavalry, composed of middle-class liberal revolutionaries, appeared at the procession in their "incredibly lovely" uniforms and "lent the celebration a special pomp."[65]

Not all of Vienna's newspapers, now freed of the harsh censorship that characterized the *Vormärz* system, were impressed with this transformed ceremony. According to one of the leading liberal organs, "the Corpus Christi procession was held without regard to the current situation, admittedly with much less pomp than in the past. Furthermore, we believe that this national performance would be easy to dispense with."[66] Viennese critics viewed this Corpus Christi procession of the revolution as a transforming event or as an unwanted reminder of the antiliberal nature of the old regime.

Already in the summer of 1848, the Habsburg military began to bring the revolutions to heel. Habsburg forces quelled uprisings in Prague and defeated Piedmont's armies by the end of July. In October, Habsburg armies bombarded Vienna into submission. Ready to consolidate these gains and to reverse concessions granted by Ferdinand in the early months of revolution, the dynasty overturned its own rules of succession. Franz had secured the succession of his eldest son, despite Ferdinand's infirmities. Franz Joseph's mother, Archduchess Sophie, Franz's brothers, and close advisors of the Habsburg family now orchestrated Ferdinand's abdication. Pressured by the family, Ferdinand's younger brother, Franz Karl, removed himself from the line of succession to make way for his son, the young and energetic Franz Joseph.

As the head of the restored dynasty, Franz Joseph consciously dedicated himself to reviving inherited traditions that had been interrupted by the revolutions, including the Corpus Christi procession. Franz Joseph did not reinstate a full calendar of imperial ceremonies and celebrations characteristic of the era of *Pietas Austriaca;* yet he did insist, as had his grandfather Franz, that all imperial celebrations that were performed be regularized and repeated with little if any variation.

Franz Joseph's first Corpus Christi procession after his accession to the throne was more than a mere return to traditional forms. The participation of much of Austria's Catholic hierarchy increased the importance of the 1849 procession. In March, the interior ministry had sent invitations to all the bishops of Austria, the "sole legitimate representatives of Catholic interests," to congregate in Vienna in April. For months, Austrian bishops and Catholic newspapers had been lobbying for such a gathering to develop an official Catholic position with regard to church-state relations in the new system.[67] Church leaders attempted to persuade the government that a Catholic Church independent of the state could more effectively use its position to educate the public in religious values and state loyalty. The Catholic hierarchy also sought to negate the desires of those seeking greater participation of priests and Catholic laity in decision-making.[68]

More than twenty Austrian bishops present in Vienna for the church conference joined with the court and army to transform the 7 June 1849 Corpus Christi procession into a celebration of the defeat of the revolution and the return of legitimate dynastic rule. Franz Joseph made his way from the imperial palace to St. Stephen's in an imperial carriage pulled by six horses and accompanied by the court. After mass, the bishops, dressed in their robes of office and carrying staves, proceeded before the emperor along the traditional route from the Great Gate of St. Stephen's to each of four altars located in the center of the city. The highest aristocrats of the realm, absent from Vienna in 1848, donned the robes and great crosses of the Habsburg house orders and walked in the procession along with archdukes, dozens of imperial body-guards, and the *Edelknaben,* sons of aristocratic families educated and serving at court.[69] During his reign, Ferdinand had either avoided participation or walked unsteadily before the Viennese population; Franz Joseph appeared the vision of strength and youth as he, head uncovered in a gesture of humility and carrying a lit candle, followed behind the archbishop of Vienna, who carried the Eucharist. The new emperor knelt at each altar as a priest read from the Gospels.

After the procession, army formations paraded before the emperor in the courtyard of the imperial palace. The Viennese population watched as the emperor proudly demonstrated that the legendary Habsburg piety remained a source of strength and stability. With the church and army at his side, he and his family would guarantee stability for all his peoples.

The day before the procession, the *Österreichischer Volksfreund,* the newspaper of the Catholic Association for Belief, Freedom, and Morals, related the triumphal feeling among church officials at the restoration of monarchy and the possibility for a reversal of Josephinist state oversight of the Catholic Church:

> Whoever is able will take part tomorrow in the Corpus Christi procession:
> such [a procession] Vienna has not yet seen. Twenty and some bishops, differ-
> ent in origin, language, custom, but united by the band of belief and the idea
> of a great Austria . . . will proceed before the canopy under which the most
> worthy Archbishop of Vienna will bear the Host, and our youthful emperor

will follow him, fulfilling for the first time in his life the exalted duty to bear witness publicly before all the people to the respect that all worldly power and glory of the present owes to the Son of Man from whom all salvation comes. In the entourage of the emperor one will catch sight of the Archduke Franz Karl, who is the subject of his son; then such is the God-given magnificence of kingship that in the face of it even the natural relationships of family step back.—Many healing thoughts on the horrifying celebration of this day a year ago will involuntarily awaken, and so we will return home . . . uplifted, excited, and warned.[70]

The Catholic press compared the barricades and violent clashes of October 1848 to this magnificent festival and published poems praising the new emperor as the "Angel of Freedom" and declaring devotion to the "unity of Austria under the hereditary Imperial House."[71]

In 1850, Franz Joseph participated for the first time as emperor in the second of the traditional Habsburg expressions of dynastic piety: the Holy Thursday footwashing ceremony, part of the four-day court observance of Easter. The master of the staff and the court prelates chose twelve poor elderly men, transported them to the Hofburg, and positioned them in the ceremonial hall on a raised dais. There, before an invited audience observing the scene from tribunes, the emperor served the men a symbolic meal and archdukes cleared the dishes. As a priest read aloud in Latin the words of the New Testament (John 3:15), "And he began to wash the feet of the disciples," Franz Joseph knelt and, without rising from his knees, washed the feet of the twelve old men in imitation of Christ.[72] Finally, the emperor placed a bag of twenty silver coins around the necks of each before the men were led away and returned to their homes in imperial coaches. Court ceremonial rules applied by the grand court master and the keeper of the ceremonial protocol governed every aspect of this ceremony, portraying the Habsburg emperor as a pious son of the church who possessed the right to rule by grace of God, by the historic tradition of his imperial house, and by his humility and concern for his subjects (figure 6).

Regular imperial participation in these rituals originated as exhibitions of the Habsburg relationship with the Counter-Reformation Catholic Church. The revived ceremonies were not simply appeals to notions of God-anointed kingship, though the power of such an appeal should not be discounted in this overwhelmingly rural and Catholic monarchy. On every great imperial occasion—the 1879 twenty-fifth wedding anniversary of the imperial couple; Franz Joseph's fiftieth, sixtieth, and seventieth birthdays; and his fortieth, fiftieth, and sixtieth jubilees as emperor—government newspapers and party organs printed depictions of the ceremonies and descriptions of the emperor's every move. Commemorative pamphlets and books in many languages cited these rituals as proof of the personal piety of the unassuming emperor. In the narrative of Habsburg legitimacy invoked

Figure 6: The Foot-washing Ceremony in the Ceremonial Hall of the Hofburg. Theo Zasche. From Franz Joseph und seine Zeit, *1898. Austrian National Library.*

since the Counter-Reformation, these qualities of the monarch conferred the right to rule on the head of the dynasty and in later decades, at least in government-sponsored publications, came to symbolize the efforts of the Habsburg state to address the material needs of the population.

The Corpus Christi procession and the foot-washing were not evidence of a revived Habsburg Catholic bigotry or of a return to a full-blown *Pietas Austriaca,* but served to remind the population of the stabilizing value of religion and of monarchy. While commemorative publications and school textbooks immortalized the personal piety and dedication of the emperor to the religious obligations of his predecessors, Franz Joseph never hesitated to attend very different religious rituals. Franz Joseph participated in Eastern Orthodox, Greek Catholic, Armenian Catholic, and Jewish (liberal and orthodox), and, after the occupation of Bosnia-Herzegovina, Muslim religious celebrations, where he was blessed by priests, ministers, rabbis, and Muslim clergy. By the 1890s, the Vienna Corpus Christi procession had become a tourist attraction. When age finally did slow Franz Joseph's legendary "elastic steps," he did not fail to emerge slowly from Michael's Gate (*Michaelertor*) of the imperial palace at the arrival of the procession. There he knelt at a special altar to hear the third section of the Gospel reading.[73] Thousands from all over the monarchy journeyed to Vienna to witness the emperor perform this seemingly ancient ritual, "the most colorful and wonderful performance that one could see in Old Vienna."[74] Many came to gawk at the

Habsburg carriages, the imperial horses, and the Knights of the Golden Fleece in their finest costumes—increasingly exotic in urban and heavily middle-class Vienna (figure 7).

Figure 7: Corpus Christi Procession in Vienna, 1894. Austrian National Library.

After revolution, the neoabsolutist regime sought to emphasize the traditional sources of legitimacy for the restored dynasty by revitalizing the imperial court and applying a stricter interpretation of court etiquette to all contact with the emperor. Even while working toward a new concordat that would free the Catholic Church from state control, Franz Joseph was uninterested in reinstating a full schedule of imperial pilgrimages, public masses, saint veneration, and the like. As explained by the son of Franz Joseph's long-time director of the ceremonial department,

> Whoever watched carefully even if only from a distance, will have to admit without reservation that the imperial court always knew how to represent; always, however, the realization of overly pompous performance and more or less theatrical effects was purposefully avoided. The emphasis lay on a strictly regulated, smooth realization of a program appropriate to the dignity of the court.[75]

Under Franz Joseph, discipline and dedication replaced the relative ceremonial laxity of his immediate predecessors and the splendor of the seventeenth-century baroque Habsburg courts. Ceremony and celebration painted the emperor as the embodiment of the qualities of the revitalized state: duty, justice, and stability. The Catholic piety of Franz Joseph, displayed year after year in the public rituals of the foot-washing and the Corpus Christi procession, proclaimed the traditional ties of the ruling house to Catholicism, the historic reality of centuries of Habsburg rule in Central Europe, and the youthful strength and firmness of resolve of the new emperor. Imperial celebration emphasized that Franz Joseph possessed the traditional qualities of the Habsburg ruler—piety and concern for the public welfare—and underscored the assertion that these qualities continued to justify Habsburg rule. Seemingly timeless imperial celebrations conveyed messages of legitimacy based on tradition and on concrete achievement: the dynasty would provide for security and prosperity in return for obedience. Over the course of Franz Joseph's long reign, the elaborate rules of court ceremony and the Catholic rituals of the foot-washing and the Corpus Christi procession became part of the legend of the benevolent emperor who worked for the good of his people despite personal tragedy.

CHAPTER 2

Nasz Pan Kajzer

Imperial Inspection Tours of Galicia 1851, 1868

> *When kings journey around the countryside, making ap-*
> *pearances, attending fêtes, conferring honors, exchanging*
> *gifts, or defying rivals, they mark it, like some wolf or tiger*
> *spreading his scent through his territory, as almost physi-*
> *cally part of them.*
>
> —*Clifford Geertz[1]*

The reorganization of the imperial court and the new commitment to strict ceremonial form and practice lent the legitimacy of tradition to the neoabsolutist program
of modernization from above. On ceremonial occasions, the new regime presented
the youthful energetic ruler surrounded by the pomp of the court, magnifying the
sacrality of the political authority he wielded and revealing him as both victorious
warlord and munificent benefactor. More than any other imperial celebrations,
inspection tours and imperial visitation of the crownlands brought the emperor and
the court into direct contact with populations and power structures far removed
from Vienna.[2] During inspection tours the emperor became, as surely as he did
when performing Catholic ceremonies in the capital, a living symbol promoting
dynastic loyalty and identification with the state he ruled. The examination of a
series of imperial journeys to Galicia illustrates how the changes from neoabsolutism to constitutional rule and from centralization to the devolution of power
affected the presentation of the imperial image.

 Franz Joseph visited Galicia a number of times over the course of his reign.
Galicia was one of the more recent acquisitions of the dynasty and provides an
ideal setting to study this transformation. Its political leadership, at first largely
antagonistic to Habsburg rule, was deemed one of the pillars of the state system
by the final third of the nineteenth century and its inhabitants were counted among

the most loyal to the House of Habsburg. Franz Joseph's trips to Galicia were not directed solely at the population of this province, but were meant to enhance the prestige of emperor and state in the eyes of the population of the monarchy as a whole.[3]

The present chapter focuses on the 1851 inspection tour of Galicia and the aborted 1868 *Kaiserreise.* The first section offers a brief overview of Habsburg Galicia. The second section examines the 1851 efforts to bring the imperial court to this distant province and to define the roles of dynasty, local elites, and the wider population within the idealized neoabsolutist system. As the final section of this chapter shows, in 1868, after the institution of the constitutional system, the planned imperial visit was designed to project a very different conception of the relationship between the imperial crown and the Polish aristocracy. Chapter 3 then concentrates on the 1880 imperial inspection tour of the province and briefly considers the emperor's 1894 visit to the Galician Provincial Exhibition in Lemberg.

Habsburg Galicia

Franz Joseph was not the first Habsburg emperor to inspect Galicia, today divided between Poland and Ukraine. Joseph II visited the province in 1773, 1780, 1783, and again in 1786.[4] These visits came shortly after the Habsburg Monarchy acquired this territory in the first partition of Poland in 1772. With the final two partitions of 1793 and 1795, Prussia, Russia, and the Habsburg Monarchy completed the dismemberment of Poland. The Habsburgs papered over this breach of historic right by naming their slice the "Kingdom of Galicia and Lodomeria," seemingly reviving medieval Hungarian claims to "Ruthenian Galicia."[5]

Like many Habsburg provinces, Galicia had an ethnically diverse population. According to the census, in 1880, 3,059,222 Poles and 2,551,594 Ruthenians (Ukrainians) lived in this province, one of the poorest of the monarchy.[6] Polish speakers accounted for well over 80 percent of the population in Galicia's western districts; Ruthenians constituted some two-thirds of the inhabitants in the east, where religious, social, and ethnic divisions reinforced each other. Most peasants in eastern Galicia were Greek Catholic Ruthenian speakers. Almost all noble landlords and the majority of the urban population were Roman Catholic Polish speakers. The annexation of Galicia also brought an estimated 200,000 Jews into the monarchy, their numbers reaching 800,000 by 1900.[7]

In most of Western Europe those recognized as nobles constituted less than 1 percent of the population. The hereditary nobility (*szlachta*) of the former Polish-Lithuanian Commonwealth included 8–10 percent of the population. Members of the *szlachta,* of Polish, Belorussian, Lithuanian, German, and baptized-Jewish origin, were imbued with a sense of "Polishness" tied to their exalted political and social position.[8] Nobles enjoyed many privileges in Poland-Lithuania, including the *liberum veto:* theoretically, any noble could negate any piece of legislation. In reality, poor nobles wielded little power, and a small number of wealthy magnate families dominated the state.

Until 1848, most Galician peasants were obligated to provide labor service, the *robot,* to noble landowners. Stefan Kieniewicz writes that around 1830 "the great lords sat in Vienna, the *szlachta* did not touch politics, the towns resounded with German and jargon [meaning Yiddish], and the peasant was "imperial.""[9] Many peasants well into the twentieth century defined themselves as "from here" rather than as "Poles" or "Ruthenians." The "Poles" were the noble landlords; non-noble non-Jews were simply peasants who attended either Roman Catholic or Greek Catholic (Uniate) churches.[10]

Jews made up a significant proportion of the population in many towns, including Cracow and Lemberg, though the numbers of town-dwelling Poles and Ruthenians increased dramatically in the nineteenth and early twentieth centuries. Many Polish landowners hired Jews to administer their estates or awarded Jews the *propinacya,* the alcohol monopoly. Often the most heated social conflicts were those between Jewish tavern owners and estate managers and Polish and Ruthenian peasants.[11]

Though far from the imperial palace in Vienna, Galicians soon came into contact with Habsburg efforts to increase the power of the crown by improving and expanding the state administration.[12] Maria Theresa's urbarial reforms, spurred on by economic pressure and peasant uprisings in Bohemia, outlawed the beating of peasants and gave peasants the right to complain of noble abuses before a state official.[13] Joseph II confirmed and expanded these reforms, ended the personal servitude of the serf (*Leibeigenschaft*), prevented landowners from arbitrarily adding land farmed by serfs (rustical land) to their own holdings (dominical lands), and guaranteed the serf the right to marry, choose an occupation, and leave the land—though in order to leave the land the peasant had to find a replacement.[14] Joseph's final peasant reform would have replaced the *robot* with cash payments both to the state and to the landowner.

These measures yielded mixed results. The reforms eliminated some of the peasants' work and tax burdens, but subjected peasants to new taxes levied directly by the state and to compulsory military service. On his deathbed, faced with pressure from the nobility, military tensions with Turkey and Prussia, revolution in Belgium, and unrest in Hungary, Joseph II renounced his last reform. Still, the enlightened absolutists had established the precedent of state intervention in the lord-peasant relationship.[15] Habsburg efforts to alleviate the harsher aspects of serfdom bolstered the myth of the Good Emperor. When Franz Joseph came to Galicia in 1894, peasant newspapers declared that Joseph II lived on in the "songs of the people as their Protector and True Father."[16]

Habsburg reforms also affected religious rights and the structure of administration and government. Joseph's Edicts of Toleration transformed the relationship of Jews to the state. Now defined as potentially useful citizens, Jews became subject to conscription and could attend public schools.[17] Vienna recognized the equality of the Greek Catholic clergy with the Roman Catholic clergy and supported improvements in the training and compensation of clergy and in the organization of the Greek Catholic dioceses.[18] Joseph's emphasis on German as the language of the unified state had its effect on Galicia as well. The administrative language of the province and of the educational system became German, and with the new administration came German-speaking officials. Vienna installed a new provincial diet of clergy, magnates, and gentry in Lemberg.[19]

As the leading advocates of the principle of legitimacy from the Congress of Vienna to the revolutions of 1848, the Habsburgs were suspicious of the activities of Polish revolutionaries and made few concessions to the desire of Polish aristocrats for home rule.[20] Many Galician Poles had supported Napoleon and later the failed 1830–31 uprising in the Russian partition. In exile in France and elsewhere, Polish revolutionaries engaged in conspiratorial activity aimed at the eventual reconstitution of Poland.[21] From 1815 to 1848, the Habsburgs did little to improve the lives of Galician peasants; yet suspicion of the nobility reinforced the perception of many peasants of the noble as enemy and the emperor as benefactor and protector.[22]

The debacle of the 1846 Polish uprising in Galicia documented anew the apparent pro-Habsburg orientation of many Polish peasants and their suspicion of the Polish nobility. Revolutionaries attempted to rally the population in the name of "Poland" against the Habsburg occupier. Instead of joining a people's uprising aimed at the restoration of Poland, rioting peasants burned manors, hanged hundreds of Polish landowners, and brought the severed heads of some to Austrian officials as a show of imperial loyalty and hatred for the Polish lords. Many Polish nobles believed that Austrian bureaucrats had encouraged the massacres. The Habsburgs used the jacquerie to incorporate Cracow into Habsburg Galicia.[23]

Polish revolutionaries fell short again in their efforts to ignite popular revolts against Habsburg rule in Galicia in 1848. Galician governor Franz Stadion supported the Greek Catholic hierarchy and the Supreme Ruthenian Council in Lemberg, leading to angry Polish assertions that Stadion had invented the Ruthenians in an effort to undermine Polish unity.[24] Stadion also issued a proclamation freeing the Galician peasantry from labor duties, upstaging calls by Polish revolutionaries for an end to the *robot*. The law for emancipation in the monarchy as a whole was passed by the Kremsier parliament, promulgated by the emperor on 7 September 1848, and communicated to the peasantry as a gift from the hand of the emperor.[25] Galician peasants abandoned the revolution; the Habsburg army crushed the rebel democrats, émigrés, gentry, magnates, and their burgher allies in Cracow and Lemberg. Many of the gains of the revolutions were reversed by 1851, but Franz Joseph did not rescind the emancipation of the peasantry.[26]

Vienna appointed conservative Polish magnate Agenor Gołuchowski governor (*Statthalter* in German; *Namiestnik* in Polish) of Galicia in 1849.[27] A wave of German-speaking bureaucrats, police, and military personnel did little to placate restless Polish nobles, however. Many, especially west Galician conservatives, viewed Gołuchowski as a traitor, only decades later acknowledging the realism of his policies.[28] The events of 1846 and 1848 increased the distaste of many aristocrats for the Habsburg regime and seemed to confirm the imperial orientation of the peasant, based as much on suspicion of the Polish landowners as on the legend of the Good Emperor.

1851—Supporting the Monarchical Principle

Franz Joseph embarked on a series of tours of his provinces following the final suppression of revolution. From 1849 to 1851, the emperor traveled to Hungary, Trieste, Bohemia, Moravia, Tyrol, Vorarlberg, Venice, Italy again, and finally to Galicia and neighboring Bukovina. The neoabsolutist regime replaced the new freedoms of the revolutionary period with harsh censorship and laws retarding the growth of civil society. In this political climate, the court and government could use the army, police, and court ceremony to project the image of the emperor as they chose, making few if any concessions to local sentiment during imperial visitations. These inspection tours were meant to impress the population with the power and majesty of the young emperor, whose will was executed by the victorious army and the expanding state bureaucracy, and who was prepared both to offer mercy and to ruthlessly quell threats to internal order. Enthusiastic crowds would provide evidence of popular acceptance of the restored dynasty.

Ultimate authority over the planning and execution of the 1851 *Kaiserreise* to Galicia and Bukovina was concentrated in the hands of two of the leading strongmen of the new regime. General-Adjutant Carl Graf Grünne, the head of the Military Chancellery and former acting grand court master, coordinated the trip.[29] Interior Minister Alexander Bach, his name virtually synonymous with neoabsolutism, accompanied the emperor. Franz Joseph personally approved all details and made minute changes, while the Polish nobility was denied an independent role in organizing events. Grünne communicated Bach's wishes and those of Franz Joseph to Galician *Statthalter* Gołuchowski, whose input was limited to the execution of the orders of the central government and the court.[30]

Grünne's main task was to recreate the world of the imperial court in a poor province far removed from Vienna, thereby defending and asserting the central tenet of the neoabsolutist governing system: the emperor was the font of all state power. The display of the magnificence of the emperor required the transportation of the court itself to Galicia. In addition to Franz Joseph, the imperial suite included Bach, Galician military commander Field Marshal Lieutenant Eduard Schwarzenberg,[31] their personal assistants, several military officers, the emperor's personal body servants, the quartermaster, court paymasters, nineteen chefs, bakers, and kitchen assistants, five servants from the imperial cellars, and seven from the court table-chamber.[32] In all, some one hundred and forty people traveled with Franz Joseph to Galicia in 1851.[33]

In 1851, train lines from Vienna did not penetrate the borders of Galicia.[34] From Troppau, the capital of Austrian Silesia, the imperial suite would have to disembark and ride in wagons and carriages for more than three weeks, dependent on the weather, to Cracow, Lemberg, Czernowitz (Chernivtsi in Ukrainian; Cernauti in Romanian), the capital of Bukovina, and back along muddy unkempt roads. Over one hundred horses pulled the twenty-three imperial wagons carrying the imperial suite.[35]

The dozens of formal meals and ceremonial events during the three-week tour of Galicia provided opportunities to impress the grandeur of the monarch onto the local scene. The hierarchical world of the Habsburg court derived its meaning in part from the physical portrayal of power relationships expressed in ceremony and celebrations. Court rankings determined the lists of those invited to the emperor's table. Few if any exceptions were made to accommodate local conditions. This strict adherence to court etiquette and the refusal of the imperial court to accredit the princely titles of many of the leading Polish magnate families created bitterness in the early stages of the preparations for the emperor's trip. Nobles left off the lists resented the fact that others, "notorious for taking the most decisive part in the revolutionary movements of the last years," received this recognition, while "calm, solid men" who had refused to take part in the uprisings of 1846 and 1848 were passed over. Some of the latter, considering themselves slighted, voiced their intentions to remove themselves from Cracow during the emperor's visit.[36]

Those who did receive invitations to the imperial table listened to music performed by military orchestras and attempted to ingest a few morsels. The Habsburgs had long abandoned the baroque practice of admitting the public to witness the emperor eat; however, no one could eat before the emperor began and all found their dishes cleared away the moment the ascetic monarch completed each course, forcing many to seek out a second meal at local establishments.[37]

The emperor's chosen accommodations (referred to as the *Hoflager*, the court camp) gave rise to more resentment on the part of the Polish nobility. The choice of *Hoflager* for the emperor was an important part of the presentation of the imperial court in the provinces. Acceptable locations typically boasted a spacious hall for hosting representative dinners and audiences, a balcony or large window from which the emperor could be seen by the gathered local populations, a grand space or square before the *Hoflager* to allow for parades and honor guards, and large stables to accommodate dozens of horses. In 1817, the court of Franz I had designated palaces and castles of great Polish nobles in and near larger towns as *Hoflager* and prepared government buildings to receive the court suite in smaller towns and villages. In 1851, Bach and Grünne deemed only post offices, military and government buildings, and the governor's mansion in Lemberg suitable to host the imperial party, a clear reflection of the neoabsolutist regime's distrust of the Polish nobility.[38]

The military and police were responsible for security. The Lemberg police observed all foreigners and staked out taverns popular with such suspicious characters as students, youths of various classes, pensioned officers, lower bureaucrats, and women of reportedly dubious morality.[39] Field Marshal Lieutenant Schwarzenberg arranged for the concentration of thousands of troops in the major towns along the emperor's route, the largest number, almost 8,000, to be billeted in Lemberg.[40] The army formations had to be available for imperial inspections and to line the streets and squares Franz Joseph would ride through during the many planned festivities. These arrangements were not meant solely as security measures. Like Joseph II, Franz Joseph always appeared in public dressed in military garb, giving visible articulation to his preference for a military lifestyle and his trust of and dependence on the army to support his regime.

In 1851, through censorship and the network of official newspapers, the government enjoyed a virtual press monopoly and could present the *Kaiserreise* to the reading public as proof of the success and popularity of the neoabsolutist program. At Grünne's request, Gołuchowski ordered all district captains (*Bezirkshauptmann* in German; *Starosta* in Polish), heads of the local offices of the provincial administration, to prepare descriptions of the emperor's reception in their counties. These reports were sent to both the provincial administration (*Statthalterei* in German; *Namiestnictwo* in Polish) and to Bach. They were to "provide an exact and detailed description" of the "journey and stay, festivities with which [Franz Joseph was] greeted, and the mood of the population . . . in order to make these reports into suitable articles" for the provincial press and for the *Wiener Zeitung,* the official organ of the Vienna government.[41]

The official mouthpiece of the Galician administration, *Gazeta Lwowska,* began raising public interest in the emperor's imminent arrival well in advance of his entrance into Biała. Ten days before Franz Joseph first crossed the border from Austrian Silesia into Galicia, the paper described the emperor's reception during his tour of the monarchy's Italian lands, each article based on reports printed days before in the *Wiener Zeitung. Gazeta Lwowska* ignored the many slights the emperor received from the Italian population and the ongoing state of emergency in Lombardy.[42] Though there had been problems preventing a coming together of crown and population in the past, acknowledged *Gazeta Lwowska,* the present trip to Italy was a "great and absolute victory for the monarchical principle." Now, "almost everywhere His Majesty is greeted with signs of sincere joy. The knightly bravery and courtesy that characterizes His sublime spirit created a most serious impression."[43] Here in Galicia, the *Gazeta Lwowska* informed the reading public, "Millions of inhabitants" will "await him [Franz Joseph] with deep feelings of honor and respect." All strata of society were eager to greet the emperor with love in their "loyal hearts."[44]

1851—The Triumphant Procession

The tone set by government propaganda, the numerous ceremonial entrances into towns and villages, and the comings and goings of the imperial suite to various points of interest provided a series of opportunities for the population to view the emperor in dramatic, heroic, and pious poses. The events and the press coverage were choreographed to impress the monarchical principle upon the population. The inspection tour heralded the new regime's priorities: the church, the bureaucracy, and the army were to be the pillars of the new order, united under and contributing to the glory of the dynasty.

Only twenty-one years old, Franz Joseph performed his role with the astounding patience and endurance that would characterize his ceremonial performance throughout his sixty-eight-year reign. His party departed from Vienna's Schönbrunn palace by train on the evening of 10 October. At 2 A.M. on 11 October, local officials, gendarmerie, and clergy greeted the emperor in Troppau, the capital of Austrian Silesia. The imperial party then headed out along the Reichsstrasse toward Galicia. The emperor's party arrived at 4:30 P.M. in Podgórze. Artillery batteries fired a salute and church bells began to ring. Before a decorated arch and a large crowd of officials and townspeople, Podgórze's oldest citizen, a ninety-six-year-old man who had welcomed Joseph II in 1786, greeted Franz Joseph in the name of the town.[45]

An even more elaborate welcome awaited the imperial party in Cracow. A delegation of landowners greeted Franz Joseph as soon as he crossed the newly renamed Franz-Joseph Bridge connecting Podgórze and Cracow. This delegation was a late addition to the schedule that accounted for almost every minute of the emperor's time. Prominent citizens of Cracow did not want the Jews of Kazimierz, who did not enjoy full and equal citizenship, to be the first Cracovians to welcome the emperor. The *Statthalterei* agreed that this "would not be entirely proper."[46] The imperial procession then continued toward Kazimierz. Soldiers, charitable organizations, seminary faculty and students, and the Jewish community lined the streets. A triumphal arch conveyed the sentiments of "The thankful Israelites to the Emperor," who hoped that the emperor would soon confirm the freedoms they had gained during the revolutions.[47]

At Florian Gate, a reminder of Cracow's medieval fortifications, school children, guilds, and peasants cheered as city council members presented a golden key and an address to the emperor. In the medieval Church of Mary, priests blessed Franz Joseph. Civil and military authorities, *szlachta,* and the academic senate of the Jagiellonian University waited for Franz Joseph at the designated *Hoflager.* "The city, especially the streets through which his Most High Majesty rode, was decorated festively . . . and at the Florian gate as well as before the Most High *Hoflager* strewn with flowers by maidens in white dresses."[48]

Franz Joseph devoted most of his schedule in Cracow and other large towns to viewing military installations, highlighting his support of the army and the role of the threat of violence in maintaining stability. Three years before, the imperial army had quelled Polish uprisings; the army now stood as proof of military occupation and the willingness of the Habsburgs to suppress all dissent. Wawel Castle was among the many military sites Franz Joseph inspected in Cracow and the surrounding region. Perched on a hill overlooking the city, this Renaissance castle had been the residence, and its church the burial place, of Polish kings. In 1851, this symbolic heart of old Poland housed a garrison of Habsburg troops. On 12 October, Franz Joseph attended mass in Wawel Cathedral, visited the tombs of the Polish kings, and toured the castle.[49]

From Cracow to Lemberg, local authorities greeted the tireless emperor at decorated arches. In larger towns, German-speaking mayors, bureaucrats, and army officers paid homage to the ruler in the name of Galician society. Franz Joseph toured the salt mines of Wieliczka and viewed military formations in Tarnów. Rabbis lifted Torahs, priests blessed Franz Joseph, and peasants cheered. Occasionally the emperor answered with a few words praising decorations and festivities—"Ach, that is very lovely."[50]

Lemberg, the administrative capital, hosted four days of festivities (figure 8). On 16 October, "The masses crowded together at the first shot from the High Fortress: cannon fire, ringing bells, and cries of joy from afar foretold the approach of the Person of His Imperial Majesty." At the *Statthalterei,* singing groups serenaded the emperor who watched from the balcony: "Grateful to God—loyal to the Lord [Franz Joseph]/We do not despair of our fate/Each content with his estate/From the heart we shout: 'May He Live Long!'"[51] The gathered crowd then sang the imperial hymn. Franz Joseph's evening survey of the illuminated town "ended the glorious day that will remain unforgettable in the annals of Lemberg."[52]

During Franz Joseph's stay in Lemberg, the city council produced a gala theater performance in his honor. Officials from the Office of the Grand Court Master assigned seats according to court rankings, transforming the inside of the theater into a reflection of the court-defined ideal social hierarchy. Audience members rose and cheered when Franz Joseph appeared in the imperial box. Franz Joseph also acknowledged the alleged loyalty of the Ruthenians, the "Tyroleans of the East." Lemberg had been the center of Ruthenian activity in support of Austria and the emperor in 1848. The Supreme Ruthenian Council, backed by Greek

Figure 8: Entrance of Franz Joseph into Lemberg. Karl von Höpflingen und Bergendorf, 1851. Austrian National Library.

Catholic clergy, collected 200,000 signatures on a petition to divide Galicia.[53] On 18 October 1851, Franz Joseph laid the foundation stone for a building to house the National Institute. A "multitude of onlookers" sang the imperial hymn.[54]

On his last night in the provincial capital, the emperor and his suite rode through illuminated streets to attend a ball sponsored by aristocrats at the Ossolineum, the Polish library founded in 1817 by Józef Maksymilian Ossoliński. Banners hung on the building declared: "Today the people with the king and the king with the people," and offered "Greetings to our king in the land of our fathers." Despite these oblique references to Polish traditions, decorations confirmed that Lemberg was not a Polish possession. The Ruthenian Greek Catholic cathedral displayed its banners in French: "Divine Heart, protect him always!" The banner hung on Lemberg's largest synagogue, lit by hundreds of lamps proclaimed in German: "See! His Majesty in all his splendor. Homage and Loyalty come together; Justice and Peace embrace each other."[55]

Evaluating the 1851 *Kaiserreise*

District captains filled their reports to Bach with descriptions of the enthusiastic response of the population to the presence of the emperor. These reports became the basis for laudatory articles published in the monarchy's network of government and heavily censored newspapers.[56] The consistent reporting emphasized the apparent widespread acceptance of the legitimacy of the renewed dynasty.

The "triumphant procession" described in the government newspapers did not, however, impress Galicia's Polish nobility. Paweł Popiel, an influential west

Galician aristocrat, described the reception for the emperor in Cracow as "loud, because there were many peasants, but cold." He and others were incensed by the imprisonment of Adam Potocki, the leading figure among the Cracow conservative nobles. "We experienced the time of the first visit of the emperor in Cracow with pain. We were more concerned with Adam Potocki [held prisoner in Wawel Castle] than with Franz Joseph in the Spiski Palace. He had not yet earned for himself the right to the gratitude of the Poles . . ."[57] As if in confirmation of Popiel's words, the emperor received and consequently ignored at least three petitions signed by magnates asking for an increase in Polish (read *szlachta*) influence in the province, the recognition of the Polish language in public life, and an easing of military and police measures.[58] *Statthalter* Gołuchowski felt his position as the representative of the crown had been compromised before the Polish nobility by the fact that he and his administration had been visibly subordinate to military authorities. Gołuchowski tendered his resignation and asked for a position in the diplomatic corps.[59] A surprised Minister President Felix Schwarzenberg brought this to the attention of the emperor, who immediately rejected Gołuchowski's resignation.[60]

The characterization of the 1851 *Kaiserreise* as a failure became part of the accepted Polish historical account of the reign of Franz Joseph and of the transformation of the relationship between the Galician Poles and the Habsburg state. In the late nineteenth century, democrats and conservatives made comparisons between the allegedly triumphant imperial visitation of 1880 and the supposed fiasco of 1851. The progressive Lemberg daily *Dziennik Polski* claimed that spontaneous expressions of state and dynastic loyalty like those welcoming the emperor in 1880 had not occurred in 1851: in 1851 homes had been decorated in imperial black and yellow at the direct request of the Galician administration; only government appointed mayors and a few dozen girls in white dresses had paid homage to the emperor.[61] In his book commemorating the 1880 *Kaiserreise,* Alexander Nowolecki wrote that "the reception [in 1851] was purely bureaucratic, the public remained aloof, even hostile. . . . The emperor stayed in administrative buildings, the public did not participate . . ."[62] According to Polish conservatives and democrats, the 1851 and 1880 imperial visits to Galicia proved that constitutional change, the devolution of power, and the Polonization of the Galician administration after 1867 had effected a sea change in the attitude of the Polish population toward the emperor and Austria.[63]

In 1851, however, eliciting a positive response from the Galician population as a whole—peasants and townspeople—was of far greater importance to Franz Joseph's government than ameliorating the wounded sensibilities of the Polish elites. Bach's intelligence apparatus assessed the attitudes of the population in very positive terms:

> Travels of his Majesty the Emperor to Italy and Galicia have given rise to expressions of the fullest satisfaction from the public. It is clear that the

imposing and winning appearance of the monarch brought forth an agreeable impression among the population of these provinces, and through this positive impression must work favorably on the securing of public order and on the expansion of sympathies for the government.[64]

The Galician district captains reported that the arrival of the emperor "was especially joyfully received by the rural population."[65] Tens of thousands of peasants traveled to villages along the emperor's route and to Cracow, Lemberg, and other large towns in order to catch a glimpse of the exalted ruler, either out of loyalty to the emperor and Austria or because the presence of the emperor was something out of the ordinary in lives full of hard work and monotony. Many hoped to slip past the military cordons and hand the emperor petitions for financial support or imperial assistance in struggles with local manors arising from the abolition of serfdom:

> Wherever the emperor appeared, he was accompanied by cheering masses, and the needy used the moments [when Franz Joseph] exited and entered his carriage to lay their petitions into the hands of the all merciful emperor, where they found merciful and comforting acceptance.[66]

The court received more than 3,500 petitions addressed to the emperor during the three-week tour of Galicia.[67] In addition to peasants, widows of soldiers and policemen begged for pension assistance, priests asked for help in repairing churches, mothers beseeched the emperor to grant mercy to sons jailed for activities during the 1846 uprising or the 1848 revolution. Franz Joseph left 2,000 gulden in Cracow and 5,000 gulden in Lemberg with instructions for the police and the governor's office to evaluate which of the thousands of petitions were deserving of imperial favor. The well-publicized charity of the emperor and his personal concern for the peasantry, illustrated by his acceptance of petitions, reinforced the notion that his state, not the Polish nobles, defended peasant interests.

Court officials and the emperor himself were very satisfied by the apparent popular affirmation of dynastic patriotism. Franz von Raymond, a court official who acted as quartermaster during the inspection tours of the monarchy's Italian lands and of Galicia, was moved by what he interpreted as genuine popular enthusiasm. As Franz Joseph appeared on the main square of Podgórze, Raymond wrote in his reports to the grand court master in Vienna, "Even those standing at the farthest reaches of the square, as if responding to one command, took off their hats. Such an unmistakable sign of respect is especially satisfying to those of us coming out of Italy," where Franz Joseph had been embarrassed by public expressions of discontent.[68] Raymond was pleased that Galicia provided a sharp contrast with the Italian experience: "at each station hundreds of people, old and young, Christian and Jew, are busy preparing the way for their emperor" even though the peasants no longer owed labor duties.[69]

Franz Joseph shared Raymond's sentiments. From Tarnów he wrote his mother that Galicia, compared to Italy, was certainly "not a very romantic land, its population is however extraordinarily good and uncivilized." The emperor was pleased with the organization of the trip and the overt displays of dynastic loyalty he witnessed:

> The garrison was mobilized, church bells, 101 cannon salute, the magistrate with the keys to the city at the city gate, school children, guilds with their banners, Jews with rabbis carrying the Torah, clergy in pontifical attire at the cathedral, the authorities gathered at the house, much shouting, especially the Jews, who made an unbelievable spectacle. The whole in order and decent.[70]

The aims of the inspection tour did not include an offer of partnership to the Polish nobility; instead, the court and the government informed the Polish nobles of their place within the new system. The court divided all of Habsburg society into social orders, each of which derived its status through its relationship with the emperor. Grünne and the court coordinated the *Kaiserreise* without the input of the Polish aristocrats. Military security, army parades, inspections of fortresses, and visits to military schools and other facilities impressed on the nobility the power of the army that had recently suppressed revolution. The Galician administration, headed by a Polish magnate but staffed largely by German-speakers, acted only as the executive arm of the Vienna government. Mayors and other officials appointed by Vienna delivered speeches, often in German, praising the monarch and devoid of any references to the economic and cultural interests of the Polish elite or of the Galician population. Petitions that contained such references and expressed hope that the new emperor would consent to the establishment of some limited forms of home rule were ignored. The apparent pro-Habsburg orientation of the peasantry reminded the nobility of the futility of any program aimed at reconstituting a Polish state.

The official interpretations of the inspection tour echoed the neoabsolutist conception of the relationship between emperor and subject. The government press had bombarded the reading public with articles describing the "manly" emperor who graced the people of Galicia with his presence and personally assured Galicia of peace and stability in return for acceptance of Habsburg rule:

> Knightly and at the same time impressive as a courteous personage, the adored monarch has awakened in the hearts of all of his subjects true patriotic inspiration, from which arises true love for Throne and Monarchy, promising to bring forth at each moment the most beautiful fruit of unshaken submissive loyalty.[71]

Despite the contentions of some historians, later characterizations of the 1851 inspection tour as a disaster by Polish conservatives and democrats reflect only the views of those who had been frustrated with the refusal of the neoabsolutist administration to increase the role of Poles in the governance of Galicia.[72] Bitterness at the exclusion of Poles from political responsibility cannot alter the fact that the 1851 *Kaiserreise* was an almost unqualified victory for the "monarchical principle."[73]

1868

Franz Joseph and Empress Elisabeth planned to visit Galicia in 1868 as one in a series of imperial tours designed to display the now constitutional emperor to the provinces. Franz Joseph's first visits to Galicia in 1851 and 1855, the latter during the Crimean War, took place within the context of neoabsolutism. In the 1850s, the court and government had ignored the desires of the Polish elites for autonomy in Galicia. In 1868, however, imperial celebration was no longer independent of political disputes concerning the constitutional system and Galician autonomy.

The humiliation of Solferino in 1859 convinced even Franz Joseph that neoabsolutism had failed to provide the monetary resources and political stability needed to pursue the dynasty's interests within or beyond the monarchy's borders. Franz Joseph now accepted the need to institute constitutional reforms. In 1848, the dynasty's first move to appease the forces of revolution was to sacrifice the most potent symbol of the *Vormärz* regime, Metternich; in 1859, the emperor dismissed Bach. Grünne and the hated police minister Johann Kempen-Fichtenstamm soon submitted their resignations.

Franz Joseph appointed Gołuchowski minister of the interior in late 1859, and this once and future Galician *Statthalter* oversaw the drafting of the 1860 October Diploma.[74] The October Diploma created (or recreated) provincial diets based on limited suffrage. The diets were given considerable influence in local affairs and were to send representatives to a weak central Reichsrat in Vienna. German liberals and other opponents of this federalist arrangement pushed for the promulgation of the February Patent in 1861, which enhanced the competence of the Reichsrat. In protest, Poles, Czechs, and South Slavs boycotted the Vienna parliament. The impotent Galician diet, in which a large number of peasants sat due largely to the sponsorship of Vienna, functioned lamely until prorogued in 1863 in the face of revolution in Russian Poland. The failure of the 1863 January uprising in Russian Poland prompted much rethinking by nobles and intellectuals who had been sympathetic to the idea of an armed struggle to restore a Polish state. When Gołuchowski was once again appointed Galician *Statthalter* in 1866, he received greater support for his program of cooperation, compromise, and dynastic loyalty than he had enjoyed in the 1850s.[75]

In the 1860s, before Prussia defeated the Habsburg armies at Königgrätz in 1866, the emperor opened negotiations with the Hungarian nobility to create a new constitutional structure that would grant Hungary a special status. Conservative Polish nobles and Polish democrats opposed a Dualist settlement that would establish in the Austrian half of the monarchy a strong central Reichsrat dominated by German-speakers. On 10 December 1866, the Galician diet (Sejm) approved an address backed by Gołuchowski; his ally, the former revolutionary democrat Florian Ziemiałkowski; archconservative magnate Kazimierz Grocholski; and leading west Galician magnate Adam Potocki. The address offered loyalty to the dynasty and the state in return for Polish hegemony in Galicia and the devolution of power to the Sejm:

> . . . Austria—in order to blossom more strongly than ever before—will become in its internal structure the most powerful expression of respect for freedom, and externally a shield of western civilization, nationality, humanity and justice. —Such a mission was our task through many centuries. Without fear, therefore, of departing from our national idea, with faith in the mission of Austria and with confidence in the durability of the changes which Your Majesty's words expressed as an immutable purpose, from the depths of our hearts we declare that we stand by You, Your Majesty, and there we wish to remain.[76]

The final 1867 constitutional Compromise that created Austria-Hungary shocked and dismayed many Poles. Franz Joseph and the Austro-German liberals ignored the pleas of the Sejm for a special constitutional status for Galicia. Franciszek Smolka's new National-Democratic Society supported street protests against the Compromise. The Polish democrats wanted to join the Bohemian Czechs in boycotting the Reichsrat. The "Mamelukes"—urban intellectuals and noble-bureaucrats led by Ziemiałkowski and Gołuchowski—secured concessions on school policy and language use, laying the ground work for "Galician autonomy."[77]

The plans for the 1868 *Kaiserreise* contrasted sharply with 1851. The court and military planners had accepted little input from the Galician administration or from Polish elites in 1851. The 1868 imperial visit to Galicia would have acknowledged the "great success of the politics of the great *Statthalter* [Gołuchowski]" and Ziemiałkowski.[78] The post-1867 Polonization of the Galician administration and concessions to Polish autonomy in Galicia increased the influence of the *Statthalter* and the Polish elites over the organization of the planned *Kaiserreise*.

Adam Potocki was named assistant court master and marshal of the journey. This prominent conservative had been in prison during the 1851 *Kaiserreise*, had written letters and petitions calling for greater Polish influence in Galicia in the 1850s, and had authored the 1866 address offering loyalty in return for Galician autonomy.[79] Once listed by Bach's network of informers among "the families and individuals of the crownland Galicia, who are politically compromised or through their ambiguous behavior have not earned any trust," Potocki was now poised to play a major role in presenting the monarch to Galician society—and

Galician society to the monarch.[80] Representatives of now autonomous Galician institutions also actively participated in the preparations. The Sejm voted a 25,000 gulden credit to prepare a grand reception for the emperor.[81] Elected mayors and members of the new diet—not appointed German-speaking officials—would represent Galician society to the imperial visitor.

In 1851, many Polish aristocrats felt slighted by the strict application of court ceremonial rules and military regulations. As a result, Gołuchowski submitted his resignation. In 1868, the *Statthalter* pleaded with the court to allow men and women "who hold no public office and therefore cannot appear at the official introductions, to be introduced" to Franz Joseph. Gołuchowski admitted that this "may not correspond to the letter of court etiquette . . . [but] it seems totally out of the question, considering the particular societal relations here and especially at such an occasion as the present one, to bring the dictates of court etiquette into full force."[82] The court responded by designating some events "court soirées," which were governed by less strict ceremonial rules.[83] The court also planned overnight stays and meals in the palaces of aristocrats.[84] In this way, the court preserved the integrity of imperial ceremony and accommodated local sentiment. The military command also responded favorably to Gołuchowski's concerns and ordered the suspension of army regulations.[85] Garrisons were not to mobilize. Only one company of honor guards would stand with officers at the train stations in Cracow and Lemberg.

The advance of the train system greatly affected the presentation of the emperor. With the completion of the line from Cracow to Lemberg in 1861, there was no longer any need for the imperial party to traverse the entire length of Galicia in horse-drawn wagons and carriages. The emperor could bypass small villages. Peasants could still see the emperor by congregating at decorated train stations along the route or by purchasing discounted train tickets to travel to larger towns.

With the concentration on large towns and noble palaces there was little practical need for an army of court officials. Yet a total of one hundred and sixty-four court officials—thirty Garde-Gendarmerie, twelve chefs, five bakers, and dozens of kitchen and table servants, including the seemingly indispensable court place-setters and imperial silver cleaners—prepared to escort the emperor on the 1868 inspection tour.[86] The anachronistic accouterments of the court—imperial wagons, chefs, and guards—no longer performed necessary functions, but were essential to the creation of a court universe removed from all connections with everyday life. The distance between the ethereal world of the court and the mundane existence of the audience for imperial ritual in Galicia made contact between emperor and subject potentially more meaningful.[87]

Months of planning virtually guaranteed a successful *Kaiserreise*. Yet, on 24 September, two days before the emperor's departure, Franz Joseph abruptly instructed the general-adjutant to inform all parties "the trip to Galicia is postponed indefinitely."[88] Kitchen staff, horses, and carriages already in Cracow returned to

Vienna.[89] Photographs and visiting cards depicting the imperial couple in supposed Polish costume intended as gifts for their various hosts were returned to Vienna, perhaps saving the emperor from embarrassment: in the portraits Franz Joseph wore a Hungarian tunic and distinctly non-Polish boots.[90] The emperor accepted Gołuchowski's resignation with little commentary.

The Galician press cleared Polish leaders of blame for the debacle. The usually sober Cracow conservative daily, *Czas,* imagined a conspiracy between Berlin and St. Petersburg against the pro-Polish changes to the structure of the monarchy that, according to *Czas,* a *Kaiserreise* to Galicia would have facilitated.[91] Lemberg's *Gazeta Narodowa* charged that the *Kaiserreise* had fallen victim to the power struggle between centralizing liberals like Cisleithanian Minister President Prince Auersperg, who opposed Galician autonomy, and the more federalist Count Eduard Taaffe.[92]

Some Polish observers and most subsequent scholarly accounts blamed Russian pressure.[93] Tsar Alexander II scheduled a visit to Warsaw—his first trip to his Polish territories since the suppression of the 1863 uprising—at the same time Franz Joseph was to be in Galicia. Comparisons of the receptions of the tsar in Warsaw and Franz Joseph in Lemberg would have been unfavorable to the Russian dynasty. Nevertheless, Russian threats failed to prevent the appointment of Gołuchowski as minister of the interior in 1860 or the appointment of Alfred Potocki as Cisleithanian minister president in 1870. It seems unlikely that Russian pressure would have been decisive in September 1868.[94]

Posters declaring that "Whoever participates in the reception is a traitor to the Nation" had marred Franz Joseph's recent trip to Prague.[95] Security reports from Galicia suggested the emperor's presence there could inspire similar public protests. The intelligence apparatus informed Vienna of plans by the Democratic Association for a Polish national demonstration in Lemberg. The police also warned that if widespread expectations for greater Polish autonomy in Galicia were not met, which they would not be, public opinion would turn against the dynasty.[96] Police reported that the "lower sectors of society" intended to greet Franz Joseph with cries of "The King of Poland Lives!"[97]

Despite ominous reports from the intelligence apparatus, a month of Sejm debates, and public protests against the *Ausgleich,* as late as 23 September preparations continued to be made for the inspection tour.[98] Franz Joseph and the central government were willing to risk open antipathy toward the *Ausgleich* as well as Russian displeasure until the moment the Sejm passed the Galician resolution on 24 September 1868.

On 22 August 1868, the Sejm opened for its first session in the new constitutional system. The Sejm majority rejected demands for a wholesale reorganization of the monarchy and adopted instead a moderate program of constitutional change.[99] The Galician resolution of 24 September protested that the Compromise "did not award our land as much legislative and administrative autonomy as its historical-political past, special nationality, level and dissemination of culture merits." The Sejm majority wanted to create a provincial government headed by a *Statthalter* responsible to the Sejm and to limit the purview of the Reichsrat and the Vienna government to matters specifically designated as common to the monarchy as a whole.[100] As Cracow conservative Józef Szujski wrote one year later, the Sejm majority endeavored to realize the stillborn federalist October diploma of 1860 and to secure the historic national dominance of Polish culture and language in Galicia against the centralizing Austro-German liberals.[101]

The resolution was unacceptable in Vienna. Franz Joseph had been crowned King of Hungary in a dramatic ceremony in Budapest on 8 June 1867 and the Dual Monarchy had become reality.[102] Although the crown was willing to make concessions, it would not write these concessions into the new constitution. Even to discuss such matters would encourage similar demands and provoke Hungarian opposition. When Gołuchowski learned that the resolution would doom the *Kaiserreise,* he renounced his earlier support of this measure and worked against its passage. The Sejm majority ignored his pleas. Advised that the Sejm "virtually demanded an autonomy totally opposed to the constitution of the empire," Franz Joseph cancelled the imperial visit to Galicia.[103]

In a letter to his mother dated 28 September 1868, Franz Joseph held the Poles who dominated the Galician diet responsible. "Unfortunately I have had to give up the trip to Galicia," wrote an incensed Franz Joseph,

> since the provincial diet, in genuine Polish irresponsibility, just now commits such incomprehensible foolishness that it was impossible for me to visit the province at this time. The lesson will, moreover, do good, and I hope to be able to make up the trip in the new year. Alfred Potocki behaved excellently in this incident, and it is refreshing to find such character in these times. Gołuchowski is completely broken by the anger over his compatriots.[104]

Whereas the 1851 *Kaiserreise* had mirrored the neoabsolutist conception of the post-revolution government and court, the plans for 1868 revealed flexibility in imperial ceremony and a willingness by the government and the emperor to allow local elites to use the imperial presence to their own advantage. The court was prepared to acknowledge the reality of social relations in Galicia and to accommodate important Polish nobles who did not have ceremonial standing. The Polish elites hoped to bolster their position in Galician society. The Galician resolution, however, by openly challenging the *Ausgleich,* convinced the emperor to postpone the trip.

Franz Joseph's 1867 crowning in Budapest acknowledged limitations on his authority to intervene in Hungarian affairs, even as it bound Hungary to the dynasty.[105] The collapse of plans for Franz Joseph to be crowned king of Bohemia in 1871 demonstrated the reality of the Compromise with Hungary as well as the refusal of the dynasty to formally acknowledge home-rule in Bohemia.[106] The cancellation of the 1868 *Kaiserreise* to Galicia must be understood in the same context.

In the constitutional era, with its political and press freedoms, imperial celebration and the display of the majesty of the emperor could not be separated from regional and monarchy-wide political disputes. The court and government alone could no longer entirely control the public portrayal of the emperor. The emperor had no choice but to cancel celebrations when the demands of the same regional elites who would be responsible for representing the emperor to the population directly conflicted with the aims of the government and the court. There would be no formal constitutional concession to Galician autonomy, and the emperor would not come to Galicia and thereby give recognition to the political elites of the province in the immediate aftermath of the passing of the Galician resolution.

Only the fall of the Austro-German liberal-dominated Cisleithanian government in 1879 and the formation of Eduard Taaffe's Iron Ring coalition created again an atmosphere conducive to the organization of another *Kaiserreise* to Galicia. The next chapter will examine the 1880 *Kaiserreise* to Galicia, revealing the possibility for successful promotion of the imperial image in the constitutional era and serious limitations on the dissemination of the symbol of the emperor as a focus for common identity in Cisleithania.

CHAPTER 3

The Ideal Monarchy

Galicia, 1880 and 1894

During Franz Joseph's 1851 trip to Galicia, the court and neoabsolutist regime carefully controlled the presentation of the emperor. From the 1860s on, the Vienna government and the imperial court had to compete with the increasingly partisan and lively press of Galicia and Cisleithania for the attention of the reading public. Enhanced public awareness of and interest in the formal political process ensured that public events as visible as the 1880 three-week imperial tour of the province and the five-day imperial visit to the Galician exhibition in 1894 would bring to the surface the struggle to define and achieve Polish (and Ruthenian) interests within Galicia and to rethink the relationship between Galicia and the monarchy as a whole. These imperial visits to Galicia forced Polish conservatives and Ruthenian intellectuals to consider how to portray themselves and Galician culture to their potential constituents in Galicia, to the emperor, and to the reading public of the monarchy.

In 1880, thirteen years after the 1867 Compromise had ushered in the era of de facto Polish autonomy in Galicia, Polish conservative nobles, who had distanced themselves from Franz Joseph in 1851, embraced the emperor. As in the past, Franz Joseph approved of every detail and insisted on some significant changes to the program, but for much of the 1880 *Kaiserreise* he was like a living statue, delivering speeches penned by Polish conservatives in settings chosen by the Polish elites. The receptions and public spectacles conveyed the conservatives' interpretation of the Galician present: the Polish conservatives, in partnership with the benevolent Habsburg dynasty, were facilitating the renewal of the Polish · nation while reinforcing Habsburg patriotism.

Polish "progressives," Ruthenian intellectuals, and Jewish leaders contested the narrative of *szlachta* leadership, Polish national unity, and imperial loyalty presented during the 1880 *Kaiserreise*.[1] Despite these challenges, the Polish conservatives considered the inspection tour a great triumph. Cheering crowds seemingly bore witness to the leadership claims of the conservatives, justifying their past, present, and future stewardship of the Polish national community in Galicia.

When Franz Joseph returned to Galicia in 1894, however, the political position of the conservatives was far less secure than it had been in 1880. Expanding suffrage and mass political mobilization altered the presentation and, more significantly, the reception of the imperial presence.

Setting the Stage

> *On 1 September 1880, from Jawiszowice to Cracow, groups of peasants crowded along the rail lines, gathering in large numbers at train stations led by priests . . . carrying church banners. At every station the numbers increased, and when the Special Imperial Court Train passed, for some time crowds ran behind enthusiastically sending cheers in honor of the emperor [Franz Joseph] to the heavens . . .*
>
> *—Czas, 2 September 1880, 1*

To a far greater degree than was the case in 1851, or would have been the case in 1868, the 1880 *Kaiserreise* to Galicia was a public event. For almost three weeks the scenes repeated themselves: cannon fire, chiming church bells, massive crowds, peasant bands on horseback, school girls in white dresses laying flowers along the emperor's path, torchlight parades, mountain top bonfires, city illuminations, serenades, court dinners, aristocratic balls, early morning prayers at cathedrals and synagogues. During Franz Joseph's 1880 inspection tour of Galicia, millions of Galicians either saw the emperor, talked with someone who did, read about his visit in the paper, or heard about it at a village reading hall or gathering, or from the local priest or rabbi.[2] Franz Joseph, liberator of the peasants, protector of the Ruthenians, patron of the Jews, granter of national rights to the Poles, drew the attention of Galicia's population to his presence.

Several factors combined to heighten public interest in the spectacle of the 1880 imperial visit to Galicia. First, the gradual expansion of suffrage for the Reichsrat, the spread of voluntary associations, improvements in the education system, and modest increases in literacy rates made Galicians more aware of happenings beyond the borders of the small towns and villages that were home to the majority of the population. Newspapers informed the public of the emperor's schedule and bombarded readers with exhortations by voluntary associations and government institutions to participate.[3]

Second, by the 1870s, the bitter memory of Habsburg participation in the partitions of Poland and the Habsburg suppression of subsequent Polish uprisings had faded and for decades Galicians had been schooled in dynastic patriotism.

Galicia's inhabitants read panegyric poems and stories about Franz Joseph and the imperial family in school textbooks, prayed for the emperor's health, attended annual celebrations of the emperor's birthday, and heard and read about the yearly Corpus Christi and foot-washing ceremonies in Vienna. The failed 1853 assassination attempt on the emperor's life, as well as Franz Joseph's 1854 wedding to Elisabeth of Bavaria, raised public sympathy for the imperial house. Though the empress did not often present herself to the public, the 1858 birth of the heir was widely publicized and Elisabeth did appear intermittently at her husband's side. The 1873 World Exhibition in Vienna, the twenty-fifth jubilee festivities in 1873, and the 1879 celebrations of the imperial couple's silver wedding anniversary provided additional opportunities for mass participation in imperial celebrations—and for the manufacture and consumption of mass-produced commemorative books and other souvenirs.[4]

A third factor affecting public perception of the 1880 *Kaiserreise* was the re-formation of the Cisleithanian government. The Czech boycott of parliamentary elections (lifted in 1879) and the curial system had assisted the German liberals in solidifying a strong majority in the Austrian Reichsrat. In 1879 the Austro-German liberals, the majority of whom had opposed the 1878 occupation of Bosnia, fell from power. Franz Joseph appointed his childhood friend Count Eduard Taaffe minister president of Cisleithania. Taaffe hoped to retain some liberals in his coalition, but soon turned to Austro-German conservatives, landowners, clericals, Czechs, and Poles to back his policies. Taaffe relied on this "Iron Ring" majority for the next thirteen years.[5] The liberals continued to believe in their imminent return to power, and the coalition partners took this threat seriously; however, the removal of the German liberals from power offered non-German elites an opening to increase their standing in Vienna and to lobby for greater devolution of power to the provinces. From June 1880 on, Taaffe's cabinet included two Galician Poles, revealing the dependence of the Cisleithanian government on the support of the Polish delegation to the Reichsrat.[6]

Finally, by 1880 a loose coalition of Polish conservative nobles, urban intellectuals, and bureaucrats had solidified its control over the cultural and political institutions of Galicia and pursued a policy of conciliation toward the dynasty and the state. This alliance became possible as the reality of Polish autonomy in Galicia reduced tensions between the Cracow conservatives and the Mamelukes (*szlachta* bureaucrats and urban intellectuals led by Ziemiałkowski and Gołuchowski). The Stańczyks (*stańczycy*), who took their name from a sixteenth-century Polish court jester, made up the core of this ascendant alliance.[7] Many of these Cracow conservatives had cultivated ties to the Polish exile organization under the Czartoryskis in Paris in the 1850s and 1860s. After the defeat of the 1863 uprising in the Russian partition, this new generation of Cracow conservatives rejected the Polish revolutionary tradition and moved toward loyalism.

In 1869, Józef Szujski, Stanisław Tarnowski, Stanisław Koźmian, and Ludwik Wodzicki published *Teka Stańczyka* (The Stańczyk Portfolio) in the Cracow journal *Przegląd Polski,* effectively announcing the existence of the Stańczyks as a coherent political faction.[8] The Stańczyks lampooned the hopes of Polish democrats for a new uprising against the partitioning powers as the foolish pipedreams of dangerous fanatics. Such fantasies, they asserted, only diverted the energies of the population from realistic goals that could strengthen Polish society. Instead, like reformers in the other Polish partitions, the Stańczyks promoted "organic work" to raise the cultural and economic status of the Polish population.[9] The Cracow historical school—Szujski, Koźmian, future Galician *Statthalter* Michael Bobrzyński, and others—provided much of the ideological underpinning of the Stańczyks' program. These historians blamed the eighteenth-century demise of the Polish-Lithuanian Commonwealth on the refusal of the *szlachta* to enact needed reforms rather than on foreign intervention. The Cracow historical school viewed anti-Habsburg demonstrations and revolutionary conspiracies as continuations of the failed policies of the past.[10]

When Franz Joseph arrived in 1880, the Polish conservatives dominated the provincial legislature, having minimized Polish peasant and Ruthenian representation in the Galician diet through the restrictive franchise and effective election manipulation. One of the original Stańczyks, Ludwik Wodzicki, served as marshal of the Sejm. Franz Joseph appointed former Minister President Alfred Potocki to the post of Galician *Statthalter* in 1875.[11] In Cracow, another Stańczyk ally, Mikołaj Zyblikiewicz, presided as mayor.[12] Stańczyks were also prominent in academic circles: Szujski was rector of Cracow's Polonized Jagiellonian University, and fellow Stańczyk and historian Józef Majer was president of the Academy of Sciences. Stańczyks controlled the leading Cracow newspaper, *Czas,* and the journal *Przegląd Polski.* In 1880, the Stańczyks were in a powerful position to advance their program of loyalism and organic work.

Orchestrating Patriotism

When Franz Joseph first came to Galicia in 1851, the appointed Galician administration merely executed the orders of the central government and the court. In 1880, the court again pursued its own agenda of upholding imperial prestige and enhancing the popularity of the emperor and loyalty to the monarchy. The Habsburg court transported the emperor's suite of some one hundred and seventy cooks, servants, officers, ceremonial guards, officials from the Office of the Grand Court Master, coachmen, and wagon washers from Vienna to Galicia. Railroad officials erected triumphal arches in the squares before the main train stations, among the grandest of the ubiquitous Habsburg public buildings distinguished by the imperial style and the "imperial yellow" finish.[13]

In 1880, however, the court and the Cisleithanian government left most decisions concerning the imperial visit to the conservatives and their allies. The Polish conservatives labored to orchestrate a series of public spectacles designed to communicate the Stańczyks' message of imperial loyalty and Polish achievement to the emperor, the Galician population, and the reading public of the monarchy as a whole. To this end, months before the emperor's arrival the Sejm created a committee to coordinate the reception, appointed Marshal Wodzicki to direct the committee, and voted 26,000 gulden for expenses.[14] Prominent conservatives, Marshal Wodzicki and the members of the *Wydział Krajowy,* the mayors of Lemberg and Cracow, Lemberg Rabbi Bernard Loewenstein, Lemberg Roman Catholic Bishop Morawski, the Greek Catholic Metropolitan Sembratovych, and Greek Catholic Bishop Stupnicki of Przemyśl (Peremyshl in Ukrainian) sat on this committee. This reception committee encouraged popular participation in the festivities and coordinated the preparations for the emperor's arrival in order to provide the emperor with a "way to get to know the people" and "the possibility for the people to approach the person of the monarch."[15]

The central reception committee called on the mayors of Cracow and Lemberg to set up affiliated organizations and offered subsidies to cover some of the costs for celebrations in these two cities. The Cracow and Lemberg committees arranged for decorations and triumphal arches to serve as backgrounds for large-scale public affirmations of imperial loyalty. The Lemberg committee, for example, decorated the city hall with statues of lions, gypsum allegorical figures of agriculture and mining, which symbolized the province's main sources of income, and a series of sculptures depicting the alleged Slavic virtues of patriotism, masculinity, and hospitality.[16] The Lemberg city administration also compelled owners to fix crumbling facades and to decorate buildings on main streets by threatening to undertake needed repairs and to bill uncooperative homeowners for the cost.[17]

Most significantly, the Cracow and Lemberg reception committees immediately began to organize citizens' guards to provide security. The Galician administration feared that the conspicuous military presence required for imperial visits and in evidence during Franz Joseph's previous tours of Galicia "would without a doubt call forth general discontent among the inhabitants of the city."[18] *Statthalter* Potocki pleaded successfully with General-Adjutant Friedrich von Mondel, the official master of the journey, to convince Franz Joseph to relax the military regulations and allow Galicians themselves, in the form of the guards, to guarantee order in the streets. To attract large numbers of townspeople to join the citizens' guard, the Cracow committee invited high officials from the Galician administration as well as leaders of voluntary associations and corporations to sit on the subcommittee organizing the guard and to influence their underlings to join the guard. Teachers, handworkers, and engineers volunteered, and the Cracow honor guard eventually numbered more than 2,000 persons. The "Regulations of the honorary citizens' guard during the visit of His Majesty in Cracow" stipulated that the guard, distinguished by blue-white or red-white ribbons and "national costume," was to keep order in the streets, which would be lined on both sides by members of various associations, schools and institutions.[19] In contrast to his previous trips to Galicia, a visible police and army presence would not surround Franz Joseph. He would trust his security to representatives of the Polish urban classes of Cracow. The guard was to be a symbol of the unity of interest and mutual respect between the emperor and the Polish population and to present the commitment of Galician society to the Stańczyks' program of loyalty.[20]

Potocki's Galician administration supported these actions in order to create an "image of a joyous atmosphere" and to establish the *Kaiserreise* as an "eternal memory" in the minds of all Galicians. The administration urged delegations from small villages to travel to the nearest train stations and peasants to congregate along the rail lines. District councils, supported by funds from the central, Cracow, and Lemberg committees, organized and outfitted mounted peasant bands to accompany the emperor's train within the borders of their respective jurisdictions. Word was leaked that the train would slow or stop wherever large crowds had gathered, inspiring a competition among local populations to catch the attention of the emperor. The Galician administration and the reception committee prompted local governments to create reception programs and to send delegations to greet the emperor in Cracow and Lemberg.[21]

The Polish conservatives wanted the expected large and lively crowds to learn that, by their mere presence at each festivity, they had affirmed the claims of the Polish conservatives to define Polish interests. At Potocki's request, Minister President Taaffe prompted the Office of the Grand Court Master to provide Władysław Łoziński, editor of *Gazeta Lwowska,* with access to all events. Potocki contended that it

> is highly desirable that the organ of the Galician administration, *Gazeta Lwowska,* receive swift, authentic, and direct dispatches and reports, and in fact the more so since this paper serves as the source for the entire unofficial Galician press, and in this way faulty or incomplete private reports would be prevented.[22]

Each notable slated to deliver a speech in the presence of the emperor had to send drafts to Potocki's administration for approval. According to Kazimierz Chłędowski, an official in the Galician administration and later Cisleithanian minister for Galicia,

> Our endeavor was, naturally, to avoid any kind of dissonance during the reception of the emperor, so that everything flowed smoothly. Speeches, with which presidents of district governments, leaders of communities and other corporations had to greet the emperor, had to be put under our censorship, so that nothing uncouth or political was expressed.

Many simply asked officials in the *Statthalterei* to write speeches for them. Łoziński, Chlędowski, and others penned such speeches as well as drafts of Franz Joseph's responses and sent them to the Cabinet Chancellery in Vienna, where they were approved without significant alterations.[23] The many speeches presented similar ideas, often using identical phrases. Mayors, county representatives, and leaders of cultural institutions attested to the "unshakable loyalty" and "patriotic devotion" of the people for the monarch who permitted Poles "free development on their own foundation."[24] The speeches tied Polish cultural progress to the relationship between Polish elites and the dynasty, thus presenting Polish identity, Habsburg patriotism, and dynastic loyalty as mutually reinforcing.

Interpreting the *Kaiserreise*

> *This trip will be a triumphal procession; it will be an unusual triumph, unique in its nature, because it will not be a commemoration of bloody victories or new conquests nor a march toward heroic and chivalrous undertakings, but it will constitute a calm and serious celebration, marking the successful rebirth of society and the deeply significant transformation of the relationship between a great land and the nation inhabiting it [on the one hand] and the glorious dynasty and the vast monarchy [on the other].*
>
> —Anton Klobukowski, Czas, 1 September 1880

On 1 September, the day Franz Joseph arrived in Galicia, Anton Klobukowski, chief editor of the Stańczyk organ, the Cracow daily *Czas,* published a long editorial in Polish and German. The editorial related the Stańczyks' interpretation of Galicia's past, present, and future to the pending arrival of the emperor. The official Vienna government press as well as Austro-German liberal organs quoted this editorial extensively.

Klobukowski divided the reign of Franz Joseph into two periods. From 1848 to 1867 antagonism and misunderstanding defined the relationship of the Poles to the dynasty and state. In stark contrast, the devolution of power to the Polish elites after 1867 had freed the Poles to develop their culture on their own terms, and Galicia had bloomed under conservative management, a golden era of Polish national achievement. By confirming the leading role of the Polish conservatives in Galicia, the emperor had transformed the dissatisfied Polish population into Austrian patriots. The expected total mobilization of Galician society during the emperor's visit would be "a splendid proof of the deep roots that the Austrian State Idea has grown here." The emperor would

> find a land in which all orders and all strata of the population would happily rally like one man around its monarch in the face of any state emergency

... [the words of the 1866 address] will not cease to be our motto: "We stand beside You, Imperial Highness, and there we wish to remain!"[25]

To quiet Polish critics of the Stańczyks' pro-Habsburg message, Klobukowski emphasized the Stańczyks' Polish national credentials, even as he justified the willingness of the conservatives to play a major role in the central parliament and government. The policy of loyalism, not "servilism," at once pro-Polish and pro-Austrian, spearheaded by Agenor Gołuchowski in the 1850s and 1860s and now championed by both the Galician administration and the Stańczyks, had secured de facto home-rule, transforming Galicia into a Polish national haven. Conservative leadership in autonomous Galicia had overcome social conflicts and replaced disagreements with a "unanimous dynastic feeling" in favor of "unification with the Austrian monarchy." Under the "Austrian scepter" national rights and "strong dynastic feelings" were united in "faithfulness to the ruling house; the one and the other will join in harmony in the reception and will be given loud expression at every step."

This editorial also addressed the ongoing conflict between the centralizing Austro-German liberals and Taaffe's coalition. The Austro-German liberal press in Vienna repeatedly charged that the continued devolution of power threatened the cohesion of the state.[26] Klobukowski turned the arguments of the liberals to the advantage of the Polish conservatives. He argued that Polish autonomy had convinced the Polish population to support a strong state and to sacrifice for the common good—and this would be manifested by popular participation in the reception of the emperor. The editorial called on the German population to accept the Poles as partners in a strong and flourishing Austria, one in which power is shifted from the center toward the provinces.

The Lemberg dailies *Gazeta Narodowa* and *Dziennik Polski* rejected the conservatives' claims to have satisfied Polish national goals and challenged the notion that the *szlachta* were the natural leaders of the province.[27] These papers, which expressed the views of Polish democrats, liberals, urban professionals, and elements of the lower *szlachta* disenchanted with Stańczyk loyalism, vehemently denied that popular enthusiasm for the emperor should be interpreted as public approval of Stańczyk policies.[28] Despite their greater emphasis on connections with Poles in the other partitions and their less enthusiastic embrace of imperial loyalty, the conservatives' Polish opponents did not agitate against the reception for the emperor. In 1880, Galicia's few democratic representatives to the Reichsrat sat with the conservatives and they were in general agreement on the desire for expanded Galician autonomy.

Austro-German and Ruthenian criticism of Polish chauvinism and of the overwhelmingly Polish character of the planned reception of the emperor drew the Polish factions (at least rhetorically) together. *Dziennik Polski* maintained that "All of us [Poles] stand under one banner." *Gazeta Narodowa* vowed that the Polish nation "sees its interests in the attachment with Austria and its ruling dynasty" and compared Galicia favorably with Russian Poland. Echoing *Czas, Gazeta Narodowa* asserted that the Poles of Galicia had come to love Franz Joseph because Austria alone among the partitioning powers had awarded the Poles "enough freedom to develop themselves."[29] Polish conservatives and democrats encouraged participation in the preparations for the reception of the emperor, pointed to the citizens' guards with pride, and countered all claims that Poles and Ruthenians could not work together for the festivities and for the province.[30]

Presenting the Emperor/Representing Galicia-Cracow

> *To the sound of all the church bells of the "Slavic Rome," to the echoes of the Bell of Sigmund from Wawel Tower, to the reverberations of a 101 cannon salute, His Most Sublime Emperor and King arrived in Cracow at 10 A.M.*
> —Czas, 1 September, 1880

The program of events centered on Cracow, the largest and most important city in western Galicia, and Lemberg, the capital and Galicia's most populous city. The series of receptions, festivities, and scripted speeches that marked the emperor's three-day visit to Cracow reinforced the conservatives' narrative of Polish achievement in the era of autonomy. In the 8 September edition of *Czas,* a feuilletonist described several particularly "splendid images" from Franz Joseph's stay in Cracow and compared the reception of the emperor with great historical moments:

> And so our impressions [of Franz Joseph's visit] will not be overshadowed by recollections of . . . royal weddings, or feudal homages at the Cracow Market Square, and no contradiction will arise between the monuments of the distant past and these images from contemporary times.[31]

The first of the "splendid images" organized by the reception committees and Potocki's Galician administration, the imperial entrance into Galicia and into Cracow, fulfilled Klobukowski's expectations: the entire province seemed united in a common celebration of the emperor and of the cultural and political development of Galicia. As newspapers informed the monarchy's reading public, crowds massed along the rail lines from the border to Cracow early in the morning on 1 September. Peasants in colorful costumes, priests dressed in their finery and holding aloft relics and banners at the head of village communities, and Jews donning fur hats and kaftans cheered the emperor and flanking Polish notables at every train station. Franz Joseph's "strong and vigorous, nearly adolescent elastic steps added grace and ease to his chivalrous, manly and noble figure" as he briefly alighted from the train several times to receive bread and salt from peasants and to kiss crosses proffered him by priests.[32]

At least 50,000 people witnessed the arrival of the emperor into Cracow.[33] Delegations from Galicia's seventy-nine districts, including many Polish and Ruthenian peasants in national costumes, greeted the emperor at the decorated train station. As a military honor guard played the state hymn, Marshal Wodzicki welcomed Franz Joseph in Polish and Ukrainian, lauding the emperor's respect for "nationality and mother tongue." Mayor Zyblikiewicz, in an elegant wagon pulled by four horses and flanked by footmen in blue and white—the colors of Cracow—led the emperor and imperial party through cheering crowds kept in order by the citizens' guard. At the Florian Gate, Franz Joseph received the golden key to the city. Mayor Zyblikiewicz hailed the emperor under whose "just scepter we are free to be and to remain Poles," who recognized "our national rights," and aided the development of "national institutions" that once again "ignite the spirit of our national life. . . . Our gratitude has no limit."[34] *Czas* boasted that Franz Joseph, who supposedly understood Polish, listened with "satisfaction" to Zyblikiewicz's Polish language speech filled with references to Polish national symbols and the achievements of Polish autonomy in Galicia.[35] The emperor's wave and glance awarded recognition to city and provincial government officials, voluntary associations, university professors, attorneys and notaries standing in assigned places along the parade route from the train station to the Market Square. Inside the Potocki Palace, Franz Joseph granted brief audiences to twenty-one groups representing important sectors of Galician society and, for the most part, led by prominent Stańczyks.[36]

Galicia's political elites commissioned a series of paintings memorializing this and other dramatic moments from the 1880 *Kaiserreise* and presented them to Crown Prince Rudolf as a wedding gift in 1881.[37] Produced by Polish history painters, these works embody the Stańczyks' vision of a timeless Galicia of ethnic and social harmony and Polish national achievement under the direction of the conservatives. Stańczyks and their allies feature prominently in the series, often dressed in anachronistic "national" costumes (some purchased from theater supply companies in Vienna). These costumes reflected the "Neosarmatian" cult of the Polish nobility, which reached its height in Cracow in this period of noble-conservative political and cultural domination.[38] In Juliusz Kossak's 1881 watercolor *The Entrance of His Majesty the Emperor into Cracow* (figure 9), for example, the aristocratically outfitted commoner, Mayor Zyblikiewicz, not Franz Joseph, is the central figure. Enthusiastic townspeople, colorfully dressed peasants, honor guards, and Polish nobles cheer and salute the mayor.[39] Franz Joseph and his suite follow behind, upstaged and out of focus. The presence of the emperor in the painting enhances the significance of Zyblikiewicz, just as the emperor's presence in Galicia was intended to reinforce the authority of the Polish conservatives.

In another scene deemed highly significant by *Czas,* on his second day in Cracow Franz Joseph declared Wawel Castle an imperial residence and agreed to

Figure 9: Entrance of His Majesty the Emperor into Cracow. *Juliusz Kossak, 1881. National Museum in Cracow.*

remove the Habsburg garrison from Wawel hill.[40] This was the perfect symbolic act to justify conservative hegemony in Galicia. Wawel's return evoked a glorious Polish past, a romantic Polish national identity, and the revival of Polish traditions in the present under the patronage of the conservatives. Franz Joseph's own words on this occasion, quoted many times over the next few weeks, expressed as much the Stańczyk program as his own sentiments: "There is great virtue in preserving important traditions of the past with high honor and in reconciling them with the responsibilities of the present." For *Czas,* Franz Joseph was no foreign prince occupying Polish lands; he was heir to Polish kings and protector of Polish national traditions: "The castle on Wawel hill, the former residence of Piasts and Jagiellonians, the present residence of the Habsburgs, will be an eternal embodiment and manifestation" of the accomplishments of "our province and nation . . . in union with the Habsburg dynasty and the Austrian monarchy."[41]

In the final image from the emperor's stay in Cracow emphasized by *Czas*'s feuilletonist, the Cracow committee produced stylized versions of two peasant festivals.[42] Crowds began forming outside of the Potocki palace the evening of 3 September, kept in order by the citizens' guard. Gas reflectors and "Bengali" lights—many imported from Vienna—illuminated the market square. Franz Joseph appeared on the balcony of the Potocki palace as military bands played the state hymn. Then, to the tune of folk songs, hundreds of peasants accompanied four decorated wagons representing the four grain types grown in the area and one wagon bearing a pyramid composed of fruits and vegetables and sporting the emperor's initials (figure 10). A peasant wedding procession followed. Peasant songs, dances, and riding maneuvers entertained the newlyweds and the emperor. Wedding guests then gathered on the ground floor of the Sukiennice, the medieval

Figure 10: Harvest Procession before His Majesty the Emperor on the Market Square in Cracow. *Tadeusz Ajdukiewicz, 1881. National Museum in Cracow.*

Cloth Hall that still dominates Cracow's Market Square, for a feast sponsored by the city. Franz Joseph walked from the Potocki palace into the crowded Sukiennice through "lines formed by the honor guard among the tens of thousands of gathered people" with no police protection, supposed proof of the close relationship between the emperor and the Galician population.[43] Franz Joseph was "face to face with the people of Cracow in this most festive moment." He handed each couple fifty gulden, made liberal use of his modest knowledge of Polish, "How are you?" and accepted petitions from old women.[44]

These pompous celebrations were only the most spectacular of the array of receptions, audiences, official lunches and dinners in honor of Franz Joseph. Among the most noteworthy festivities, six hundred peasant riders, their costumes and mounts subsidized by the Cracow committee, "spontaneously" accompanied the emperor's wagon on his return to Cracow from a nearby military school. More than two thousand invited notables crammed into the Sukiennice for a gala ball. Franz Joseph also visited the Jagiellonian University and the Academy of Sciences, viewed by many in the Prussian and Russian partitions as Polish national institutions, and received praise from the Stańczyk directors of these institutions for permitting the use of the mother language and for raising the level of Polish culture in Galicia.

With justification, the conservatives proclaimed the emperor's visit to their stronghold a resounding success. In 1851, at least according to disgruntled Polish nobles, only military parades and state bureaucrats had greeted Franz Joseph when he arrived in Cracow. In 1880, the imperial visit to Cracow was instead a monumental *tableau vivant,* bringing to life the Stańczyks' vision of Polish progress under conservative patronage, a vision legitimized by the presence of the emperor and the fervor of the crowds. "Neither the emperor or anyone else heard a false note during the three days" of the emperor's visit to Cracow. *Czas* attributed the enthusiastic reception of the emperor to the achievement of national autonomy for the Poles in Galicia. "We saw at each step the administrative [*Statthalterei*] and autonomous [*Wydział Krajowy*] authorities leading the population together, in conformity and in unity with one idea and one feeling." Poles and Ruthenians, Catholics and Jews, aristocrats, urban professionals, and peasants all performed the roles assigned them by the Polish conservatives in what conservative journalists described as a mass demonstration of imperial loyalty and popular support for the conservatives' agenda.[45]

Although the emperor's schedule included some visits to military installations, these were few and did not detract from the overwhelmingly Polish nature of the festivities. Inspections of troop formations were limited in 1880 to the seven days the imperial party spent at fall maneuvers outside of Przemyśl in between his visits to Cracow and Lemberg.[46] The media paid considerably less attention to the maneuvers than to the imperial celebrations in the towns, but the *Wiener Zeitung* did publicize details of the journey from Cracow to Przemyśl. Through the eyes of the emperor, the *Wiener Zeitung* correspondent introduced the German-reading audience to the exotic eastern districts of Galicia and effectively confirmed the Polish conservatives' conception of Galician society. At each station from Cracow east,

> From miles away the population hurried here, in order to at least see the imperial train fly by. His majesty the emperor lingered the entire time at the window of the wagon, tirelessly observing and waving. Nobles, peasants, clergy, rabbis, townspeople, officials, school children, flower girls, miners, music associations, village fiddlers, in short all orders, associations, and all in massive numbers in the middle of the forest of flags and banners, in bright groups, splendid church holy objects, precious antique Torahs . . . an ever changeable, changing panorama. . . . From the Jaroslaw station on, Ruthenian peasant mounted bands appeared. . . . Everywhere the same enthusiasm, everywhere perfect order. . . . A whole people without difference in order and confession honored the emperor in a most imposing fashion.[47]

Franz Joseph in Lemberg: Conservative Hegemony Challenged

> *Cracow and Lemberg stand next to one another, as past and present.*
> —Fremden-Blatt *(morning edition), 11 September 1880*

While old Polish castles, medieval squares, the Jagiellonian University, and an almost purely Polish population defined Cracow as the self-confident center of

Polishness in Galicia, Lemberg, the largest city in eastern Galicia, represented the progress experienced by the province under the Habsburgs. Fewer than 20,000 people lived in this provincial town before the Habsburgs acquired the area in the late eighteenth century and designated Lemberg the capital of Galicia. Spurred on by the expansion of government administration, the population of this urban island in rural eastern Galicia rose to at least 104,000 by 1880.[48]

Lemberg was young architecturally. In the 1850s and 1860s, the bulk of the old city walls had been razed, new public and private buildings erected, and broad avenues planned. Some Viennese architects worked in Lemberg, and many Lemberg architects studied in the imperial capital.[49] In the era of Polish autonomy (1867–1918), Lemberg changed from a German-speaking to a Polish-speaking city. The language of the university and of government administration became Polish, and Lemberg was the seat of the only elected Polish-speaking representative body on the territory of the defunct Polish state.[50]

In 1880, the Polish conservatives dominated cultural and political life in Cracow and western Galicia. Eastern Galicia had a far more mixed and complicated political and ethnic landscape. Here, social conflicts intensified ethnic divisions. Polish magnates owned huge tracts of land, while the majority of the population consisted of Ruthenian-speaking peasants, many of whom could still remember the humiliation of the labor services and other indignities they endured until the peasant emancipation of 1848. Religion also divided Ruthenians from Poles. Though acknowledgement of papal authority separated the Greek Catholic Ruthenians of Galicia from Orthodox Russians, the Eastern Rite distinguished Greek Catholics from the mainly Roman Catholic Poles.[51]

The provincial capital itself had a Polish majority, a large Jewish population, a long-standing Armenian community, and a significant number of German speakers. Lemberg was also the center of Ruthenian intellectual life in Galicia. Ruthenian political and cultural activists were increasingly divided into two rival factions.[52] Labeled "Moscophiles" by the Polish press, Russophiles emphasized the relationship of the Ruthenians to the Great Russian people and desired cultural and/or political unity with Russia. Russophile priest Ivan Naumovych founded the Kachkovs'kyi Society in 1874, which soon spread its publications and reading rooms throughout eastern Galicia. Russophiles also controlled important newspapers, including *Slovo,* a Lemberg daily, and *Nauka,* a rural paper edited by Naumovych.[53] National populists rejected this Russian orientation. Through Prosvita (Enlightenment), an association founded in 1868, national populists endeavored to spread Ukrainian national identity among the peasants through publications in the Ukrainian vernacular and a network of reading rooms in small towns and villages.[54] In 1880, national populists founded the newspaper *Dilo* (The Deed) in direct opposition to *Slovo* (The Word).

An estimated 100,000 people witnessed the emperor's entrance into Lemberg and the same number roamed the streets of the illuminated city on each night of the emperor's stay. Tens of thousands traveled to Lemberg from distant towns and villages to glimpse the emperor.[55] Lemberg's population, prompted by the Lemberg reception committee, decorated houses and public buildings with flags, flowers, carpets, and banners. Galician choirs performed special Polish and Ruthenian cantatas of welcome, and a torchlight parade of some 10,000 entertained the emperor on his first night in Lemberg. Appearances at official receptions, gala balls, and important Galician autonomous institutions like the Galician diet (figure 11) crowded Franz Joseph's program during his four-day stay in Lemberg.

As in Cracow, the Polish nobles endeavored to demonstrate and encourage the acceptance by the peasantry of *szlachta* leadership. The *szlachta*-controlled Agricultural Society sponsored a banquet in the Jesuit Gardens for all the peasants who had traveled to Lemberg to represent their counties in an audience given by the emperor. Magnates such as Prince Adam Sapieha, president of the Agricultural Society, and Dawid Abrahamowicz, a wealthy east Galician noble-landowner and powerful political figure, personally served pierogi, beer, and cigars to 250 peasants. Ruthenian and "Mazurian" (Polish) peasants toasted each other, Sapieha, and the emperor.[56]

In Cracow, festivities had followed the schedule authored by Potocki and the central reception committee. In Lemberg, some events did not conform to the will of the Polish conservatives. Franz Joseph's own desire to show himself as the father and caring guardian of all of his peoples and the refusal of Polish political activists, the Lemberg Jewish community, peasants, and Ruthenians to accept their assigned roles in the Polish conservative-produced presentation of Galician society spoiled the all-Polish tenor of the inspection tour in the eastern districts of the province.

Figure 11: His Majesty the Emperor in the Building of the Provincial Diet. *Henryk Rodakowski, 1881. National Museum in Cracow.*

Lemberg's Polish political establishment, including Polish democrats and other political activists opposed to the Stańczyks' moderate program of organic work, supported the preparations for the emperor's arrival in the province.[57] The Lemberg dailies *Gazeta Narodowa* and *Dziennik Polski,* for example, printed calls for Poles to join the honor guard in the capital. Still, Polish critics of the conservatives did endeavor to infuse the festivities with a Polish national message opposed to Stańczyk loyalism. Jan Dobrzański, editor of *Gazeta Narodowa,* organized the theatrical presentation for Franz Joseph in the Lemberg theater.[58] This theater production, which included performers from the Russian partition, Polish dances, and a song expressing a strident Polish national stance, did not please the guest of honor. Franz Joseph left after an hour. Whether Franz Joseph's early exit reflected his anger at an open display of Polish solidarity with brethren beyond the Habsburg border or his usual boredom with the arts, the emperor's apparent displeasure and the resulting scandal led to the replacement of Dobrzański as director of the Lemberg theater, a result that pleased the Polish conservatives.[59]

In response to requests from the Jewish community, Franz Joseph added a visit to the liberal Lemberg Temple to the official schedule, which already included an imperial visit to the main orthodox synagogue.[60] The court had ignored Jews during the emperor's 1851 visit to Galicia. After 1868, however, Jews enjoyed full rights as citizens under the Basic Laws. Imperial etiquette now acknowledged the status of Jewish clergy and religious institutions, and the emperor publicly recognized Jews as loyal subjects. On 13 September, with General-Adjutant Mondel, *Statthalter* Potocki, and many Polish notables in his party, Franz Joseph visited the synagogues. "In both synagogues the emperor and the suite kept their heads covered" while rabbis blessed Franz Joseph.[61] Inside the temple, girls in white scattered flowers before the emperor and the president of the Jewish community acclaimed the "Protector of our freedoms and rights."[62]

A more direct threat to the conservative message of harmony arose from the Galician peasantry. The Polish conservatives interpreted choreographed celebrations like the peasant harvest festival in Cracow as genuine peasant expressions of imperial loyalty and approval of conservative policy. The conservative press discouraged the public from handing lists of grievances and petitions for imperial favor directly to the emperor, arguing that such actions undermined the *szlachta*-controlled institutions of Galician autonomy.[63] The citizens' guard attempted to wave people away; yet, "Many times the emperor, seeing hands extended toward him with white rolls of paper, ordered his carriage to halt and magnanimously received the petition from the hand of the supplicant."[64] More than 9,000 petitions reached the hands of court officials during the trip to Galicia and Bukovina. Court officials cited deepening rural poverty, the widespread knowledge that Franz Joseph had increased the amount of money he gave out in response to such requests, and the 1879 celebrations of the twenty-fifth wedding anniversary of the imperial couple for inspiring so many to seek assistance directly from the emperor.[65]

Court official Joseph von Kundrat advised Franz Joseph to distribute funds to petitioners and Galician charities liberally, because "the political importance, which lies in the impression left on the population, cannot be overlooked."[66] Kundrat also persuaded Franz Joseph to donate 2,000 gulden for the construction of a grammar school in Krysowice, a largely Ruthenian village that had no school for its 180 children of school age. The gift obligated local landowners to contribute operating costs. Kundrat believed this gift would "produce with modest means a permanent monument to the presence of Your Majesty that at the same time will be suited to preserve the feelings of gratefulness toward Your Majesty."[67] Naumovych's peasant-oriented *Nauka* interpreted this action as imperial condemnation of the Galician school board, which ignored the educational needs of Ruthenian children.[68]

Ruthenian associations staged the most serious challenge to the conservatives. In July, the Ruthenian Council (*Ruska Rada*) convened a meeting of Ruthenian voluntary and political associations in order to form a separate Ruthenian reception committee.[69] This committee called on Ruthenians throughout eastern Galicia to decorate their homes with the Ruthenian colors of blue and yellow and to greet the emperor with cries of "*Slava!*" and "*Mnohaia Lita!*"[70] Newspaper notices urged peasants to travel to Lemberg in national dress in order to prevent their "Polish brothers, from presenting Galicia before the eyes of the emperor as an overwhelmingly Polish region."[71] After all, *Dilo* insisted, "[W]e still live in Austria and not in Poland."[72]

Rival Ruthenian factions disagreed on how best to greet the emperor. In mid-August, *Slovo* published an appeal to convene a Ruthenian political gathering in Lemberg in early September. The gathering was to develop a list of grievances that would be handed to the emperor.[73] The national populists, however, swayed the majority on the Ruthenian reception committee to "welcome the emperor as the protector of freedom and equality with enthusiastic festivities" rather than with grievances. The populists wanted the events planned by the Ruthenian committee to prove to the Poles, the emperor, and the population of the monarchy that the Ruthenians existed, were loyal to Austria and to the Habsburgs—not to the tsar as charged by the Polish press—and would not allow themselves to be represented and governed by Poles.[74]

Two events added to the official agenda at the prompting of the Ruthenian committee and Metropolitan Sembratovych became public assertions of Ruthenian "national culture."[75] At 6:45 A.M. on 13 September, crowds of Ruthenians and over 400 priests from towns and villages across Galicia welcomed the emperor at St. George, the Greek Catholic Cathedral (figure 12). *Dilo* termed this event the largest gathering of "Ruthenian priests and the Ruthenian nation at a national celebration."[76] Franz Joseph's visit to the Ruthenian National Institute on 14 September took on even sharper national tones. In the great hall, decorated with banners and portraits of the emperor, Vasyl' Kovals'kyi, president of the National Institute, member of the Sejm, the Reichsrat, and in later decades, the Supreme Court in Vienna, praised the emperor for protecting all that was "sacred and precious" for the Ruthenians: "our nationality, our ecclesiastical rite, our language, our script, our customs and our ways . . . the more than 1,000-year-old heritage of the Ruthenian nation."[77] Kovals'kyi introduced representatives from the most important Ruthenian associations to the emperor, including the Prosvita and Kachkovs'kyi societies.[78]

Figure 12: The Welcoming of His Majesty the Emperor in the Greek Catholic Cathedral St. George. *Antoni Kozakiewicz, 1881. National Museum in Cracow.*

Ruthenian participation in the *Kaiserreise* did not begin and end with these two festivities. From Lemberg to the border of Bukovina, Ruthenian peasant riders rode along the tracks, flanking the imperial train.[79] Ruthenian peasants and Greek Catholic priests massed at every station along the route. Despite efforts by Potocki's administration to "use all means to ensure that the rural population backs away from this inappropriate intention," Ruthenian peasants traveled to Krysowice with petitions for imperial assistance.[80] *Nauka* reported that Franz Joseph heard "from the lips of these peasants" about the abuses of the

Galician autonomous administration and usurers.[81] In Kolomea (Kolomyya in Ukrainian; Kolomyja in Polish; Kolomey in Yiddish), Franz Joseph visited rival Polish and Ruthenian (organized by the Kachkovs'kyi Society) agricultural and "ethnographic" exhibitions. The latter was only added to the official schedule during Franz Joseph's stay in Lemberg. The Polish press reported with pleasure that the emperor did not appear to smile during his brief visit to the shabby Ruthenian exhibition, though the constant downpour might have had some effect on his good humor.[82]

In the end, the Ruthenian factions declared the *Kaiserreise* a victory for the Ruthenian people. Ruthenians had shown their loyalty to dynasty and state to be at least the equal of the Poles. "Just as the Ruthenians have distanced themselves from any presentation of their justified complaints during the emperor's stay, neither did the monarch give the slightest occasion for the suspicion that the Ruthenian nation is less in his heart than the other nations of Austria."[83]

The Ruthenian interpretation of the *Kaiserreise* incorporated an understanding of Habsburg and Galician history at odds with the master narrative presented by the Polish conservatives during the inspection tour. For the Polish conservatives, the emperor's popularity resulted directly from the achievement of Polish autonomy in Galicia. Before 1867, they repeatedly argued, the Galician population had been cool toward the dynasty and the state. For its part, the Ruthenian press looked to earlier times to confirm the support of the Habsburg dynasty for the Ruthenian people. Joseph II, the Ruthenians claimed, had favored the Greek Catholic Church and moderated serfdom. Franz Joseph had proven himself, like Joseph II before him, a defender of the Ruthenian people. Franz Joseph had confirmed the end of the *robot* in 1848, donated land and money to assist in the building of the National Institute, and had set its foundation stone during his first visit to Galicia in 1851. The Ruthenian press juxtaposed the respect of the dynasty for the Ruthenian nation with the suppression of Ruthenian rights by the Poles.

Ruthenian associations, like the Polish conservatives, orchestrated a display of "national culture" to represent themselves and their place in Galician society to the emperor, the Galician public, and the population of the monarchy as a whole. Though the cooperation of the Ruthenian associations in preparation for the emperor's arrival did not overcome the divisions among competing factions, the successful mobilization of thousands of peasants set a precedent for future political action.

The Stańczyk Achievement

Despite the grumbling of the Polish democrats, the thousands of petitions presented directly to the monarch, and the separate Ruthenian reception, the conservatives declared the *Kaiserreise* a victory for their vision of Galician society. The enthusiastic crowds and the lack of military security defined the trip as a triumph of Stańczyk organization and seemed to prove the success of loyalism and organic work.

After the emperor's departure from the province, *Przegląd Polski* editor Stanisław Tarnowski restated the Polish conservatives' message, proclaimed by Klobukowski on 1 September, and repeated throughout the festivities in honor of the emperor: The conservatives had provided the framework for the development of Polish culture and the achievement of Polish national interests within autonomous Galicia. The *Kaiserreise,* this "truly historic occurrence," had aroused not a "pale ghost wrapped in a shroud," as some had defined the Polish people. Instead, the *Kaiserreise* revealed "a nation, as one person, tired, weakened, poor, but unshaken in its being, hale and in possession of the will and capacity for life ... with spirit and body joined, a complete organism." The healthy development of the Polish nation depended on a new relationship between Galicia and the monarchy: Galicia, "a crownland, once a partitioned land attached to Austria, today joined to it of its own conviction and action with the noble and wise emperor." Tarnowski, like the Stańczyk historians, argued that the new relationship between Galicia and the monarchy had resulted from the turn away from dreams of revolution to a new "Austro-politics."[84] *Czas,* the Stańczyk organ, pointed to the concrete achievements of conservative stewardship and looked forward "to greater Polish control in Galicia and a strengthening of the state." *Czas* also compared Galician autonomy, an achievement of the conservatives, with the suppression of Polish culture in the Russian partition.[85]

Government newspapers, the German liberal press, and the court itself acknowledged the Polish conservatives' triumph. For the *Fremden-Blatt,* constitutional government, by requiring the participation of all citizens in political life, had resulted in the "total reconciliation of the Poles with the Austrian imperial idea." The *Fremden-Blatt* credited the wise governance of the emperor and Potocki for this great "Austrian Kaiserfest." The imperial visit confirmed that "[T]he Poles of Galicia have broken with the politics of dreams and illusions and have no other desire than to utilize their Austrian imperial state rights for their development."[86] Even harsh critics of the Polish conservatives, like the *Wiener Allgemeine Zeitung,* came to similar conclusions:

> The Galician *Kaiserreise* has come to an end, and it will remain long and strong in the memory of all who had the good fortune to experience it. Not one false note disrupted the beautiful festivities in Cracow and Lemberg, and one can only say that the Austrian idea has celebrated a magnificent triumph in our great northeastern crownland.[87]

For its part, the court was satisfied that the trip had been a triumph for the dynasty. In secret reports, Court Ceremonial Director Loebenstein, the highest court official accompanying the emperor, repeatedly noted the enthusiasm of the crowds.[88] General-Adjutant Mondel, the official director of the journey, was overwhelmed by the "authentic joy" of the "cheering masses" and the decorations in every street and square.[89] Galician autonomy had, in the view of the court, bolstered the prestige of the dynasty and loyalty to the state.

Franz Joseph and the 1894 Galician Provincial Exhibition

> *In the person of the emperor, the Empire itself appears in Lemberg. Can anyone doubt that this trip by the emperor will have a beneficial and lasting impact? Even the widest strata will become aware in a lively way of the inner identification with the Empire.*
>
> —Fremden-Blatt, *7 September 1894*

Franz Joseph returned to Galicia several times after 1880. With the exception of his visit to the 1894 Galician Exhibition in Lemberg, however, he came only to attend military maneuvers and made few additional public appearances. These visits did not inspire multiple large-scale public celebrations.[90] Franz Joseph's 1894 five-day stay in Lemberg, which was preceded by five days of military maneuvers in Landskron, appears on first blush to have been as spectacular and politically significant as the 1880 tour of the province.

Politically, the imperial visit to Galicia in 1894 was intended to proclaim once again the close relationship between the emperor and his subjects. Several ministers from the Cisleithanian cabinet accompanied Franz Joseph to Lemberg, underscoring the increased importance of Galician support for the governing coalition after Taaffe's 1893 fall from power. On the eve of Franz Joseph's arrival in Lemberg, the *Fremden-Blatt*, the organ of the foreign ministry, labeled the "understanding of the empire with the Poles, and the Poles with the empire . . . one of the great ideas" adhered to by Franz Joseph in the constitutional era. The *Fremden-Blatt* applauded *Statthalter* (and later Cisleithanian Minister President) Kazimierz Badeni for his efforts at reconciling Ruthenians and Poles, part of the brief and already fraying "new era" in the relationship between these two national communities. The paper predicted that the emperor's visit would showcase the "patriotic cooperation" of the Poles with other "old-Austrian" parties and the end of national tensions in the province.[91]

The emperor's visit intensified efforts already underway to use the Galician exhibition for political profit. In the months before the emperor's arrival, the press department of the Cisleithanian Ministerial Council planted favorable articles about the exhibition in the Galician and Viennese press in an effort to rouse public expressions of imperial loyalty. Minister President Alfred Windischgrätz believed there would be "advantages" to "drawing the attention of the Austrian public outside the borders of Galicia." Badeni agreed that the exhibition could "strengthen and deepen the coalition idea in the consciousness of the population."[92]

As in 1880, Polish elites and the Galician administration authored the emperor's program, organized a citizen's guard (the military and police maintained a very low profile), and assigned roles to associations and corporations.[93] The imperial court train halted briefly (no more than ten minutes per stop) at several towns on the way to the provincial capital.[94] Villagers, priests, and government officials gathered at each decorated train station for a glimpse of the imperial visitor. The train did not stop from Rzeszów to Lemberg, but priests, bureaucrats, and bands of peasant riders lined the tracks.[95]

Lemberg was the only town Franz Joseph visited for more than a few minutes. During his stay in Lemberg, Franz Joseph watched thousands of pupils parade before him, signed his name in Polish in a church guest book to the acclaim of the Polish press, gave audiences, received petitions, and praised the city illuminations: "It is really an unforgettable impression."[96] Ruthenians welcomed Franz Joseph at the Greek Catholic Seminary; the Jewish community greeted the emperor at the opening of a new orphanage for Jewish children.

Historian Stefan Kieniewicz termed the 1894 Galician Exhibition "a great manifestation of the unity and vitality of the Polish nation." Tens of thousands of Lemberg residents and visitors cheered Franz Joseph as he rode through the decorated city and toured the exhibition each day of his visit to the provincial capital, seemingly confirming that Galician society remained loyal to the emperor and, therefore, to the Polish conservatives.

The official organ of the Galician administration, *Gazeta Lwowska,* printed photographs and illustrations of Franz Joseph and documented every word uttered and step taken by the imperial guest during his stay in Lemberg.[98] The Cracow conservative *Czas* credited the close relationship between the crown and the Polish leadership of Galicia for the economic and technological development of the province documented in the exhibition. This conservative paper quoted Franz Joseph's words to Adam Sapieha, the president of the exhibition, as evidence of this relationship (figure 13): "We can always count on you."[99] Polish democratic/ nationalist papers compared Galicia favorably with Russian Poland and lauded the development of the Polish nation in Galicia under Franz Joseph.[100]

By 1894, however, the convergence of factors which had led to the success of the 1880 *Kaiserreise* had broken down. The Polish conservatives still dominated the Sejm and the delegation to the Reichsrat; yet, though peasants and burghers continued to line the streets for the emperor, outside of the festivities themselves the conservatives could no longer unify society behind their vision of Polish identity and imperial loyalty. Polish social democracy was raising its profile in town and village; Ukrainian nationalists and socialists were vigorously seeking supporters among the Ruthenian peasantry and the (still modest in size) urban intelligentsia.[101]

The Galician administration and the interior ministry in Vienna feared that public opposition to the status quo could mar the imperial visit and took measures to shadow "suspicious" characters.[102] The Social Democrats of Lemberg attempted to schedule a mass public meeting in a central square in the city on the morning of 9 September in order to ask the ministers if they were prepared to institute election reforms. As the organizers certainly expected, the police banned the meeting in the name of public security.[103] Issues of the social democratic *Naprzód,* the democratic *Nowa Reforma,* the radical *Kurjer Lwowski,* as well as the Ukrainian nationalist *Dilo* and *Halyczanin* were confiscated for insulting the emperor, a sign that Franz Joseph's presence could not paper over serious political and social divisions.[104]

Many peasants were no longer content to seek fulfillment of their interests through the mediation of the conservative elites. In the 1880s and 1890s, peasant publications, credit unions, voluntary associations, and celebrations enhanced peasant solidarity.[105] By 1893, the activities of rural activists, like Father Stanisław Stojałowski and the Potoczek brothers, had led to the foundation in 1893 of the first Polish peasant political organization in Galicia, the *Związek Stronnictwa Chłopskiego* (Peasant Union).[106]

Rural activists intended to use the exhibition to define their own heroes and to express their own definitions of the Polish nation. Polish-speaking peasants were drawn to the exhibition by the huge panorama painting commemorating the centenary anniversary of the near legendary Battle of Racławice and the peasant warriors who fought under Kościuszko against Russian forces in the name of Poland. Months before the opening of the exhibition, Stojałowski's press organs

Figure 13: Adam Sapieha Greets Franz Joseph at the Galician Exhibition, 7 September 1894. Lajos Halmi, 1898. Austrian National Library.

Wieniec and *Pszczółka, Związek Chłopski,* the left-liberal *Kurjer Lwowski,* edited by Henryk Rewakowicz, and *Przyjaciel Ludu,* the peasant-oriented organ of secular nationalist activist Bolesław Wysłouch, called on peasants to come to Lemberg to view the panorama and to participate in a peasant political meeting at the end of August meant to establish a unified peasant political movement directed against the ruling elites.[107] These newspapers regularly attacked the conservative elites for their timidity, servility, and abandonment of Polish national goals. The five-day stay of the emperor in Lemberg and the imperial visits to the exhibition did not constitute the main interest of the peasant visitors to Lemberg—although many thousands did cheer his every move.

By 1894, Polish and Ukrainian/Ruthenian peasants, socialists, and nationalists defined their programs in direct opposition to the conservative elites and their narrative of Galician unity and state loyalty. The contrast between the secure and legitimate hierarchy of orders presented during imperial rituals and ceremonies and the reality of Galician interest-group politics was too great to make effective propaganda. The imperial presence still evoked displays of dynastic loyalty; however, the conservative Polish elites could no longer translate this dynastic patriotism into acceptance of their claims to speak in the name of Galicia or to define Polish national interests.

The 1894 Galician Exhibition was not the only provincial fair Franz Joseph attended in the 1890s. Similar difficulties plagued Franz Joseph's visits to exhibitions in Bohemia in 1891 and in Hungary in 1896. At each, Franz Joseph confirmed the role of local elites and business people in pushing forward progress, sought to associate the dynasty with economic and cultural achievement, and strove to avoid offending or favoring particular nationalities. As was the case in Galicia, however, Franz Joseph's brief visits did not transform these events into long-running patriotic manifestations. Hungarian and Czech nationalists proclaimed the exhibitions to be triumphs for their respective nations. Bohemian Germans boycotted the 1891 exhibition, and Franz Joseph balanced his schedule with a trip to Reichenberg, one of Bohemia's most important German-dominated towns. Croats, Romanians, Serbs, and others, offended by their depiction in the quaint ethnographic section of the Hungarian Millennium Exhibition, called for boycotts, burned Hungarian flags, and signed manifestos (much of this protest activity took place outside of Hungary in Serbia, Romania, and Vienna).[108]

––––––––

In the wake of the 1848 revolutions, Franz Joseph and the Habsburg court revitalized the mythic status of the emperor. During the 1851 *Kaiserreise,* the court and central government controlled the image of Franz Joseph through the government monopoly on the media and over the choreography of the trip. The court's claim to be the arbiter of social hierarchy, the ubiquitous military presence, and the rejection of Polish requests for a greater say in the administration of the province combined to produce this neoabsolutist assertion of the monarchical principle. In 1880, Franz Joseph and Taaffe depended on the Polish Circle in the Reichsrat to support the Iron Ring. Never wholly comfortable with the liberal governments of the 1860s and 1870s, Franz Joseph backed Taaffe's efforts to join the monarchy's elites in a stable parliamentary majority. The Iron Ring offered the possibility of maintaining the power and prestige of the dynasty by creating political stability and financial resources to buttress Austria-Hungary's diplomatic position. In this context, imperial celebration now depended on the will and the action of regional notables to bolster dynastic loyalty.

In 1880, there were few direct challenges to the narrative of Galician unity, Habsburg loyalty, and conservative leadership. Polish democrats criticized the moderation of the Polish conservatives, but they also acknowledged the advance of the Polish nation under the Habsburg scepter. The Ruthenian reception did mar the display of unity. Ruthenians organized their own reception for the emperor and redefined the emperor as a symbol of Ruthenian national pride. They charged that the Poles denied them the national equality guaranteed by the emperor as protector of constitutional rights. However, Ruthenian peasants may have dressed in Ruthenian national garb and greeted the emperor with traditional Ruthenian cheers, but they did so within a framework largely created by the Polish elites.

Franz Joseph's recognition of Galicia's Jews and of Ruthenian cultural societies and his distribution of charity to the poor did not overshadow the central message of the 1880 imperial visit to Galicia. Dependent on the Polish conservatives for support in the Reichsrat, the court and the Cisleithanian government worked closely with the Polish elites to create a "spontaneous" display of popular enthusiasm for emperor, fatherland, Austria, and Polish conservative leadership of Galicia. That court and government were more than satisfied with the inspection tour does not alter the reality that the 1880 *Kaiserreise* to Galicia was Polish not Habsburg theater.

The triumph of the Polish noble elites was short-lived, however. Mass political parties and pressure groups no longer willing to defer to *szlachta* leadership transformed the Galician political landscape by the 1890s. Successful organization by Social Democrats, peasant activists, National Democrats, and Ukrainian nationalists undermined the ability of the Stańczyks to define Polish national interests and to equate these interests with those of all inhabitants of Galicia. The crowds still came out for the emperor in 1894; however, already at the moment of their triumph in 1880, the conservative Stańczyk nobles were fighting a rear-guard battle against social and political forces beyond their control. These forces would increasingly express their skepticism toward conservative loyalism and the notion that Polish national interests could be fulfilled within a noble-dominated Habsburg Galicia.

CHAPTER 4

Imagining Austria

The Cult of the Emperor during the Great Jubilee Year of 1898

> One cannot easily or immediately banish entirely from the world this factional striving for much greater autonomy—enthusiasm for independence–, but one certainly must endeavor to use all permissible and promising means to defeat such strivings, to render them harmless, or even to channel them in better directions. . . .
>
> Just as Our House will also offer the most tenacious resistance against such tendencies, so it will want neither to overlook nor to overestimate those manifestations which national feelings—whether German, Slavic, Hungarian, Romanian, or Italian—have been able to bring to pass over the course of the centuries, but most especially in the last decades.
>
> —Franz Joseph to Franz Ferdinand, 7 February 1903[1]

National tensions like those visible during Franz Joseph's trips to Galicia in 1880 and 1894 intensified in the later 1890s. In this 1903 letter to his nephew and heir, Franz Ferdinand, Franz Joseph expressed his belief that the political crises caused by national separatism, while serious, should and could be successfully opposed. The emperor directly addressed Franz Ferdinand's concern that Hungarian meddling and the radical rhetoric of irresponsible nationalist politicians threatened the unity of the army. However, Franz Joseph would likely have used similar words to discuss the atmosphere of crisis facing Cisleithania on the eve of his fiftieth jubilee in 1898.

In his first years as emperor, Franz Joseph oversaw the revival of the court, insisted on preserving Habsburg traditional celebrations, and demanded adherence to the rules of court etiquette (unless he personally intervened). Before 1898, he rarely authorized expensive and pompous imperial celebrations aside from regularly performed ceremonies and festivities like the Corpus Christi procession and the foot-washing or the many imperial inspection tours of the provinces. At the same time, Franz Joseph and his advisors were cognizant of the fact that Cisleithanian politics in the late nineteenth century were marked by the rise of a new kind of mass and special-interest "politics in a new key."[2] The 1898 jubilee year came at a time of intensified national and social conflicts, and Franz Joseph and his advisors recognized the need to ameliorate such tensions or "channel them in better directions."

In the last decades of the nineteenth century, decades characterized by heightened political tension as well as popular celebrations of national and state heroes and workers' holidays in the monarchy and throughout Europe, the Habsburgs could not counter the perception that visible signs of public approval of and devotion to state, government, and dynasty were necessary confirmations of the health of political society. The Russian monarchy's "scenario of power" merging conquest, violence, and autocracy with, by the nineteenth century, a dynastic claim to embody the essence of the Russian people, could not serve as a model for Franz Joseph. The Habsburg emperor was committed to upholding the constitutional order. Obvious populist appeals, like the attempts by Emperor William II of Germany to associate himself directly with the German nation, were alien to Franz Joseph, who was predisposed to reject the concept of popular sovereignty.[3] The merging of dynastic imagery with national identity would, in any case, have been explosive in the multinational Habsburg Monarchy. Nonetheless, elements of traditional Habsburg self-presentation could be and were adapted to appeal for a renewal of dynastic and state patriotism.

This chapter, the first of three treating aspects of the 1898 jubilee celebrations, examines patriotic actions undertaken by the court, the Catholic Church, the Joint Army, the government, and the imperial family. There was no Habsburg department of propaganda to coordinate a systematic program of patriotic propaganda. Still, the Habsburgs and their closest supporters did convey consistent messages about the importance of the Habsburg ruler as a symbol of stability and as a focus for a common supranational patriotism. Court celebrations distanced the emperor from divisive government decisions and associated him instead with economic and cultural progress. At the same time, Franz Joseph, his supposed gentle nature magnified by the ceremony that governed his public performance, became the symbol of an idealized Austria in which the economic and national interests of all citizens could be reconciled if the population emulated the monarch's alleged Christ-like piety, charity, and concern for the public welfare.

Spectacular Imperial Celebrations, 1854–88

A number of large-scale officially sanctioned spectacular imperial celebrations had, of course, taken place prior to 1898. In April 1854, hundreds of thousands of Habsburg subjects rushed to glimpse the many scripted events of the wedding of Franz Joseph and Elisabeth of Bavaria, from the arrival of Elisabeth by steamship at the Danube port of Nußdorf on 22 April to her formal entrance into Vienna accompanied by the entire *Hofstaat*. A popular festival in the Prater, a ball in the imperial palace for the political and economic elite of the capital, parallel celebrations in the provinces, newspaper coverage, and commemorative publications projected an image of unity, renewal, restoration, and imperial benevolence.[4] The court developed similar programs for the 1873 twenty-fifth anniversary of Franz Joseph's accession to the throne and the imperial couple's silver wedding anniversary in 1879. Some events, like the Habsburg family's 1879 *tableau vivant,* were limited to the imperial family and the cream of court society.[5] Commoners holding positions in government, army, and state bureaucracy received recognition in the imperial audiences marking these celebrations.[6] The imperial family also showed itself to adoring crowds, thus proclaiming the continued centrality of the dynasty in the life of the (now) constitutional monarchy. Franz Joseph and Elisabeth rode out into the illuminated city in the evenings and attended large-scale public events like the 1879 dedication of the Votive Church, built just off the Ringstrasse with funds collected after the failed 1853 assassination attempt.[7]

In 1888, Franz Joseph explicitly forbade government and court promotion of his fortieth jubilee. Instead, he called on Habsburg subjects to make the jubilee a solemn day of contemplation and a time to offer charity to the poor.[8] With no official jubilee festivities, the unveiling of the Maria Theresa monument between the court museums of natural science and fine arts on 13 May, the 170th anniversary of her birth, was the most important imperial celebration in 1888 (figure 14). The museums had been constructed directly across the Ring from the imperial palace and asserted the imperial character of newly expanded Vienna.[9] The monument depicts Maria Theresa as the mother of the state and associates the dynasty with progress. Statues of advisors and military officers who helped rebuild the army and the state administration, enlightened thinkers who reformed the legal system and public education, and artists and scholars active during her reign surround the raised and oversized figure of Maria Theresa (figure 15).[10] The court invited several thousand guests to the elaborate unveiling ceremony. A special theater performance in the opera house that evening presented an opportunity for the court to reaffirm its vision of the ideal hierarchy of society. The court assigned the opera's two thousand seats based on court rankings.[11]

A political demonstration the night before the unveiling marred the dynastic celebration. On 12 May, a week after Pan-German leader Georg von Schönerer had been convicted for storming the offices of the *Neues Wiener Tagblatt* in retaliation for alleged insults to the House of Hohenzollern, Schönerer's followers held a rally on behalf of their leader and his wife.[12] Several hundred rowdy German nationalists then marched to the Ring and, in front of the still-veiled monument

Figure 14: Unveiling of the Maria Theresa Monument, 13 May 1888. Austrian National Library.

Figure 15: Maria Theresa Monument, photograph by author.

to the Mother of the Peoples, sang the German nationalist "Wacht am Rhein," a symbolic attack on the multinational monarchy and its supranational dynasty.[13]

The Catholic intellectual Karl von Vogelsang, editor of *Das Vaterland,* expressed regret at the decision to discourage popular festivities in honor of the emperor's fortieth jubilee.[14] Vogelsang believed that "in our days, where the monarchical principle has to struggle against strong attacks . . . it is in fact to be recommended to stand up publicly at each fitting opportunity" to convince the next generation of the "good deeds of the monarchy." Such expressions of dynastic loyalty would have proven that the imperial house continued to enjoy the support of the population. Instead, the Pan-German demonstration, growing partisan strife, and national conflict overshadowed what should have been an opportunity for bolstering public support for the monarchy.[15]

Parliamentary Paralysis

The 1898 imperial jubilee took place in the context of the expansion of the Cisleithanian suffrage and the related political crises of the late 1890s. Often accused of "muddling through," Taaffe had largely succeeded in keeping the tensions between federalists (Slavs, German Clericals, and Conservatives) and centralists (German liberals and nationalists) from breaking out into open conflict during his 1879–93 tenure as Cisleithanian minister president.[16] In 1882, hoping to ease the formation of a stable parliamentary coalition, Taaffe lowered the amount of paid taxes that qualified citizens to vote in the second and fourth curias to five gulden, opening the formal political process to tens of thousands of previously excluded "five-gulden men."

After the fall of Taaffe's coalition over proposals to further expand the suffrage—Taaffe's Polish conservative, Slav, and German Clerical allies resisted these efforts—German-Slav tensions intensified. In 1895, German-speakers in Cisleithania were infuriated by the creation of a Slovenian-language high school in Cilli, a majority German-speaking town located in the midst of a Slovene ethnic hinterland in the province of Styria. This incident provoked ever more radical political rhetoric from factions and parties seeking the votes of Austro-Germans, including those newly enfranchised. As Pieter Judson has argued, the galvanization of the Austro-German public by this seemingly insignificant incident revealed a "new sense of a larger German identity in Austria . . . anchored in local social experience of social conflict." This new sense of embattled national identity resulted from and spurred on a new mass politics as nationalist political leaders rhetorically connected such local controversies with state-level political struggles.[17]

Like Taaffe before him, Kazimierz Badeni, minister president from 1895 to 1897, hoped to forge parliamentary majorities by expanding the franchise.[18] He pushed through the addition of a fifth curia based on universal manhood suffrage in 1896 and lowered the tax requirements to vote in the second and fourth curias.[19] The 1897–99 crisis over the Badeni language ordinances promulgated in April 1897 proved that modest suffrage expansion was not the hoped-for panacea. Among other provisions, the language ordinances required officials in the Bohemian administration to verify their ability to work in both Czech and German by 1901. Violence broke out in Bohemia, Graz, and Vienna as many Austro-Germans feared the loss of their previously protected position in Cisleithania. Political factions jockeyed for votes by portraying themselves as the most uncompromising toward ethnic rivals. Czech politicians tried to harness popular discontent with the perceived ethnic arrogance of the Austro-Germans. Pressed by Georg von Schönerer's Pan-Germans as well as Austro-German deputies from Bohemia, Austro-German representatives obstructed the workings of the Cisleithanian parliament, leading to the forcible removal of deputies by the police, the dismissal of Badeni, the appointment of Count Franz Anton Thun as minister president, and the reliance of Franz Joseph on article 14 of the constitution to rule by decree.[20]

Political factions willing to exploit ethnic tensions were not the only political movements aided by the expansion of the suffrage. Officially created at Hainfeld in 1889, the Social Democratic Party proved adept at taking advantage of the new electoral realities. By the mid-1890s the party was in fact a loosely connected association of ethnically and regionally based social democratic parties. The party demanded the reorganization of the state to accommodate competing national interests, the institution of universal (manhood) suffrage, and an end to all privilege. The revolutionary rhetoric of the party, despite its evolutionary program, assured it the enmity of conservatives and radical nationalists.

The Social Democrats delivered harsh criticisms of the state and its recent history, but the party did not, as an institution, advise its adherents to distance themselves from popular public patriotic celebrations.[21] The party did, however, mobilize its members for alternative public festivities, such as the March celebrations of the martyrs of 1848 and the commemoration of May Day. The Social Democratic press also published daily notices glorifying the fiftieth anniversary of the "workers' revolution" of 1848. "Today begins the jubilee year of the revolution in Austria," proclaimed the *Arbeiter-Zeitung* on 1 January 1898:

> In the course of the year, we will have many opportunities to describe fully or in brief outline individual events of the jubilee year, and from March on, day after day to bring before the comrades the happenings during the revolutionary epoch in chronological order.[22]

Staging Patriotism: The Court and the 1898 Jubilee

Whether inspired by the need to confront parliamentary paralysis, the preparations by the city government of Vienna for the 1898 jubilee, the criticisms leveled by Vogelsang and others in 1888, or the successful jubilees of Victoria in 1887 and

1897, Franz Joseph broke with his stated reluctance to approve of extravagant and ephemeral festivities.[23] Franz Joseph continued to call on his subjects to celebrate him and his house "with acts of charity" even as he set in motion court preparations and specifically approved of court and government promotion of the 1898 jubilee.

In the summer of 1897, Franz Joseph assigned the task of overseeing the development of spectacular court festivities commemorating his fiftieth jubilee to Franz Ferdinand, recently recovered from several years of illness that had cast doubt on the succession.[24] Always protective of his authority as head of the House of Habsburg, Franz Joseph insisted on personally approving even the smallest details of the projected festivities. Practical control over the celebrations lay with the Office of the Grand Court Master. Heinrich Loebenstein von Aigenhorst, the ceremonial director, authored the program of celebratory events.[25]

The court's jubilee program was to commence on the morning of 29 November 1898 with a mass and Te Deum in Vienna's Cathedral of St. Stephen. The court scheduled a jubilee theater production in the court opera house for the evening of 1 December. An "Homage of His Majesty by the Imperial Family" in the Marble Hall of the imperial palace was to welcome in the 2 December jubilee itself. Later in the day at a less than spontaneous "Homage of the Peoples" in the Spanish Riding School, Franz Ferdinand would praise the emperor in the name of the peoples of the monarchy before silent invited guests, including delegations from the provinces. The court celebrations were to conclude with a "soirée at court" in the court opera theater.[26]

The invitation lists displayed the minimal ceremonial accommodations made to take account of the reality of popular participation in politics and of the importance of the middle classes in society. Most of the available space in the Spanish Riding School and St. Stephen's Cathedral was reserved for foreign dignitaries, army officers, clergy, *hoffähig* aristocrats, *Geheime Räte, Kämmerer, Truchsesse,* and high court officials. Small delegations from both houses of the parliament, representatives from the provincial legislatures and from the capitals of Vienna and Budapest, as well as groups representing organizations like the Red Cross, would pay homage to the glory of the ruler in the name of rest of Habsburg society. Those not invited to the events could only observe the emperor surrounded by foreign princes and the imperial court as he made his way to and from the various festivities.[27]

Of the official jubilee celebrations, all canceled after the murder of Empress Elisabeth on 10 September, the jubilee theater production was the court-controlled event designed to be witnessed by the largest audience. Due to its public character, the theater production offered an opportunity to make a definitive jubilee statement. The organizers hoped to bolster state patriotism and to agitate against ethnic and social division by blending together traditional elements of Habsburg legitimacy with reminders of concrete achievement in the present. The court intended the production to be performed a minimum of five or six times in the court opera theater, since "a great portion of the population of Vienna will want to see the production."[28] More than two thousand people could attend each performance in this great opera house. For the first presentation of the play, the court planned to reserve the central boxes for the imperial family and selected aristocrats, high government officials, and bureaucrats.[29] The potential audience was not limited to residents of and visitors to the Cisleithanian capital. Seats were set aside for Viennese and provincial journalists, ensuring that the reading public would find detailed descriptions in provincial newspapers. The play would also be published and, presumably, in the years ahead schools and local communities would perform it on the emperor's 4 October name-day and other imperial occasions.[30]

The evolution of the 1898 jubilee theater production will remind those familiar with Robert Musil's unfinished modernist masterpiece, *The Man Without Qualities,* of the Parallel Action.[31] In the novel, Ulrich, the title character, joined a committee seeking to organize festivities for the upcoming (and never realized) seventieth jubilee of Franz Joseph's reign. Ulrich's unfocused committee failed to develop a convincing central idea that would instill the Parallel Action with meaning. The actual court committee that produced the 1898 jubilee production had an even more daunting task than the mere creation of a patriotic play. The court and Cisleithanian government sought to exalt Franz Joseph and the imperial house without making references that could exacerbate national tensions or be used by political factions for partisan advantage.

In December 1897, the court solicited proposals for the jubilee production from several patriotic playwrights.[32] The proposals had to conform to a framework provided by Franz Ferdinand. The Office of the Grand Court Master was to "bring to production a *patriotic play* that should correspond to the sublime occasion, and in which living scenes from the past of the Most High Imperial House should be presented, and on which the entire membership of the court theater, opera house, and ballet was to collaborate." The production was to take under two hours to perform and was to include dance intermixed with dialogue and tableaux vivants.[33] Gustav Mahler, the director of the court opera, Paul Schlenther, the director of the court theater, and August Freiherr Plappart von Leenheer, the general intendant of the court theaters, were unimpressed with the proposals submitted in late January 1898. Though "patriotic," none brought out the historical significance of great moments in Habsburg history or ordered their scenes to fully reveal the glorious development of the Habsburg state to the satisfaction of these critics.[34]

Court and government officials then intervened directly in the creative aspects of the proposed production. In an extraordinary sitting, attesting to the perceived importance of the theater presentation, the grand court master Rudolf von und zu Liechtenstein; the second grand court master, Prince Alfred Montenuovo; the common minister of foreign affairs and of the imperial house, Agenor Gołuchowski (the son of the former Galician *Statthalter*); the Cisleithanian minister president, Franz Graf von Thun und Hohenstein; and Plappart met on 22 March 1898 to determine the "disposition" for the jubilee theater production.[35] They began by evaluating a list of great moments in "Austrian state history" and the "history of the House of Habsburg" drawn up by Plappart and Joseph Alexander von Helfert, a prominent patriotic historian.[36] These moments were to serve as the inspiration for a series of "living scenes" to be incorporated into the theater production:

1. The 1282 investment by Emperor Rudolf von Habsburg of his sons with his Austrian lands.

2. The acquisition of Tyrol by Duke Rudolf IV in 1365.

3. The 1515 double marriage of the grandchildren of Maximilian I.

4. The joining of the crowns of Hungary and Bohemia to those of the Austrian inherited lands by Ferdinand I, 1526–27.

5. Emperor Rudolf II's court at Prague, 1676–12.

6. Ferdinand II during the Thirty Years' War.

7. Leopold I and the lifting of the Turkish Siege of Vienna in 1683.

8. Maria Theresa, holding her infant son Joseph, asking for and receiving Hungarian promises of assistance at the Hungarian Landtag in 1741.

9. The declaration of the Victory of Kolin and the founding of the Order of Maria Theresa.

10. Maria Theresa with Franz Stephen in the circle of the Habsburg family, servants of the state, soldiers, and scholars.

11. Kaiser Joseph II at the plow, the lifting of *Leibeigenschaft,* the Edict of Toleration, and the founding of the Burgtheater.

12. Emperor Franz I's entrance into Vienna after the First Paris Peace in 1814; Congress of Vienna.

13. The wedding of Emperor Franz in 1830.

14. Ferdinand the Good riding in an open coach through the streets of Vienna to the acclamation of the public on 15 March 1848.

15. Arrival in Nußdorf of the steamship bearing Princess Elisabeth of Bavaria in 1854.

16. Emperor Franz Joseph: Vienna World Exhibition in 1873; the 1879 Makart Procession in honor of the silver wedding anniversary of the imperial couple; unveiling of the Maria Theresa monument in 1888.

17. Final Tableau; Apotheosis; the expansion of the imperial palace; city regulation and Greater Vienna.

According to the minutes of the meeting, Thun led the ensuing "lively discussion" about the "meaning" of the scenes. After carefully weighing "political
and other considerations" with regard to the "prevailing trends of the day," the
committee chose a handful of scenes with "the greatest subtlety." Most were
quickly rejected as undignified or unpoetic. At Thun's insistence, the committee
deemed unacceptable all references to Franz Joseph's predecessor, Ferdinand, the
revolutions of 1848, and "historical moments of recent and the most contemporary
times." The foreign minister and conservative Polish magnate Gołuchowski opposed the scene of Joseph II at the plow and convinced the committee to present
instead the less radical Maria Theresa together with her son. Gołuchowski also
pushed for the inclusion of the Congress of Vienna, an event of "world historical
importance" when Austria "constituted the political center of Europe if not the
world" and which had ushered in an "epoch of peace."

In the end, with Plappart basing his views on artistic criteria, Gołuchowski
hoping to portray the monarchy as a great (and conservative) power, and Thun
eager to avoid stirring up ethnic tensions, the committee agreed on an opening
and six tableaux. The chosen scenes conveyed, in the view of the committee, the
proper message of imperial patriotism: the late-thirteenth-century investment of
the sons of Rudolf, the first Habsburg Holy Roman Emperor, with the Austrian
lands; the double wedding of 1515 in Vienna's St. Stephen's Cathedral; the second
siege of Vienna in 1683; the Pragmatic Sanction; Maria Theresa and Joseph II; and
Franz I and the Congress of Vienna. The final scene would "allegorically glorify
the Ruling Majesty and bring an apotheosis that in a certain sense illustrates the
crowning achievements and deeds of the Habsburgs fulfilled by Emperor Franz
Joseph I." The Apotheosis, a great metaphor of unity and harmony of the peoples
of the monarchy, would present Franz Joseph as the benevolent father of his
subjects and as patron of art, culture, and industry.

After this meeting, the grand court master contracted Christiane Gräfin Thun-
Salm, an author of light fiction and patriotic one-act plays, to craft a melodramatic
story to knit together the chosen scenes.[37] Thun-Salm centered her play, *The
Emperor's Dream,* on pious Emperor Rudolf I, familiar to her audience through
the legend of his encounter with the Host discussed in Chapter 1. The choice of
Rudolf was sure to remind the audience of Franz Joseph's annual participation
in the Holy Thursday foot-washing and the Corpus Christi procession, ritualized
displays of Habsburg self-sacrifice, humility, and piety—qualities Franz Joseph
and all members of the House of Habsburg supposedly shared.

The production opens with nobles flocking to the imperial palace in Vienna
to pay homage as Rudolf invested his sons with his Austrian lands in 1282. Concerned about the fate of his lands, Rudolf sleeps fitfully. Future appears to him and
guides him through the succession of brief scenes. During each scene, soldiers,
burghers, and tavern keepers explain the importance of the historical moment,

and after the dialogue sets the tone, a tableau vivant is revealed in the background as the orchestra plays appropriate music or the choir sings of battles, peace, and Habsburg glory. The first Habsburg Holy Roman emperor remains unsatisfied, however. He has not yet seen what he holds most important:

> All the peoples united by my scepter
> I have loved as only a father can.
> The ruler who has the love of the people,
> He is the best and such a one I wish to be.
> Let me see if also in future days
> The distant grandchildren feel as do I.

In response, Future sings the praises of Rudolf's future heir:

> It glitters in the golden light of fifty years
> The crown, that your noble offspring bears,
> Beloved by the people, as never was another ruler
> When you hear the jubilation that envelops him,
> Coming from thousands and thousands of hearts—
> Then lay down your tired head in peace!
> What you have planted, you see it bloom again.
> The love that once founded the power of Habsburg,
> This love also binds people and ruler.[38]

Love and Loyalty, played by members of the court theater company, then transport Rudolf to the celebration of Franz Joseph's imperial jubilee. Modern cities, art, science, handicrafts, trade, and commerce flourish under this emperor's steady hand, and all the people of the monarchy "Thank our Kaiser, whom we all love!/Hail to him and to beloved Austria!" Pleased and moved, Rudolf gestures to the imperial loge, convinced that his great descendant would fulfill his dreams for his people and his house.

As Rudolf sinks back into sleep, the play culminates in the magnificent apotheosis. This final scene blends together decorations and "allegorical figures of the present," such as *Bohemia, Hungaria,* and *Galicia* wearing provincial colors and bearing the shields of the Habsburg provinces. This vision of the monarchy as a harmonious mosaic of peoples and cultures moving into the future with confidence, guided by the experience of the sacred House of Habsburg, reaches a crescendo with the collective singing of the state hymn.[39]

The planned December 1898 performances were canceled after the murder of Elisabeth. Still, *The Emperor's Dream* was published and recommended for sale by newspapers, including the *Neue Freie Presse,* which noted that the play stood out from among the many jubilee publications due to Thun-Salm's "Meaningful verses, lovely language, and the fresh living image of folk scenes."[40] A shortened version of the play was performed in Vienna's court opera house as part of a special theater presentation honoring Franz Joseph's 1908 sixtieth jubilee celebrations. More than two thousand people attended each of six performances between 2 December and 8 December (two of these performances were added to the scheduled four in order to accommodate public demand for tickets). According to the correspondent of the *Illustrirtes Wiener Extrablatt* who attended the first performance, when the audience sang the *Gott erhalte*

> The emperor appeared profoundly moved.
> It was a moment of such solemnity, that it touched everyone deep in their souls. Whoever was a witness to this homage will never lose this moment from his memory.[41]

The narrative of Habsburg family and state history contained in this play, developed with the assistance of a professional historian, tailored to properly address issues of the day by politicians like Gołuchowski and Thun, and penned by the author of popular patriotic publications, couched the Habsburg answer to the problems of the day in the form of a traditional allegory of dynastic glory. The theater production associated Franz Joseph with his great predecessor, Rudolf. In the production, Franz Joseph became the symbol of an idealized monarchy of harmony, national cultural fulfillment, and economic progress. This play, like all the official court events, was designed to depict the emperor as a ruler who cared for the needs of all citizens, irrespective of social status or self-designated national/ethnic affiliation. In 1898, the monarchy did not seek to supplant nationality with state patriotism, but to project ethnic identity as an essential aspect of dynastic loyalty within a harmonious Austria.

However, in order to display the emperor, the dynasty, and the monarchy in a harmonious image of ethnic peace and cultural progress, this panegyric play had to lift Franz Joseph out of time: the decade of neoabsolutist rule following the revolutions of 1848–49 could not be emphasized in a constitutional era when Franz Joseph was guarantor of civil rights; the emperor could not be associated with policies and governments considered anathema by competing ethnic and political factions. Only by distancing Franz Joseph from the actions taken by his governments over the course of his reign could the message of tolerance and unity be conveyed in a way appropriate to maintaining imperial dignity and to avoiding an exacerbation of national passions. Franz Joseph became, then, a focus of popular dynastic loyalty and a symbol of an idealized Austria existing above the compromises and complications of the real world.

The Death of the Empress

On 10 September, Luigi Luccheni, an Italian anarchist, stabbed and killed Empress Elisabeth in Geneva. Grief-stricken, Franz Joseph ordered the immediate cancellation of all officially planned jubilee events and mourned the loss of his wife, murdered less than ten years after his only son had committed suicide at Mayerling.[42] The murder, the transfer of the body of the empress from Geneva to Vienna, and the official mourning darkened the final months of the jubilee year. During these months, the human qualities of the emperor-martyr, enhanced and magnified by grief for his wife expressed during traditional Habsburg mourning ceremonies, came to the fore.

Franz Joseph's dedication to court ceremony had been matched by Elisabeth's rejection of her designated roles in Habsburg imperial festivities. After her arrival in Vienna in 1854 at the age of sixteen, Elisabeth soon rebelled against the strictures of Habsburg court etiquette. She seldom participated in the Holy Thursday ceremonies. She only reluctantly took part in the 1873 jubilee and World Exhibition events and, after the death of her son Rudolf in 1889 and the 1890 marriage of her youngest daughter, Maria Valerie, Elisabeth ceased to play a public role altogether.[43] By refusing to appear in public at her husband's side within the framework of Habsburg court etiquette, Elisabeth never became a symbol of state unity while alive, though she did enjoy a considerable measure of popularity in the Hungarian half of the monarchy.[44]

Elisabeth's lifeless body became subject to the regulations she had long sought to flee and became a focus of official and unofficial appeals for dynastic and state patriotism. In Geneva, in accordance with court dictates and with the wishes of the emperor, the body of the empress was placed in a coffin with a glass top, enabling court and government officials to confirm the identity of the deceased for the official death certificate. The coffin was then sealed in a sarcophagus and set on a pedestal inside a wagon of a special court train; the sarcophagus was visible to all onlookers through large windows. From the border of the monarchy to Vienna, church bells rang and civil and military authorities gathered at every station to honor the empress as the train rolled slowly past. Since the late 1850s, Elisabeth had largely avoided her husband's many tours of the crownlands, but now, in death, her final imperial progress "locate[d] the society's center and affirm[ed] its connection with transcendent things by stamping" Habsburg territory "with ritual signs of dominance" as surely as had Franz Joseph's many visitations.[45]

The train arrived at night at Vienna's West Station on 15 September and the empress was transferred in a solemn procession to the Hofburg.[46] The sarcophagus was displayed to the public for one and a half days in the Hofburg Chapel. Hundreds of dignitaries and representatives from institutions and associations traveled to Vienna to place wreaths at the base of the sarcophagus. At 4 P.M. on 17 September, church bells all over the monarchy chimed as the funeral procession in Vienna, complete with white horses pulling imperial coaches draped in black cloth, made its way from the imperial palace to the Capuchin Church, the location of the burial chambers of the Habsburg family. Newspaper reports agreed that the crowds lining the streets were greater than any in living memory.[47] The male members of court society joined the emperor for the vigil evening on 19 September and the three traditional services for the dead (*Seelenamte*) on 20, 21, and 22 September. The vault was then closed to the public until several Habsburg coffins had been rearranged and Elisabeth's placed next to that containing the remains of her son Rudolf.

Court rules and associated directives issued by state authorities produced manifestations of official mourning in every province. Entertainments staged by the court or presented on property administered by the court were canceled. The Ministry of Interior requested that all private theaters close for Elisabeth's internment. The coaches of the imperial family and of court society were draped in black for the designated six months of ceremonial mourning (*Hoftrauer*). Court regulations specified the proper clothes to be worn throughout the mourning period by military officers, court society, as well as state and provincial government bureaucrats.[48] The Cisleithanian Ministry of Religion and Education directed schools to hold special ceremonies dedicated to the loss of the empress on 17 September. Millions of pupils attended religious services and school directors explained the importance of this tragedy "in a patriotic fashion."[49]

There were indications that the murder of the empress and her burial had succeeded, at least temporarily, in uniting the population of the monarchy in a common experience of mourning. In Hungary, where Franz Joseph's jubilee had not been officially acknowledged and Elisabeth was seen as an ally of the Hungarian nation, signs of mourning were as prevalent as they were in Cisleithania. Austro-Hungarian citizens packed churches and synagogues for services in memory of the empress. Town and city governments followed the lead of the court and the Vienna city government and hung black flags from masts, streetlights, and government buildings.[50] Local governments and voluntary associations sent messages of sympathy to the emperor. Lengthy newspaper articles described in great detail the wounds inflicted on the empress, the train carrying her body to Vienna, and the traditional funeral ceremonies.[51]

The organs of almost every political party printed editorials about the loss of the beloved empress, though of central importance in most of these editorials was the health of the emperor. Franz Joseph, it was alleged, was

> acknowledged in all of Europe as a model of the virtues of a ruler, venerated in the entire civilized world as a prince of peace, His Majesty Emperor and King, to whom on the occasion of his fast approaching golden jubilee, with the affection of their entire hearts, the people extend wreaths of their feelings and gratefulness at the feet of his throne![52]

Peasant, liberal, and Christian Social papers detailed signs of the emperor's grief, from his reaction to the news, "nothing is spared me in this world," to his collapse on Elisabeth's sarcophagus. Editorials expressed hope that in mourning the monarchy would overcome political differences, so petty and insignificant when compared to the bonds uniting the peoples with the person of the emperor and the common fatherland he ruled.[53]

Yet, despite the outward signs of unity in mourning, even the death of the empress became an opportunity for the expression of competing political agendas. Rival social and political factions incorporated the empress into their preexisting explanations of and prescriptions for the crises confronting the Habsburg state. German liberal newspapers in Bohemia, for example, declared that Austro-German burghers mourned "in honorable fashion for the loss of the empress" and affirmed that "The old love and devotion to the imperial house, the adulation for the emperor" continued to exist; however, the same editorials blamed divisions in society on the Social Democrats and the Czechs, who threatened the German liberals with social revolution and ethnic defeat.[54]

Perhaps most ironically, Vienna's anti-Semitic Christian Socials claimed Elisabeth, personally liberal-leaning and a devotee of the poetry of German-Jewish poet Heinrich Heine, as a martyr to the Christian Social cause. For the Catholic *Das Vaterland,* commenting on the massive crowds standing silent on the streets as the coffin of the empress was carried to the Hofburg from the train station, the empress "embodied a divine idea: The idea of Christian Authority."[55] The Vienna Christian Women's Association (*Frauenbund*) defined the empress as "the truly loving spouse—the concerned, tender mother—the adored, deified grandmother—the gentle good ruler . . . she exchanged the golden crown with the crown of the martyr!"[56] This fervently anti-Semitic organization, unable to embrace the living empress, organized a special gathering devoted to her memory during which the Christian Social mayor Karl Lueger and the leadership of the *Frauenbund* raged against the dangerous progression from liberalism to radicalism to social democracy to anarchism—and created a fund in her name for Christian orphans. The *Frauenbund* joined the calls for the addition of an Elisabeth Chapel to the proposed Jubilee Church (figures 16 and 17 show the completed Jubilee Church and a relief on the outside of the Elisabeth Chapel; see Chapter 6 on Lueger, the Christian Women's Association, and the Christian Social manipulation of the 1898 jubilee).[57]

In the 1890s, politicians in Bohemia and Hungary railed against every perceived challenge to provincial autonomy, fearing that political rivals would accuse them of failing to protect the national honor. The funeral of the empress could not escape this kind of scrutiny, and in fact gave rise to two challenges to the court's control over imperial ceremonies that forced court officials to defend the ability of court ceremonial to represent the constitutional reality of the Dual Monarchy.

The coat of arms on the empress's sarcophagus originally bore the Latin inscription: "Elisabeth, Empress of Austria." In order to avoid a possible dispute with Hungarian officials, the court ceremonial director ordered that it be immediately changed to "Elisabeth, Empress of Austria and Queen of Hungary." Incensed that the shield now identified Elisabeth as "Queen of Hungary" but not as "Queen of Bohemia," Prince Georg Lobkowitz, marshal of the diet of Bohemia, complained to the minister president and to the grand court master. Lobkowitz, like many Bohemian autonomists and Czech nationalist politicians, was eager to force the court to acknowledge a direct relationship between Bohemia and the Crown. If it could be demonstrated that the emperor ruled Bohemia only as Bohemian king—similar to his official status as king of Hungary—than this could legitimize demands for greater provincial autonomy.

Just weeks after the murder, Franz Joseph was forced to adjudicate this dispute over the proper title for his deceased wife. He fully endorsed the position of the court, which Ceremonial Director Loebenstein based on the emperor's official title used since 1868. According to Loebenstein, "empress" encompassed all of Elisabeth's titles that referred to the lands represented in the Cisleithanian parliament and, therefore, implied "Queen of Bohemia." In the future the late Elisabeth would be referred to as "Her Majesty, Empress and Queen Elisabeth," avoiding the issue of her full title and hence avoiding further controversy over the relative importance of the crownlands.[58]

The efforts made by the court to head off potential Hungarian complaints over Elisabeth's title did not prevent Hungarian minister president Baron Dezső Bánffy from protesting that the funeral ceremonies had a "tendentious Austrian character" and that Habsburg court ceremony did not adequately represent the

Figure 16: Kaiser Jubilee Church, photograph by author.

Figure 17: Elisabeth Frieze on the Jubilee Church, photograph by author.

fact that Elisabeth was equally Hungarian queen and Austrian empress.[59] Pressed by Thun and Gołuchowski, Loebenstein dismissed these charges. The court, he wrote, had added Elisabeth's royal Hungarian title before anyone had viewed the sarcophagus.[60] Available seats had been evenly divided between representatives from Hungary (from the Budapest parliament and the city council) and from Cisleithania. The small size of the Capuchin Church, not malicious intent toward the Hungarians, prevented many who had traveled from Hungary for the funeral from attending the ceremony inside the church. The only possible solution to the limited seating in the Capuchin Church would have entailed holding the ceremony in St. Stephen's Cathedral. Had the court made this alteration, the empress would have been transferred first to the cathedral and then to the Capuchin Church, forcing Franz Joseph to endure two ceremonies and another funeral procession.

> Aside from the fact that it would have been questionable whether His Majesty would have deigned to bestow his permission to deviate from the old tradition, who would have had the heart to propose to the bereaved husband an extension of the ceremony of mourning, just so the self-confidence of a few persons would not have been affected or so a larger number of mourning guests could have attended the consecration inside the church instead of outside?[61]

The court, Loebenstein contended, had in fact succeeded in adapting ceremonial precedents to the post-1867 political system. As the 1896 millennium celebrations in Hungary and the preparations for the fiftieth jubilee in Austria had confirmed, the traditional Habsburg ceremonial was capable of meeting the requirements of large spaces and of reflecting the constitutional structure of the Dual Monarchy.[62]

The death and burial of Elisabeth intensified a trend already evident in the official and semi-official presentation of the emperor during the jubilee year. During the decade of neoabsolutism, the court had presented the emperor as the youthful renewer and legitimate heir to Habsburg greatness. In the constitutional era and after the suicide of Rudolf in 1889 and the murder of the empress, the emperor was no longer the strong, youthful face of a powerful state rising from the ashes of revolution to new and greater heights. Court ceremony surrounding the jubilee and the death of the empress made revelations of Franz Joseph's personal pain and human suffering more powerful. Franz Joseph was now both idealized ruler—prince of peace, first soldier, living embodiment of the benevolent state— and idealized human being, dedicated to working for the good of his subjects, a model of suffering and patience, bowed but not broken by personal tragedy.

Jubilee Message from the Catholic Hierarchy

The image of the emperor as Christ-like martyr and sublime moral model dominated the final months of the jubilee year. Nowhere was the presentation of the emperor as suffering martyr more powerfully communicated to a large proportion of the population than in the jubilee pastoral letter issued by the Catholic hierarchy of Cisleithania, authored by Cardinal Schönborn of Prague, and signed by thirty-nine archbishops and bishops.

The Habsburg family had long utilized religious imagery to defend and advertise its right to rule in Central Europe. The mythic story of Rudolf and the Host and the allegedly miraculous relationship between the imperial house and the Virgin (monuments to such a relationship can be seen all over Central Europe in the form of Maria columns erected in the seventeenth century) received annual confirmation in the foot-washing and the Corpus Christi procession. Franz Joseph and his government revived these Catholic rituals and also recreated the relationship between the state and the Catholic Church in the first years after the revolutions, negotiating the 1855 concordat, which undid (at least temporarily) many of the Josephinian church reforms. The church hierarchy promised to spread the values of unity and imperial loyalty through religious services and religious education in return for recognition of church autonomy. The concordat ceded to the Catholic Church influence over marriage, education, and funerals even for non-Catholics.

After 1860, however, the Austro-German liberals who dominated the government of Cisleithania for most of the first two decades of constitutional government attacked the privileged position of the Catholic Church. Already in 1861, new laws guaranteed rights to Protestants. In the late 1860s, the liberal government of Karl von Auersperg passed bills creating confessional equality in marriage, conversion, and other matters previously considered within the purview of the Catholic Church. When the Ecumenical Council promulgated the doctrine of papal infallibility in 1870, Franz Joseph himself finally negated the concordat.[63]

Even after the abrogation of the concordat, Catholicism remained a key part of the ceremony surrounding the emperor. As Archduke Albrecht explained in 1881 to the young Franz Ferdinand, at the time second in line to the throne, the most important duty of all members of the Habsburg family was to embody the "ideal of the pious Christian."[64] Over the course of Franz Joseph's sixty-eight-year reign, religious services and religious elements were always intertwined with imperial celebrations. Franz Joseph continued to participate in Catholic ceremonies, and the life-cycle events of marriage, birth, and death for members of the imperial family always included Catholic Church services.

In 1898, the Catholic hierarchy, a historic ally of the dynasty, under attack from Schönerer's *Los von Rom* movement and its authority within the church threatened by Catholic clergy associated with the Christian Social Party, directed priests and bishops to read the special jubilee pastoral letter from every Catholic pulpit in Cisleithania on 27 November, the first Advent Sunday. The majority of the citizens of the monarchy were Catholic, and millions attended these services. Many more, Catholic and non-Catholic alike, read excerpts from and comments on the pastoral letter printed in newspapers sold in every city and town in the monarchy.[65]

The pastoral letter interpreted Franz Joseph's role in the history of the monarchy in terms corresponding to the unrealized court program of festivities. Priests and bishops told their congregations that Franz Joseph, called to the throne by "divine Providence," had rescued the state from the chaos of revolution "with a strong hand," "faith in God," and "confidence in the future of Austria." Like the jubilee theater production, the letter reminded all believers that the emperor had ascended the throne filled with respect for ethnic difference and had called on the "tribes" of the monarchy to work with him for the good of the common fatherland. According to the Catholic hierarchy, Franz Joseph, true to his principles, had labored ceaselessly for fifty years to improve the lives of all his ungrateful peoples.

The church implicitly compared Franz Joseph to Christ and appealed for an end to ethnic conflict and partisan division. According to the pastoral letter, God had set Franz Joseph on his earthly throne. Franz Joseph was wise and merciful; Franz Joseph punished the guilty and rewarded the good. The emperor ministered to the weak, and he answered prayers sent to him in the form of petitions for charity. Franz Joseph suffered for his just cause. The death of his son and wife did not shake his dedication to the future of Austria and his belief and trust in God. Only this Christ-like ruler could ameliorate the many conflicts within the "great Austrian family of peoples."

The messages conveyed by the court on the one hand and the Catholic Church on the other diverged over the nature of the existing state. The 1898 jubilee theater production defined the history of the monarchy as the history of the Habsburg family, which culminated in the person of the good emperor, Franz Joseph. Future revealed to Rudolf an ideal of ethnic and social harmony and economic progress under Franz Joseph as though this vision corresponded to reality in 1898. In his 1903 letter to Franz Ferdinand quoted at the beginning of this chapter, Franz Joseph expressed his own belief that national conflicts and parliamentary paralysis were not nearly as threatening as they appeared and that the future was still a Habsburg future.

The Austria depicted in the pastoral letter was quite different. The letter did not deny or paper over the seriousness of the political crises affecting the monarchy by maintaining that all lived in harmony. In the pastoral letter, "Austria" and "Austrian patriotism" became a matter of faith. The episcopal letter directly acknowledged national tension, the growth of a new politics of attack and division, and the threat these trends posed for the coherence of the state. The church's prescription for the problems plaguing the monarchy was a deceptively simple one: all Christians were urged to set aside division and petty squabbling and recognize each other as children of the common imperial father. The church implored the faithful to cleanse themselves of hatreds, to dedicate themselves to the common good, to give to charity, to show their faith in God, and to follow in the footsteps of the Christ-like emperor-martyr. "Would we not have been spared the troubles and evil had his example and his convictions found imitation everywhere?" Only by acting in the image of Franz Joseph could the idealized Austria become a reality:

> The good of the whole is possible only through the harmonious arrangement of the individual parts; but also the parts receive life and strength from the whole. The happy development of the individual nationalities (*Volkstämme*) is dependent on the power and strength of the whole monarchy, and to strengthen it and preserve it in its full splendor is the constant concern of our emperor. So should the Austrian empire of peoples represent a magnificent mosaic, in which all parts take a deserved place and by doing so contribute to the beauty of the whole.

The Catholic hierarchy demanded that the faithful end the selfish pursuit of ethnic goals while ignoring the real interests of their fellow children of the good emperor: "That is the true Austrian patriotism."

The connection between the dynasty and religion was not, of course, limited to Roman Catholicism. On inspection tours Franz Joseph kissed relics, attended mass, and was blessed by clergy of all stripes. As a commemorative publication produced under the auspices of Franz Ferdinand asserted, "Like the hatred based on difference of race, confessional intolerance is also against his temperament (*Sinn*)." He attended church on holidays,

> surrounded by the whole overwhelming splendor his court is able to display. Franz Joseph does not, however, disdain to admit the most modest clergy of

a Jewish community to the audience chamber, [the clergyman's] head covered according to the rules of his religion, in order to plea for the blessing
of heaven on his beloved ruler.[66]

The practical wisdom of Franz Joseph's recognition of *organized* religion as a
stabilizing force in the monarchy was demonstrated by the response of religious
institutions to every state and dynastic holiday. The emperor was evoked from
pulpits and bimas on his birthday, name-day, jubilees, the death of members
of the imperial house, and the marriage of his son. At the same time, it must
be acknowledged that the power and authority of the church hierarchy over its
flock and even over the clergy was under siege in this period. Catholic political
movements antagonistic toward the church hierarchy and openly anti-Semitic
such as the Christian Social Party attracted ever-greater numbers of followers
among the lower clergy and the general Catholic population. Members of the
clergy were prominent in even some of the more radical nationalist movements
of the day—in direct contradiction to the spirit of the jubilee pastoral letter. In
this socially conservative monarchy, however, the impact of religious leaders,
including the Catholic clergy, describing dynastic loyalty as a religious impera-
tive should not be underestimated.

The Pillar of the Regime: The Armed Forces and the Jubilee

Like the Catholic Church, the most ubiquitous of all common institutions of
Austria-Hungary, the Joint Army, also appealed for increased loyalty to emperor
and fatherland and a lessening of ethnic conflicts during the 1898 jubilee year.

Throughout his long reign, Franz Joseph never forgot that the Habsburg army
had defeated revolution and ensured the existence of the monarchy in 1848–49.
Franz Joseph constantly displayed his preference for a military lifestyle. He
surrounded himself with military advisors and insisted that the formal aspects
of military discipline be strictly adhered to. Military discipline became part of
the ceremony that regulated all aspects of his public life. Like Joseph II, Franz
Joseph appeared in public almost exclusively in military uniform (exceptions
included his many hunting trips and visits to foreign countries). Franz Joseph
even participated in the foot-washing and the Corpus Christi procession dressed
as First Soldier of the realm, uniting his roles as holy Habsburg ruler and commander-in-chief of the armed forces.[67]

The 1867 Compromise creating Austria-Hungary provided for a common
Ministry of War to oversee the Joint Army under the direct control of the emperor-
king. The emperor-king possessed the sole power of command over the military,
but the provisions of the Compromise concerning the Joint Army and the Hungarian, Austrian, and Croatian National Guards had to be renewed each decade,
by definition subjecting military matters to political debate.[68] Every ten years,
Hungarian politicians agitated for increasing the role of the Hungarian National

Guard and for the use of Hungarian as the language of command in units of the Joint Army recruited from Hungarian soil. Czech politicians repeatedly called for the creation of a Bohemian national guard. Still, the joint Army was a very visible symbol of state unity. The officer corps was supranational in ideology and multiethnic in personnel. Loyalty to the person of the emperor was at the core of the dynastic patriotism drilled into the members of the armed forces, recruited by conscription after 1868. Though the rank and file spent less time in this school of dynastic loyalty than did the officers, the Joint Army was, as Oscar Jaszi wrote, "the chief supporter and maintainer of the monarchy."[69]

The Joint Army played a very prominent and public role in all of the 1898 jubilee celebrations. As was the case every year, military bands paraded through the streets of towns and villages, awakening the population (as early as 4:30 A.M.) with the sounds of military marches on the emperor's 18 August birthday. Military honor guards were a common feature at local celebrations and at major festivities in large cities in Cisleithania.

At the specific request of the military command, the grand court master integrated into the 1898 court jubilee program the unveiling of a monument to Archduke Albrecht, general inspector of the armed forces until his death in 1895. Albrecht was the protector of imperial traditions and the archconservative in the imperial family. This archduke had issued the order to fire on the crowds in March 1848, and it was to him that Franz Joseph entrusted the political education of his son and heir, Rudolf—at least until Elisabeth assumed control over the crown prince's education. Albrecht was the last Habsburg to successfully lead troops in the field. Franz Joseph had failed as a battlefield general in his one major attempt, at Solferino in 1859; Albrecht had led his forces to victory at Custozza in June 1866. Though the statute of the House of Habsburg, codified in 1839, awarded Franz Joseph great power over his family, family members often dreaded and feared Albrecht.[70]

Contributions from officers and enlisted men funded the construction of the Albrecht monument. Franz Joseph demanded that no undue pressure be exerted on his notoriously underpaid officers and soldiers. Yet the lists of contributions made from a number of military formations were suspiciously uniform: each soldier of a particular rank "voluntarily" contributed the exact same amount, and this sum was often deducted from military pay over the course of several months. For example, all officers of the Infantry School of Budapest "volunteered" to have 6 percent of one month's salary automatically deducted to demonstrate their patriotic feelings and love for the deceased army inspector and archduke.[71]

The unveiling of the Albrecht monument was the only item listed in the official court program for the 1898 jubilee, which was postponed after Elisabeth's death rather than canceled.[72] The monument was eventually placed on the grounds of the imperial palace complex in the center of Vienna. The army leadership feared that any other location chosen in the city would have prompted Hungarian complaints that such a location was a direct attack on Hungarian autonomy and, therefore, on the provisions of the Compromise.[73]

Despite the official mourning due to the death of Elisabeth, the military leadership planned a special jubilee program for 2 December. On the morning of the jubilee itself, all members of the armed forces, aside from those on watch, were expected to attend religious services in churches and other houses of worship. The commander of the Second Corps ordered that "also those military persons who participated in the parade in Olmütz on the occasion of the accession of the emperor on 2 December 1848 attend [the religious services] as a corporation."[74]

After religious services, the soldiers and officers, dressed in parade uniforms, gathered in their garrisons all over the monarchy for the distribution of jubilee medals. By the 1890s, the minting of commemorative medals and coins had become common practice for the organizers of major state, local, and ethnic celebrations. The city of Vienna, to name just one example, had distributed several hundred such medals in 1879 in honor of the twenty-fifth wedding anniversary of the imperial couple.[75] However, the sheer volume of commemorative medals handed out by the state in 1898 dwarfed all previous distributions. On Franz Joseph's birthday, the *Wiener Zeitung* announced that the emperor, in his role as commander of the armed forces, had issued an army order to produce a jubilee-commemorative-medal for the armed forces and the gendarmerie. The emperor declared this medal a "renewed demonstration of my devotion [to] and grateful recognition of those who served me—and therefore the monarchy—in joy and sadness in truest and most pure fulfillment of duty." All those serving in the armed forces and thousands of retired solders and officers were eligible for this medal. Those who had been in active service for at least fifty years received a gold medal, all others bronze.[76] On 2 December, the military handed out more than three million of these tokens of the supposed bond between soldier and emperor-king (figure 18).[77]

At these ceremonies, during which the soldiers wore solemn reminders of the ongoing official mourning for the murdered Empress Elisabeth and received their jubilee medals, the Joint Army also distributed the thirteen-page *Commemorative Pamphlet for the Soldiers on the Occasion of the Fiftieth Jubilee of His Majesty Franz Joseph I,* "dedicated by the officers to the enlisted men." This pamphlet was written before the assassination of the empress and, according to the *Fremden-Blatt,* was published "in every provincial language."[78] Rank-and-file soldiers served in active service for only three years, too short a time, perhaps, to fully adopt the supranational ethos of the career Habsburg military officer.[79] The pamphlet, like the jubilee medal, was intended to instill in enlisted soldiers and noncommissioned officers a sense of corporate identity and supranational dynastic loyalty. The pamphlet was, in effect, an attempt to immunize the Joint Army against the threat of radical nationalism.

Figure 18: Jubilee Commemorative Medal for the Armed Forces, 1898. Photograph by author.

The pamphlet depicted Franz Joseph as the patron saint of the armed forces. The emperor cared for the welfare of his soldiers, had relied on this most loyal institution to suppress revolution and defend the state from foreign threats, and trusted the armed forces to meet future challenges. Sitting on the "God-entrusted throne" of the Habsburgs, the "first soldier of the monarchy" understood and worked to meet the needs of his beloved soldiers. The brochure credited the emperor with improvements in armaments, uniforms, pay, and benefits and the reduction of harsh punishments. Franz Joseph raised the reputation of the military in the greater society by creating medals honoring valor and service and by ensuring that veterans had priority for employment in government and government-supported institutions. Franz Joseph, himself a veteran, directed the government to found homes for war invalids and institutions to provide financial assistance to families left behind by the fallen. Out of benevolence, Franz Joseph had reduced active service to three years from eight, instituted universal conscription—thereby eliminating (at least in theory) exemptions for the wealthy and highborn—and created an army based on duty and bravery and merit:

> Just as each enjoys the benefits of his fatherland, each person has the duty to defend the monarch and the fatherland to the last drop of blood, and rank and wealth frees none from this obligation. Whether born in a palace or in a hovel, son of a prince or of a poor day laborer, all are equal when it is time to defend the fatherland.[80]

The pamphlet did not limit its stated justifications for an intensification of patriotic devotion to practical matters that affected the daily life of the ordinary soldier. National separatism could potentially reduce the effectiveness of a multinational military force, and opposition to separatism and radical nationalism was at the core of the military's jubilee message. The pamphlet urged the soldiers to retain their patriotism, gained during their active duty, after the end of their service and to teach this patriotism to their children:

> Hold tight to your duty, do not let yourself be led astray by demagogues, by coarse agitators and rebels, who only lie to you and deceive you! . . .
>
> Our exalted ruler's protection and care encompasses all of his people; like children to a father, each is as near to his heart as the other; He will bring right and justice to each, no matter how great the hindrances; but like a father our Emperor and King must be able to count on the loyalty of His [subjects]—irrespective of language and nation, of tribe and confession—in the face of any danger, at any time![81]

The military's 2 December program of religious services and distribution of jubilee medals and pamphlets delivered a message of dynastic loyalty. The pamphlet handed out to soldiers all over the monarchy exhorted them to resist the lure of nationalism and to maintain their discipline and loyalty to emperor and fatherland after the end of their service. The military portrayed the emperor as a model of dedication to duty, who alone promised to ameliorate the dangers threatening the monarchy and to assure the welfare of each individual citizen.

Pushing Patriotism: The Cisleithanian Government and the 1898 Jubilee

In sharp contrast with 1888, the Cisleithanian government also acted to promote the 1898 jubilee, complementing the efforts by the court, the Catholic Church, and the Joint Army. Already in the first days of January, official government newspapers, from the *Fremden-Blatt* and the *Wiener Zeitung* published in Vienna to the official organs of the provincial governments like Galicia's *Gazeta Lwowska,* declared 1898 a year of "joy for His Majesty and the peoples living under His scepter." *Gazeta Lwowska* and other regional official newspapers published daily notices of "the most important happenings from the epoch of the reign of His Majesty" that touched directly on the lives of the people of the region, and by doing so intended "to create a single great expression of homage and devotion to the person of His Most August Jubilant."[82] The flood of newspaper articles highlighted the allegedly steadfast character of the emperor, his quietly heroic qualities of generosity and kindness, the magnificent traditions of the imperial house, and the concrete achievements of his governments. Editorials credited Franz Joseph's support for advances in art, science, and culture over the last fifty years.

The government press cited the emperor's reticence to approve costly festivities, his own long record of personal charitable contributions, and thousands of charitable actions initiated in honor of the jubilee by local governments and private citizens as proof of the bond between emperor and people. The official press organ of the Galician administration, for example, noted that in accordance with the emperor's wishes, communities and institutions in the province had founded hospitals, schools, and homes for orphans, as well as insurance funds in the name of the emperor in 1888. Large-scale celebrations would capture the attention of the public throughout the jubilee year of 1898, but the paper prompted the population to again greet the jubilee with acts of charity in imitation of the generous emperor.[83] The government supported such actions, received an overwhelming response from the population, and defined these actions as proof that the state, like its living symbol, endeavored to address the material needs of the population (the next chapter will discuss charitable contributions made during the jubilee year in greater detail).

In addition to the daily articles connecting the personal qualities of the emperor with the actions of the state on behalf of its citizens over the course of the last fifty years, the government minted several categories of commemorative medals. The 18 August issue of the *Wiener Zeitung* announcing the creation of the military jubilee medals also announced the creation of another officially produced and distributed commemorative medal. The "Jubilee Medal for State Civil Servants," a "new demonstration of My good will and My fatherly affection for the entire body of the state civil bureaucrats and servants," was given out to all state employees currently in service on 2 December 1898 as well as those no longer in state service who had worked for at least ten straight years in the state bureaucracy. Franz Joseph also agreed to Foreign Minister Gołuchowski's request to issue a "Medal of Honor for Forty Years of True Service." This medal recognized "persistent and conscientious performance of duty" irrespective of "rank, of estate, and of gender." This was the only medal awarded by the government to people outside of state, court, or military service. It was fitting that men and women who had worked for forty years in public or private service should receive a medal minted with the image of the emperor, who was himself legendary for his dogged commitment to duty.[84]

The individuals receiving the most decorations during the jubilee year were not to be found, however, in the ranks of the military or the state bureaucracy, but rather in the court administration itself. In October, Franz Joseph approved the creation of one final commemorative jubilee medal: the Jubilee-Court-Medal. Those who had served "around the Most High Person" or in the court administration at any time over the last fifty years were eligible for this medal, minted in gold, silver, and bronze versions. The grand court master ordered 7,395 of the Jubilee-Court-Medals. Some 2,663 members of the court, including the *Oberst-hofchargen,* the *Hofdienste,* hundreds of imperial body-guards, and hundreds of officials employed in the *Hofstäbe* received both the Jubilee-Court-Medal and the Jubilee-Commemorative-Medal for the Armed Forces.[85]

The Jubilee-Commemorative-Medal for the Armed Forces, the Jubilee Medal for State Civil Servants, and the Jubilee-Court-Medal were handed out to several million government officials, military personnel, and court officials in thousands of local ceremonies on or around 2 December.[86] The ceremonies provided individuals with publicly affirmed social prestige. Each medal was a badge of honor, graced by the visage of the emperor, the living symbol of the state. Medals were distributed in public ceremonies, which were described in local and regional newspapers.

Though the sheer volume of medals may have diminished their value, many individuals and institutions left off the lists to receive these medals were eager to prove that their own patriotic credentials were worthy of similar reward. A self-described "true patriot, expert, and friend of the Catholic clergy," for example, wrote anonymously to the director of the cabinet chancellery asking that Franz Joseph issue a jubilee medal for the Catholic clergy. The critic reasoned that Catholic priests, who offered special daily prayers for the emperor and who "cultivate a sense of loyalty for the imperial house and imperial patriotism," deserved acknowledgment of their importance to the state to the same degree as did state bureaucrats and members of the armed forces.[87]

The government was not interested in deepening the patriotic feelings of only the adult population. Through the Ministry of Religion and Education, the Cisleithanian government ensured that school children were indoctrinated in dynastic and state loyalty. In 1897 and 1898, the *Verordnungsblatt für den Dienstbereich des Ministeriums für Cultus und Unterricht* periodically listed patriotic pamphlets, plays, and books deemed suitable for use in the classroom. The ministry also issued instructions to each provincial school board concerning 2 December school commemorations. The ministry directed that schools cancel classes and arrange mandatory special religious ceremonies "as far as possible for each confession." After the completion of the religious services, all students and teachers were to gather in the school or another "suitably large space" for a jubilee celebration. At these assemblies, the school director or a member of the faculty was to deliver a speech emphasizing the importance of the day and of the government of Franz Joseph in a "dignified manner corresponding to the comprehension and emotional level of the young people." The commemoration was to end with the collective singing of the first verse of the imperial hymn. Many schools also planned pageants, plays, and musical programs.[88]

The government of Cisleithania issued its final 1898 official interpretation of Habsburg history and call for Habsburg patriotism in the 2 December *Kaiser Jubilee Festblatt* of the *Wiener Zeitung* (figure 19). The aging, steadfast emperor-martyr, father of all the peoples, and symbol of a compassionate modernity had, by 1898, replaced the earlier image of Franz Joseph as neoabsolutist font of all power, magnanimous and distant benefactor, and emperor-renewer. According

*Figure 19: Kaiser Jubilee Fest-Blatt,
Wiener Zeitung, 2 December 1898.
Austrian National Library.*

to this commemorative publication, Franz Joseph began his reign as a youthful prince, with "unclouded vision" and "eager energy." The new emperor forged peace in a time of chaos and confusion. Over time, through his great achievements, such as the new constitutional structure of the monarchy and the modernization of Vienna, Franz Joseph earned the devotion of all of the many nationalities. His policies assured peace and produced a better life for all the peoples of the monarchy despite his own tragic personal life. "Above all the blows of fate, however, the monarch raised his deep piety, the powerful push to marshal all of his strengths for the fulfillment of his difficult tasks." The sublime ideal human nature of the emperor remained the fulcrum of the state: "So in the course of the past decades, the beloved monarch has become a shining model of the strongest dedication to duty, selflessness, self-sacrificing efforts for the common good." Though the murder of the empress "transformed the clear laughter of jubilee happiness into the dreary tears of deep sympathy," now, on the day of the jubilee itself,

> The enmity of political parties is stilled and the strife of national and social division is overcome before the unifying love for the celebrated monarch. May this be a sign bringing blessings for the future of our dear fatherland! . . . May he experience that all the peoples of the monarchy work together with Him on the completion of the splendid edifice of our beloved fatherland, mindful of His lofty motto: "Viribus unitis!"[89]

The Imperial Family and Dynastic Patriotism

After the death of the empress, the imperial family itself also publicized the image of the benevolent and wise emperor pained by personal tragedy and dedicated to the public good. The statute of the House of Habsburg subjected all members of the imperial family to the absolute power of the head of the House of Habsburg. Constitutional rule did not diminish the dictatorial authority of the monarch over his family. No member of the family was free to travel, marry, or act in the public sphere without the express approval of Franz Joseph. Archdukes and archduchesses who married commoners or even nobles whose rank was insufficiently exalted faced expulsion from the family, loss of title, and exile. Those members of the family who did not possess large inheritances were dependent financially on the largess of Franz Joseph, who doled out allowances from funds he controlled. Franz Joseph also insisted that members of the imperial family comport themselves at all times according to the strictest interpretation of court etiquette and obey his commands without delay or complaint.[90] Only with Franz Joseph's approval did members of the imperial family lend their names as "protectors" of patriotic actions, festivities, institutions, art exhibitions, and publications.[91]

Two commemorative books produced in the final months of 1898 under the "protection" of individual members of the imperial family can be seen, therefore, as official jubilee publications. Both the lavish *Viribus Unitis: The Book about the Kaiser,* edited by Max Herzig under the protection of Franz Joseph's daughter Marie Valerie, and the equally impressive *Franz Joseph and His Times: A Cultural-Historical Look at the Francisco-Josephine Epoch,* edited by J. Schnitzer under Franz Ferdinand's protection, brought together a number of prominent artists, writers, and important government figures who contributed articles that, collectively, presented a coherent vision of Austrian patriotism and dynastic loyalty. Neither was aimed at a wide audience. Each was several hundred pages in length, prohibitively expensive, and filled with portraits and drawings commissioned specifically for the publication or taken with permission from artworks owned by the imperial house.[92] At least one observer of the "flood of publications" celebrating the jubilee declared that these two commemorative books "surpass everything that has until now been achieved in this field and under such circumstances in Austria."[93]

Though the two books are very different, they delivered a similar message. The chief aim of the books was not to overwhelm the reader with the majesty of the emperor, but to construct a portrait of Franz Joseph's personality and character (or, rather, an idealized portrait of him as the most pure of human beings), and to associate advances in art, culture, and industrial development with the hardworking symbol of state unity.

Max Herzig hoped *Viribus Unitis* would deepen the population's "love and devotion to the emperor." Many other patriotic publications produced during 1898, some of which are treated in Chapter 5, described the development of the state and various institutions over the previous fifty years. Herzig wanted to produce a book centering on the emperor himself, to show the world

> how the first in the empire day after day worries over his peoples and is the first at work, how the Most High Warlord strives unceasingly to preserve the security and prestige of the monarchy, and where possible to enhance it, how the emperor travels, hunts and otherwise uses the time dedicated to relaxation.[94]

This book purported to depict realistically the personality of the emperor. In fact, *Viribus Unitis* reads like an updated version of a medieval chronicle of saints' lives, reiterating the two central characteristics that publications during the jubilee attributed to Franz Joseph. The book called on the reader to see in Franz Joseph both a sublime ruler and the embodiment of the average person full of goodness, virtue, and love for family. Almost miraculous anecdotes of Franz Joseph's generosity, bravery, dedication to duty, and performance of ceremonies are juxtaposed with his prowess at the hunt, and his ability to seem like one of the people. The book includes artistically rendered texts of poems and songs dedicated to the emperor as well as illustrations of Franz Joseph performing the Catholic ceremonies associated with the House of Habsburg. Franz Joseph is both "heir to a hundred Caesars" and "due to his personality, the most honored ruler in the world."[95] The book was reissued in 1908 with additional paintings, and became the subject of the only 1908 jubilee exhibition enjoying the protection of Franz Joseph himself.[96]

The two-volume *Franz Joseph and His Times* presented a related vision of the role and importance of Franz Joseph, melding together the many potential sources of dynastic and state patriotism. The book includes illustrations of Franz Joseph with his grandchildren, depicts him as a protector of children, and presents a benevolent elderly emperor working hard at his desk before a painting of the ever-youthful Elisabeth (figures 20 and 21). The authors of the many chapters did not, however, concentrate on the personality of the emperor. Leading government officials, military officers, and prominent historians treated various aspects of economy, state, and society under Franz Joseph's watch. The articles are filled with statistics demonstrating the advance of society over the course of the previous fifty years. The chapters include portraits, drawings, and paintings of the subject at hand—whether the development of the city of Vienna into a worthy capital city or the modernization of the armed forces.

Franz Joseph and His Times presented the cultural, political, and economic advances of the past half-century within a unified narrative: the Francisco-Josephine Era. The articles in these volumes awarded Franz Joseph colossal charisma by associating him with events, trends, and developments for which he bore little

Figure 20: The Kaiser and His Grandchildren, Eugen Schroth. From Franz Joseph und seine Zeit, 1898. Photographic reproduction made by author at the Library of Congress.

Figure 21: The Emperor at His Desk, Theodor Zasche. From Franz Joseph und seine Zeit, 1898. Photographic reproduction made by author at the Library of Congress.

direct responsibility. Franz Joseph, these volumes proclaimed, stood as a beacon of stability in a changing world; he alone guaranteed that the benefits of progress would accrue to each of his subjects. This publication applied the traditional themes of the legend of Rudolf to Franz Joseph and to the half-century of his rule. Franz Joseph's personal qualities, in these volumes defined as devotion to duty, justice, and charity, justified the continued centrality of the Habsburg dynasty in the life of the state. Franz Joseph was "Most High Warlord [*Kriegsherr*]" and "Prince of Peace [*Friedensfürst*]" (figure 22). Bowed by the loss of his wife, "He is a Christian in the noblest meaning of the word."[97]

Figure 22: The Prince of Peace, *H. Rauchinger. From* Franz Joseph und seine Zeit, *1898. Photographic reproduction made by author at the Library of Congress.*

Schnitzer's work was directed at the future: the past and present had been managed for the benefit of all by the almost omniscient emperor, and the future would, therefore, be best entrusted to the wisdom of the Habsburg family: "unfortunately, political and national rivalry breaks out from time to time with great passion; [the peoples] find themselves again only in love and adoration for the monarch; based on rich experience, [everyone knows] that his heart beats for all his subjects with equal warmth."[98]

The art incorporated into *Viribus Unitis* and *Franz Joseph and His Times* reflected the idealization of the past, positive evaluation of the present, and orientation toward the future common to these two projects. These books demonstrated anew that the most "modern" artists of the age were prepared to apply their talents to glorify the dynasty. Koloman Moser, a leading Viennese Secession artist, contributed the title page and several colorful illustrations to *Viribus Unitis* (figures 23, 24, and 25). Moser also added whimsical allegorical decorative elements and stylized renditions of the shields of Hungary and each of the lands and kingdoms represented in the Reichsrat. Another of Vienna's *Jugendstil* masters, Josef Hoffmann, later one of the founders of the Wiener Werkstätte, designed the elaborate cover of

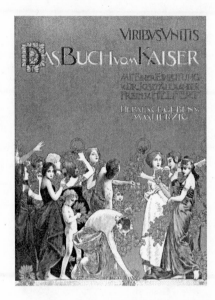

Figure 23: Title Page, Koloman Moser. From Viribus Unitis, 1898. Austrian National Library.

Figure 24: Hymn, Koloman Moser. From Viribus Unitis, 1898. Photographic reproduction made by author at the Library of Congress.

Figure 25: Illustration by Koloman Moser. From Viribus Unitis, 1898. Photographic reproduction made by author at the Library of Congress.

Figure 26: Cover of Luxury Edition, Josef Hoffmann. From Viribus Unitis, 1898. Photographic reproduction made by author at the Library of Congress.

Figure 27: Title Page, Heinrich Lefler. From Franz Joseph und seine Zeit. Austrian National Library.

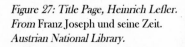

Figure 28: Alphonse Mucha illustration in Franz Joseph und seine Zeit, 1898. Photographic reproduction made by author at the Library of Congress.

the "luxury" edition (figure 26). Some of the monarchy's most innovative artists also contributed to *Franz Joseph and His Times.* Artist Heinrich Lefler produced the cover page (figure 27). *Jugendstil* decorative elements and illustrations by the Czech art nouveau master Alphonse Mucha and others frame poems as well as photographs of cities, buildings, and important persons (figure 28).

Mucha, Moser, and Hoffmann were certainly not the only contemporary artists who worked on imperial projects like these commemorative publications. Otto Wagner, the leading secessionist architect, must be counted among the artists most eager to seek out patriotic commissions. In his pre-Secession phase, Wagner designed the historicist podium and tent from which the imperial couple viewed the 1879 procession honoring the imperial couple's silver wedding anniversary. He created the decorations for Vienna's 1880 celebration of Franz Joseph's birthday, including the massive representations of *Austria* and *Vindobona* set up in the Praterstern. Wagner wrote essays on the progress of modern architecture under Franz Joseph for many jubilee publications. He also designed the address offered to Franz Joseph in honor of the 1898 jubilee by the Academy of Fine Arts in Vienna and sat on the jury for the competition to design the jubilee exhibition pavilion for the city of Vienna. Fittingly, a magnificent secessionist portrait bust of Franz Joseph decorates the entryway to Wagner's most famous building in Vienna, the Postsparkasse (figure 29).[99] In their decorative illustrations and settings glorifying Franz Joseph, Vienna's "modern" artists confirmed the continued relevance of the dynasty in the modern world.

During the jubilee year of 1898, the court, the Catholic Church, the army, the Cisleithanian government, and the Habsburg family took action to promote the emperor as a symbol of state unity. Court imagery continued to place the emperor within the context of the court ceremonial system. Brigitte Hamann argues that "The strict adherence to the ceremonial obscured the individuality of the ruler with all of his possible deficiencies and weaknesses and demanded that he completely

Figure 29: Franz Joseph Portrait Bust in Entrance Stairs to Otto Wagner's Postsparkasse, Vienna. Photograph by author.

recede behind his high office."[100] This obscuring of the human characteristics of the emperor reached its apex with the planned jubilee theater production. Actors prepared to become previous Habsburg rulers and allegorical figures like Future and Austria, but no one would portray Franz Joseph. He existed above and beyond even this idealized presentation of Habsburg history. At the same time, however, from the opening days of the jubilee year and especially after the death of Elisabeth, Franz Joseph was cited as the living embodiment of humble Christian piety and goodness, of duty and perseverance, who stood as a model for all his subjects.

These two visions of Franz Joseph—the sublime ruler lacking individual characteristics and existing above the realities of everyday life and the ideal human being, the embodiment of Christian morality—communicated "simultaneously the importance of the dynasty and the concept of unity among its polyglot subjects."[101] The emperor, wounded by the inability of his peoples to rise above ethnic divisions, was evoked time and time again during the jubilee year as a symbol of the state. The Habsburg Monarchy, like its sacred and much tried ruler, existed above partisanship, concerned itself with the legitimate interests of all its citizens, and championed progress even as it provided stability in changing times; yet Franz Joseph's state could not complete its mission unless all its people came to reject the politics of exclusion.

CHAPTER 5

Consuming the Emperor

Charity, Jubilee Kitsch, Popular Celebration, and Provincial Festivities

> *The widespread cult of the Habsburg dynasty reached vil-*
> *lage homes, where portraits of the emperor and empress,*
> *bought for groschen at the bazaar, hung on the walls, in*
> *bookstores, and general stores. It was the fashion to have*
> *porcelain plates, mugs, pipes with busts of the imperial fam-*
> *ily, post cards of the imperial palace in Vienna, and prints*
> *of the emperor and his family.*[1]
> —Piotr Babczyszyn, activist for Polish Socialist Party (PPS)

Public participation in imperial celebrations in the pre-constitutional period had been limited, for the most part, to reactions to the physical presence of the emperor (inspection tours), to extraordinary imperial celebrations (such as the 1854 wedding), and to local festivities marking these and other state/dynastic holidays organized by central, regional, and local governments as well as religious institutions. Beginning in the 1860s, with the establishment of constitutional government and the accompanying rapid growth of civil society, local elected governments, voluntary associations, and notables sponsored and organized literally thousands of so-called "patriotic actions" (*Loyalitätskundgebungen*) to commemorate Franz Joseph's birthday and name-day and other events in the lives of members of the imperial family. At times officials spurred these local festivities on, yet often the initiative for them arose from unofficial sources.

Even as political rhetoric sharpened and political cohesion proved frustrat-ingly elusive, manifestations of popular support for and identification with the state and its living symbol, Franz Joseph, greeted the 1898 jubilee. Evidence of popular participation in imperial celebrations cannot, however, be unambigu-ously interpreted as evidence of mass acceptance of the official jubilee message of patriotism and imperial loyalty. Imperial celebration had moved far beyond the controlled world of the court and was open to manipulation and interpretation. Some of the most prominent events of the jubilee year illustrated both the widespread acceptance of the emperor as a symbol of Austrian patriotism and the severe limitations that proscribed the successful promotion of a truly "Austrian" identity within Cisleithania. Furthermore, though the court and the Cisleithanian government sought to "channel" popular commemoration of the imperial jubilee to counter problems facing the monarchy, the successful marketing of the imperial image complicated attempts by the center to associate the imperial image with a single hegemonic narrative of progress, unity, and peace under the Habsburg scepter. The increase in the production and consumption of jubilee-related souvenirs and *kitsch,* though evidence of a common culture of imperial celebration, dictated that the kind of central control over the imperial image evident during the 1851 *Kaiserreise* to Galicia could not be repeated in 1898.

Certainly, Franz Joseph was not the only European ruler whose jubilees and birthdays became occasions for massive public celebrations and for the sale of vast quantities of monarchical souvenirs. During Victoria's great jubilee as empress and queen in 1887, for example, manufacturers looking to cash in on the growing popularity of the queen brought out a rash of mass-produced jubilee products. Her image burnished by Benjamin Disraeli and other British politicians seeking an expansion of the British Empire and stability at home, Victoria had become a powerful symbol of British identity by the late nineteenth century. According to Thomas Richards, the immaterial body of Victoria—the transcendent body of the eternal monarch, inherently conferring charisma on the anointed ruler—declined in importance as the real power and influence of the British monarch declined. At the same time, her material body—associated during her jubilee year with accomplishments with which she had little contact, from the accretion of colonies to the development of industry—gained in charismatic significance. During Victoria's 1887 jubilee year, established and newly formed institutions and associations evoked Queen Victoria as their patron. Advertisers and manufacturers took advantage of the material charisma of Victoria by creating jubilee products bearing her image or by portraying her touching, buying, and viewing commodities offered for sale. In turn, the figure of Victoria, her sacred status as queen and empress bolstered by association with tangible achievements in the material world, bequeathed a heightened importance and prestige to the prevailing values and material culture of middle-class Victorian society.[2]

Unlike Victoria, Franz Joseph continued to occupy the leading position in the political structure of the monarchy. In the Habsburg constitutional system, the emperor retained a great deal of formal and informal authority. Franz Joseph reigned and ruled: he was at once chief of the ruling house that had created the state, symbol of historic continuity with a distant mythic past, and first servant of the state, the living embodiment of the bureaucracy, army, and government he directed.[3] Despite this difference, like Victoria, his person gained in importance in the constitutional era through association with concrete achievements. As the first and most dedicated servant of the state, economic, political, and cultural achievements credited to the protection of the emperor were also, by definition, achievements credited to the state.

This chapter explores the attempts by the Cisleithanian government to influence public interpretation of the jubilee and looks at how the image of the emperor took on heightened significance through the popular experience of the jubilee. The first section considers jubilee activities centered on charity. Individual and group donations in honor of the jubilee as well as local festivals designed to gather funds for charities or to announce the creation of new charitable institutions were among the most pervasive of all popular jubilee activities and offer some clues into popular reaction to the officially propagated image of the benevolent emperor. The association of local charitable actions with the emperor and the jubilee increased the importance of otherwise minor and isolated activities by viewing them in association with monarchy-wide jubilee events. In turn, local jubilee charity drives associated the benevolent emperor with attempts to tackle economic and social problems at the local level. By equating charity with imperial loyalty, the government and the court sought to define actions undertaken by voluntary associations, individuals, and corporations to provide resources to the needy as a great collective plebiscite in favor of dynasty and state.

The second section examines the proliferation of jubilee-related consumer products. The Cisleithanian government was committed to spreading images of the emperor during the jubilee year; however, the government and the court also struggled to protect the imperial image from association with questionable products. The Cisleithanian government tried to influence the content of inexpensive commemorative publications in order to present to the widest possible readership the proper image of the emperor as "Father of all His Peoples." The final section briefly considers imperial celebration at the local level.

Giving in the Name of the Emperor

During the decade of neoabsolutism, the state couched its claims to legitimacy in updated "traditional" forms. Franz Joseph toured his provinces, participated in the Corpus Christi procession, and preserved the system of court rankings and court etiquette. Even before the establishment of constitutional rule, however, Franz Joseph's regime based the legitimacy of the state at least in part on service to the citizenry. Imperial celebrations and ceremonies presented Franz Joseph to the public as the energetic renewer of the monarchy and guarantor of stability and security. Franz Joseph always appeared as the commander-in-chief of the modernizing armed forces and became legendary as a dedicated bureaucrat, the ideal model for the state bureaucracy, which, in theory, met the legitimate interests of the populace.

State finances could not, however, meet the needs and expectations of the population. Franz Joseph's own charitable contributions, publicized in the official media, merged his personal generosity with the commitment of the state to address the economic difficulties facing his subjects. Franz Joseph's dedication to the centuries-old Habsburg tradition of charity and piety transformed him into a living symbol of the good intentions of the financially limited, but inherently benevolent, state.[4]

On every imperial celebration and in response to economic downturns and natural catastrophes, Franz Joseph made large and very public donations to the needy and to institutions supporting the public welfare. In commemoration of his wedding to Elisabeth of Bavaria in 1854, for example, Franz Joseph donated 200,000 gulden from his private accounts to aid the poor in each of his provinces.[5] The city of Vienna followed his lead, collecting funds to distribute five hundred gulden to each of forty poor couples.[6] Popular commemorative books emphasized the emperor's acts of charity and those of the city of Vienna as proof of the compassionate nature of the young emperor and of his concern for his subjects' welfare. Through Franz Joseph, the revitalized Habsburg state displayed its commitment to improving the lives of all citizens.

From his first years as emperor, Franz Joseph directed the government to encourage the public to display loyalty to emperor and fatherland by joining in charitable actions rather than squandering precious funds on pompous parades and public celebrations.[7] As the decades passed, the emperor favored individuals, institutions, and local governments that marked imperial celebrations with actions designed to improve public welfare with Habsburg orders, titles, and letters of recognition. The number of charitable actions, insurance funds, building funds, parks, schools, public buildings, and churches founded, named, and/or constructed in honor of Franz Joseph increased with each passing imperial birthday, but truly became a ubiquitous feature of the Cisleithanian landscape after the institution of constitutional rule. The 1873 twenty-fifth jubilee and the 1879 twenty-fifth wedding anniversary provided occasions for a multitude of such efforts. Hoping to encourage such activity, in advance of his fortieth jubilee in 1888 and his fiftieth in 1898 Franz Joseph ordered his government to issue forceful statements discouraging celebrations and calling on the population to direct scarce resources to address the needs of the population.[8]

Franz Joseph's 1898 call for jubilee charity drew a great response from the public.[9] The Interior Ministry recorded that 1,307 charitable foundations named after the emperor were created and/or were the recipients of 12,501,522 gulden in honor of the 1898 jubilee. The 314 recorded contributions and fund drives for building projects and charities affiliated with religious institutions represented slightly more than 1,505,480 gulden. Some 3,603,056 gulden in funds, buildings, and land were donated for educational institutions and for educational purposes. More than 600 humanitarian institutions received 10,945,008 gulden in funds and property. Another 1,723 actions were undertaken for "humanitarian and [for the] public interest" and counted 11,066,531 gulden in contributions. According to the official figures, Habsburg citizens, communities, and voluntary associations contributed a total of 39,621,600 gulden and 9.5 crowns to commemorate the 1898 jubilee.[10]

Government newspapers reported in detail on large and small-scale acts of jubilee charity, citing donations as evidence of popular identification with state and dynasty. The Ministry of Religion and Education even awarded institutional support to the efforts of C. Henop to publish two volumes overviewing this outpouring of patriotic charity. According to government-sponsored publications like Henop's, isolated and otherwise relatively insignificant charitable actions united participants with a much broader community of Habsburg patriots.[11]

Charitable actions tied to the jubilee created opportunities for local notables, business leaders, and voluntary associations to raise their own profile by association with actions favored by the popular emperor. Prominent among the many jubilee charitable actions undertaken at the local level were funds, with titles like "Kaiser Franz Joseph Jubilee Insurance Fund," set up by middle-class professional and industrial associations to assist their less fortunate members. Prague Hair Stylists-Shavers-and-Wig-Makers, Bohemian Czech doctors, teachers in Budweis, and Austria's Association of Animal Doctors were among the many institutions that created jubilee funds to support widows and orphans left behind by deceased colleagues.[12] Chambers of commerce, like those in Linz, the capital of Upper Austria, and Brody in Galicia, created modest insurance funds for poor business people.[13] Associations of state employees also requested use of the emperor's name for newly created insurance funds for their members.[14] Military veteran associations in every crownland established jubilee insurance funds. Typically ranging from 1,000–2,000 gulden, the interest from these modest sums was to be paid out annually to poor veterans or to widows and orphans of fallen warriors.[15]

Wealthy capitalists and industrialists were also eager to fund jubilee charities. Certainly many enjoyed the publicity derived from such contributions and hoped to receive appointment to one of the Habsburg house orders. Among the largest of these donations, members of the Rothschild family donated 5,000 gulden to poor schoolchildren of Vienna[16] and 150,000 gulden for the construction and upkeep of an orphanage in Moravian-Ostrau.[17] Baroness Clara Hirsch, who headed a foundation created by her husband, offered 1.5 million gulden in no-interest loans for poor handworkers and tradespeople throughout the monarchy.[18] Galician industrialist Moses Gartenberg set up a new hospital named after the emperor and turned it over to the control of the Jewish community in Drohobycz.[19]

Arthur Krupp, owner of the Berndorf Metal Works, suggested that every citizen of the monarchy donate one gulden, and that these millions be used to build "Children's Refuges" in each crownland for poor workers' children. In this way, the jubilee could be used to ameliorate sharpening class tensions and, at the same time, involve the entire population in a single patriotic action. Minister President Thun rejected this proposal; however, Krupp's suggestion does reflect what appears to have been a widespread attitude held by leading industrialists.[20]

Manufacturers and bankers sought to use jubilee charity to persuade workers and nationalists that their interests could be accommodated within the existing economic and political structure of the monarchy. In an effort to enhance its profile and demonstrate loyalty to the monarchy, the Austrian-Hungarian Bank announced its "Imperial and Royal Franz Joseph 1898 Jubilee Donation" of 500,000 gulden. The bank divided its contribution among twenty-two different charities, including hospital construction funds as well as the widow and children's funds created by voluntary fire departments and military veteran associations.[21] The Nobel Dynamite Corporation in Vienna donated 50,000 gulden for the support of its workers and announced another 50,000 gulden in other charitable donations.[22] The owners of porcelain factories in Bohemia dedicated 140,000 gulden to a jubilee pension and insurance fund for their workers and to a fund for widows and orphans of deceased employees.[23]

Many of the jubilee funds created in 1898 were the result of fund-drives for buildings to be used for educational, humanitarian, or religious purposes by local populations—and to be named after the Jubilant. Jubilee construction, while addressing local concerns over education, poverty, and urban renewal and beautification, resulted in permanent monuments to the benevolence of the emperor.

From Bukovina to Tyrol, buildings, parks, town squares, and lookout towers were decorated with obelisks, plaques, busts, and stone monuments and unveiled in local jubilee ceremonies. The incomplete Interior Ministry records include requests to use the imperial name or image on no fewer than thirty-seven schools, twenty-one hospitals, eight water lines, and eight churches.[24] These figures do not include the many synagogues, churches, schools, and monuments named/renamed/unveiled during the jubilee year in Galicia, such as the 1898 jubilee plaque put up in the Old Synagogue of Lemberg commemorating the emperor's 1880 visit.[25] Nor do the existing Interior Ministry records note the unveiling in Moravian-Weisskirchen of what the *Neue Freie Presse* termed "the first free-standing image of the emperor in a public place." The white marble monument, designed by a Viennese sculptor, depicted the emperor in the robes of the Order of the Golden Fleece and holding a scroll inscribed with his 1848 motto: Viribus Unitis (With United Strength), a reflection of the official jubilee message of multinational harmony.[26]

Those seeking to put up such permanent markers to the honor of the emperor could choose from a wide assortment of premade Kaiser decorations. Newspapers and magazines carried advertisements urging individuals, associations, and lo-cal governments to decorate buildings and parks with Kaiser busts, statues, and plaques designed by well-known artists and mass produced by manufacturers in Lower Austria and Bohemia. Though the number of full statues of Franz Joseph put up in 1898 hardly rivaled the one-a-week pace of Victoria statues unveiled during her 1887 jubilee, Kaiser busts and plaques certainly kept pace.

Charitable donations, buildings, and monuments dedicated to Franz Joseph for his jubilee, mostly organized by voluntary associations or professional organi-zations or built with funds donated by wealthy individuals and large institutions, were not the only evidence of popular participation in jubilee charitable actions. Literally thousands of small-scale jubilee festivals were held all over Cisleitha-nia, attended by millions of people. Many of these local activities were in fact fund-raising events for the sponsoring institutions or for designated charitable organizations. Such events were spread throughout the jubilee year, though the majority of them were concentrated around the emperor's birthday, 18 August, and the official 2 December anniversary in order to take advantage of the "jubilee spirit."

Vienna was one of the centers of such activity. The Office of the Governor of Lower Austria counted over five hundred patriotic charities, acts of loyalty, and jubilee-related celebrations, most of which took place in the imperial capital.[27] The groups sponsoring such events represented all sectors of Vienna's middle-class and lower-middle-class networks of clubs, professional and voluntary associa-tions, guilds, and local governmental institutions. Voluntary associations, many affiliated with Vienna mayor Karl Lueger's Christian Social movement as well as more established organizations, rented out restaurants, halls, and various eating and drinking establishments for their events.[28] Some associations, like the Zither Club of Austria, canceled plans for evenings of music and festivities after the assassination of the empress.[29] Others had scheduled their celebrations before the 10 September murder or for later in the year. Many such events held in the weeks surrounding 18 August took place in Vienna's beer and wine gardens and other outdoor venues. A number of large-scale sports-related Kaiser Festivals took place as well. Among others, the First Vienna Football Club sponsored a Kaiser-Jubilee-Football Tournament, and bicyclists organized special jubilee races.[30]

Jubilee celebrations sponsored by voluntary associations typically included concerts, honorific speeches, humorous skits, pageants, Kaiser-lotteries, and the collective singing of the imperial hymn. Entrance fees and money from the lotter-ies and charity bazaars were added to existing insurance funds, given to favorite charities, or put in the general funds of the organization.[31] Though the assassina-tion of the empress forced the cancellation of many local festivities scheduled for the last months of 1898, few voluntary associations, from the Jewish-Socialist Handworker's Association in Lemberg to Vienna's Nicotine Society, could resist the expectation that they sponsor at least one patriotic gathering or festivity like those described above during the great imperial celebrations of the following years—the emperor's seventieth birthday in 1900, his eightieth in 1910, and, above all, his sixtieth jubilee year in 1908 (figure 30).[32]

Figure 30: Flyer for the Savings Association and Smoking Club "Nicotine" 1908 Jubilee Festival. Provincial Archives of Lower Austria (NöLA).

Buying and Selling the Emperor

Like their British counterparts during Victoria's 1887 jubilee in England, Habsburg manufacturers viewed the inclusion of the imperial image, the Habsburg coat of arms, or the state insignia as a commercially advantageous addition to their product lines. However, indiscriminate use of the imperial image was not possible in the Habsburg Monarchy. A number of laws and decrees designed to defend the dignity of the imperial family applied to the *Gelegenheitsindustrie,* perhaps best translated here as the imperial *kitsch* industry.

Article 14 of the decreed constitution of March 1849 guaranteed the "Holiness, independence from oversight [*Unverantwortlichkeit*] and inviolability of the emperor." Building on this article from a constitution never fully put into force, article 63 of the 1852 Penal Code stated that

> Whoever violates the reverence for the emperor, whether done by personal insult [*Beleidigung*], by abuse, slander, or mockery brought before the public or before many people, by publications, communication and distribution of

pictorial representations or writings, is guilty of the crime of lèse majesté and is to be sentenced to one to five years at hard labor.[33]

Attacks on the dignity of the emperor—irreverent speech, writings, symbolic portrayals, the failure to show respect to the emperor or a member of the imperial family, or physical attacks—were punishable by stiff prison sentences. In the late nineteenth century, judges sympathetic to ethnic politics occasionally lightened sentences of impulsive and youthful nationalists who distributed anti-Habsburg literature or defaced pictures of the emperor; however, this article of the penal code remained in force until 1918.[34]

Manufacturers sought to satisfy (and stimulate) the market for Kaiser products long before the 1898 and 1908 jubilees, as evidenced by the proliferation of souvenir portrait busts of the imperial couple made for the imperial wedding in 1854 and for the 1879 twenty-fifth wedding anniversary (figures 31, 32, and 33). In the 1880s, the Cisleithanian government faced a dramatic increase in requests for permission to use the emperor's name or image or the Habsburg family or state insignias for local festivities, voluntary associations, buildings, products, and insurance funds and acted to streamline the evaluation process for such requests. In 1886, in anticipation of the 1888 jubilee, the emperor issued instructions to enforce an 1858 decree, which applied article 63 to the commercial use of the imperial image:

1. Business trademarks, which consist exclusively of the image of their majesties or of members of the imperial family, cannot be used for the labeling of commodities.

2. Such trademarks, which make use of the images of their majesties or of members of the imperial family not exclusively, but rather in conjunction with other distinguishing marks . . . require imperial approval prior to their use.[35]

Acting in direct response to inquiries from provincial authorities in Prague and Vienna, the Ministry of the Interior issued new instructions in December 1897 and January 1898 concerning requests to use of the images of Franz Joseph and the Habsburg state insignia on products to be sold during the 1898 jubilee year. These instructions were reissued in anticipation of the 1908 jubilee. Some of these instructions and many related documents are badly damaged or missing from the General Administrative Archives in Vienna, apparently casualties of the 1927 fire in the Palace of Justice. However, by considering examples from both the 1898 and 1908 jubilees, it is possible to reconstruct how the Cisleithanian government attempted to protect the reputation of the monarch even as it encouraged the spread of the "jubilee spirit."[36]

Some of the criteria used in evaluating requests for the use of the imperial name and image can be inferred from wine-growing inspector Alois Stelzl's

Figure 31: 1854 Ceramic Portrait Busts of Franz Joseph and Elisabeth. Austrian National Library.

1897 application to name his latest invention the "Kaiser-Jubilee-Plow." Stelzl contacted the *Statthalter* of Styria, who in turn sought clarification from the Ministry of the Interior in Vienna. In its response, the ministry informed the Styrian *Statthalter* that products could carry the imperial name only if made from quality materials and "suitably constructed." Should the plow meet these requirements, the *Statthalter* was to send official notice of approval to Stelzl. The ministry also warned, however, that the imperial image could not be used in a "purely commercial advertisement"—there would be no cartoon images of Franz Joseph selling plows as there were of Victoria selling carpets and other products during her 1887 jubilee.[37]

The patriotic value of some mass-produced items apparently trumped concerns about the need to guard the dignity of the imperial image. For example, the Interior Ministry agreed to a 1908 request to produce children's aprons in the colors of the monarchy (black and yellow) and decorated with a portrait of Franz Joseph in medallion form. The ministry concurred with manufacturer Kamil Faltin of Rumburg that patriotic "aprons decorated in this fashion could exert an influence on the intensification and promotion of the patriotic feelings of the affected children," and therefore should not be considered "inappropriate" to carry the imperial image.[38]

The Interior Ministry did deem some commodities, irrespective of quality, unworthy of association with the imperial family. Concern with the prestige of the imperial house led the Lower Austrian governor to reject the Austria-American Rubber-Factory Corporation's request to "equip and put on the market rubber

Figure 32: 1879 Bronze Portrait Bust of Franz Joseph. Photograph by author.

Figure 33: 1879 Bronze Portrait Bust of Elisabeth. Photograph by author.

balls with the picture of His Majesty the Emperor." In fact, the governor's office made it clear that "use of the image of His Majesty the Emperor on rubber balls is not permissible, because these objects do not appear appropriate to bear the imperial image." The governor ordered the provincial administration to be on the lookout for this kind of product.[39]

Using similar logic, the Interior Ministry insisted that the imperial insignia and image could not be associated with disposable materials. The Interior Ministry denied a 1908 request from a Bohemian fish packing company to use the image of the emperor on its products. Citing the 1898 instructions, the ministry ruled that the use of the imperial image on "items of daily use" such as "unsuitable, throw-away packaging, paper products of lower quality, envelopes, labels, and the like is not to be approved."[40] For similar reasons, the ministry did not permit Julius Kohler to put the imperial coat of arms and the double-headed eagle on cigarette tips and cartons in 1908.[41] The ministry tried to ensure that association with throwaway commodities and packing materials would not diminish the symbol of state unity.

Despite rejecting many uses of the imperial image, the Ministry of the Interior did deem "appropriate" and "patriotic" an impressive variety of mass-produced jubilee items that were sold in every province of the monarchy. Popular participation in jubilee events scheduled for the emperor's birthday and for the 2 December anniversary, as well as the many pageants, parades, and festivals that took place throughout the year, created markets for companies specializing in patriotic products. Manufacturers in Vienna, Prague, and elsewhere seeking to maximize their jubilee sales took out advertisements in the monarchy's major newspapers and contacted city councils and other potential customers.

Some producers created items designed specifically for large-scale celebrations and government offices as well as middle-class and wealthy patriots. Many firms sold special lighting equipment for the 2 December illumination; others offered window decorations with the imperial coat of arms and the imperial eagle, at, it was often noted, reasonable prices.[42] Cisleithanian minister president Thun pressed provincial governors to purchase items from Prague's J. B. Pichl.[43] Pichl sold jubilee medallions and bronze, iron, and gypsum plaques to preserve the memory of this great occasion for "present and future." The plaques, Pichl's brochures asserted, were equally well suited for "estate and palace, for office and school, for civil as for military, for interior rooms, great halls, and for the outside of private and public buildings." Pichl's products were "Majestic lasting adorations of the jubilee year!" Convinced, Vienna's jubilee commission (discussed in the next chapter) ordered one large medallion, two smaller ones, and a papier-mâché double eagle from this Bohemian manufacturer.[44] In 1898, the *Neue Freie Presse* informed its readers that Ernst Wahliss's porcelain warehouse offered four different sizes of a mass-produced bust of the emperor designed by the "artist's hand." Wahliss recommended his products, "the most splendid version in ivory" for all "imperial-royal state offices, imperial-and-royal Officers' Clubs, city governments, voluntary associations, and the like." Wahliss also tantalized his novelty-seeking customers with "completely new" jubilee "jewelry and ashtrays, especially lovely and original."[45]

Photographers, lithographers, and publishers produced a plethora of inexpensive portraits of the emperor. These mass-produced portraits of Franz Joseph often decorated even modest peasant homes.[46] In 1898 and 1908, firms like J. Ulmann and Son offered

> an artistic portrait of His Majesty that, up to now, for the most part, could only
> be seen in the wealthiest circles. In honor of the patriotic festivities on 18 Au-
> gust and 2 December we are fulfilling the heart-felt wishes of all patriots.

Ulmann produced this portrait of Franz Joseph in his coronation robes as "a fabulous illumination-transparency, made of lasting material in water-retardant colors," certainly the "most beautiful souvenir of the jubilee year for big and small."[47] The Cisleithanian government supported efforts by photographers to distribute mass-produced portraits of the emperor to public institutions throughout the monarchy. The imperial-and-royal court and chamber photographer Carl Pietzner, for example, received permission to distribute several thousand copies of a photograph portrait he made of Franz Joseph to public schools.[48] A similar action was undertaken by the photography, art, and publishing house of R. Lechner, which received government backing for its efforts to sell to local and regional governments reproductions of photographs of Franz Joseph, in wood, imitation mahogany, and gold-gilded frames.[49]

Merchants sold a dizzying array of jubilee products that seem to have slipped past the efforts of the Cisleithanian government to protect the grandeur of the imperial image. In 1898 and 1908, newspapers in Vienna and Galicia advertised Kaiser Franz Joseph Jubilee Carpets,[50] Kaiser-Jubilee-Pocket Knives,[51] and Kaiser Jubilee Bitter, the latter to assist with eating and digestion difficulties.[52] Stores sold Kaiser stamps, portraits, cups, mugs, ashtrays, scissors (with portrait-medallions of the emperor and empress), and even bread-crumb grinders (figures 34–37 display a variety of Kaiser items sold during the jubilees).

Despite the popularity of jubilee souvenirs, at least a few businesses overestimated the market. In the weeks after the 2 December jubilee and before Christmas, at least one enterprising business advertised "very tasteful" bronze, nickel, gold, and silver busts of the imperial couple, as "lovely and practical Christmas and New Year's gifts."[53]

The extensive catalogue of available jubilee products, often sold and distributed in schools, provided some justification for the distaste expressed by the Pan-German *Ostdeutsche Rundschau*:

Figure 34: Advertisement for Kaiser-Jubilee-Bitter, Correspondenz-Blatt, Nr. 9, 1898. Austrian National Library.

"Hardly a week goes by in which my children do not come home from school with some kind of jubilee ware and demand money from me to purchase it." So a family father from the countryside writes us, whose income is just adequate to meet the basic needs of life. . . . Aside from the fact that the method of selling such products is by means of force since the teacher recommends them, so this method is also suited to give rise to jealousy in the poor children whose parents have no money left for such things and to make the social inequalities between rich and poor downright tangible. To endeavor to teach patriotism in this fashion is senseless.[54]

Figure 35: 1908 Jubilee Postcard, Koloman Moser. Austrian National Library.

Figure 36: 1898 Jubilee Stamps, Koloman Moser. Austrian National Library.

Figure 37: Window of a Vienna Antique Shop, 1997. Photograph by author.

Reading about the Emperor

Though the Pan-German newspapers criticized all "black and yellow" jubilee products as evidence of misplaced and false patriotism, their greatest criticism was directed at the most widely distributed of all jubilee souvenirs: commemorative jubilee pamphlets, books, brochures, and special newspaper editions published and sold in every province of Cisleithania by the hundreds of thousands.[55] Publishing houses put out several types of jubilee publications. Some, like the great commemorative books discussed in Chapter 4 and produced under the protection of members of the imperial house, were extravagant, printed on thick paper, filled with well-written articles by government ministers, generals, and well-known writers and with original drawings, paintings, and engravings created by leading secessionist and academic artists. Publishers also rushed out inexpensive pamphlets for jubilee-related festivities, with as many pages devoted to advertisements as to articles and stories related to the emperor and the jubilee. Among the most popular of all jubilee publications were patriotic books and plays directed toward children and largely concentrating on the life of the emperor. A number of more scholarly jubilee publications, sponsored by Catholic-aristocratic-patriotic societies, liberal voluntary associations, and publishing houses seeking a broad readership depicted the emperor and the meaning of the jubilee in very different ways.

The mass production and consumption of brochures and pamphlets commemorating the imperial house did not originate in 1898. Few panegyric books were published in the first years after 1848. However, by the early 1850s, the emperor's travels throughout the monarchy, his birthdays, and the failed attempt on his life in 1853 were all marked by such publications, some of the profits often directed toward charity.[56] Beginning with the imperial wedding of 1854, publishing houses competed to put out inexpensive books describing the events surrounding imperial celebrations, some funded by the government. Many such publications were obvious attempts to cash in on the growing popularity of Franz Joseph. Some, like J. F. Boehringer's *Austria's Days of Joy* and Adolph Carl Naske's *Commemorative Book of the Wedding Celebrations,* sold tens of thousands of copies.[57] Newspapers, like the *Wiener Allgemeine Theaterzeitung,* printed descriptive articles detailing every moment of the festivities, and illustrated newspapers published in the monarchy and abroad provided, with a few weeks' delay, images of all the major events (figure 38). The audience for such publications in the 1850s, however, was still relatively small. Even the most inexpensive publications were beyond the reach of the rural poor, and literacy rates in the Habsburg Monarchy were too low in the 1850s to provide a great number of consumers eager to spend their modest incomes on such souvenirs.

In the last decades of the nineteenth century, literacy rates increased, reading societies spread, and newspapers found new and larger audiences. Publishers took note of the reading public and began to produce large numbers of commemorative publications for every great imperial celebration. In 1879 and 1888 hundreds of such books and pamphlets were published in many languages and sold in stores in every province. The ability to utilize new technologies and swiftly take advantage of sudden public interest in events was demonstrated after the murder of Empress Elisabeth. Within days after her death, the imperial *kitsch* industry produced and sold a large number of items related to the empress, including inexpensive portraits found in shop windows all over the monarchy. Hawkers sold

Figure 38: Elisabeth Arrives at Nußdorf,
Wiener Illustrirte Zeitung, 6 May 1854.
Austrian National Library.

"instant" commemorative pamphlets and souvenirs to the crowds lining the streets of Vienna for Elisabeth's funeral procession.[58] Some of the jubilee publishers drew attention to their ability to swiftly churn out brochures as a marketing tool. The editor of the official commemorative album for the Jubilee Exhibition, for example, informed his readers that this brochure was "*A triumph* of the Austrian graphic industry: *A magnificent work produced in eight days.*"[59]

After 1867, the Cisleithanian government continued to apply Article 63 of the 1852 Penal Code to protect the image of the emperor, threatening those insulting the emperor with imprisonment. In the constitutional era, however, aside from direct attacks on the imperial family, the monarchy's publishing houses were free to publish treatments of the jubilee and the emperor offering a wide variety of perspectives. The Cisleithanian government did endeavor to indirectly influence the way the emperor was portrayed. Writers of popular jubilee pamphlets and books often lifted and embellished anecdotes and stories of the emperor's life from the laudatory articles in the government network of official and semi-official newspapers. These papers, widely read and often greatly respected, presented the emperor and the jubilee in terms similar to the planned jubilee theater production discussed in the previous chapter.

Through the Ministry of Religion and Education, the Cisleithanian government was able to exert considerable influence over the presentation of the emperor in books and pamphlets directed toward children. The Cisleithanian school system provided a vast and captive market for patriotic publications. Schools handed out jubilee brochures, organized patriotic pageants and plays, and encouraged pupils to purchase commemorative items. Writers who hoped to receive the ministry's recommendation for the adoption of their writings by teachers and school directors tailored their work accordingly.[60]

A number of otherwise undistinguished writers who can perhaps best be categorized as professional patriots—for the most part schoolteachers, army officers, and government bureaucrats—authored publications for children on every possible imperial occasion. Dr. Leon Smolle was one of the most prolific of these patriotic writers. Between 1880 and 1908, this schoolteacher wrote no fewer than eight commemorative Kaiser books. In 1880, Smolle published his 10-kreuzer 32-page *Kaiser Joseph II. For the People and the Youth of Austria,* which was recommended by the liberal *Konstitutionelle Vorstadt-Zeitung* for schools and institutions.[61] Smolle's first Franz Joseph publication was his 1888 *The Book about Our Emperor,* published by A. Pichler's Widow and Son in Vienna, "bookseller for pedagogic literature," and signed by its author on the emperor's birthday.

Smolle's books and pamphlets were typical of those produced for children and approved by the Ministry of Religion and Education. Smolle made clear his intended audience in his introduction to his brochure for the 1888 jubilee:

In plain words, in the following lines we have tried to sketch a living picture of our emperor, which above all is intended to work warmly and stimulatingly on the receptive hearts of the youth, in order to be welcomed in the circles of Austrian schools and family.[62]

Smolle and other patriotic authors left out potentially controversial events, perhaps fearing rejection of their work for distribution in schools. Smolle glossed over neoabsolutism and averred that the creation of constitutional Austria-Hungary resulted from the long-held intentions of the emperor—rather than from mismanagement, military defeat, and financial collapse. Deeming politics "the future task of the historian," Smolle instead concentrated on the "personal qualities and characteristics" of this "shining example." This focus on the personality of the emperor, drawn through repetition of hagiographical accounts of anecdotes from the emperor's life and reproductions of Franz Joseph as a child, youth, and aging grandfather, was common for books aimed at raising the dynastic and patriotic feelings of children for emperor and fatherland (figures 39 and 40 show portraits of Franz Joseph as a boy and as the newly minted emperor, often found in patriotic publications oriented toward children).

Figure 39: Archduke Franz Joseph Plays with Toy Soldiers: Portrait as a Small Child, *Ferdinand George Waldmüller. Museum of the City of Vienna.*

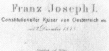

Figure 40: The Constitutional Emperor of Austria, etc. 1848. *Museum of the City of Vienna.*

Smolle and his rivals depicted Franz Joseph as a perfect human being, a model for young people, and a focus for patriotic feelings. In line with government emphasis on public charity, Smolle highlighted Franz Joseph's generosity, retelling the tale of the five-year-old Archduke Franzi lifted by his grandfather, Emperor Franz, to place money in the pocket of a soldier on guard duty. Smolle's Franz Joseph embodied the values of self-sacrifice and bravery. In Smolle's brief account of the Battle at Santa Lucia, the young steel-willed archduke fought with great courage under Radetzky's command.

Even as emperor, Smolle's Franz Joseph remained a model for all good citizens. Smolle's munificent Franz Joseph rewarded the kindness of peasants who, not recognizing him in his hunting clothes, addressed him in familiar terms and lent him assistance as a fellow man of the forest. A similar lesson is learned from the account of the old woman who begged Franz Joseph (this time mistaken for an army officer) to intercede with the emperor to release her last living son from the army to help her keep the family farm. Stories of Elisabeth and the imperial children depict Franz Joseph as a caring father figure. Smolle included chapters on the jubilee of 1873, "The Emperor as Person," and the 1879 silver wedding anniversary celebrations. The generosity of the great ruler, unveiling of monuments, and evidence of popular acclaim of and sympathy for the emperor filled the pages of Smolle's books.

Altered passages in the later versions of Smolle's works incorporated the Habsburg family tragedies of Mayerling and Geneva and the great jubilee events of 1898. These later versions portrayed the emperor, in line with the official 1898 jubilee message, as father of the peoples and accentuated the emperor's personal charitable donations and the patriotism of the public as expressed by mass participation in public festivities and activities to further the public good.[63] By 1898, even in books printed before the murder of Elisabeth, the emperor had become the grandfatherly figure he would remain in the public imagination until his death in 1916 and beyond.

Many of the commemorative books and pamphlets authored by Smolle and his competitors were written in German and translated and distributed in the provinces.[64] Smolle's works appeared in Czech, Polish, and German.[65] Johann Emmer, author of commemorative books for 1879, 1880, 1888, 1898, and 1908, published brochures for children and more elegantly produced books for adults in Italian, Czech, and German. Joseph Eichler and Eduard Jorden's 1888 work, *Our Kaiser: Commemorative Publication for the Patriotic Youth,* was reissued in 1898 in German and Polish versions (figures 41 and 42).[66] Many popular and inexpensive publications were written in Slovenian, Ruthenian, Polish, Czech, and other languages.[67] Some producers of these children's books, like the Nowy Sącz publisher of Izydor Poeche's *Sedziwy Jubilat,* offered discounts for bulk orders.[68]

Figure 41: Title Page, Unser Kaiser,
1898. Austrian National Library.

Figure 42: Title Page, Nasz Cesarz,
1898. Austrian National Library.

Jubilee plays were also widely disseminated among schoolchildren, and some received the support of the Ministry of Religion and Education. Many schools performed Christiane Gräfin Thun-Salm's *The Emperor's Dream,* though not on 2 December 1898 due to the death of Elisabeth. Alfred Freiherr von Berger's *Habsburg,* like Thun-Salm's play, included a sleeping Kaiser and a pageant of great moments from the Habsburg past.[69] In May 1898, the German People's Theater in Vienna performed Berger's work, according to the cultural commentator in the liberal organ *Neue Freie Presse,* a "fine work, in language and performance far beyond the usual commemorative plays, which captivated the participation of the public until the end."[70] The city of Vienna distributed 200,000 copies of Berger's play as a jubilee souvenir to Vienna's schoolchildren.

A number of writers and composers also issued slim volumes of poems and musical compositions that were sold and/or handed out through the schools.[71] The back pages of Smolle's books, for example, often included advertisements for publisher Pichler's other patriotic publications, like the musical pageants *Austria's Jubilee Tones* and *My Fatherland, My Austria!*, which were intended for sale to school directors for jubilee, imperial birthday, or name-day celebrations.

These publications oriented toward the youth market echoed the descriptions of Franz Joseph's character and significance found in government publications and projected in the proposed court festivities. Though the books devoted only a few pages to imperial ceremony, preferring to stress anecdotes that might attract the attention of children, the Franz Joseph of patriotic children's publications was more a collection of idealized values and qualities than a real human being.

This saintly Franz Joseph was to be loved and admired for his perfect human character, piety, dedication to duty, and commitment to the public good even in the face of personal tragedy. Imperial celebrations were described as moments of great historical significance and Franz Joseph was presented as the living symbol of the common fatherland.

Just as jubilee commodities sporting the imperial image and the state insignia did not escape criticism, Smolle and his fellow professional patriots attracted acerbic attacks. The *Freie Lehrerstimme,* the organ of Social Democratic teachers, termed the attempts to "awaken patriotism" among the youth with anecdotes from the life of the emperor as "hypocritical Byzantinism."[72] Patriotic performances could not escape the wrath of those hypersensitive to perceived ethnic slights. Lemberg's Catholic-conservative *Głos Narodu* derided Berger's play for its presumptions of German superiority and its negative depiction of Ottokar, the Bohemian king defeated by Rudolf, the first Habsburg Holy Roman emperor.[73] This criticism, like that levied against the flood of jubilee commodities bearing the emperor's name and image, did little to slow the purchase, distribution, and public performance of commemorative publications. Nor did the scattered harsh critiques of organized youthful patriotism in the form of pageants, parades, choral performances, and the like prevent the mainstream press from citing such performances as evidence of the next generation's commitment to dynasty and state.

The Cisleithanian government had much less influence over patriotic publications written for an adult audience. Some popular commemorative books and pamphlets for adults presented Franz Joseph in terms similar to those found in the books produced for children. Other works had more scholarly pretensions. Many of the latter were produced by voluntary associations and interpreted the importance of the emperor and the jubilee in accordance with the prevailing ideology of the sponsoring association. Here it suffices to look briefly at publications produced by two dissimilar associations: the patriotic-conservative Austrian People's Publications Association (ÖVV); and Concordia, the German-liberal professional writers' and journalists' association in Vienna.

In 1848, a group of state bureaucrats, the former abbot of the Schottenstift, historians, and aristocrats founded the ÖVV, originally named the Association for the Distribution of Publications for the Enlightenment of the People. The founders supported the neoabsolutist program of the first decade of Franz Joseph's rule. They wanted to counter what they perceived as the corrupting influence of the revolution and the new liberal press freed by the lifting of state censorship. The ÖVV sought to "develop religious and moral feelings, to spread knowledge of interest to the public, to maintain and promote love of the fatherland and to promote the education of the people for state institutions and laws."[74]

In the first years after Franz Joseph's accession, the association published a number of almanacs, pamphlets, and books to teach the population about the lives of important figures in Habsburg history, the Habsburg family itself, and the peoples and lands united by the Habsburg dynasty. In later decades, the ÖVV abandoned its publications intended for those close to the "illiterate classes" and focused instead on inspiring patriotism and devotion to emperor.[75] According to Dr. Hans Maria Truxa, who served in 1898 as the vice president of the association and was a knight of the Kaiser Franz Joseph Order, this patriotic organization hoped to foster "the fear of God and genuine religious sentiment, love of fatherland and of the hereditary Ruling House."[76] This conservative association enjoyed the protection of Archduke Ferdinand of Toscana, had its publications regularly accepted by Franz Joseph, and received a small stipend from the emperor.

In 1898, the membership of this association was determined to confront the political crises of the day with an appeal to dynastic patriotism. To this end, the ÖVV published several commemorative books, including *On the Second of December*, edited by the president of the association, Joseph Alexander von Helfert. Helfert, the conservative and respected historian, had served as undersecretary in the Ministry of Religion and Education from 1848 to 1861 and, in this capacity, had pushed the ministry to adopt educational materials that portrayed the Habsburg dynasty as a binding force in the state.[77] Helfert had also provided the court with the heroic moments in Habsburg history that served as the basis for the 1898 jubilee theater production eventually authored by Thun-Salm. Helfert contributed chapters to both of the great commemorative albums produced under the auspices of the imperial family, *Viribus Unitis* and *Franz Joseph and His Times*.

While works by Smolle and others avoided controversial subjects and emphasized Franz Joseph's sublime qualities, *On the Second of December* interspersed poems and illustrations with articles denouncing national conflict. The general message of the book was similar in tone to the messages portrayed in the jubilee theater production and in the Catholic pastoral letter but pursued here with greater scholarly force.

Helfert and the other contributors argued that the weak and small peoples of Central Europe had no hope to survive against the incursions of larger and more powerful nations without the protective shield provided for centuries by the Habsburg family. Without Habsburg protection, many nationalities would have disappeared long ago, argued the authors of this volume, absorbed by powerful neighbors in the course of history. To nurture and create a zone of security and harmony in which the peoples could thrive was Franz Joseph's great task. Only "conviction from out of the midst of the battling nationalities themselves" could lead to a solution of the nationalities conflicts. The nationalities needed to realize that their national cultures could only be preserved within the Habsburg Monarchy: "Austria-Hungary's entire nature relies on the harmonious peaceful coexistence of the various peoples united here."[78]

The ÖVV did not ignore the character of the emperor. Echoing the court and government jubilee messages, the book pictured Franz Joseph as strong but caring, a soldier and a man of peace, a pious and tolerant man. Franz Joseph was an example for everyone to follow because of his sublime character. "Genius can move the world, can rip it apart; the noble character holds it together and seeks reconciliation."[79] Not surprisingly, *Das Vaterland* commended this book, Helfert, and the ÖVV for dedication to morality and dynasty. According to this Catholic newspaper, "men of all classes of society, scholars, artists, princes of the church, nobles," middle-class notables, and archdukes were listed on the member roles of this organization.[80]

A second elegant ÖVV 1898 publication, the *Kaiser-Jubilee-Poetry-Book*, did not attempt to portray the character of the emperor or the history of the monarchy over the past fifty years.[81] In conscious imitation of the early-nineteenth-century German romantic academics who collected folktales in the countryside, this volume brought together "50 years of Austrian literature" written in the "high German language and in all German-Austrian dialects" to spread love of "Heimat" to the Austro-German population. For Truxa, the editor of this volume, "In no other land of the earth are Prince and People so deeply bound one to the other as in our much beloved, if at times severely tried, Austria!"[82] Professional patriots like Bohemian German schoolteacher Karl Eichler, priest and teacher Wenzel Wächtler, Julius Laurencic, and Hermine Camilla Proschko collected poems, short stories, and songs dedicated to emperor and fatherland and written over the past fifty years. The poems and songs acclaimed Franz Joseph

> The prince of peace,
> The noblest ruler,
> The most self-sacrificing monarch,
> The father of his peoples,
> The patron of all noble endeavors,
> **The protector of all patriotic poets and writers**.

These ÖVV publications offered readers an alternative to national conflict: instead of national competition, all nationalities should seek common cause and mutual understanding under the protection of the common father-emperor.

The Vienna association Concordia produced the most highly touted of all jubilee commemorative publications, *Kaiserblatt*. Major Viennese newspapers with ties to Concordia as well as the official and semi-official press repeatedly advertised *Kaiserblatt*, available in 60-kreuzer and 1-gulden editions. Concordia sold over 40,000 copies of this commemorative volume. According to one report, the first edition sold out within a few hours.[83] The profits from the sale of the book established a new fund for widows and orphans of deceased Concordia members.

Unlike the ÖVV, Concordia, the professional society of Austrian writers and journalists (Austro-German), had opposed censorship and supported the freedoms gained in the revolutionary months of 1848. Refounded after the lifting of neoabsolutist press and assembly controls in 1859, Concordia created a pension fund to meet the needs of professional writers and journalists (Concordia did not admit women, prompting Maria von Ebner-Eschenbach to found the Association of Women Writers and Artists in 1885). Franz Joseph, whose government had once banned Concordia, donated land for the association headquarters in Vienna and contributed considerable sums for its activities.

The editors and publishers of the *Neue Freie Presse, Neues Wiener Tagblatt*, and most other major Viennese newspapers and journals joined Concordia. At the turn of the century, the Viennese press could be roughly divided between the Concordia press—German, liberal, largely owned and/or staffed by Jews—and anti-Semitic newspapers like the *Reichspost, Deutsches Volksblatt*, and *Ostdeutsche Rundschau*. In the era of anti-Semitic success at the ballot box in Vienna, the Christian Social and Pan-German nationalist press denounced Concordia as "Judaized" and considered the organization a symbol of Jewish control of the Viennese media.[84]

The cover illustration of a youthful, vibrant, secessionist-style female figure of *Austria* watched over by a realistic portrait profile of the emperor sets the tone for Concordia's *Kaiserblatt* (figure 43). This publication, typical of commemorative publications brought out by voluntary and professional associations, did not center on Franz Joseph as the father of all the peoples and did not seek to convince its readership to disdain national conflict in favor of ethnic reconciliation. Instead, Concordia remade Franz Joseph in its own image. The opening pages announced the book's intention to document the Vienna of fifty years before and

Figure 43: Cover Page, Heinrich Lefler. From Kaiserblatt. *Austrian National Library.*

"what Vienna has become during the reign of Franz Joseph."[85] The book was an ode to liberal values. *Kaiserblatt*'s Franz Joseph was the patron of Austro-German liberal ideals of cultural progress and economic advance, his fifty-year reign a half-century marked by liberal achievement.

The chapters of *Kaiserblatt,* penned by academics, Concordia journalists, and artists, including the architect Otto Wagner, portrayed the monarchy as a state progressing toward a better future under the benevolent protection of Franz Joseph. "To Our Kaiser," the book's opening poem by Ferdinand von Saar, whose works could be found on the pages of many jubilee publications and jubilee special newspaper editions, depicted Franz Joseph as the champion of liberalism. The emperor stood like a rock, unshaken by the changing world: "In you alone is comfort to be found/Before you all feel themselves equal."[86] Franz Joseph and the state were the patrons and protectors of science and discovery: "All the nationalities [*Volkstämme*] are represented in these works, all have the right to rejoice in these accomplishments."[87] The transformation of Vienna from a walled town to a modern city was portrayed as the work of Franz Joseph in league with Vienna's previous liberal governments. *Kaiserblatt* evaluated the decade of neo-absolutism, the most anti-liberal period of Franz Joseph's reign, in terms of the expansion of trade and commerce resulting from Franz Joseph's modernization program. The contributors to *Kaiserblatt* portrayed Franz Joseph as a dedicated adherent to liberal economic and legal reform. *Kaiserblatt* credited him with the democratization of government and society. Other articles depicted Franz Joseph as a supporter of modern theater, music, art, and architecture.

Many less ideologically driven works were designed to attract a large market and, by doing so, also projected a jubilee message of tolerance, ethnic diversity, and common love for the joint fatherland. These jubilee publications intended for adults bolstered the official jubilee messages of unity, harmony, and progress of all peoples and lands under the benevolent emperor. Some authors and publishers developed clever marketing ideas to induce the public to buy more of their pamphlets. One such scheme was Julius Laurencic's *Our Monarchy.* This publication consisted of twenty-four separate issues. Consumers could purchase one or all of these pamphlets, which, when bound together, made an impressive jubilee souvenir. Each issue had twenty-four pages—twelve pages of photographs and twelve pages of text—and each covered a different theme.

The first issue of *Our Monarchy, The Austrian Crownlands at the Time of the Fifty-Year Jubilee of His Imperial and Royal Apostolic Majesty Franz Joseph I,* consisted of pictures of major buildings in the capitals of each crownland of Cisleithania. This issue gave many what was sure to be a first look at the major cities of the monarchy. Each subsequent issue brought together writers and artists to consider various aspects of culture, history, and architecture in all the crownlands: "a national project of peace [*Friedenswerk*] in the fullest sense of the word."[88] In order to ensure that most residents of Habsburg Austria could read this patriotic "nonpartisan" work claiming to treat equally all national and religious groups without prejudice (and to ensure the maximum possible market for this series of publications), each page was printed in Czech, German, Polish, and Italian (figure 44).

Figure 44: Cover Page, Unsere Monarchie. *J. Laurencic, editor. Austrian National Library.*

Local Jubilee Celebrations

Jubilee charities, products, and commemorative books were permanent reminders for millions of Habsburg citizens of the celebrations. A large proportion of Cisleithanians also participated in local jubilee festivities. Town and city jubilee programs concentrated around the two most important dates of the jubilee years: Franz Joseph's 18 August birthday and the 2 December anniversary of his accession to the throne. Prominent in the programs were dedications of new insurance funds and jubilee schools, parks, and other public spaces. Local governments scheduled jubilee sittings of city councils, parades, public festivals in town parks, and town and village illuminations. Many town councils, voluntary societies, and business owners presented elaborately decorated addresses of congratulations to local representatives of the provincial administrations to be forwarded to the court in Vienna (figures 45 and 46). Town jubilee programs coordinated patriotic actions sponsored by religious institutions, schools, military institutions, and

Figure 45: Cover of Address of Congratulations from the Galician Town of Nadworna to Franz Joseph, 1898. Austrian National Library.

Figure 46: Address of Congratulations from Residents of Nadworna (in Polish and Ukrainian), 1898. Austrian National Library.

military veteran associations into integrated jubilee programs communicated to the population in local journals, newspapers, and public notices.

The jubilee program of the city of Lemberg was typical of provincial city celebrations. The Lemberg city council announced a list of its jubilee-related charitable donations in October. The city council earmarked 300,000 gulden to fund the new Franz Joseph City Institution for the Incurable. The formal establishment of this new hospice became the centerpiece of the jubilee celebrations scheduled for 1 December and 2 December. Members of the city council commenced city jubilee festivities by attending the official opening ceremony for this facility on 1 December at 10 A.M. [89]

The opening ceremony for the new facility for the incurable was only one of many items crowding the schedule of jubilee events in Lemberg. On 1 December, the evening before the jubilee itself, many decorated their homes with Austrian flags. At 8 P.M. the military bands of the four infantry regiments stationed in Lemberg gave a concert of marches and patriotic songs, including the state hymn, before parading through the streets of the city. Military bands played reveille on the streets early in the morning on the day of the jubilee itself, marking the day as one dedicated to patriotic activity.

On 2 December, beginning at 8 A.M., churches and synagogues held special services. Lemberg, seat of three Catholic archbishoprics, boasted three Catholic cathedrals: Roman Catholic, Greek Catholic, and Armenian Catholic. Members of corporations, associations, government representatives, and the public at large filled synagogues and each of the three cathedrals to capacity, listening to priests and rabbis extol the generous and hard-working monarch, the model for the good citizen. The officer corps took part in jubilee services at the Jesuit Church, and soldiers received their jubilee medals. At 10 A.M. city council members dedicated a new church, funded by the city in honor of the jubilee.

As in other provincial capitals, following the religious services, clergy, government officials, university professors, school directors, members of the city council, the Jewish community, veterans' associations, and other institutions attended a celebratory audience in the palace of the *Statthalter.* The *Statthalter* handed out jubilee medals to civil servants and to those qualifying for the special medals for forty years of public or private service. Later in the day, in a hall decorated with a bust of Franz Joseph the mayor of the city spoke about Franz Joseph's "knightly" character and the good he had done for the province before handing out 5,000 honorary city medals to cheers for the Jubilant.[90] In decorated assembly halls, school directors throughout the city spoke to pupils of patriotism and the devotion of the emperor to the welfare of his peoples.

On the evening of 2 December, though Franz Joseph had requested that all official celebrations be cancelled, local communities organized illuminations all over the monarchy. "Bengali" lighting illuminated town centers and special jubilee decorations. From Vienna to Czernowitz, "from palaces to the most humble little houses,"[91] Habsburg subjects set candles in their windows, displaying "glowing signs of their heartfelt sympathy for the jubilee Kaiser."[92] Lemberg was no exception. Public buildings, banks and other private institutions, as well as most homes, were decorated and lit up with lamps and electric lights. Tens of thousands of residents came out onto the streets to look at the decorations.[93]

A similar series of events took place in cities throughout Cisleithania. In other towns, city theaters performed special jubilee theater productions. In Cracow, for example, the main theater presented an "Apotheosis of the Monarch." The stage was decorated with special curtains with the colors of the state and the province. On a pedestal in the midst of the stage, surrounded by plants and flowers, stood yet another bust of the emperor—perhaps purchased from producers in Lower Austria or Bohemia. Actors costumed as *szlachta* and as peasants gave homage to the inanimate emperor.[94]

As the discussion of jubilee events in Lemberg suggests, religious services featured prominently in local programs in every corner of Cisleithania, melding together religious faith, local and regional identity, and dynastic patriotism. In 1898, religious services were held for the emperor's birthday, and name-day and for the death of the empress. In late November, Catholic priests read the episcopal letter written by the Cisleithanian Catholic hierarchy from pulpits in every province. On 2 December, schools were let out so children could attend yet another round of special services in honor of the emperor held at their respective religious institutions. Those packing houses of worship knew that in neighboring villages and towns and in cities across Cisleithania millions of their fellow citizens were, at the same moment, joining them in a common expression of dynastic patriotism.

In Lemberg and elsewhere, no religious communities participated in local imperial celebrations with more open enthusiasm than Cisleithania's Jewish communities. The Jews of the monarchy have often been termed the "only true Austrians." Though this is certainly an overstatement (there were certainly many others who considered themselves "Austrian" and many Jews who were less than enthusiastic about the House of Habsburg), orthodox and liberal Jews were prominent among the crowds eager to view the emperor during inspection tours and were also among the thousands cramming Vienna's inner city during the Corpus Christi procession.

Individual Jews and Jewish communities responded to the emperor's many requests for acts of charity to commemorate imperial celebrations. Jews contributed to the building of the Votive Church, erected synagogues, schools, and community buildings in the emperor's name in commemoration of the imperial wedding.[95] Jewish charities handed out food to the poor (usually irrespective of confession) on the emperor's birthday. Jewish communities and individuals hoisted black-and-yellow flags and illuminated their properties on 18 August, 2 December, and other imperial occasions, held parades, sponsored charitable *Volksfeste,* and attended musical evenings dedicated to the emperor. Jewish community publications lauded the emperor's accomplishments in foreign and domestic policy as well as his personal characteristics in similar terms to editorials printed in the government and non-Jewish press.

To many Jews, the emperor was the symbol of the constitutional guarantees of equality before the law and freedom of religious observance. On 2 December 1898, hundreds of thousands of Jews in Cisleithania heard sermons similar to that delivered by C. Horowitz, assistant rabbi of the old synagogue in Cracow. Horowitz proclaimed it a "religious obligation for each Jew to thank God that we have the good fortune to be subjects of a just and wise emperor." Franz Joseph, he noted, worked to ameliorate the social and political strife threatening the monarchy and guaranteed the Jews their "natural and Godly rights." As Catholic sermons compared Franz Joseph implicitly or explicitly to a suffering Christ, Horowitz and other rabbis compared Franz Joseph to King David, who ruled with wisdom.[96] Vienna's Jewish leaders praised Franz Joseph, whose belief in God gave him strength and who, because he recognized the "image of God" in every person, protected the "human rights" of all citizens."[97]

The identification of much of the Jewish population with the emperor and the state was enhanced by repeated acts of imperial favor toward the Jewish population. According to a source close to Franz Joseph, one evening when the emperor complimented the loyalty and charity of several prominent Jews, a dinner guest, Prince Waldemar of Denmark, reportedly asked in shock,

> "Your Majesty is not a philosemite?"
>
> "Certainly I am," responded Franz Joseph in high spirits, "and with good reason! The Popes have long been the best protectors of the Jews! And should I be in this more Catholic than the Pope?"[98]

Whether or not this conversation actually occurred, it would not have been out of character. Franz Joseph invited rabbis to his dinner table and visited synagogues and Jewish hospitals. He received delegates from Jewish communities and organizations and individual Jews in the audience chamber of the Hofburg. In years witnessing the growth of a vigorous political anti-Semitism in Vienna and elsewhere in the monarchy, Franz Joseph was credited with holding back its worst excesses, as demonstrated by his initial refusals to confirm Karl Lueger as mayor of Vienna.[99]

For many Jews, Franz Joseph symbolized an ideal Austrian state, one of tolerance and equality, one of constitutional and individual rights, one of cultural progress and enlightenment—a curious set of ideas to associate with one of the most conservative rulers in Europe.[100] However, Franz Joseph's rejection of the very modern phenomena of racism and nationalism and his public gestures of recognition toward Jews made him a sympathetic figure for Jews seeking greater acceptance and acculturation into the broader society and for those committed to more traditional social and religious lifestyles.[101]

Millions of Habsburg citizens participated in jubilee religious services, building dedications, voluntary society-sponsored festivals, local charity drives and illuminations. Voluntary and professional associations, the bedrock of middle-class sociability, incorporated imperial patriotism as part of their schedule of events and entertainments.[102] Wealthy industrialists, large corporations, banks, city governments, and town councils sponsored charitable events. These charitable actions and local festivities defined the ideal Habsburg political culture—one in which people of diverse nationalities, religions, and social classes, bound together by shared devotion to emperor and fatherland, joined together in the spirit of self-sacrifice and good citizenship. Government newspapers and patriotic publications interpreted the outpouring of jubilee charity as evidence of the yearning of the population for an end to partisan strife and a renewal of dynastic and state patriotism.

Government efforts to control the image of the emperor had some success in preventing the kind of commodification of the monarch that marked Victoria's

1887 jubilee. Consumers could not purchase Kaiser rubber balls (though they could buy Kaiser bread grinders). Government-approved plaques, busts, and portraits of the emperor graced public spaces, schools, hospitals, mountain tops, and modest homes all over Cisleithania. Mass-produced patriotic books and pamphlets for children focused on Franz Joseph as an idealized human being, one for children to emulate, brave, tolerant, hard-working, generous—the model for good citizenship in this multinational state. Publications for adults considered the past fifty years as a single bloc of time, "the Francisco-Josephine era." These publications linked cultural, economic, and social progress with the imperial person. They credited Franz Joseph with achievements for which he bore at best limited responsibility.

The reality, of course, was much less clear. Those organizing charitable actions often did so out of a desire to gain social recognition, to enhance the profile of a particular voluntary association, or, like Krupp and other industrialists, to prevent social revolution. Perhaps more ominously, some sponsors of jubilee charitable actions used imperial celebrations to sharpen national divisions. In eastern Galicia, for example, the local jubilee illuminations on 2 December 1908 became an occasion for Polish-Ruthenian national competition. Hundreds of thousands of Galicians purchased inexpensive transparent portraits of the emperor and placed them in windows, turning the entire province into a sea of light honoring Franz Joseph. A committee elected by the city council of Lemberg and including representatives from charitable institutions organized the sale of these "illumination cards." Produced in Lemberg, the transparencies carried a portrait of Franz Joseph below the Hungarian and Austrian crowns separated by "2 December" (written in Polish) and "1848–1908." Rzeszów, Cracow, Stanisław, Sanok, and other town councils ordered the lithographs from the Lemberg committee at the bulk rate of 30 crowns per thousand and sold them for 10 hallers each. These town governments and the Lemberg committee pledged to use the proceeds from the illumination cards to support local schools, libraries, museums, and charities. Ruthenian newspapers, however, urged their readers to purchase portraits printed by the Ruthenian Pedagogic Society and with text written in Ruthenian characters. The proceeds from these transparent Ruthenian Kaiser portraits would fund Ruthenian schools and not be used for "Polish aims."[103] Though it is far from certain that peasants thought of their patriotic purchases as expressions of national identity, many Ruthenian and Polish intellectuals viewed the illuminations in honor of the "Father of all the Peoples" as a plebiscite on national identity within Galicia.[104]

Habsburg jubilee commemorative products transformed the emperor, who had hesitated as long as possible to share his authority with representative institutions, whose government was blamed by ethnic factions for national insults, and who shared a great deal of the blame for the faults of the 1867 Compromise, into the embodiment of the middle-class values of discipline and concern for the public good. Local celebrations throughout Cisleithania seemed to unite the population in love of dynasty and fatherland. Events in Galicia and elsewhere, however, revealed the ambiguous nature of patriotic activities. Those attending a Nicotine Society Kaiser Smoke-Fest in Vienna and Galician peasants taping transparent Ruthenian and Polish Kaisers to their windows might have acted out of dynastic patriotism. Nevertheless, the image of the benevolent emperor had clearly become available to those pursuing agendas that ignored or were in opposition to the official rhetoric of peace, harmony, and fulfillment of national interests within the great family of the peoples under the all-loving and all-beloved emperor-father.

CHAPTER 6

Monopolizing Patriotism

Vienna, Karl Lueger, and the 1898 Jubilee

In 1898, the imperial court, the Cisleithanian government, the army, the Catholic Church, and the imperial family itself used the public arena as never before to defend the legitimacy of the imperial house and the state it ruled. Publications, sermons, charitable actions, and celebrations marking the fiftieth anniversary of Franz Joseph's accession to the throne seemed to confirm the centrality and importance of the dynasty to the lives and livelihoods of all Habsburg subjects. This activity was not without precedent, but the multiplication of efforts was a significant innovation and these efforts were, as the previous chapter has argued, far from fruitless. In the 1880s and 1890s, however, the franchise expanded, wider sectors of the population became participants in the formal political process, and organized political parties promoted agendas opposed to the ideal monarchy of tolerance, adherence to legitimate authority, and imperial loyalty depicted in official and semi-official sources. In this context, imperial celebration became part of an increasingly partisan public discourse about the state and the future of Habsburg society.

Due to the cancellation of official court celebrations after the murder of Empress Elisabeth, festivities organized and/or hosted by Karl Lueger's Christian Social Vienna city government in the summer and in December went unchallenged as the most extravagant events of the jubilee year. Lueger and the Christian Socials attempted to manipulate the jubilee for partisan advantage, embroiling the celebrations in political controversy.

Though he began his career in the liberal camp, Lueger won Vienna's mayoralty by uniting artisans, house-owners, shopkeepers, white-collar workers, Catholic intellectuals and clergy, and others moved by anti-Semitic rhetoric in a powerful political and social movement. In 1848 only 200 Jewish families were legally tolerated in Vienna, and in 1857 Jews made up only 6,000 of Vienna's total population of some 500,000. However, the achievement of legal equality under the constitution of 1867 resulted in a great influx of Jews from Bohemia,

Galicia, and elsewhere in the monarchy to Vienna. In 1900, Jews constituted over 145,000 of Vienna's 1,674,957 inhabitants. In 1910, more than 175,000 of Vienna's two million residents were Jews, and Jews formed approximately 8.6 percent of the city's population—some 12 percent of the population if one excludes the outlying districts incorporated into Vienna after 1890. Christian Socials cited the prominence of Jews in the liberal middle classes as "proof" of Jewish culpability for the alleged evils of liberal hegemony in the capital city: 22 percent of all law students and 48 percent of medical students at the University of Vienna in 1890 were Jews; Jews constituted over half the members of Concordia, the most prestigious journalists' professional association.[1]

Many artisans, excluded from urban politics by the curial suffrage scheme and challenged by competition from foreign and domestic manufacturing, viewed with suspicion the successful entry of Jews into the professional middle classes. Artisans were not the only Viennese residents, however, who viewed Jews as the main victors of the failed revolutions of 1848, the force behind the hated German Liberals, the evil geniuses of the Social Democratic Party, and the corrupt capitalists responsible for the 1873 stock market crash and the decline of the crafts.[2] Anti-Semitism proved a powerful political tool for Lueger's Christian Social Party. Lueger's party claimed to protect the Christian values of the lower middle classes from the godless socialists and to represent those resentful of the perceived arrogance of the anticlerical Austro-German Liberals.[3]

In 1898, Lueger's Christian Socials controlled the Vienna city council and wielded considerable authority in the Lower Austrian diet. Building on Vienna's earlier city-sponsored imperial celebrations, Lueger and the Christian Socials developed an 1898 jubilee program designed to bolster their own political power. Not only did Christian Social jubilee celebrations reassure the emperor and the central government of the loyalty of the party, but Lueger and the Christian Social Party used every possible opportunity to define themselves as the only true political representatives of the patriotic German Christian middle classes in Habsburg Austria. Christian Social Party leaders employed anti-Semitic rhetoric to amplify their attacks on the patriotic credentials of rival political parties during the jubilee year. The first section of this chapter overviews Vienna's official participation in imperial celebrations from 1848 to 1898. The next sections look in greater detail at the Christian Socials and the imperial jubilee year of 1898, from the Christian Social rejection of commemorations for the martyrs of 1848 to the party's jubilee program and the Kaiser Jubilee Exhibition.

The Liberal City and Imperial Celebrations

The Christian Social jubilee program of 1898 was not the first attempt by city politicians to make political use of imperial celebrations. Lueger could and did build on precedents set during the era of liberal domination of city politics from the 1860s until the Christian Social election victories of the 1890s.[4]

In 1863, 1864, and 1865 liberal majorities on the Vienna city council sponsored festivities in the Prater to celebrate Franz Joseph's birthday.[5] These Kaiser-festivals portrayed the emperor who had suppressed liberal revolution in 1848 as the protector of the new constitutional order, which was dominated, in Cisleithania, by German liberals. Fireworks, a Kaiser-lottery, military bands, and theater performances honored Franz Joseph as the "standard-bearer of German reform."[6] Choirs sang German national songs written by early-nineteenth-century German romantic nationalist Ernst Moritz Arndt, such as "What Is the German Fatherland?" and "Hail to You, My Fatherland." These celebrations of the *constitutional* emperor represented a "powerful victory" for "progress" and for the "German" people of Vienna.[7] Exclusion from the new German Empire diminished the liberals' eagerness to commemorate the emperor's birthday. The city of Vienna did not sponsor imperial birthday celebrations from 1866 until 1880; Prater festivities were limited to decorations and amusements organized by businesses located in the park.[8]

Vienna's most extensive program of imperial celebration prior to 1898 came in April 1879. The city council developed a week-long program of festivities rivaling the official court celebrations in honor of the twenty-fifth wedding anniversary of the imperial couple. Artist Hans Makart's magnificent historical/allegorical procession around the new Ringstrasse, a symbol of the expansion and modernization of the imperial capital under liberal leadership, was the undisputed highlight of these celebrations.[9] Close to half a million people, including an estimated 200,000 visitors to the imperial capital, witnessed this spectacle.

Historical processions were the rage of the day, but Makart outdid his German rivals and solidified his reputation as the leading historicist artist.[10] Makart and his team of artists clothed some 8,000 Viennese in costumes evoking the proud independent German towns of the late Middle Ages. Stylized medieval Germans on decorated wagons represented industries, artisan trades, and even the railroads (figure 47). The imperial couple watched from a special podium designed by Otto Wagner that overlooked the Ring just outside the gates of the imperial palace. Ostensibly in honor of Elisabeth and Franz Joseph, Makart's *Festzug* proclaimed the central role of the "progressive" and "productive" classes in society. This display of urban self-confidence unofficially opened the Ringstrasse and served as a self-referential celebration of liberal achievement.

In accordance with the emperor's often stated wishes and in a continuation of trends evident since the mid-1860s—with the notable exception of the 1879 festivities—Vienna's city council voted against sponsoring "magnificent festivals" to commemorate the 1888 fortieth jubilee. Instead the liberals supported

Figure 47: "Train Group" from Hans Makart's 1879 Festzug.
Austrian National Library.

modest acts of public charity, enabling them to appear to address the material needs of their constituents while celebrating a patriotic event. Most prominently, the city council created a foundation with 100,000 gulden dedicated to assisting "craftspeople who have fallen into an emergency situation."[11] The city also published a commemorative album portraying the development of the city under liberal stewardship, *Vienna 1848–1888. Commemorative Album for 2 December.* Essays in this self-congratulatory publication posing as an ode to the emperor celebrated liberal championship of universal freedoms, the liberal program of urban autonomy, and the resultant transformation of Vienna into a modern capital:

> May this book take its place as a monument to the emperor's care for the capital of his empire—but also as an honorable witness for an understanding and goal-conscious *Bürgerschaft*, worthy of the greatness of its task.[12]

The liberal city government began considering projects for the 1898 jubilee as early as 1892.[13] Mayor Prix proposed the construction of a museum, funded with 500,000 gulden of city funds, to display the city's large artistic and historical collections and to house its library. This city museum was to hold a jubilee exhibition on the development of Vienna during the reign of Franz Joseph—the era of liberal hegemony and the transformation of Vienna into a modern capital.[14] Mayor Prix's death on 28 February 1894 brought this project to a standstill, despite lobbying efforts by the Austrian Association of Engineers and Architects, the Vienna Society of Artists (*Wiener Künstlergenossenschaft*), and other organizations.[15]

Prix's death also signaled the end of liberal majorities in Vienna. Four times in the following years Franz Joseph refused to confirm the popular Karl Lueger as mayor. The emperor viewed him as a dangerous demagogue and had little sympathy for anti-Semitism.[16] Minister president Badeni, originally opposed to Lueger's confirmation, recognized the futility of this position and made a deal with the Christian Social leader. After the municipal elections in February and March 1896, Lueger received an audience with the emperor, and Joseph Strobach, a leader among the powerful Vienna landlords (*Hausherren*), was installed as mayor. On 31 March 1897, the city council once again voted Lueger mayor, and

Franz Joseph confirmed the election on 16 April. Lueger would not relinquish the office until his death in 1910.[17]

Lueger had made his own debut in the politics of imperial celebration in 1880 when he and Ignaz Mandl led the short-lived United Left.[18] Only a minority of the city council dared to vote against Lueger's motion to sponsor a *Volksfest* in the Prater for Franz Joseph's fiftieth birthday. Franz Joseph initially opposed the festivities; however, after the conclusion of the celebration minister president Taaffe communicated the emperor's appreciation for the event.[19] Lueger's first exercise in using the image of the emperor for political gain had largely succeeded. He had associated himself with Austrian patriotism, defined patriotism to suit his own ends, and forced acceptance of this definition by political rivals and by the emperor himself. As mayor, Lueger would again produce imperial celebrations for the benefit of his own political faction.

Sharpening the Christian Social Message

Outside of Vienna the Christian Social Party did not fare well in the battle for the support of the monarchy's ethnic Germans at the outbreak of the Badeni language crisis. The Christian Socials were, at first, reluctant to join with radical German nationalists in a unified German camp opposed to the Czechs. Christian Social leaders seized the occasion of the jubilee year to define their party as the only major political force that vowed to protect Austro-German interests while proclaiming loyalty to state and Kaiser.

In the first months of 1898, the Christian Socials wielded their own publicly proclaimed imperial loyalty as a political weapon. The language of political attack, anti-Semitism, and dynastic devotion expressed by Christian Social leaders in the opening days of 1898 previewed the tactics the party would use throughout the jubilee year. Already on 4 January, the Christian Social *Reichspost* labeled Pan-German nationalists "anti-Austrian-German-Radicals" who distanced themselves from the emperor and desired above all "to become a vassal state of the German empire." The Social Democrats would celebrate the "deeds of the revolutionaries" of 1848, as would the "Jewish-Liberal party." The Christian Social Party was the only political choice possible for patriotic German Christians in Habsburg Austria: "All in the land who value being Austrians, who think and feel as Austrians, who are filled with love and devotion for the person of our *JubelKaiser*" should join with the Christian Socials and work for a year of peace to honor the emperor.[20] In the same spirit, the *Österreichische Frauen-Zeitung,* the organ of the Christian Social Vienna Women's Association, called on Vienna's many Christian clubs and institutions to come together for a great unified Christian *Kaiserfest.* This great festival, which never took place, would have demonstrated

that the Christian Social Party really means the people of Vienna. . . . Would not such a singular celebration be a renewed victory celebration for the Christian Social Party and at the same time a defeat for its defamers?[21]

Public celebrations of the fiftieth anniversary of the outbreak of the 1848–49 revolutions bolstered the efforts of Christian Social Party spokespersons to portray theirs as the only truly patriotic political organization. Franz Joseph came to the throne in the midst of revolution, and the imperial jubilee was, therefore, also the jubilee of a failed revolution, defeated by Franz Joseph's government and army. Liberals, democrats, Social Democrats, and Pan-Germans scrambled to portray themselves as the sole heirs of the martyrs of 1848. Some claimed to be patriots and supporters of the dynasty as well as adherents of the revolutionary ideals defeated by the dynasty in 1848–49. By celebrating the emperor's jubilee *and* those killed by the victorious reaction, however, these political groupings opened themselves up to attacks by the Christian Social Party, which publicly identified itself with the imperial jubilee and rejected the commemoration of the fallen revolutionaries.

The competition to control public memory of 1848–49 reached its acme on 13 March, fifty years after Archduke Albrecht ordered his forces to fire on the crowds gathering in the Herrengasse. During the decade of neoabsolutist reaction, government controls over political expression had not permitted public commemorations of the losers of 1848. In the relative political freedom of the 1860s, the liberal city council did little more to keep the memory of revolution alive than erect an obelisk in the central cemetery dedicated to the March martyrs.[22] As the suffrage expanded in the 1880s, the liberals and their political rivals increasingly felt the need to appeal to a wider audience of potential voters by claiming the heroes of 1848 as their ideological ancestors. Beginning in 1889, Vienna's city council decorated the obelisk with flowers each 13 March, and, in the 1890s, the growing Social Democratic Party called on its adherents to join in an annual pilgrimage to the obelisk. In January 1898 and again in early March, Lueger's Christian Social majority rejected proposals by the liberal minority requesting that the mayor and city council gather in the central cemetery, give speeches in the name of the city of Vienna, and lay a wreath at the base of the obelisk.[23]

With no official representation from the city of Vienna, the commemorations of the fallen on 13 March 1898 seemed to reveal a patriotism gap between the Christian Socials and their political rivals. In a display of orderliness bordering on the absurd, Vienna's political groupings, with the conspicuous exception of the Christian Socials, made the pilgrimage to the obelisk at designated times prearranged with the Vienna police. Leaders delivered fiery speeches proclaiming themselves true to the goals of the dead heroes; crowds raised flags, sang songs, and then exited quietly to make way for the next scheduled faction to arrive.

The first group reached the obelisk at noon. Ludwig Vogler represented the

"Progressive Union" in the city council, and democratic ideologue Ferdinand Kronawetter, a former member of Lueger's United Left who remained a staunch opponent of anti-Semitic politics, spoke to a small group composed of radical democrats and delegations from a few Social Democratic district organizations. The group then proceeded to the Jewish ("Israelite") section of the cemetery to lay a wreath at the grave of Adolf Fischhof, the physician who played a prominent role in the 1848 events.[24]

Several hundred Austro-German nationalists, including two of the editors of the Pan-German organ, the *Ostdeutsche Rundschau,* and members of the German Nationalist faction of the city council arrived at the obelisk at 2 P.M. Many sported the German nationalist symbol, the blue cornflower. The main speaker, parliamentary representative and leading Pan-German politician Karl Hermann Wolf, described what he termed the German nationalist aims of the 1848 revolution. Representatives of the University of Vienna's German nationalist dueling fraternities placed wreaths at the base of the obelisk before leaving the cemetery.

Some 200 anarchists followed dutifully on the heels of the German nationalists. The anarchists sang "The Red Flag" and raised a cheer to international revolution before laying a wreath with the inscription "To the True Warriors of the Year 1848, from the Anarchists of Austria."

Finally came the Social Democrats. An estimated 50,000–200,000 men, women, and children, most displaying red carnations, gathered at designated points in all of Vienna's districts before marching silently to the cemetery. Hundreds of party members wearing red armbands kept order and Social Democratic bicyclists maintained communication between the long lines of workers and their families. At the monument itself, socialist leader Karl Hoeger declared 13 March 1848 the greatest day in Austrian history and labeled the middle classes betrayers of the glorious proletarian revolution of 1848. Thousands swore to "hold the martyrs holy," listened to speeches in German, Czech, and Polish, sang workers' songs, and placed almost 200 wreaths at the base of the obelisk.[25] Later that evening, in many locations throughout the city, Social Democrats gathered to commemorate the occasion.

The Christian Socials used the coincidence of the fiftieth anniversary of the revolution and the fiftieth jubilee of Franz Joseph's accession to position themselves as the only party worthy of the support of loyal German-Austrians. In early March, city council member Albert Gessmann, the most influential member of the Christian Social leadership aside from Lueger himself, criticized all Christian Social rivals for their lack of dynastic patriotism and their support of allegedly Jewish interests to the supposed detriment of Austro-German Christians.[26] Despite their anti-Semitic bluster, Gessmann charged, glorification of the revolution proved the Pan-Germans to be in league with the Jew-liberals, the only real winners from the tragic events of 1848. He raged against the eagerness of the "liberal party of the *Judenschaft*" and the Pan-Germans to celebrate a revolutionary movement that "empowered *Judentum* and liberalism to further oppress the people." The Jews had been at the forefront of a revolution that directed its energy against the church and, therefore, against the interests of the Christian inhabitants of Austria. According to Gessmann, the "people of Austria have harvested bitter fruits" by trading absolutist oppression for Jewish domination.[27]

The political gatherings in the cemetery prompted the *Reichspost* and other Christian Social newspapers to denounce the "Freethinking family, father liberalism, daughter Social Democracy, and base democracy." Those who celebrated the revolution, the paper charged, could not lead the German-Christian-Austrians to true freedom. The self-appointed German nationalists did not act for the good of the Austro-Germans, but only aided the Jew-liberals and *"Juden-Soci"* who endeavored to undermine Christian society. According to the Christian Social press, true "patriots" avoided such disloyal demonstrations and insults to the emperor and would instead "celebrate the return of the day on which our beloved monarch" came to the throne.[28]

The Christian Social Jubilee

While the Christian Social abstention from the 13 March festivities sharpened the profile of the party against its rivals, the Vienna city council's jubilee program more directly served the aims of Christian Social politics. On 8 February 1898, Lueger himself introduced a motion containing the program for Vienna's commemorations of the jubilee. Passed unanimously, Lueger's city council program for the jubilee was a marked departure from previous, liberal practice and, though at first blush a grab bag of unrelated items, the program formed a coherent whole that advanced Christian Social politics under the cover of nonpartisan imperial loyalty. The city council pledged the following:

1. To produce an official city council address. The address, to be executed in an artistic fashion, would be delivered by a delegation led by the mayor and was to reaffirm the loyalty and gratefulness of the city to the emperor.

2. To reserve one million gulden to fund the construction of a city Franz Joseph Jubilee Children's Hospital.

3. To provide 500,000 in city funds to create the City of Vienna Emperor Franz Joseph Jubilee Insurance Institution.

4. To provide (limited) financial and moral support for the building of a Jubilee Church.

5. To produce a jubilee commemorative medallion.

6. To participate in the jubilee exhibition.

7. To sponsor as yet undefined jubilee celebrations, including an undefined homage of the schoolchildren.

8. To support the Kaiser Jubilee and Fifth Austrian United Shooting Festival.

9. To organize a general illumination of Vienna on 1 December.

10. To distribute commemorative publications to all of Vienna's schoolchildren on 2 December.

11. To elect a jubilee commission to include the mayor, the two vice-mayors, and thirty-six members of the city council. This jubilee commission would then execute the city jubilee program.[29]

Lueger's comfortable anti-Semitic majority on the city council ensured that his people would control the jubilee commission (item 11). Elected by the city council in March, the commission eventually expanded to forty members, not including Lueger himself, and his two vice-mayors, Joseph Strobach and Joseph Neumayer.[30] The full commission met for the first time on 15 March and divided into four subcommittees with the following division of responsibilities:

Committee I) Produce the official city address and the commemorative medal; coordinate the participation of the city in the jubilee exhibition; distribute a commemorative publication to all of Vienna's schoolchildren.

Committee II) Coordinate all arrangements for the Kaiser Jubilee Children's Hospital; the foundation stone to be laid during the jubilee year.

Committee III) Create the city insurance institution.

Committee IV) Organize an unspecified homage of the schoolchildren, coordinate the city's participation in the V. Austrian and Kaiser Jubilee Shooting Competition, arrange the general illumination of the city of Vienna on 1 December, and, added at Lueger's request, prepare the opening ceremonies for the jubilee exhibition.[31]

Aside from a handful of aging liberals, like former mayor Dr. Eduard Uhl and Dr. Ludwig Vogler, anti-Semites dominated the membership of the jubilee commission and the four subcommittees. Prominent anti-Semitic politician and sculptor Karl Constenoble and Dr. Theodor Wähner, editor of the Christian Social newspaper *Deutsche Zeitung,* sat on committee I. Leopold Tomola, the chair of committee IV and a dedicated Christian Social activist, advocated the forced separation of Jewish and Christian pupils in Vienna's public schools.[32] Dr. Klotzberg, elected to the city council as a liberal and in 1898 a devoted follower of Lueger, and Karl Schuh, a member of the anti-liberal Central Union of House Owner Associations, also played prominent roles on the commission. These and other Christian Social members guaranteed that the city's jubilee program would benefit the Christian Social Party.[33]

Only a few of the items on the city council program were Christian Social innovations. Even before the constitutional era, official presentations of addresses on important occasions had become standard procedure in the monarchy. The production of commemorative medals for major public anniversaries and celebrations was also a well-established practice by the 1890s. The jubilee church, the jubilee exhibition, and the shooting festival originated outside of Christian Social circles, and illuminations had accompanied imperial celebrations for at least a century. These items, however, and those that were genuine innovations or significant departures from previous practices, combined to produce the most extensive and expensive list of city-sponsored imperial celebrations yet undertaken by a city government.

The Christian Socials had long avowed that they, unlike the current Cisleithanian government, cared for the needs of the population. In the early 1890s, the liberal majority had considered constructing a jubilee hospital as part of a projected city jubilee program. Lueger doubled the amount of money the city committed to this effort, making the children's hospital the most expensive single item on the jubilee program.[34] The *Reichspost* cited this item as further evidence of the Christian Social dedication to social reform and faulted the state for its failure to provide properly for its citizens.[35] The eventual dedication of the jubilee hospital and the yearly awarding of eighty-four insurance annuities to poor children in a special 2 December ceremony in the town hall (item 3) offered Lueger many occasions to display his and his party's alleged concern for the welfare of Vienna.[36]

The drive to collect funds to build a jubilee church (figures 16 and 17), originally the idea of the papal representative and supported by the cardinal-prince-archbishop of Vienna, became embroiled in anti-Semitic politics. The jubilee church was to be built in Vienna's second district, long home to the largest concentration of Jewish inhabitants within the city limits.[37] Some Christian Social sympathizers described the drive to collect funds for the jubilee church as a Christian crusade against the powerful Jews. In 1897, Heinrich Apfelthaler wrote Lueger seeking his support for several jubilee projects, including the construction of the jubilee church. Apfelthaler appealed to Lueger's anti-Semitic sentiments: "The construction of this landmark of our exalted religion would dam up this settlement of Semites."[38]

More strident public rhetoric was used in the fund drive for a Kaiser jubilee city theater. Though not listed on the official city program, the effort to collect money to build the theater became a Christian Social rallying cry throughout the year. Already in January, the *Reichspost* complained about the flood of patriotic jubilee plays by Jewish authors: "Whether Julius Loewy [author of a play performed at a festival in Kahlenberg] is the right man as playwright to inspire the Christian folk to patriotism and to love of the imperial house may be easily doubted." The jubilee theater would provide a forum for exclusively German "Christian religious and patriotic performances" in order to "emancipate" art and culture from the grip of the corrupting and anti-Christian Jew.[39]

Not surprisingly, the Christian Social press welcomed the city jubilee program as a blueprint for "genuine Christian, social, Charitas." "One thing is certain," the *Reichspost* asserted, "[Lueger] has gained for himself in the last weeks new trust, new love in the Christian *Volk*."[40] The *Frauenbund*'s *Österreichische Frauen-Zeitung* crowed that even the "Jew-liberals" could not dare to oppose this "Christian" and patriotic program. Lueger's jubilee program demonstrated that Vienna would not become a "Judenstadt" but would "remain the cozy, charming, genuinely German and *Kaisertreu* city that it has been since ancient times. This God will ensure!"[41]

Christian Social Lessons in Patriotism

The most innovative and controversial item in Lueger's program was the homage of the schoolchildren. The liberals had limited even their extensive 1879 silver wedding anniversary program to a procession of adults, a city ball, and some relatively modest charitable contributions. Lueger and the Christian Social city council, however, orchestrated a display of popular patriotism by utilizing fully the power of the city administration. Lueger and his city council worked through the city school system to choreograph a march of over 70,000 pupils around the Ringstrasse and to distribute self-promoting jubilee publications to all of Vienna's schoolchildren. As Richard Geehr has written, "Lueger knew the political value of children."[42]

Though there were no Viennese precedents for an organized display of youthful patriotism, there was at least one recent example of royal celebration involving large numbers of children. The editorial staff of the London *Daily Telegraph* contributed 8,000 pounds and sponsored a Children's Festival in Hyde Park in honor of Victoria's fiftieth jubilee in 1887. The newspaper invited 30,000 thirteen-year-old children, chosen for good behavior from London's elementary, state, and public schools, to participate in this event. The children marched to the park four abreast, in two columns, each one and a half miles long. The *Daily Telegraph* treated the children to a series of games, theater performances, and sporting events. Aristocratic women provided the children with food and drink. Victoria and members of the royal family visited the festivities, held under the official protection of the Prince of Wales. Lueger and committee IV requested information about this event from Sir Edward Lawson, editor of the *Daily Telegraph*. Lueger and the commission decided, however, not to treat the children of Vienna to an entertainment, but to use the children to display the supposed dynastic devotion of the Viennese—and of Lueger's city government.[43]

Brushing aside the fears of some school officials that hours of marching in the sun would be detrimental to the health of the children, Vienna's city council began to plan a procession of the schoolchildren.[44] Though Schönbrunn offered "romantic surroundings," the committee determined to hold the event on the Ring, "our often used and every time reliable *via triumphalis.*" The Ringstrasse was central enough for all children to avoid excessive commutes, and wide enough to allow twenty-four children in a row, reducing the time to pass before the emperor to approximately one hour.[45] Undoubtedly, the organizers were also pleased with the possibility of using the Ringstrasse, in the past host to liberal festivals like the 1879 Makart procession as well as more recent Social Democratic marches, for a Christian Social spectacle of patriotism.

The city council jubilee commission moved to ensure that the memory of the event would remain in the minds of the children—and their parents—long after the last pupil had returned home from the procession. Committee I produced medals that were distributed to each pupil participating in the procession. At Lueger's insistence, this subcommittee also developed a commemorative publication. This pamphlet was eventually handed out to all of Vienna's schoolchildren on 2 December and included photographs of the procession, the text of Lueger's speech to the emperor that opened the procession, and the emperor's reply.[46]

The choreography of the procession was designed to show the patriotic youth of Vienna to the emperor and the population in the best possible light—though the council was not willing to spend large sums of money on this event. Each school district would form two sections, one of boys and one of girls; each row would consist of twenty-four children. The first row of boys was to carry small flags, the first row of girls to wear sashes. The sashes and flags were to be in the colors of the city of Vienna, Lower Austria, and the imperial black and yellow.[47] The jubilee committee IV planned to provide each child with only one roll and a glass of water during the hours necessary to gather and arrange the pupils for the procession. To reduce costs further, the commission decided not to costume tens of thousands of children. Instead the commission instructed the teachers designated to keep order and the youthful marchers to don their "Sunday clothes."[48]

In 1880, Polish nobles in Galicia had turned to Vienna for the necessary accouterments of patriotism and the costumes and other items needed to present "genuine" Polish culture to the visiting emperor (see Chapter 3); in 1898 the Vienna city council looked to Germany for costumes and other products fitting for a display of Habsburg patriotism. As soon as the program of city jubilee festivities was announced in February, companies began lobbying the jubilee committee to purchase their products in order to produce the best possible display of imperial loyalty. The city council accepted the bid of a Munich firm to provide the costumes for the trumpeters who would precede the children. This firm, Diringer, had recently supplied the historical costumes and other paraphernalia for such extravaganzas as the seventieth birthday party of the archduke of Baden, city anniversaries in Karlsruhe and Krems, and a historical procession in Hanover.[49]

Concerned that a public manifestation of sympathy with the Social Democrats or German nationalists could mar this expression of Christian Social patriotism and leadership, the jubilee commission ordered school directors to ensure that no children display red sashes or red carnations (signs of solidarity with the Social Democratic Party sported by the tens of thousands of workers who filled the cemetery on 13 March). The city council also forbade children from wearing the blue cornflower or sashes in the German national colors of black, red, and yellow, evocative of radical German nationalism.[50]

These orders drew predictable sarcastic responses from the Social Democratic and German nationalist press. The Pan-Germans were disdainful of this ban, since in any case they preferred not to associate themselves with a demonstration of patriotism; however, they took issue with the city council declaration that these symbols were in and of themselves "provocative":

> If the cornflower and the red carnation are provocative to Herr Rossner [an official in the mayor's office involved in the details of the procession arrangements] and Herr Dr. Lueger, others might take offense at the white carnation [the symbol of political Catholicism]. This [flower] was declared, however, at least implicitly as a suitable flower for a festival of homage.[51]

These comments were not the opening skirmishes in the public relations war between the Christian Socials and the Pan-German nationalists and Social Democrats over the jubilee celebrations and the use of the children of Vienna as props in a Christian Social patriotic performance. Pan-German leaders Schönerer and Wolf decried the upcoming procession on the floor of the central parliament on 7 June. They condemned Lueger for risking the health of children to prove his patriotic credentials.[52] In the weeks preceding the procession, the Social Democratic press lambasted the Christian Socials and their misuse of children to bolster their own political fortunes and to obscure their failure to deal with important issues affecting the lives of the workers and poorer citizens of Vienna. Social Democrats lampooned the procession as the "Path of Misery of the Vienna Schoolchildren." Instead of gathering to play games and to receive catered food, as had been the case in London during Victoria's 1887 jubilee, Vienna's children would be forced to march for hours in the sun and would receive only a cup of water and a roll from the hands of the unscrupulous Christian Socials.[53] "The Christian Socials want to parade with the children of *other* people" in order to misuse them for the advantage of the ruling classes.[54] The Social Democrats also attacked the Christian Socials for forcing poorly paid teachers, constantly under pressure from Lueger's party for supposedly disseminating Marxist values to Vienna pupils, to appear in black coats and top hats for the procession. The Christian Socials, the *Arbeiter-Zeitung* charged, recognized only "black-tie patriotism."[55]

Despite the opposition of the Social Democratic Party and of German nationalist groupings, the procession itself, postponed from 17 June to 24 June due to bad weather, "succeeded happily beyond all expectations."[56] In Lueger's choreography the emperor became a prop affirming his and his party's patriotic credentials. Before 10 A.M., the members of the imperial family and other dignitaries took their places in the special imperial tent (*Kaiserzelt*) and flanking tribunes set up outside the Burgthor and facing out toward the Ring. Eight men dressed in gala costumes accompanied Lueger, who wore his golden chain of office; this new mayoral ceremonial pomp rivaled the splendor of the emperor himself.[57] Members of the jubilee commission also joined the mayor as he waited for the emperor. Franz Joseph rode from the Hofburg to the Burgthor in his imperial carriage, accompanied by three adjutants. After an exchange of formal greetings between Lueger and the emperor, Franz Joseph removed his hat, as did the thousands near the *Kaiserzelt,* and a choir of 1,000 children sang the first verse of the state hymn.

A mounted herald bearing Vienna's banner, the four trumpeters on foot dressed in medieval costume, and the members of committee IV with sashes in the red and white of the city of Vienna opened the one-and-a-half-hour-long procession. The children, drilled for weeks prior to the procession itself, performed with near perfect discipline. As each group of children passed the emperor, the first row of boys lowered their flags. All the children turned their heads toward the emperor and took off their hats and caps (figure 48). "Thousands of throats" resounded with cheers.

Predictably, Social Democrats and German nationalist spokespersons were quick to denounce the procession as a cynical political ploy. For the *Arbeiter-Zeitung,* the procession did not display the unity of purpose of the Viennese population, but rather showed the economic gulf between the rich and poor: the children of workers' families did not have suitable clothing and their attire and demeanor in the procession underscored their abject poverty. Some 200 children needed medical care during the course of the procession, proving to the Socialists that the Christian Social "experts [*Fachmänner*] in patriotism" had no qualms about sacrificing the health of children for awards and titles.[58] "What is patriotism? Before the procession one believed that it was a feeling of belonging to the native soil, to the hereditary People." But, remarked the *Freie Lehrerstimme,* the procession revealed that "patriotism is not a feeling, but a skill that has to be taught and learned, like playing the piano." Children apparently had to be drilled in marching and cheering to instill patriotism: "*In Austria, it is truly an art to be patriotic.*"[59] The Pan-German press was equally vicious. The *Ostdeutsche Rundschau* labeled the procession "patriotic abuse of children" created by "organizers addicted to [official recognition]." The Christian Socials were "only patriotic when it costs nothing."[60]

The German nationalists and Social Democrats reacted not only to the procession, but to the descriptions and interpretations of the procession presented in the Christian Social press. The Christian Social press, and Lueger himself in numerous publicized speeches, continually juxtaposed their party's patriotic commitment, as allegedly evidenced by the jubilee program and the procession, with the lack of patriotism of their rivals. The Christian Socials also used the event to proclaim that, in fact, the majority of Viennese citizens actually shared the Christian Social value system. According to the *Reichspost,* "today's performance may stand *not only in Austria, but in the whole world as one of a kind,* that the future generation pays homage to the monarch." In his speech to Franz Joseph before the procession began, "Mayor Dr. Lueger, whose black-and-yellow imperial and loyal sentiments are not questioned even by his opponents, was the translator of the patriotic meaning of this significant homage of the future urban population before the monarch." The *Reichspost* expressed the pleasure of the Christian Social leadership that 70,000 children marched in the face of the "socialist Hebrews."[61]

The emperor usually limited his own remarks at public events to stock phrases, repeating endlessly: "How lovely, I am so pleased." Rare, spontaneous expressions of emotion from the emperor received widespread attention, and Franz Joseph's words to Lueger at the procession were no exception: "It was something extraordinary. It is a comfort to me in this year of many difficulties."[62] Editorial writers dissected this seemingly innocuous phrase for hidden meaning

Figure 48: 1898 Procession of the Children. Austrian National Library.

on the front pages of the monarchy's major newspapers. German-language papers (with the exception of the Social Democratic press) blamed Czech and Pan-Slav "chauvinists" for hurting the emperor so deeply that he could not maintain his usual public stoicism. German-speaking journalists charged that Czech nationalists had provoked the emperor's emotional words by seeking to rob the German speakers of Bohemia of their language rights and traditional (and well-deserved) economic, political, and cultural dominance in this province.[63]

Sponsorship of imperial celebrations in the Cisleithanian capital enabled the Christian Socials to demean their rivals and yet appeal to a nonpartisan patriotism all good German-Christians should share. Christian Social commentary affirmed the sentiment of the German nationalist camp by rhetorically defending Austro-German interests against the encroachments of the Slavs in the monarchy. Christian Social spokespersons, however, also argued that their party, and their party alone, was prepared to counter threats to German Christian values and private property by rallying the population to the imperial banner. Lueger himself said before a special sitting of the city council, "The adults joined in today's homage of the little ones: were the adults not in agreement, then the little ones could not have made this homage."[64] For the Christian Socials, the participation of the children, including the sons and daughters of Vienna's working classes, proved that even Social Democratic voters rejected the doctrinaire positions of their party's "Jewish" leadership. Poor and middle-class children had marched hand in hand before the emperor because a common "feeling of love for the legitimate Ruling House makes all class differences disappear." The people were united in "patriotic exuberance."[65]

Responding to Social Democratic commentary concerning the abject poverty of the children of the workers on display during the procession, the Christian Social press blamed the poor themselves for this state of affairs. The workers had children out of wedlock, wasted money, and drank excessively in Jewish-owned taverns and had only themselves to blame for their misery.[66] Journalists sympathetic to the Christian Socials wrote that attacks on the Christian Social jubilee program by the allegedly Jewish controlled *Arbeiter-Zeitung* and the "traitors" of Schönerer's Pan-German nationalists only revealed the "true faces" and "real intentions" of these "enemies of the Catholic Habsburg Empire."[67]

Government newspapers as well as German-language independent papers extolled the procession as an expression of popular imperial loyalty. The Cisleithanian government termed the procession proof of the "golden wedding" between the emperor and the peoples of Austria and appealed to the population to work together to make the jubilee a "Family Festival."[68] The popular *Neuigkeits-Weltblatt* was optimistic that the "wisdom of the monarch will likely succeed and overcome the present crisis and lead the empire over all dangers that even now threaten it!"[69] The *Reichswehr* complained that "foreign" music had accompanied this "Austrian festival for an Austrian Kaiser," but lauded the event as an expression of the positive influence of military values on society and the development of an Austrian loyalty in the population:

> Command creates discipline, this Corps Spirit . . . that for each individual— and such can one discern in almost all schools—is equally important as one's own honor. The Procession of Homage of the Vienna schoolchildren was a look into the future—God be praised!—one full of hope![70]

The liberal *Neue Freie Presse,* however, judged that the 1879 Makart *Festzug* had been a greater triumph. In 1879, all sectors of society had united for the festival, the most elaborate imperial celebration since the Congress of Vienna; in 1898, divisions in the monarchy could not be overcome by a public display, as evidenced by the emperor's emotional words. The liberal press blamed this change on Taaffe and Badeni and the transformation of the relationship between the German population of Austria and the Cisleithanian government. Even the *Neue Freie Presse* conceded, however, that mass participation in jubilee events suggested that the population, despite the activity of Slavic nationalists and Schönerian agitators, in fact remained united behind the emperor.[71]

Conveniently for Lueger, the procession of the children was the first of three elaborate public jubilee festivities that took place in Vienna during the same week. The day after the procession, the imperial family itself and members of the aristocracy presented Franz Joseph with a colorful homage of the hunters at Schönbrunn palace. As in the rest of Europe, many Habsburg aristocrats, including the emperor, were avid hunters.[72] For this celebration, several thousand hunters, for the most part wealthy nobles and their employees, cheered the emperor with the "hunter's greeting." Two days after the procession of the children, the Kaiser Jubilee and Fifth Austrian United Shooting Festival (*Bundesschiessen*) opened with a historical procession around the Ring. The vast majority of participants were Austro-Germans, a fact used by German-language newspapers as evidence of a special relationship of the Austro-Germans with the emperor and the state. Franz Joseph did not attend this event, leaving Franz Ferdinand to accept the homage of the participants and to wish them well during their upcoming competition. Newspapers and commemorative jubilee publications grouped these three events together as highlights of the jubilee year. The fact that Vienna hosted the largest jubilee celebrations in the monarchy enhanced Lueger's endeavors to associate Christian Social Vienna with imperial loyalty.

Completing the Program

The Christian Social press continued to emphasize the German, *Kaisertreu,* and Christian credentials of their party during the remainder of the jubilee year. On Franz Joseph's sixty-eighth birthday, Christian Social editorials encouraged Franz Joseph, a "German Prince, as you have termed yourself," to "rely on the most true of your peoples who are under your scepter! It was the German heart, it was German spirit that preserved the House of Austria."[73] On 2 December, the Christian Social leaders vowed to stand by their emperor, despite the erosion of the "justified hegemony of Germandom" in the monarchy.[74]

As promised by the city program, Christian jubilee celebrations did not end with the procession of the children. Lueger personally added a "festival of the peoples" to the events the city planned to sponsor in November and December. Invited guests were to arrive at the gothic town hall in late November dressed in historical costumes reflecting all the crownlands and all of the monarchy's peoples, thus portraying Lueger's Vienna as a pillar of support for the multinational imperial state.[75] This event, like other public festivities, was canceled after the murder of Elisabeth. Despite the ban on public festivities, however, Lueger and the city government quietly persuaded house owners and district notables to establish informal committees to arrange a "spontaneous" illumination of Vienna.[76] In December, the jubilee commission distributed to Vienna's schoolchildren several hundred thousand copies of the pamphlet immortalizing Lueger's speech to the emperor and Franz Joseph's response opening the procession.[77] Each pupil also received a copy of a play by Alfred von Berger glorifying Franz Joseph and the Habsburg dynasty courtesy of the mayor.[78] Finally, on 2 December, Lueger presided over a special sitting of the city council and invited guests in the People's Hall of the town hall. Here, Lueger again wrapped himself and his party in the flag of patriotism, attacking the government for its failures, and claiming for himself the mantle of defender of the emperor's stated goals of providing support for the health and welfare of the population.

As Chapter 5 documented, thousands of local governments and voluntary associations throughout Cisleithania hosted commemorations during the jubilee year. In Vienna, Christian Social clubs organized small-scale patriotic gatherings of Christian Social believers. Prominent among these events were those sponsored by the Vienna Christian Women's Association (*Christlicher Wiener Frauenbund*) and the Christian Social Worker's Association.

In 1897, women closely associated with the Christian Social movement founded the *Frauenbund*. The original statute of the *Frauenbund* declared that "the association is not political." The association pledged to "spread Christian fundamental values in the family" and to support "Christian craftsmen." The *Frauenbund* accepted applications only from "women and grown girls of the Christian religion."[79] One of the most openly anti-Semitic of the network of Christian Social clubs, the *Frauenbund* never missed an opportunity to denounce "international Jewry."[80] The Vienna police and the Lower Austrian provincial administration were suspicious of the "anti-Semitic tendencies" of this allegedly nonpolitical association.[81] The president of the association, Emilie Platter, a Protestant, enjoyed the full support of Lueger; the mayor often praised her and the

Frauenbund as a "great bulwark on the field of battle."[82] The *Frauenbund* served as an effective support organization for the Christian Social Party.

Many of the women participated in Christian Social gatherings, election campaign events, and public celebrations—including those organized by the city of Vienna for the emperor's jubilee.[83] The *Frauenbund* mobilized its members to attend jubilee festivities (members appeared in white dresses) and held its own birthday celebration in honor of Franz Joseph in August. The *Frauenbund* newspaper, the *Österreichische Frauen-Zeitung,* urged women to participate in the fund drives for the jubilee church and the jubilee theater. Throughout the year, the *Österreichische Frauen-Zeitung* repeatedly compared the patriotism of the German, Christian inhabitants of Vienna to the suspicious beliefs held by Jewish-Liberal-Socialists and Jew-serving Pan-German nationalists.

In late November and early December, the *Frauenbund*'s district sections held music-lecture evenings. Though not officially billed as jubilee events, many of these became, in effect, combination patriotic celebrations and anti-Semitic rallies. In Neubau, for example, Frau Singer, the chair of the local section of the *Frauenbund,* spoke about the murder of the empress and the need for women to cultivate "love of fatherland" and "loyalty to the dynasty." Christian Social notables like Reichsrat delegate and anti-Semitic city council member Josef Gregorig, Albert Gessmann, vice-mayor Josef Neumayer, and others attacked the opposition press, urged the women to shop only at Christian stores, and called on the members of the *Frauenbund* to remain politically active in support of Christian Social goals. All present cheered the glorious emperor on the occasion of his jubilee. Lueger himself did not speak, instead leaving early to attend Christian Women's meetings in other districts.

The same evening, the Währing section of the association scheduled its gathering at the pub *Zum Wilden Mann.* Leopold Tomola, the chair of the jubilee commission subcommittee that had organized the procession of the children, delighted the audience with his call for separating Jewish and Christian pupils in the schools in order to save innocent Christian children from the "poison" of their Jewish classmates. Later in the evening, Monsignor Scheicher, a regular contributor to the anti-Semitic newspaper of the lower clergy, the *Correspondenz-Blatt,* attacked the Schönerian Pan-Germans for their false nationalism and called on all true Germans to unite and battle Jewry (*Judentum*). *Frauenbund* leader Therese Ruzicka then appealed to her fellow members not to purchase Christmas presents from Jewish-owned stores. Finally, to the cheers of the crowd, Lueger arrived to wish all present a happy holiday.[84] At another such event, Lueger thanked everyone for illuminating their homes on 2 December and vowed that with "loyalty to Kaiser and empire" they would defeat their enemies.[85] The imperial hymn officially closed the proceedings at each gathering.[86]

The jubilee celebration of the Christian Worker's Association even more explicitly united anti-Semitism, German identity, dynastic and state loyalty, and Christian Social politics. The Christian Social Party viewed the Social Democrats as their main rivals in the new political landscape, which was characterized by the expansion of the suffrage. To counter the Social Democratic network of labor organizations, Leopold Kunschak, termed by a biographer of Lueger "one of the most versatile and talented organizers of the younger generation of Christian Socials," founded the Christian Social Workers' Association in the 1890s.[87] On Monday, 28 November 1898, just three days after the German nationalists and the Social Democrats had distanced themselves demonstrably from the jubilee sitting of the Reichsrat, Kunschak's new organization held an "imperial devotion of Christian Social workers." The ceremonies commenced with a special mass in St. Peter's Church, followed by a gathering of over 3,000 members of the Christian Social network of voluntary associations in the Hall of the People of the city hall.

Before the crowd of Christian Social luminaries, Lueger himself derided the Social Democrats and the "Schönerians" for opposing jubilee celebrations: "Even here one can observe who celebrated the jubilee in our Austria-Hungary and who did not celebrate it. . . . It deserves to be confirmed at today's occasion, that the Jew-Magyars helped to undermine the jubilee celebrations." Lueger grouped together the Magyars, Jews, Schönerians, and Social Democrats and opposed their antipatriotic activity with the "loyalty to the hereditary monarchy," defended by Christian workers and middle classes, "until all enemies are brought to their knees." At the same time that Lueger attacked all other parties, he rhetorically differentiated the ministers and government of Cisleithania from the emperor. While loyal and respectful of the latter, the Christian Social Party savaged the former for failing to uphold the ideals of the dynasty as the Christian Socials defined them. Enthusiastic cheers greeted Lueger's words, and his speech was followed by the state hymn.[88]

The 1898 Kaiser Jubilee Exhibition in Vienna

The single most significant jubilee event not organized or planned by the Cisleithanian government, Habsburg court, or the city of Vienna was the 1898 Kaiser Jubilee Exhibition (figure 49). The exhibition, the first of the great jubilee events held in Vienna, opened on 7 May and ran until December in the Prater, drawing several million visitors and providing a much-needed boost to Vienna's tourist industry.[89] The exhibition brought together all of the strands of jubilee activity discussed in this and previous chapters: government promotion of jubilee harmony, imperial pomp, the spread of the cult of the emperor through jubilee-related products, popular participation in patriotic activities—and Lueger's politics of patriotism. Lueger's city council was not the chief sponsor of the exhibition; nonetheless, the city council succeeded in integrating this long-running event into the Christian Social calendar of patriotism.

This strange jubilee event drew spectators from all over the monarchy and was reviewed in the pages of major provincial newspapers. The Kaiser Jubilee Exhibition, perhaps more than any other single jubilee event, demonstrates at once the spread of the cult of the emperor and the difficulties the Cisleithanian government and the imperial court faced in projecting a single, dominant interpretation of the jubilee's significance.

According to its president, Count Dominik Hardegg, the Kaiser Jubilee Exhibition displayed the special virtues of the Austrian citizen that paralleled the superior qualities of the emperor himself. In Hardegg's view, every item exhibited, from plumbing equipment to school supplies to beer, was a gift to the emperor, "whose own life's work is everything that today blooms and bears fruit in this monarchy . . . the Kaiser is the source of everything."[90] This "cultural-historical event of the first rank" evidenced the continued vitality of the "life force" of the state.

The reality of the exhibition was much more prosaic. The great spectacle did attract the attention of readers in every province and provide more "proof" of the "spontaneous" popular outpouring of patriotism. At the same time, the exhibition was not a mere reflection of the official jubilee message, which urged all citizens to cultivate their national identities through their loyalty to the benevolent emperor and to the state, which sought only to bring his wishes for improving the lives of his subjects to fulfillment.

In the late nineteenth century, exhibitions were common events in Europe, spurred on by the world's fairs, the first of which was held in 1851 in London's Crystal Palace.[91] In mid-century, such exhibitions provided entertainment, introduced new products, educated visitors about the state and the wider world, and drew international attention. Though the 1873 world's fair held in Vienna was considered a flop, tens of thousands of tourists traveled to Vienna and frequented Vienna's hotels,

Figure 49: 1898 Kaiser Jubilee Exhibition, Prater Park. Austrian National Library.

restaurants, and shops.[92] The 1888 Kaiser Jubilee Exhibition in Vienna sponsored by the Lower Austrian Trade Association (*Niederösterreichischer Gewerbe-Verein*), though modest in comparison to the 1898 Jubilee Exhibition, brought together hundreds of manufacturers and businesses from Vienna and beyond to create a great spectacle of commerce and entertainment. Provincial exhibitions in Bohemia, Galicia, and Hungary in the 1890s spotlighted economic progress and Polish, Czech, and Hungarian "national" achievements.[93]

The 1898 jubilee year inspired many Cisleithanian professional associations, trade and industrial societies, art academies, and agricultural institutions to organize exhibitions. These jubilee exhibitions displayed products affirming the progress made in diverse realms of production, and offered opportunities for local and regional economic elites to gain the attention of provincial populations. In Vienna rabbit-, canary-, and dog-breeding associations held jubilee exhibitions. The secessionist movement sponsored a *Jugendstil* Kaiser jubilee art exhibition and the Society of Fine Artists in Vienna installed its exhibition in the Kunstlerhaus and the Musikverein. The Chess Club of Vienna sponsored an international Kaiser jubilee chess exposition and tournament. The Club of the Friends of Coins and Medallions in Vienna also organized an exhibition, officially opened by Joseph Alexander von Helfert in April.[94] Franz Joseph's visits to many of these various exhibitions created occasions for parades, speeches, orchestras, the gathering of cheering crowds, and the singing of the *Gott erhalte.*

As early as 1892, the leaders of the arts and crafts division of the Lower Austrian Trade Association began planning for a great all-Austrian jubilee exhibition that would express "patriotic devotion and grateful love of our Emperor," who had "led Austria up from the deepest medieval-like conditions to the light of a modern culture state [*Kulturstaat*]." The association, like the producers of Concordia's *Kaiserblatt,* wanted to showcase middle-class achievement. The organizers envisioned a

> great general Austrian Exhibition in order to demonstrate the unparalleled revolution and upswing that industry, trade, arts and crafts, agriculture, transportation, trade, science and education, welfare and administration, in short the entire spiritual, material, and humanitarian life of Austria experienced during the half-century reign of our emperor.[95]

Despite overwhelming institutional support from the central government and business circles, the plans of the Trade Association to hold an all-Austrian exhibition were soon abandoned.[96] Two arguments doomed the ambitious project to create a single great spectacle in Vienna displaying the material progress of the entire monarchy. First, provincial governors, including those of Lower Austria and Bohemia, expressed deep reservations about the depth of support in the business community for such a project. Industrialists cited "exhibition weariness" that had set in during the past few years as exhibition followed exhibition on the provincial, state, and international levels. These industrialists believed that such exhibitions brought advantages only to those introducing new products never before seen. All other exhibitors would face a certain financial loss.

National conflict also played a role in the abandonment of the project. Provincial governors feared that a centrally organized exhibition would inflame nationalist passions. Count Franz Anton Thun, then *Statthalter* of Bohemia, a province wracked by political struggles between Czech and German nationalists, was concerned that due to the sensitive "political-national standpoint the idea of the projected exhibition will [be less than] sympathetically if not downright hostilely received."[97] In Galicia, the press voiced similar sentiments.[98]

In late 1896, assured of the full support of Badeni's government, the association renewed its push for a jubilee exhibition, though one pared down from the original all-Austrian concept. The organizers now proposed a more modest Vienna industry and trade exhibition designed specifically to boost Vienna's troubled economy:

> . . . in order to begin new life and impulse into the producing circles, it is an undertaking that Vienna needs for its trade . . . and to revive the mutual relationships with the rest of the crownlands, which threaten . . . to reduce their business visits to the most necessary and unavoidable.[99]

At first, even this modest proposal did not gain the sympathy of the Christian Socials, who viewed the liberal Trade Association with suspicion. Delegates from the city of Vienna attending the initial organizational meeting to discuss the exhibition in October 1896 made clear their hostility to the undertaking and to those sponsoring this event. The Vienna delegates demanded that all exhibitors agree to use only German-language signs to reflect the Austro-German character of the city. Lueger's delegates also objected to all speeches that justified the need for the exhibition with references to the difficult "political and social situation" in the monarchy and the need for economic progress. The Christian Socials viewed such comments as veiled criticisms of the Christian Social leadership in Vienna.[100]

Eventually Lueger took a more positive view of the exhibition, which presented him with a perfect opportunity for displaying himself as the popular and *Kaisertreu* leader of the imperial capital. The city council's jubilee program offered only modest financial support to the event, but committed the city to erecting a pavilion in the exhibition and participating in opening ceremonies. The Vienna pavilion housed items from Vienna's historical collections, including portraits of past mayors (Lueger had his portrait made for the pavilion as well), a model of Vienna before the city walls were demolished in 1857, a new model of the expanded modern metropolis, and a statue of Franz Joseph surrounded by plants (figure 50).[101]

As had been the case in 1894, the Cisleithanian government saw the exhibi-

Figure 50: Pavilion of the City of Vienna, Kaiser Jubilee Exhibition. Austrian National Library.

tion as an opportunity to point to the achievements of the state and to bolster state patriotism through the celebration of the popular emperor. Badeni himself served as the honorary president of the section of the exhibition devoted to advances in welfare, judged by the Christian Social *Reichspost* to be "Probably the most notable, generally interesting and in addition entirely newfangled section of the exhibition."[102] Dr. Anton Loew and the many government officials who headed subdivisions of the welfare exhibit hoped "to create a complete picture of the Austrian welfare institutions and how these same developed during the reign of His Majesty, our beloved Emperor Franz Joseph." Prompted by the central government, provincial hospitals, police departments, orphanages, homes for the elderly, the Red Cross, research institutions, fire departments, schools, and universities loaned more than 30,000 items to the welfare exhibit. This part of the Jubilee Exhibition aimed to present Austria at the forefront of European-wide developments in health and public welfare, exhibiting everything accomplished "during the glorious reign of our all beloved monarch for the advancing of the most precious good of the state, the life and health of state citizens."[103]

The first of the great jubilee events, and therefore the first chance for Lueger to pose as patriotic host, the 7 May exhibition opening found a privileged place in "instant" publications and in commemorative books printed in the second half of the year. Newspapers from Vienna to Lemberg detailed the ride of the emperor from the Hofburg around the Ring up the Praterstrasse and to the South Portal of the Rotunde, the great round structure erected for the 1873 world's fair. An estimated 200,000 people lined the streets (figure 51). Lueger's jubilee commission topped the masts along the Ringstrasse with flags and assisted in arranging places along the streets from the Hofburg to the Praterstern for Vienna's voluntary associations

Figure 51: Opening of the Kaiser Jubilee Exhibition, Illustrirtes Wiener Extrablatt, 8 May 1898. Austrian National Library.

joined by just under 30,000 military veterans and voluntary firemen, mostly from German-speaking regions of Cisleithania.[104] Lueger reserved a prominent position near the Vienna pavilion for several hundred white-clad members of the *Frauenbund* (figure 52).

Many who came out for the event were entertained by a dramatic act of patriotic devotion. A journeyman tower repair worker named Hubert Frankel, an "extremely solid worker and brave family father," climbed the great tower of the Votive Church at dawn and planted a black-and-yellow imperial flag (figure 53).

Figure 52: Karl Lueger and the Vienna Christian Women's Association greet Franz Joseph at Vienna's Pavilion, Kaiser Jubilee Exhibition, Illustrirtes Wiener Extrablatt, 12 May 1898. Austrian National Library.

Frankel's wife had sewn the 164-centimeter-wide and six-meter-long banner, which read: For the Commemoration of the Fiftieth Jubilee of His Majesty the Emperor Franz Joseph I 1848–1898. Frankel's employer, Joseph Pircher, had done the same on the emperor's birthday in 1886.[105]

Figure 53: Hubert Frankel Raises the Jubilee Banner on the Tower of the Votive Church in Vienna, Illustrirtes Wiener Extrablatt, 11 May 1898. Austrian National Library.

Despite the pomp of the opening ceremonies, the exhibition did not concentrate on incidents from the life of the emperor. Franz Joseph served more as tour guide than as the focus of the many subdivisions of the exhibition. Journalists used the emperor's frequent visits to describe for their readers exhibition highlights.

Franz Joseph's two-hour visit to the welfare exhibit provided an occasion for newspapers to inform their readers about the items Franz Joseph perused, from plumbing equipment to exhibits displaying "modern" "care for the insane."[106] Franz Joseph's inspection of the land and forest economy exhibit introduced readers to improvements in animal breeding. The Neue Freie Presse followed the emperor on his long stay in the section devoted to nutrition and refreshments. Here, the emperor, or any other tired visitor, could sit and enjoy beer from Pilsen or Budweis, wine from Tyrol, and sparkling wine from Styria, or could find sustenance at Dombacher's Giant Barrel (figure 54) or the Sacher Pavilion.[107.]The pavilion of the Vienna Brewmasters, the Neue Freie Presse assured its readers, particularly impressed the monarch.[108]

In the weeks and months ahead, the monarchy's reading public joined Franz Joseph as he toured the exotic Bosnian pavilion (figure 55), a favorite of the Vienna press, as well as exhibitions of clothes, work, jewelry, and crafts. Other subdivisions of the exhibition displayed items related to sport and the sports industry,

Figure 54: Jubilee Giant Barrel, Kaiser Jubilee Exhibition. Austrian National Library.

Figure 55: Main Street of the Jubilee Exhibition with Bosnian Pavilion. Austrian National Library.

the development of the city of Vienna during the past fifty years (with a strong focus on Mayor Lueger), the regulation of the Danube, the Vienna police, baked goods, and air travel. The Urania housed a scientific theater, demonstration and experiment halls, and "the flame," a model of a crematorium.[109]

The Hall of Youth, which endeavored to present a complete picture of the development of education in Cisleithania, contained one of the few displays directly related to the person of the emperor. Schoolteachers led their classes to one or more of the daily showings of Leon Smolle's slide show, "From the Life of the Emperor," based on his popular commemorative pamphlets (discussed in detail in chapter 5). The show included slides of paintings and drawings depicting Franz Joseph in many of the most well-known of his heroic moments: the generous Archduke Franzi; the brave, strong Franz at the battle of Santa Lucia; the young emperor and his bride in 1854, and so on.[110]

Patriotism was also central to the entertainments of "Kaiser Week." Several days of special concerts, decorations, nighttime illuminations, and choirs, which, combined with special prices for city transportation and trains to Vienna from the provinces, made these August days surrounding the emperor's 18 August birthday among the most crowded of the exhibition run.[111]

Certainly, those who visited the exhibition were well aware that the emperor had been there before them, had seen the same items, and had expressed his approval of this splendid display of Austrian ingenuity focused on public welfare and gastronomy. The loquacious emperor, the news media reported, occasionally pleased his hosts by remarking, "That is truly extraordinarily interesting."[112]

Journalists from all of the major newspapers rushed to review the exhibition. According to the savvy Christian Social press, the exhibition, which Lueger had originally opposed, embodied the "proverbial" loyalty that the Viennese, under Christian Social leadership, have for their emperor.[113] The Christian Social press was not alone in its efforts to place its stamp on the events. The *Neue Freie Presse* quoted Franz Joseph's opening remarks, in which he spoke of "productive classes," as a welcome acknowledgment of the achievements of the former liberal leadership of Vienna and of the Cisleithanian parliament.[114]

Critics did not ignore the obvious gap between the all-Austrian rhetoric used to advertise and describe the exhibition and the reality of the items on display. German nationalists pointed out the absence of any common Austrian spirit in the exhibition. For them, the exhibition did not provide evidence that all the peoples were ready to work together under the Habsburgs, but only revealed "that the Germans are to thank for all of the cultural advances in Austria." According to the Pan-Germans, "Austria's importance in the economic life of the peoples," despite the claims of the Slavs and the ongoing "Judaization" (*Verjudung*) of Austrian culture, derived only from the German *Volk*.[115]

The Galician press gave the exhibition a mixed reception. Democratic *Słowo Polskie* and the official *Gazeta Lwowska* described the huge crowds and the pomp and excitement of the opening celebrations. These papers commended the jubilee exhibition for surpassing the 1873 world's fair and the many pavilions as the work of talented new architects.[116] The clerical-nationalist *Głos Narodu* criticized the supposed Jewish control over food concessions, but still lauded the exhibition: "next to this magnificent dynastic celebration the socialist holiday of the first of May looked so sad."[117] The leftist *Kurjer Lwowski* took a far more skeptical view of the exhibition. With some justification, *Kurjer Lwowski* complained that "the Vienna exhibition neither gives a picture of economic development of Austria, nor of one Austrian province" nor did it display the history of the state over the past fifty years. Instead, this paper charged, the Vienna jubilee exhibition was only a collection of items available for purchase every day in the shopping streets of Vienna.[118]

In the late 1890s, the symbol of the emperor—interpreted and promoted by the imperial court and the government as the fulcrum of the state, the living embodiment of unity and tolerance in the multinational monarchy—was contested and redefined by political parties endeavoring to present their own interpretations of the Habsburg past, present, and future to potential voters. The Christian Social Party used the commemorations of the 1848 revolution, the city jubilee program, and the procession of children to attack their rivals and to wrap their own party in the black-and-yellow flag of Habsburg patriotism. Christian Social leaders spoke to large gatherings of Christian women, workers, and Christian Social associations, calling on all good Christian Socials to "buy only from Christians, to raise the children Christian and patriotic, and to reject the unwholesome Jewish press."[119] God and Kaiser became symbols of the Christian Social Party claim to be the sole defender of the Christian-German-patriotic middle classes.

Ritual speeches, award presentations, and group singing combined to create a predictable and powerful Christian Social ceremony granting a sacred status to the party elite and offering a common identity to those in the audience who joined their leaders in songs and cheers. Christian Social Party leaders deemed all opposed to their party's interpretation of imperial loyalty—German nationalists, liberals, and Social Democrats—traitors to the ideal Austria imagined in Christian Social Party publications. The other political parties worshipped the revolutionaries of 1848, who allegedly ushered in Jewish domination, but the Christian Social Party mobilized large sectors of the population in support of German-Christian identity within a framework of imperial loyalty. The Christian Socials alone stood for Christian values and Christian patriotism. The Christian Socials even used the Kaiser Jubilee Exhibition—a great tourist draw if far from the all-Austrian patriotic extravaganza originally planned by its liberal organizers—to enhance their party's patriotic profile.

For the Christian Social leadership, the fact that the emperor was a living being and not just an inanimate marble bust decorating the stage during patriotic gatherings was almost an inconvenience. The Christian Socials preferred to remake the emperor in their own image, to set him in the context of their own propaganda, and to use him to legitimize their dominant position in Vienna. Official celebrations and publications portrayed the "good Austrian" as one who treasured his/her own ethnicity but understood that the emperor was father of all the peoples and protector of all religions in the lands represented in the Reichsrat. Christian Social jubilee celebrations and jubilee rhetoric, on the other hand, married virulent anti-Semitism, German identity, and imperial loyalty into a new and exclusionary definition of the Good Austrian.

Conclusion

"Who are you? Who asks to enter here?"

"I am his Majesty the emperor of Austria, king of Hungary. I am the Emperor Franz Joseph Apostolic king of Hungary, king of Bohemia, king of Jerusalem, grand prince of Transylvania, grand duke of Tuscany and of Cracow, duke of Lorraine and of Salzburg . . ."

"I do not know him. Who asks to enter here?"

Only when, on his knees, [grand court master] Prince Montenuovo began again: "I am Franz Joseph, a poor sinner, and I beg God for mercy," did the voice behind the door give permission to enter: "Enter, then."[1]

The devotion to ritualized duty that had organized Franz Joseph's life framed even his last hours and structured the rituals surrounding his internment. On 20 November 1916, after reading through reports from the front and just before falling asleep for the last time, Franz Joseph ordered his body-servant to return to him at 3:30 A.M. the next morning—since the outbreak of the First World War he had risen each morning even earlier than his previous habit of 4:30 in order to conduct the business of state. Immediately after his death, his body was dressed in the uniform of a field marshal and displayed for several days in the Hofburg. Thousands of Viennese were let in to the court chapel to view the deceased emperor. On 30 November the *Hofstaat,* foreign dignitaries and princes, and members of the imperial family joined the procession from the imperial palace around the Ring and through the inner city to St. Stephen's for the funeral service (Figure 56). The funeral procession then walked the short distance to the Capuchin church, where, according to legend, Grand Court Master Montenuovo spoke for the emperor in the traditional exchange with the Capuchin abbot, confirming the pious character of the deceased ruler, before the body could be received into the Habsburg family crypt.

His death and internment reflected the dual nature of his reign. Franz Joseph did not live outside of the times; the emperor was not a baroque demi-god, but rather a pious and charitable human being whose personal qualities, like those attributed to Rudolf I, justified his place on the throne. He had been Prince of Peace, Warlord, and First Bureaucrat. He had rejected luxury in his personal life and devoted himself to duty. His asceticism, thrift, and simplicity had continued trends long discernible within the Habsburg family. At the same time, Franz

Figure 56: Franz Joseph's Funeral Procession Leaving the Hofburg. Museum of the City of Vienna.

Joseph's commitment to court ritual separated him from other mortals, bolstering the significance of his persona.

The vitality of Habsburg imperial ritual declined in the years before Franz Joseph's death. Yet, at its height, as jubilee events in Bohemia in 1898 attest, the imperial cult could inspire acts of loyalty, even if it could not paper over deep divisions in Habsburg society. In 1898, Czech- and German-speaking Bohemians named schools, horse races, new wings of hospitals, town squares, and military-veteran relief funds after Franz Joseph.[2] Signs of opposition to the imperial message of unity, however, were also in evidence. Large-scale Czech celebrations of Jan Hus and František Palacký competed with jubilee celebrations in the summer months, and several dozen flyers sporting the image of an ox-head with the imperial initials "FJI" were distributed in Prague on Franz Joseph's birthday.[3]

The September death of the empress underscored Franz Joseph's image as a long-suffering and well-intentioned martyr to peace and harmony, but even the 1898 anniversary of Franz Joseph's accession to the throne was not spared from partisan bickering. On 25 November Pan-German members of the Reichsrat walked out of the parliamentary chamber just before the special jubilee sitting. Pan-German leader Georg von Schönerer raged against the alleged pro-Slav and anti-German orientation of the government:

> ... I and my colleagues in conviction will not be present in the next so-called Jubilee-Sitting, since in our opinion men with German national convictions cannot participate in declarations of loyalty and manifestations of homage at this time and for as long as the illegal coercive [Badeni] language ordinances exist . . .[4]

The Pan-Germans were not the only representatives to boycott the jubilee session. The Social Democrats also, if more quietly, absented themselves from the Reichsrat commemoration.[5]

The day before the jubilee sitting, Galician peasant, Jewish, and social democratic deputies traded charges and counter-charges for some ten hours over the state of emergency that had been instituted in the western counties of Galicia during the summer and fall months in response to a wave of anti-Jewish riots.[6] The violence evidenced the challenge to conservative hegemony raised by the spread of social democracy in Galicia and the rise of peasant parties. Beginning in May, anti-Semitic thugs rioted in the western districts of the province, some apparently inspired by propaganda spread during a heated election campaign that Franz Joseph's son Rudolf was alive and had given permission for peasants to beat Jews and destroy Jewish property.[7] In August, the peasant newspaper *Związek Chłopski*, which blamed the riots on Jewish tavern keepers for allegedly corrupting the peasantry with drink, indebtedness, and bad morals, addressed the rioting in a birthday address to the emperor:

> Your Majesty! The grace of almighty God has brought you to the fiftieth anniversary [of your] accession to the throne! Lower yourself to remember your faithful Galician people, and how at one time you mercifully consented to order the liberation of this people from the yoke of serfdom—just so may you now mercifully consent to order the lifting of the law of *propinacya* [the alcohol monopoly, often administered by Jews] in Galicia.[8]

On 26 November, the day after the jubilee sitting, the bitter negotiations between the two halves of the monarchy on renewing the Compromise once again dominated the headlines.

The official celebrations for the 1908 sixtieth jubilee were designed to outdo those planned (and cancelled) for 1898. With no tragedy in the imperial family, the official program of festivities—from a court soirée to a court theater production—were carried out. Wilhelm II even led the princes of the German states and the mayors of the free cities of the German Empire to Vienna for a special homage to Franz Joseph. Government newspapers printed more patriotic editorials; the government, court, and army again minted millions of jubilee medals eventually handed out in ceremonies in every corner of Cisleithania on 2 December. The Cisleithanian government attempted, with some limited success, to join charitable activity undertaken throughout the monarchy into one unified action labeled "For the Child."[9] Habsburg citizens contributed large amounts to charity. More hospitals, schools, and parks were named after Franz Joseph; professional patriots produced another wave of commemorative books. Millions of citizens participated in *Volksfeste,* small patriotic gatherings, and religious celebrations in honor of the emperor.[10] City governments, voluntary societies, manufacturers, bakers, and candy-makers sent decorated addresses of congratulations to the emperor (in figure 57, the frame around the address, the imperial insignia, and the likeness of Franz Joseph are formed from sugar paste). Karl Lueger mobilized the resources of the city of Vienna for a series of celebrations, including another mass patriotic performance by the children of the city. This time 80,000 children participated in a pageant for the teary-eyed emperor in the gardens of Schönbrunn Palace while actresses from the Burgtheater portrayed Vindobona and Austria. With no court mourning, illuminations transformed all the lands and kingdoms represented in the Reichsrat into a sea of patriotic fire.

Figure 57: 1908 Address from Confectioner Julius Hava. Austrian National Library.

Figure 58: Harvest in Podolia, Galician Group, 1908 Kaiser-Huldigungs-Festzug. From Kaiser-Huldigungs-Festzug Wien Juni 1908. Eine Schilderung und Erklärung seiner Gruppen. Wien, 1908.

The most elaborate single jubilee event of 1908 was the *Kaiser-Huldigungs-Festzug* in Vienna, organized at the instigation of the city government by a commission led by Graf Hans Wilczek and dominated by liberal-leaning Habsburg-loyal nobles and notables once close to Franz Joseph's son Rudolf. Over 12,000 marched around the Ring in this colorful extravaganza. The first part of the procession depicted scenes from Habsburg history, with characters often portrayed by their descendants. The highlight of the procession was the spectacular "ethnographic" section. Delegations from the crownlands, dressed in decorative versions of peasant and national costumes designed by provincial artists, many astride horses or posing on lavishly adorned wagons, participated. Peasant groups from Bosnia and Galicia, dubbed "the largest and most beautiful of the subgroups due to the elegance and variety of the costumes," drew the cheers of the crowds (figure 58).[11] Some 300,000–500,000 witnessed the *Festzug*, many thousands drawn to Vienna from all parts of the monarchy by advertisements in provincial newspapers offering Ringstrasse views of the *Festzug* and hotel rooms at discount rates.[12] Programs, brochures, commemorative books, and souvenirs were sold throughout the monarchy, and articles in provincial newspapers spread details about this and other events to millions outside the Cisleithanian capital. The message was clear: all the peoples of the monarchy could enjoy the security to develop their national cultures under the watchful eye of the Prince of Peace, Franz Joseph.[13]

The keeper of the ceremonial protocol recorded his hopes that this great demonstration of dynastic patriotism revealed the true feelings of a population often seemingly divided by insurmountable national and political divisions:

> Although it cannot be the task of the Keeper of the Ceremonial Protocol to go beyond the description of court ceremonial proceedings and to also relate the impressions and atmosphere, still it is permitted to him in this case to say that the 12th of June 1908 will establish a lasting memory for young and old; since entirely aside from the fantastic success of this splendid act of homage, for weeks, not only in Vienna, but in the entire monarchy, a festival mood has reigned, which has triggered the warmest interest even in the most distant foreign lands.
>
> Everyone prepared themselves for the greatest Kaiser-Homage, and in this era of upsetting party passions and national hatreds, all peoples saw only the image of the Kaiser framed with the glorious light of devotion and true love, and as the nationalities in great strong groups in most clear joy passed by, there were few eyes that remained dry.[14]

However, even the 1908 homage procession, conceived as a great statement of supranational unity, failed to meet the expectations of its creators. The Bohemian Czechs boycotted the procession over a dispute concerning a Czech theater performance in Vienna. The Polish delegation threatened to join the boycott when they learned that the historical group depicting the 1683 siege of Vienna would have Jan II Sobieski, the king of Poland who came to Vienna's rescue, ride behind Habsburg emperor Leopold I. Eventually it was agreed that King Sobieski and Emperor Leopold would ride side by side, diffusing this petty conflict. Ruthenians complained of the overrepresentation of Poles in the delegations, which they saw as yet another attempt by the Polish elites to portray Galicia as a purely Polish province.[15] Finally, the procession, representing Cisleithania, included no Hungarian delegation. In Hungary Franz Joseph was recognized only as Hungarian king. The absence of representatives from the Hungarian half of the monarchy demonstrated the complicated and problematic nature of the structure of the Dual Monarchy.

Special editions of the mainstream press devoted their coverage of the event to detailed descriptions and illustrations of the procession; however, reviews of the procession were not uniformly positive. The *Neue Freie Presse,* for example, highlighted the absence of the Czechs and the dispute in the Galician groups, and stressed that the procession only demonstrated again the central role of the Austro-Germans in the life of the monarchy and the threat of Slavic nationalism to the integrity of the state.[16]

During the 1908 jubilee year, liberals honored the emperor as the patron of liberal ideals; Christian Socials proclaimed their imperial loyalty while attacking Jews and political opponents. In Bohemia, most of the dozens of Kaiser busts, statues, and plaques unveiled in 1908 expressed Austro-German national sentiment rather than supra-national ideals.[17] Many Bohemian Germans perceived the rising power and influence of Czechs within Bohemia as a grave threat to their previously protected position and marked towns and regions as German territory with monuments to the emperor. Choirs singing in German, German voluntary societies, and Austro-German women in white dresses joined in the unveilings. Mayors spoke of the Germanness of Franz Joseph and their hope that the Cisleithanian government would again realize the contributions of Germans to the culture and economy of the state.[18] Perhaps most telling, in the intermission of the court theater production in the court opera in Vienna, just after the presentation of a revised and shortened version of Thun-Salm's *The Emperor's Dream* and just before a series of dances depicting the ethnic diversity and harmony of the monarchy, Franz Joseph was informed that a state of emergency had been declared in Prague as a result of violent Czech-German street confrontations. In Bohemia, by 1908, national conflict threatened to overwhelm the jubilee spirit.[19]

However, it is too easy to be blinded by the cynical Vienna press or the fact that national and social conflicts were not erased by spectacular imperial celebrations and to interpret jubilee celebrations as nothing more than failed attempts to bolster a non-existent patriotism. Certainly imperial celebrations served to highlight divisions in society, but these difficulties did not, for the most part, reflect antagonism toward the emperor or the state itself. The culture of imperial celebration was well entrenched. The most outspoken opponents of centrally organized celebrations like the 1908 *Festzug* or the 1898 jubilee exhibition, with the exception of the radical Pan-Germans who for all their dramatic extremism enjoyed only modest popularity, did not reject the notion of state unity or of loyalty to the crown. If the dream of ethnic harmony proved elusive and complicated efforts to stage truly supranational celebrations, millions of Czech, German, Polish, and Ruthenian speakers continued to commemorate the emperor, even if they often did so within their respective national communities and therefore experienced imperial celebrations as part of their national orientation.

The official messages transmitted to the population by the 1908 procession and the 1898/1908 jubilee theater production did not assume the end of national consciousness, and the fact that national conflict continued to exist did not detract from the attractiveness of a message calling for national self-expression and supra-national loyalty. Both the jubilee play, written in 1898 and performed in 1908, and the 1908 homage procession had portrayed the monarchy as a haven for the cultivation of national cultures. National identity and supra-national loyalty were to coexist. Polishness/Czechness/Germanness was defined as an important element of a higher loyalty to the imperial house and through the dynasty to the larger "Austrian" community and to the state itself. In 1900 (Franz Joseph's seventieth birthday), 1908, and 1910 (his eightieth birthday), Habsburg citizens continued to show loyalty to the emperor by participating actively in birthday celebrations and charity drives. On 2 December 1908, surveying the official and popular celebrations that took place during the jubilee year, the keeper of the ceremonial protocol could still write with conviction that "Whatever storms and thunder clouds have arisen, in one feeling all joined together: in the sincere fervent love for the Monarch!"[20]

The demise of imperial celebration—and the demise of the monarchy itself—came as a by-product of the devastation wrought by the First World War, not as the result of nationalities conflicts. Imperial celebration in the constitutional era tried at once to distance Franz Joseph from political controversies and to associate him, and through him the state he led, with concrete improvements in the lives of the populace. Court celebrations ignored specific historical events, but portrayed Franz Joseph as the Father of the Peoples. Official and semi-official sources proclaimed the emperor the guarantor of constitutional rights, patron of the armed forces, and prince of peace. Franz Joseph, who championed economic and cultural advance, assured his peoples that social and economic change could be reconciled with tradition. Perhaps most importantly, the emperor's adherence to ceremonies rooted in the legend of Habsburg piety and charity made him the symbol of a state that strove (if with mixed success) to meet the material interests of the population.

Even the benevolent Father of the Peoples, however, could not be the Prince of Peace in the midst of war. During World War I, the aging emperor could not dedicate bridges, attend balls, or walk in magnificent processions while his subjects were dying on the front and hungry at home. With war rationing and the creation of a war-driven economy, petitions to the court asking for financial assistance from the emperor became too numerous to meet with even token amounts.[21] The gap between the narrative of Habsburg legitimacy based on the notion of the state as the executor of the benevolent will of the emperor and the reality of the dislocation caused by war became too great. When Franz Joseph died, the emperor once hailed as the living embodiment of the "Austrian Idea," the creator of peace and prosperity, and the guarantor of ethnic and social interests had become something his grand court masters had tried to prevent throughout his long reign: Franz Joseph had become largely irrelevant to lives preoccupied with survival.

Franz Joseph would seem an unlikely subject for a study of charisma. Franz Joseph lacked the wise foresight and personal magnetism of Maria Theresa; he had none of the erratic brilliance of Joseph II. He was not a great speaker or dramatic man of the people. Nonetheless, this study of imperial celebration has been a study of the charisma of Franz Joseph. Clifford Geertz defines charisma as "a sign of involvement with the animating centers of society."[22] Under Franz Joseph, the Habsburg court endeavored to reassert the charisma of the emperor, to symbolically return him to the "center of things," from which the dynasty had been banished by revolution. The renewal of court ceremony reaffirmed the sacred nature of the political authority wielded by the pious emperor whose right to rule had been acknowledged by God and church. Imperial rituals and celebrations were opportunities to reinforce imperial loyalty and to communicate ideas about the unity of the state through the promotion of the imperial image.

In the first decade of his reign, the court and government allowed relatively little public competition to define the symbol of the emperor. Censorship and police controls limited the development of a public sphere and retarded the growth of political movements. The print media celebrated the youthful emperor whose strong hand guaranteed order and peace. The young Franz Joseph symbolized the vigorous centralizing neoabsolutist state.

After the institution of constitutional government, the dynasty had to confront the increasing political mobilization of society. In Cisleithania, the German liberals and the dynasty both claimed to control the fate of the monarchy; both claimed the power to ensure unity and stability. Under Taaffe, faced with the rise of national movements, the court and Cisleithanian government presented imperial loyalty and "Austrian" patriotism as complementary rather than as an alternative to ethnic identity. This vision meshed well with the goals of the Polish elites, and in many ways the 1880 imperial inspection tour of Galicia represented the ideal monarchy Taaffe's system sought to create: a working political system based on the mutual interests of the dynasty, its government, and provincial elites secure in their own power. However, this ideal political system never existed in practice. Facing constant pressure from below to deliver on national and social demands, the Polish conservatives used the presence of the emperor to symbolically confirm their own political authority.

In the 1890s, with the expansion of the electoral franchise, peasant, nationalist, and socialist leaders felt compelled to offer competing interpretations of imperial celebrations, incorporating Habsburg or alternative heroes into alternative narratives of the monarchy's past, present, and future. Local and provincial elites also sought political advantage, cultivating the image of the emperor to bolster their own positions. Lueger's Christian Social Party, for example, used imperial celebrations to define Austro-German identity as compatible with Habsburg patriotism. The Christian Socials declared themselves to be the only loyalist representatives of the Austro-German national community and defenders against the threats of radical nationalism and the socialist challenge. More radical and less successful political factions did make some symbolic statements countering dynastic patriotism. Schönerer's German nationalists denied the possibility of German-Austrian imperial loyalty and refused to participate in patriotic manifestations. Nationalists, socialists, and liberals paid tribute to the revolutionaries of 1848 rather than Franz Joseph, the beneficiary of the conservative reaction.

The decision in 1898 to break with the emperor's own reticence and appeal directly to the population for imperial loyalty was a reaction to the perceived danger of nationalism. Official publications did not denounce national culture and identity, but offered respect and loyalty for the emperor as a means of fulfilling legitimate ethnic interests and ameliorating national tensions. Imperial celebrations presented both the larger-than-life ceremonial persona and the supposedly moral and quietly heroic qualities of Franz Joseph, the tireless and self-sacrificing father of all the monarchy's peoples. The court, government, church, and army reaffirmed the central importance of the dynasty and associated Franz Joseph, and through him the state, with the concrete achievements gained by each national and social group through Austrian unity and peace.

This was not a simple message to convey. The Dualist system complicated the efforts of the center to foster a unified patriotism. In the Hungarian half of the monarchy, Hungarian liberals increasingly defined Franz Joseph as a symbol of Hungarian national pride, rather than as the symbol of a fatherland held in common with the many peoples living in the lands and kingdoms represented in the Reichsrat. In Cisleithania, nationalities conflicts and social tensions belied the promise of ethnic peace and harmony under the Habsburg scepter.

Yet, the outpouring of voluntary expressions of imperial loyalty all over Cisleithania suggested to sponsors of imperial celebrations that the message of unity did resonate with much of the population. The continued attraction of imperial celebrations also mirrored other trends within the monarchy in the decades before World War I. These years were marked by intensifying national conflicts as well as by vigorous participation in electoral politics at the local and regional levels, expansion of public services, state administration, and public education systems, and active service by millions of Habsburg citizens in the armed forces and military reserves. The monarchy was becoming a modern state, and its population was actively participating in modern citizenship.

Under Franz Joseph, the potential constituencies of national movements and of all the parties represented in the Reichsrat prayed for the emperor's health on his birthday, traveled many miles to witness the imperial visage passing by on a train, donated money to build churches and fund charitable institutions in the name of the ruler, bought postcards, cups, pamphlets, portraits, and stamps on the occasion of imperial jubilees. Although the constitutional government, imperial court, church, and army could no longer monopolize public discussion of the importance of the dynasty, imperial celebrations grounded loyalty to the dynasty in the natural order of things, claimed the past, present, and future for the House of Habsburg, and seemed to confirm, at least for a moment, the existence of an imagined community of "Austria."[23]

NOTES

Introduction

1. Many towns in the Habsburg Monarchy had multiple place names. In order to avoid privileging particular national claimants, I employ English place names—Cracow, for example—whenever possible. In cases where English names do not exist and where two or more national movements laid claim to the area, I list the major variants on first usage and thereafter refer to the town by the German name used by the central administration in Vienna. I use the names given by local inhabitants for towns that were not subject to such national rivalry.

2. DALO, 350/1/3006/16 [Pr. 2191, 27 December 1908. Imperial-Royal Presidium of the Governor to Lemberg Police-Direction]. Podhalicz's original letter from 4 November is held in TSDIA-L: 146/4/3140/52–54. Today, trains crawl the distance from Lemberg to Vienna in 18–24 hours.

3. Imperial celebration encompasses the rules of court etiquette, ritualized ceremonies that took place among small groups within the imperial palace, public church processions in which the emperor played a specific role, and large-scale public festivities such as the emperor's birthday, jubilees, and inspection tours.

4. On nationalism and public space, see Harald Binder, "Making and Defending a Polish Town: 'Lwów' (Lemberg) 1848–1914," *AHY* (2003); Robert Nemes, "The Politics of the Dance Floor: Culture and Civil Society in Nineteenth-Century Hungary," *Slavic Review* 60/4 (2001); *Staging the Past: The Politics of Commemoration in Habsburg Central Europe, 1848 to the Present*, ed. Maria Bucur and Nancy M. Wingfield (West Lafayette, 2001); Alice Freifeld, *Nationalism and the Crowd in Liberal Hungary, 1848–1918* (Baltimore, 2000); Patrice M. Dabrowski, "Folk, Faith and Fatherland: Defining the Polish Nation in 1883," *Nationalities Papers* 28/3 (September 2000). The essays collected in the two-volume *Speicher des Gedächtnisses*, ed. Moritz Csáky and Peter Stachel (Wien, 2000, 2001) consider national and supranational collective memory in Central Europe. See also Alon Confino, *The Nation as a Local Metaphor: Württemberg, Imperial Germany and National Memory, 1871–1918* (Chapel Hill and London, 1997) and John Gillis, ed., *Commemorations: The Politics of National Identity* (Princeton, 1994). Scholarship on collective or public memory draws from Pierre Nora and Maurice Halbwachs: Nora, *Realms of Memory: The Construction of the French Past*, (New York, 1996–1998), originally published as *Les Lieux de mémoire* (Paris, 1984–1992); Halbwachs, *On Collective Memory* (Chicago, 1992). See also David Schacter, ed., *Memory Distortion: How Minds, Brains and Societies Reconstruct the Past* (Cambridge, Mass., 1995).

5. This is forcefully argued in Jeremy King, *Budweisers into Czechs and Germans: A Local History of Bohemian Politics, 1848–1948* (Princeton, 2002).

6. Clifford Geertz, "Centers, Kings, and Charisma: Reflections on the Symbolics of

Power," in Geertz, *Local Knowledge: Further Essays in Interpretive Anthropology* (New York, 1983), 123–124.

7.   Gary B. Cohen, "Neither Absolutism nor Anarchy: New Narratives on Society and Government in Late Imperial Austria," *AHY* (1998) (1), 37; James Shedel, "*Fin de Siècle* or *Jahrhundertwende:* The Question of an Austrian *Sonderweg,*" in *Rethinking Vienna 1900*, ed. Steven Beller (New York, 2001). On the German *Sonderweg,* or special path to modernization, see above all David Blackbourn and Geoff Eley, *The Peculiarities of German History: Bourgeois Society and Politics in Nineteenth-Century Germany* (New York and Oxford, 1984).

8.   According to Joachim Whaley, "The Habsburg monarchy embodied the antithesis of the major historical force of the nineteenth century, namely nationalism." Whaley, "Austria, 'Germany', and the Dissolution of the Holy Roman Empire," in Ritchie Robertson and Edward Timms, eds., *The Habsburg Legacy* (Edinburgh, 1994), 9. See also Solomon Wank, "Some Reflections on the Habsburg Empire and Its Legacy in the Nationalities Question," *AHY* (1997), 131–146; A. J. P. Taylor, *The Habsburg Monarchy, 1809–1918* (London, 1948). Alan Sked discusses historians' treatment of national strife within the monarchy in *Historians, the Nationality Question, and the Downfall of the Habsburg Empire* (London, 1981) and *The Decline and Fall of the Habsburg Empire 1815–1918* (London, 1989).

9.   Peter Alter, *Nationalism*, 2nd ed. (London and New York, 1994); E. J. Hobsbawm, *Nations and Nationalism since 1780: Programme, Myth, Reality* (Cambridge, 1990); Ernest Gellner, *Nations and Nationalism* (Ithaca, 1983); Benedict Anderson, *Imagined Communities: Reflections on the Origin and Spread of Nationalism* (London, 1983); Miroslav Hroch, *Social Preconditions for National Revival in Europe* (Cambridge, 1985).

10.   For a convincing refutation of this argument, see Rogers Brubaker, *Nationalism Reframed: Nationhood and the National Question in the New Europe* (Cambridge, 1996), 13–22.

11.   Anthony Smith, *The Ethnic Origins of Nations* (Oxford, 1986), 13.

12.   Alexander Motyl, "From Imperial Decay to Imperial Collapse: The Fall of the Soviet Empire in Comparative Perspective," in Richard Rudolph and David Good, eds., *Nationalism and Empire: The Habsburg Empire and the Soviet Union* (New York, 1992), 15–43; Solomon Wank, "The Disintegration of the Habsburg and Ottoman Empires" in Karen Dawisha and Bruce Parrott, eds., *The End of Empire? The Transformation of the USSR in Comparative Perspective* (Armonk, 1997).

13.   John Boyer, *Political Radicalism in Late Imperial Vienna: Origins of the Christian Social Movement, 1848–1897* (Chicago, 1981), xiv. Cohen quotes this passage in "Neither Absolutism nor Anarchy," p. 38.

14.   Gary Cohen, *Education and Middle-Class Society in Imperial Austria, 1848–1918* (West Lafayette, 1996); Michael Palairet, "The Habsburg Industrial Achievement in Bosnia-Hercogovina, 1878–1914: An Economic Spurt That Succeeded?" *AHY* (1993); John Komlos, *Economic Development in the Habsburg Monarchy and in the Successor States* (Boulder, 1990); David Good, *The Economic Rise of the Habsburg Empire, 1750–1914* (Berkeley, 1984); John Komlos, *The Habsburg*

Monarchy as a Customs Union: Economic Development in Austria-Hungary in the Nineteenth Century (Princeton, 1983).

15. Marsha Rozenblit, *Reconstructing a National Identity: The Jews of Habsburg Austria during World War I* (Oxford and New York, 2001).

16. Above all, see King, *Budweisers in Czechs and Germans.*

17. Eric Hobsbawm, "Mass-Producing Traditions: Europe, 1870–1914," in Eric Hobsbawm and Terence Ranger, eds., *The Invention of Tradition* (Cambridge, 1983), 263–307.

18. John Plunkett, *Queen Victoria: First Media Monarch* (Oxford, 2003).

19. Scholarship on the post-unification imperial German court is much more extensive than that on the Habsburg court. German historians have considered the erosion of legitimacy of the imperial German court system among the upper nobility, yet point to the surprising flexibility and power of the Hohenzollern imperial cult as a mode of identification in German society. Isabel Hull, "Prussian Dynastic Ritual and the End of Monarchy," in Carole Fink, Isabel Hull, and MacGregor Knox, eds., *German Nationalism and the European Response, 1890–1945* (Norman, 1985), 13–41; Elizabeth Fehrenbach, "Images of Kaiserdom," in John C. G. Röhl, ed., *Kaiser Wilhelm II: New Interpretations* (Cambridge, 1982), 269–285; Röhl, *Kaiser, Hof und Staat: Wilhelm II und die deutsche Politik* (Munich, 1987). Werner Blessing's study of the Catholic Wittelsbachs' royal cult provides an interesting comparison with the Habsburgs': Blessing, *Staat und Kirche in der Gesellschaft. Institutionelle Autorität und mentaler Wandel in Bayern während des 19. Jahrhunderts* (Göttingen, 1982); Blessing, "The Cult of Monarchy." On the Russian dynasty's claim to embodying the Russian people, see Richard Wortman, *Scenarios of Power: Myth and Ceremony in Russian Monarchy,* vols. 1, 2 (Princeton, 1995, 2000).

20. Oscar Jaszi, *The Dissolution of the Habsburg Monarchy* (Chicago, 1929), 433. According to Jaszi, the state schools, though avoiding any reference in textbooks that might offend various national groupings, did little to foster a common identity. Schoolbooks presented the history of the state only through history of the Habsburg family. Curricula placed little emphasis on the role of the peoples in their own history. However, I would argue that school textbooks as well as official publications greeting various imperial celebrations did offer some "civic education convincing the various peoples of the monarchy of the necessity and advantages of a mutual, economic and cultural co-operation," if not "under the patronage of a free federal state," as Jaszi would have preferred, at least under the patronage of the imperial family and the government appointed by the Habsburg emperor.

21. Important works on the Habsburg and other premodern European courts include: Jeroen Duindam, *Vienna and Versailles: The Courts of Europe's Dynastic Rivals, 1550–1780* (Cambridge, 2003); Karin J. MacHardy, *War, Religion and Court Patronage in Habsburg Austria: The Social and Cultural Dimensions of Political Interaction, 1521–1622* (New York, 2003); *The Princely Courts of Europe: Ritual, Politics and Culture under the Ancien Regime, 1500–1750*, ed. John Adamson (London, 1999); Peter Burke, *The Fabrication of Louis XIV* (New Haven, 1992); Marie Tanner, *The Last Descendant of Aeneas: The Habsburgs*

and the Mythic Image of the Emperor (New Haven, 1992); Christina Hofmann, *Das spanische Hofzeremoniell von 1500–1700* (Frankfurt, 1985); August Buck and Georg Kauffmann, eds., *Europäische Hofkultur im 16. und 17. Jahrhundert* (Hamburg, 1981); Hubert Ch. Ehalt, *Ausdrucksformen absolutistischer Herrschaft: Der Wiener Hof im 17. und 18. Jahrhundert* (Wien, 1980); A. G. Dickens, ed., *The Courts of Europe: Politics, Patronage and Royalty, 1400–1800* (London, 1977); Norbert Elias, *Die höfische Gesellschaft; Untersuchungen zur Soziologie des Königtums und der höfischen Aristokratie mit einer Einleitung: Soziologie und Geschichtwissenschaft* (Berlin, 1969); Ernst Kantorowicz, *The King's Two Bodies: A Study in Medieval Political Theology* (Princeton, 1957); and Ludwig Pfandl, "Philipp II. Und die Einführung des burgundischen Hofzeremoniells in Spanien," *Historisches Jahrbuch* 58 (1938), 1–33.

22. Richard Wortman, *Scenarios of Power;* Karl Ferdinand Werner, ed., *Hof, Kultur und Politik im 19. Jahrhundert* (Bonn, 1985); Wilentz, ed., *Rites of Power;* Thomas Richards, *The Commodity Culture of Victorian England: Advertising and Spectacle, 1851–1914* (Stanford, 1990). For festivals and the French Revolution: Mona Ozouf, *Festivals and the French Revolution* (Cambridge, 1988); and Lynn Hunt, *Politics, Culture and Class in the French Revolution* (Berkeley, 1984).

23. The most extensive recent study of Franz Joseph's court, for example, documents the career of his last grand court master, Alfred Montenuovo, looks at his role in Viennese culture as the overseer of the court opera, the court theater, and the art and natural history museums on the Ringstrasse, and concentrates on his biography and relations with members of the imperial family. Margit Silber, "Obersthofmeister Alfred Fürst von Montenuovo. Höfische Geschichte in den beiden letzten Jahrzehnten der österreichisch-ungarischen Monarchie (1897–1916)" (Ph.D. Diss., University of Vienna, 1987). A number of articles treat aspects of the structure and ceremony of the Habsburg court. Franz Dirnberger, "Das Wiener Hofzeremoniell bis in die Zeit Franz Josephs. Überlegungen über Probleme, Entstehung und Bedeutung," in *Das Zeitalter Kaiser Franz Josephs,* 1. Teil: *Von der Revolution zur Gründerzeit 1848–1880* (Wien, 1984), 42–48; Brigitte Hamann, "Der Wiener Hof und die Hofgesellschaft in der zweiten Hälfte des 19. Jahrhunderts," in Karl Möckl, ed., *Hof und Hofgesellschaft in den deutschen Staaten im 19 und beginnenden 20. Jahrhundert* (Boppard am Rhein, 1990), 61–78. The most comprehensive overview of the structure of the Habsburg court remains Ivan Žolger, *Der Hofstaat des Hauses Österreich* (Wien, 1917).

24. On Franz Joseph's imperial visitations, see Petra Promintzer, "Die Reisen Kaiser Franz Josephs (1848–1867)" (Ph.D. Diss., University of Vienna, 1967). Considerably more interesting are two articles by the late Wrocław historian Zbigniew Fras: "Mit dobrego Cesarza," *Polskie mity polityczne XIX i XX wieku* (Wrocław, 1988), and "Podróże cesarza Franciszka Józefa I do Galicji," in Mark Czapliński, Romualda Gelles, and Krystyna Matwijowski, eds., *Z dziejów Galicji, Śląska, Polski i Niemiec. Prace ofiarowane Profesorowi drowi Adamowi Galosowi w siedemdziesiątą rocznicę urodzin* (Wrocław, 1994). See also: Steven Beller,

"Kraus's Firework: State Consciousness Raising in the 1908 Jubilee Parade in Vienna and the Problem of Austrian Identity," in Wingfield and Bucur, *Staging the Past;* Andrea Blöchl, "Die Kaisergedenktage: Die Feste und Feiern zu den Regierungsjubiläen und runden Geburtstagen Kaiser Franz Josephs," in Emil Brix and Hannes Stekl, eds., *Der Kampf um das Gedächtnis. Öffentliche Gedenktage in Mitteleuropa* (Wien, 1997); Werner Telesko, "Die Wiener historischen Festzüge von 1879 und 1908. Zum Problem der dynastischen Identitätsfindung des Hauses Österreich," *Wiener Geschichtsblätter* 51(3): 133–146; Elisabeth Grossegger, *Der Kaiser-Huldigungs-Festzug Wien 1908* (Wien, 1992); James Shedel, "Emperor, Church, and People: Religion and Dynastic Loyalty during the Golden Jubilee of Franz Joseph," *The Catholic Historical Review* 76(1) (January, 1990), 71–92; and Martin Hecher, "Hans Makart und der Wiener Festzug von 1879" (Ph.D. Diss., University of Vienna, 1986). Andrew Wheatcroft, *The Habsburgs: Embodying Empire* (London, 1995) provides an overview of Habsburg self-presentation from its origin until the present day and includes brief discussions of imperial celebrations.

25.   Steven Beller portrays Franz Joseph's failures as among the main causes of the monarchy's demise in *Francis Joseph* (London and New York, 1996); Alan Palmer, *Twilight of the Habsburgs: The Life and Times of Emperor Francis Joseph* (London, 1994); Jean-Paul Bled devotes a chapter of his excellent biography of Franz Joseph to the imperial court, Bled, *Franz Joseph,* trans. T. Bridgeman (Oxford, 1987). E. Conte Corti's 1950s three-volume biography of Franz Joseph and Joseph Redlich's *Emperor Francis Joseph of Austria: A Biography* (New York, 1929) also briefly discuss the Habsburg imperial court.

26.   Laurence Cole, "Vom Glanz der Montur. Zum dynastischen Kult der Habsburger und seiner Vermittlung durch militärische Vorbilder im 19. Jahrhundert" *Österreichische Zeitschrift für Geschichtswissenschaften* (1996) (4): 577–591; István Deák, *Beyond Nationalism: A Social History of the Habsburg Officer Corps* (Oxford, 1990).

27.   Laurence Cole, *'Für Gott, Kaiser und Vaterland': Nationale Identität der deutschsprachigen Bevölkerung Tirols 1860–1914* (Frankfurt and New York, 2000); T. Mills Kelly, "Taking It to the Streets: Czech National Socialists in 1908," *AHY* 29(1) (1998); Nancy Wingfield, "Pitched Battles in Public Places: How the Bohemian Lands Became Czech, 1880–1948" (unpublished manuscript); Hugh Agnew, article in preparation, "The Flyspecks in Palivec's Portrait: Francis Joseph, the Symbols of Monarchy, and Czech Popular Loyalty"; Andras Gerő, *Francis Joseph, King of the Hungarians* (New York, 2001); Alice Freifeld, article in preparation: "Empress Elisabeth as Hungarian Queen: The Uses of Celebrity Monarchism"; Patrice Dabrowski, *Commemorations and the Shaping of Modern Poland* (Bloomington, 2004).

28.   Peter Urbanitsch, "Pluralist Myth and Nationalist Realities: The Dynastic Myth of the Habsburg Monarchy—a Futile Exercise in the Creation of Identity?" *AHY* 35 (2004); Moritz Csáky and Klaus Zeyringer, eds., *Inszenierungen des kollektiven Gedächtnisses* (Innsbruck, 2002); Waltraud Heindl, "Idole und Erinnerung. Gedanken zu (religiösen) Mythen in Zentraleuropa," in Csáky

and Zeyringer, eds., *Pluralitäten, Religionen und kulturelle Codes* (Innsbruck, 2001); Ernst Bruckmüller, "Die österreichische Revolution von 1848 und der Habsburgermythos des 19. Jahrhunderts," in Hubert Lengauer and Primus Heinz Kucher, eds., *Bewegung in Reich der Immobilität* (Wien, 2001); Csáky and Zeyringer, eds., *Ambivalenz des kulturellen Erbes: Vielfachcodierung des historischen Gedächtnisses* (Innsbruck, 2000); Valdis Baidins, "Franz Joseph, Kaisertreue and Loyalty in the Late Habsburg Empire" (Ph.D. Diss., University of Washington, 1999); Bruckmüller, "Österreich: An Ehren und an Siegen reich," in Monika Flacke, ed., *Mythen der Nationen. Ein europäisches Panorama* (Berlin, 1998), 269–293; Leopold R. G. Decloedt, ed., *An meine Völker: Die Literarisierung Franz Joseph I.* (Bern, 1998). These and other works on Habsburg dynastic myths owe much to Claudio Magris, *Il mito absburgico nella letteratura austriaca moderna* (Torino, 1963).

29. On the imperial image in Hungary, see Andras Gerő, *Francis Joseph.*
30. According to Wortman, the elite included within the ceremonial world of the court "took on something of the sacral aura as well." Wortman, *Scenarios*, v. 1, 4.
31. See Geertz, "Centers, Kings, and Charisma."

Chapter 1

2. By November of 1848, Habsburg armies had suppressed uprisings in Galicia, Bohemia, the Italian lands, and Vienna. The Hungarian forces suffered a series of defeats at the hands of the Habsburg armies under Julius Haynau in the summer of 1849. By that time, however, Franz Joseph had already requested Russian intervention. The Hungarian military commander, Arthur Görgey, surrendered to the Russian, not the Habsburg army. See István Deák, *The Lawful Revolution: Louis Kossuth and the Hungarians, 1848–1849* (New York, 1979). On the revolutions of 1848–1849, see Jonathan Sperber, *The European Revolutions, 1848–1851* (Cambridge, 1994); John R. Rath, *The Viennese Revolution of 1848* (Austin, 1957); Priscilla Robertson, *Revolutions of 1848: A Social History* (Princeton, 1952).

2. On Franz Joseph's education, see Bled, *Franz Joseph*, 5–8; Egon Caesar Conte Corti, *Vom Kind zum Kaiser: Kindheit und erste Jugend Kaiser Franz Josephs I. und seiner Geschwister* (Graz, 1950).

3. Though some historians argue that Schwarzenberg did not in principle oppose constitutional government, Franz Joseph and Karl von Kübeck, head of the *Hofkammer* and later president of the Advisory Council, were never reconciled to the idea of ministerial responsibility to any representative body: Alan Sked, *The Decline and Fall*, 137–149; Bled, *Franz Joseph*, 55–56, 68–69; Rudolf Kiszling, *Fürst Felix Schwarzenberg* (1952). Franz Joseph was delighted to follow Kübeck's advice and end all pretense of constitutional rule in 1851: "We have thrown the constitution overboard and Austria now has only one ruler." Francis Schnürer, ed., *Briefe Kaiser Franz Josephs I. an seine Mutter, 1838–1872* (Munich, 1930), 166.

4. Harm-Hinrich Brandt, *Der österreichische Neoabsolutismus: Staatsfinanzen und Politik 1848–1860*, 2 vols. (Göttingen, 1978). Neoabsolutism remained in

place until military defeat and financial crisis in 1859 convinced the emperor of the need for real constitutional reform.

5. Richard Wortman, *Scenarios of Power.* For a comparison of the Habsburg and Romanov monarchies, see Orest Subtelny, "The Habsburg and Russian Empires: Some Comparisons and Contrasts," in Teruyuki Hara and Kimitaka Matsuzato, eds., *Empire and Society: New Approaches to Russian History* (Sapporo, 1997), 73–92.

6. The British dynasty completely dispensed with magic healing only after the Hanoverian succession in the early eighteenth century. The Bourbon kings of France continued to heal scrofula with the royal touch until the eve of the French Revolution. Charles X attempted a restoration of the practice when he tried to heal the afflicted at his coronation in 1821. See Marc Bloch, *The Royal Touch* (Paris, 1924).

7. From 1453–1806, the only time a Habsburg failed to win election as Holy Roman emperor was in the midst of the War for Austrian Succession. Backed by Frederick the Great, Charles Albert of Bavaria gained the crown in 1742. When this emperor expired in 1745, the Habsburg position was strong enough to win the crown for Maria Theresa's husband, Franz Stefan of Lorraine. Charles Ingrao, *The Habsburg Monarchy, 1618–1815* (Cambridge, 1994), 154–156; Adam Wandruszka, *Das Haus Habsburg. Die Geschichte einer europäischen Dynastie* (Wien, 1978).

8. For details, see Żolger, *Der Hofstaat des Hauses Österreich;* Dirnberger, "Das Wiener Hofzeremoniell bis in die Zeit Franz Josephs"; Ehalt, *Ausdrucksformen absolutistischer Herrschaft;* Hofmann, *Das spanische Hofzeremoniell;* Tanner, *The Last Descendant of Aeneas.*

9. Anna Coreth, *Pietas Austriaca. Österreichische Frömmigkeit im Barock* (Wien, 1982), 6.

10. On Leopold's personal piety and the Austrian baroque, see R. J. W. Evans, *The Making of the Habsburg Monarchy, 1550–1700* (Oxford, 1979), 117.

11. Jeroen Duindam, *Vienna and Versailles;* Karin J. MacHardy, *War, Religion and Court Patronage in Habsburg Austria;* Coreth, *Pietas;* Elisabeth Kovacs, "Kirchliches Zeremoniell," 109–142; On Ferdinand II, Ferdinand III, and Charles VI, Ingrao, *The Habsburg Monarchy,* 36–39, 120–126.

12. According to T.C.W. Blanning, "In Charles VI, baroque imperial culture had found its last and most splendid representative." Blanning, *Joseph II* (London and New York, 1994), 32.

13. Coreth, *Pietas,* 6.

14. On the festivals, theater, and baroque piety of the Habsburg courts in first half of the eighteenth century, see Karl Vocelka, *Glanz und Untergang der höfischenn Welt. Repräsentation, Reform, und Reaktion im habsburgischen Vielvölkerstaat* (Wien, 2001), 185–235.

15. Peter Baumgart, "Der deutsche Hof der Barockzeit als politische Institution," in Buck, Kauffmann, Spahr, and Wiedemann, eds., *Europäische Hofkultur,* vol. 1, 25–43; Ehalt, *Ausdrucksformen absolutistischer Herrschaft,* 118.

16. Ehalt, *Ausdrucksformen absolutistischer Herrschaft,* 118. Ehalt follows the work

of Norbert Elias, *Die höfische Gesellschaft. Untersuchungen zur Soziologie des Königtums und der höfischen Aristokratie* (1969). In *Vienna and Versailles,* Jeroen Duindam challenges many of the assertions made by Elias, arguing that they were based on the French model but were not as relevant to the much less ostentatious Habsburg court. John Adamson questions the understanding of early modern court ceremony and celebration as a means for enforcing and regulating autocracy. Adamson, "The Making of the Ancien-Regime Court, 1500–1700," in *The Princely Courts of Europe. Ritual, Politics and Culture under the Ancien Regime 1500–1750,* ed. Adamson (London, 1999), 7–41.

17. Karl Vocelka, *Glanz und Untergang,* 32.
18. Wheatcroft, *The Habsburgs,* 220–224.
19. On Jansenism and the Catholic Enlightenment in the Habsburg Monarchy, see Peter Herrsche, *Der Spätjansenismus in Österreich* (Wien, 1977); Blanning, *Joseph II,* 41–51; Kovacs briefly discusses Jansenism in the Habsburg context, "Kirchliches Zeremoniell," 129–130.
20. Ingrao, *The Habsburg Monarchy,* 189–190. James Van Horn Melton, *Absolutism and the Eighteenth-Century Origins of Compulsory Schooling in Prussia and Austria* (Cambridge,1988).
21. Georg Kugler, "Die Entwicklung der Kleidung am Wiener Hof im 18. und 19. Jahrhundert," in Kugler, ed., *Uniform und Mode am Kaiserhof* (Wien, 1983), 28.
22. Blanning, *Joseph II,* 64.
23. Kovacs, "Kirchliches Zeremoniell."
24. Despite her willingness to transform the state and to defer to her advisors, who included leading cameralist and enlightened thinkers like Josef von Sonnenfels (born of a Jewish family), Maria Theresa never overcame her prejudice against Jews. She considered forcing Jews from Bohemia and did expel Jews from Prague for a short time. Near the end of her life, she relaxed some travel restrictions on the Jews of Trieste. Joseph II's Edicts of Toleration for the Jews, issued separately for each province, must be viewed in the context of his reforms aimed at strengthening the state. Jews could now attend German-language schools, enter the civil service, be admitted to universities, and join guilds. Jews also became subject to conscription. Joseph intended these reforms to transform Jews into "productive" citizens. Joseph expected Jews, once educated and as-similated into the broader culture, to convert to Catholicism. Louis Dubin, *The Port Jews of Habsburg Trieste: Absolutist Politics and Enlightenment Culture* (Stanford, 1999); Blanning, *Joseph II,* 72–75; William O. McCagg Jr., *A History of Habsburg Jews, 1670–1918* (Bloomington, 1992), 19, 26–30; Robert Wistrich, *The Jews of Vienna in the Age of Franz Joseph* (New York, 1989).
25. Ingrao, *The Habsburg Monarchy,* 199–200. As Blanning points out, the "Jose-phinian reforms" began before Joseph. Jansenists and other church reformers worked with Maria Theresa to begin to curb the display and sensuality of the baroque. Blanning, *Joseph II,* 44–46.
26. Joachim Whaley, "Austria, 'Germany', and the Dissolution of the Holy Roman Empire," in Robertson and Timms, eds., *The Habsburg Legacy,* 3–12.

27. On the acceptance of middle-class values in the self-presentation of European dynasties, see Heinz Dollinger, "Das Leitbild des Bürgerkönigtums in der europäischen Monarchie des 19. Jahrhunderts," in *Hof, Kultur, und Politik im 19. Jahrhundert,* ed. Karl Ferdinand Werner (Bonn, 1985). Andrew Wheatcroft has written that Franz's ruling system "was designed to blur the lines of initiative and responsibility for the execution of the autocracy." Franz Joseph, on the other hand, was eager to assert himself and to defend his prerogatives at all times. Wheatcroft, *The Habsburgs: Embodying Empire* (London, 1995), 251, 268.

28. Many of the legendary tales of Franz Joseph's personal aseticism reflected his true nature. For example, Franz Joseph did in fact sleep on an unadorned iron bed. Bled, *Franz Joseph,* 199.

29. On the structure and history of the Habsburg court, see Żolger, *Der Hofstaat des Hauses Österreich;* Silber, *Obersthofmeister Alfred Fürst von Montenuovo; Österreichischer Bürgerkunde. Handbuch der Staats- und Rechtskunde in ihre Beziehungen zum öffentlichen Leben,* vol. 1, 66–91.

30. Franz Joseph signed the orders appointing Grünne acting *Obersthofmeister* on 3 December 1849. HHStA, OMeA, Varia, 1848–1895, ct. 373, Folder 1, 1848 [Enthebung des Obersthofmeister Graf Dietrichstein].

31. Ferdinand's death in 1875 provided Franz Joseph with a financial windfall. He immediately increased the funds allotted to each member of the imperial family.

32. HHStA, OMeA 1849/r. 121/12, ct. 575 [Prs. 1278].

33. According to Hannes Stekl, the court employed 4,236 people in 1847—this number includes 2,228 servants and day laborers in addition to those employed in the four *Hofstäbe* and the administrators of the family fund. In 1847, the greater *Hofstaat* also included 2,513 people who boasted membership in one of the Habsburg house orders and 2,136 who held imperial titles ranging from *Geheimer Rat* to titular chaplain. See Hannes Stekl, "Der Wiener Hof in der ersten Hälfte des 19. Jahrhunderts," in *Hof und Hofgesellschaft in den deutschen Staaten im 19. und beginnenden 20. Jahrhundert,* ed. Karl Möckl (Boppard am Rhein, 1990), 24–25.

34. Żolger, *Der Hofstaat des Hauses Österreich,* 154.

35. For example, in 1902 Grand Court Master Rudolph Liechtenstein chaired a committee to sort out the rankings of various branches of the Windischgrätz family. Other aristocratic families had expressed their concern that their own ranking would suffer if this matter were not taken up by the court. See HHStA, ZA, SR, Nepallek-Handakten, ct. 21. Though the grand chamberlain officially proofed the rankings, the grand court master applied the rankings and adjudicated disputes between aristocratic families over their standing at court.

36. Kugler, ed., *Uniform und Mode am Kaiserhof,* 112.

37. See Bled, *Franz Joseph,* 213. Younger sons of impoverished nobles filled the ranks of the Hungarian Body-Guard.

38. HHStA, OMeA 1849/r. 121/12, ct. 575 [Prs. 1278, Übersicht der in Folge ah. Handschreibens vom 26. April 1849 vom k.k. Obersthofmeisteramt vorläufig zu treffende Verfügungen].

39. HHStA, OMeA 1849/r. 121/12, ct. 575 [Prs. 1278, 27 April 1849. Franz Joseph

to Grünne; Grünne to Dräxler, 27 April 1849]. This professionalization of the court cannot be separated from the professionalization of the state bureaucracy undertaken in the same period. See Waltraud Heindl, *Gehorsame Rebellen: Bürokratie und Beamte in Österreich 1780 bis 1848* (Wien, 1991).

40. Before Franz Joseph's accession, the *Hofdienste* included: master of the kitchen (*Oberküchenmeister*), master of the silver chamber (*Obersilberkämmerer*), master of the staff (*Oberstabelmeister*), master of the hunt (*Oberjägermeister*), general director of court construction (*General-Hofbaudirector*), prefect of the Court Library (*Hofbibliotek Präfect*), count of the court music (*Hofmusikgraf*), and the master of ceremonies (*Oberceremonienmeister*). After 1849, there were only four high ceremonial posts under the *Obersthofmeister:* the *Oberküchen-meister, Oberceremonienmeister, Oberjägermeister,* and *Obersilberkämmerer* (occasionally over the next 50 years, the *Oberstabelmeister* would be listed among the *Hofdienste* in the court calendar, so though somewhat demoted, this position did not disappear entirely as a ceremonial post). HHStA, OMeA 1849/r. 121/12, ct. 575 [Prs. 1278, Übersicht der in Folge ah. Handschreibens vom 26. April 1849 vom k.k. Obersthofmeisteramt vorläufig zu treffende Verfügungen]; See *Hofschematismus* for 1848 and 1855.

41. HHStA, OMeA 1849/r. 121/12, ct. 575 [Prs. 1278, Übersicht der in Folge ah. Handschreibens vom 26. April 1849 vom k.k. Obersthofmeisteramt vorläufig zu treffende Verfügungen].

42. HHStA, OMeA 1849/r. 121/12, ct. 575 [ad. 1278, Prs. 26 April 1849, Allerunter-thänigster Vortrag des treugehorsamsten ersten Obersthofmeisters-Stellvetreter Grafen von Grünne. Eine Reorganizierung des Hofhaushalts betreffend]. Franz Joseph approved every section of this memorandum.

43. HHStA, ZA, SR, Nepallek-Handakten, ct. 22 [Prärogativen und Vorrechte eines kk Ersten Obersthofmeisters].

44. More than most of his predecessors, Alfred Montenuovo, Franz Joseph's last grand court master, played an important role in the cultural life of Vienna through his stewardship of the court theater and court opera house. Montenuovo also oversaw the plans for rebuilding the Hofburg. Silber, *Obersthofmeister Alfred Fürst von Montenuovo.*

45. An ever increasing number of court officials achieved the academic title of doctor. The creation of sickness insurance and the rise in pay and other benefits enjoyed by court officials attests to the dependence of these officials on their income to cover their living expenses. This trend toward professionalization accelerated after the creation of the constitutional state of Austria-Hungary in 1867. The court endeavored to regularize its pay and benefit structure in order to offer the same levels of compensation to its officials as the state did to state bureaucrats. The court restructured its system of pay and promotion in 1871–1872, instituted an insurance fund for widows and orphans of court employees in 1869, and created a pension fund in 1874. For details on pay and benefits in the court apparatus, see HHStA, OMeA, Status Books.

46. The Office of the Grand Court Master calculated the annual budget for the entire court apparatus. HHStA, OMeA, 1855/r. 136, ct. 673.

47. Liechtenstein insisted that court officials wear elements of the court uniform that

had long since been deemed unnecessary, prompting at least one older official to complain about the stockings once again required of court employees. HHStA, ZA, SR, Varia 1848–1895, ct. 373, Folder 2 [Raymond to Liechtenstein, 14 June 1851; Kundmachung, August 1849].

48. There were fewer than 300 *Geheime Räte* in 1847, and Franz Joseph did not greatly expand the number of those possessing this title. In 1868, most likely at the urging of liberal Karl Wilhelm Auersperg, minister president of Cisleithania, Franz Joseph ordered that cabinet ministers of both halves of the monarchy be awarded the title "Excellency" and be ranked among the privy councillors. AVA, Ministerrats-Präsidium, 1865–1869, ct. 8 [No. 178, Jan. 8, 1868].

49. William D. Godsey Jr. discusses the pedigree examination and Habsburg court society in "Quarterings and Kinship: The Social Composition of the Habsburg Aristocracy in the Dualist Era," *Journal of Modern History* 71(1) (March 1999), 56–104. On the loosening of the standards for the pedigree examination under grand chamberlain Count Rudolph Wrbna und Freudenthal in the first decades of the nineteenth century, the tightening of the standards in the 1830s, and the move from twelve to sixteen noble ancestors as the requirements for the chamberlain title after 1898, see Godsey, "'La société était au fond légitimiste': Émigrés, Aristocracy, and the Court at Vienna, 1749–1848," *European History Quarterly* 35(1) (2005), 63–95, and "Oberstkämmerer Rudolph Graf Czernin (1757–1845) und die 'Adelsrestauration' nach 1815 in Österreich," *Études danubiennes* XIX(1/2) (2003), 59–74.

50. The Order of the Star-Cross arose out of an allegedly miraculous incident that occurred during the height of *Pietas Austriaca*. A splinter, believed to be from the true cross, survived a fire that damaged much of the imperial palace in 1668, though its metal frame melted in the heat. Empress Eleonore, who survived the death of her husband, Ferdinand III, was the first leader of this order. See Coreth, *Pietas Austriaca*, 43.

51. Those receiving this and other high titles had to pay a special tax unless freed of this obligation by the emperor. In its 1898 publication of the rules for the attainment of the *Kämmerer* title, the Office of the Grand Chamberlain again based the qualifications for this title on the imperial patent of 31 May 1766. *Directiven für das Einschreiten um die allergnädigste Verleihung der k. und k. Kämmererswürde*, (Wien, 1898), 8. At the time of Maria Theresa's death in 1780, there were 1,500 chamberlains. By 1900 their numbers had increased modestly to 1,600. Georg Kugler, *Des Kaisers Rock* (Wien, 1989), 52.

52. HHStA, ZA, SR, Nepallek-Handakten, ct. 23 [*Bestimmungen über die Hoffähigkeit und den Hofzutritt zum internen Amtsgebrauche*, 2nd ed. (Wien, 1902), 5]. Polish, Hungarian, and Italian nobles contested the rules governing *Hoffähigkeit* and *Hofzutritt*. These nobles insisted that their historic privileges had always included access to the court and membership in court society.

53. Baron Hermann Tinti regretted that due to marriages below their stations many families among the "historic aristocracy" that continued to play a role in "society" were no longer welcomed at court. He suggested that the *Kämmerer* title be reserved for those families who possessed the imperial titles of baron, prince, and count and could prove their noble status for at least 150 years. This would

place the emphasis on the depth rather than breadth of one's noble ancestral tree. Tinti also called for a distinction between the nobles of historic standing and those newly created. See Tinti, *Hoffähigkeit. Eine Studie*, 2nd ed. (Wien, 1904).

54. According to Brigitte Hamann, after the establishment of constitutional government, "all *Geheimräte, Hofräte*, and ministers were by definition *hoffähig*." Hamann, "Der Wiener Hof und die Hofgesellschaft in der zweiten Hälfte des 19. Jahrhunderts," in Karl Möckl, ed., *Hof und Hofgesellschaft in den deutschen Staaten im 19 und beginnenden 20. Jahrhundert* (Boppard am Rhein, 1990), 76. The same information is provided in *Österreichischer Bürgerkunde. Handbuch der Staats- und Rechtskunde in ihre Beziehungen zum öffentlichen Leben*, vol. 1, 91. See also Kugler, *Uniform und Mode*, 91–122.

55. On the Habsburg house orders, see Kugler, *Uniform und Mode*, 20–37, 91–122; Stekl, "Der Wiener Hof," 22–23.

56. On 2 December 1898, the government announced that 4,404 people had been awarded state or court titles and various ranks in the Habsburg house orders. *WZ*, 2 December 1898. Pan-German and Social Democratic journalists often employed identical phrases when mocking the ever-growing number of orders handed out on imperial celebrations. *OR*, 28 November 1898; *AZ*, 1 December 1898, 3–4; *AZ*, 3 December 1898.

57. Reichsrat representative Dr. Menger refused to accept an award of the Order of the Iron Crown in 1898 from the hands of an allegedly Slav-friendly government. This rare rejection of an imperial order captured the attention of the press, demonstrating the singular nature of his principled stance. *DZ*, 3 December 1898, 7; *NFP* (morning edition), 2 December 1898.

58. HHStA, NZA, 1849, ct. 85 [Prs. 2750, 9 August 1849].

59. Andrea Blöchl discusses the celebration of the emperor's birthday in "Die Kaisergedenktage."

60. On these two annual events, see Bled, *Franz Joseph*, 217–218.

61. For Joseph II, the wearing of military uniform signified his rejection of baroque display. Franz Joseph combined a commitment to imperial celebration with adherence to military discipline. In 1908, Kaiser Wilhelm II led Germany's princes to Vienna to pay homage to Franz Joseph on his sixtieth jubilee. In the habit of wearing the uniform of army units of visiting princes and monarchs whenever possible, Franz Joseph changed uniforms no less than eight times in one day as he greeted a series of German princes in conformity with ceremonial regulations in the imperial palace. See Eugen Ketterl, *Der alte Kaiser wie nur einer Ihn sah. Der Wahrheitsgetreu Bereicht des Leibkammerdieners Kaiser Franz Josephs I* (Wien, 1929), 140.

62. Redlich, *Emperor Francis Joseph of Austria* (1929), 11–12.

63. This brief discussion of Habsburg piety is drawn chiefly from Coreth, *Pietas;* and Kovacs, "Kirchliches Zeremoniell."

64. *Österreichisches Volksblatt*, 24 June 1848, 35.

65. *Allgemeine Theaterzeitung*, 23 June 1848.

66. *Volksfreund. Zeitschrift für Aufklärung und Erheiterung des Volkes*, 22 June 1848, 172.

67. Gottfried Mayer, *Österreich als katholische Grossmacht. Ein Traum zwischen Revolution und Liberaler Ära* (Wien, 1989), 149. Though the Catholic hierarchy was far from pleased with the revolution, after the 25 April grant of civil freedoms by Emperor Ferdinand, the hierarchy aimed at securing similar freedoms for the church as an institution. Church leaders wished to be exempted from state controls, yet desired influence over education and marriage. DA, BIKO, 1836–1849, ct. 1, Folder 1/3 1838–1848 [Memorandum des Episcopates der mähr. Kirchenprovinz über die wünschenswerthe Gestaltung der Verhältniss der katholischen Kirche in der constitutionellen Monarchie]. The 1849 bishops' conference reiterated the church's support for the state's use of force to "save the civil order from collapse and to protect the European culture from the influence of a new unheard of barbarism." DA, BIKO, 1836–1849, ct. 1, Folder 1/4 1849 [Einleitende Erklärung der Versammelten Bischöfe, 30 May 1849]. A 17 June letter, endorsed by thirty-six of the monarchy's bishops, blamed the revolutions on Josephinism. Improper religious education and organization led people to radical nationalism, splitting families over language; only "Christendom" holds the key to the "true worth of humanity." DA, BIKO, 1836–1849, ct. 1, Folder 1/4 1849. On the church's opposition to Josephinist reforms, see also *Wiener Kirchenzeitung,* 31 March 1849, 157.
68. DA, BIKO, 1836–1839, ct. 1, Folder 1/2 1838–1848 [Ministry of the Interior, 31 March 1849].
69. The Corpus Christi procession was an order procession. Those with the highest rankings in the Order of the Golden Fleece walked in the most provileged positions.
70. *Österreichischer Volksfreund,* 6 June 1848, 384. The gathering of bishops in 1849 began the negotiations that eventually led to the 1855 concordat with Rome.
71. *Österreichischer Volksfreund,* 13 June 1848, 398; *Österreichischer Volksfreund,* 16 June 1848, 401.
72. The kings of Bavaria participated in similar Catholic rituals. On the royal cult of the Wittelsbachs, see Werner Blessing, *Staat und Kirche.*
73. In 1912, the ailing Franz Joseph did not attend the church services before the Corpus Christi procession, but joined the procession for the third reading outside the Hofburg. HHStA, NZA, 1912, ct. 207 [Dispositionen anläßlich der Fronleichnamsprozession am 6. Juni 1912]. The first page of the official publication for the 1908 Kaiser-Homage-Procession describes the seventy-eight-year-old emperor as a man "little bowed by the burden of the years, on foot and on horse almost as fit as a youth, with clear eyes, lucid mind." *Der Kaiser-Huldigungs-Festzug. Eine Schilderung und Erklärung seiner Gruppen* (Wien, 1908).
74. Eugen Ketterl, *Der alte Kaiser,* 92.
75. Egon Frieherr Loebenstein von Aigenhorst, "Das Zeremoniell unter Kaiser Franz Joseph," in Eduard Ritter von Steinitz, ed., *Erinnerungen an Franz Joseph I Kaiser von Österreich Apostolischer König von Ungarn* (Berlin, 1930), 399–400.

Chapter 2

1. Geertz, "Centers, Kings, and Charisma," p. 125.
2. For a brief overview of Franz Joseph's many imperial visits prior to 1867, see Petra Promintzer, *Die Reisen Kaiser Franz Josephs.*
3. Franz Joseph often extended his trips to Galicia to include short visits to Bukovina. This chapter considers only the tours of Galicia. For an overview of Franz Joseph's trips to Bukovina, see Raimund Friedrich Kaindl, *Unser Kaiser in der Bukowina: 1851, 1855, 1880. Ein Festblatt zum sechzigjährigen Regierungs-Jubiläum* (Czernowitz, 1908). Profits from the sale of this publication were donated to the "Kaiser Franz Joseph Jubilee Stipend for Christian-German students at the University of Czernowitz."
4. Johann Polek, *Joseph's II Reisen nach Galizien und der Bukowina und ihre Bedeutung für letztere Provinz* (Czernowitz, 1895), 1.
5. Galicia-Volhynia was one of the duchies of medieval Rus'. The Habsburgs did not attach their new Polish lands to the Crown of St. Stephen. The western districts of Habsburg "Galicia" had never been part of Ruthenian Galicia, while much of Ruthenian Galicia proper came under Russian control, including the town of Volodymyr, the origin of "Lodomeria."
6. "Ruthenian" (*rusyny* in Ukrainian; *Ruthenen* in German) is used here to distinguish between an ethnic designation (Ruthenian) and the national orientations of Ruthenian leaders and factions. In this I follow John-Paul Himka, *Religion and Nationality in Western Ukraine: The Greek Catholic Church and the Ruthenian National Movement in Galicia, 1867–1900* (Montreal, 1999).
7. Leila P. Everett, "The Rise of Jewish National Politics in Galicia, 1905–1907," in Andrei S. Markovits and Frank E. Sysyn, eds., *Nationbuilding and the Politics of Nationalism: Essays on Austrian Galicia* (Cambridge, 1982), 149–150, n. 2. The Habsburg censuses did not offer the possibility of choosing Yiddish. Before 1867, the vast majority of Jews were counted as German-speakers; the majority of Galicia's Jews were numbered among the Polish-speakers in 1880.
8. On the Polish *szlachta,* see Norman Davies, *God's Playground: A History of Poland* (New York, 1982), vol. 1, 201–255, and vol. 2, 321–372.
9. Stefan Kieniewicz, *Adam Sapieha* (Lwów, 1939), 23.
10. Peasant politician Wincenty Witos recalled that "The peasant never forgot even for a moment that the Polish *szlachta* kept him in serfdom for six hundred years, and only the emperor ended serfdom and gave him rights and freedom." Witos, *Moje Wspomnienia* (Warsaw, 1981), 87–88. Piotr Babczyszn remembered that even peasants who came to define themselves as Poles continued to express their love of the emperor and indifference toward the reestablishment of a Polish state. Babczyszn, *Od Gniezny i Seretu po Łynę Odrę i Nysę. Wyspomnienia. Tom I: Loszniów—Trembowla (1890–1914).* Ossolineum manuscript 15336/II. Keely Stauter-Halsted argues for a much more nationalized Galician Polish peasantry in *Nation in the Village: The Genesis of National Identity in Austrian Poland, 1848–1914* (Ithaca, 2001).
11. On the Jews of Galicia, see *Focusing on Galicia: Jews, Poles, and Ukrainians, 1772–1918,* Israel Bartal and Antony Polonsky, eds. (Oxford, 1999). On this

social conflict, see John-Paul Himka, *Galician Villagers and the Ukrainian National Movement in the Nineteenth Century* (Edmonton, 1988).

12. On the reforms of Maria Theresa and Joseph II see, among others, P. G. M. Dickson, *Finance and Government under Maria Theresia, 1740–1780* (Oxford, 1987); T. C. W. Blanning, *Joseph II* (London and New York, 1994); Derek Beales, *Joseph II* (Cambridge, 1987); Roman Rosdolsky, *Untertan und Staat in Galizien: Die Reformen unter Maria Theresia und Joseph II* (Mainz am Rhein, 1992).

13. Stefan Kieniewicz, *The Emancipation of the Polish Peasantry* (Chicago, 1969), 36–37.

14. Kieniewicz, *Emancipation*, 37–38; Davies, *God's Playground*, vol. 2, 141–142. Joseph's reforms also affected labor service and expanded the peasants' right to sue the lord before state officials. These officials received their salaries from the local nobility and were, therefore, subject to pressure from the *szlachta*.

15. Kieniewicz, *Emancipation*, 38–39; Edith Murr Link, *The Emancipation of the Austrian Peasant 1740–1798* (New York, 1949).

16. *Związek Chłopski*, 15 September 1894, 115.

17. Joseph II sent German-Jewish reformer Herz Homberg to Lemberg to bring "enlightened" Jewish learning to the Jews of this most backward province. Homberg did not meet with a positive reception among the Hasidic population of Galicia. See Mayer Bałaban, "Herz Homberg in Galizien," *Jahrbuch für jüdische Geschichte und Literatur* 19 (1916); McCagg, *A History of Habsburg Jews, 1670–1918* (Bloomington, 1992), 111–112.

18. Ivan L. Rudnytsky, "The Ukrainians in Galicia under Austrian Rule," in Markovits and Sysyn, eds., *Nationbuilding*, 25.

19. Piotr Wandycz, *The Lands of Partitioned Poland* (Seattle, 1974), 12. In this period, less wealthy nobles increasingly moved to urban centers. Many lawyers, doctors, and urban professionals who defined themselves as "democrats," "liberals," and "progressives" counted themselves with pride among the hereditary *szlachta*.

20. In reality, the Congress of Vienna made little attempt to restore the status quo ante. Imperial princelings deposed by Napoleon were not returned to power; the Holy Roman Empire was not restored.

21. Wandzycz, *Lands;* Stanisław Grodzicki, *W królestwie Galicji i Lodomerii* (Kraków, 1976), 136–197.

22. Jerome Blum, *Noble Landowners and Agriculture in Austria, 1815–1848* (Baltimore, 1948). When Franz I traveled to Galicia in June 1817, he was welcomed by cheering peasants with poems praising "YOUR concern for the good of the peoples." HHStA, ZA, SR 23 [Franciszek Lgocki, "Odgłos wdzięczności Galicyanów z okoliczności dobroczynnych odwiedziń Najjaśniezszego Franciszka Igo," 1817].

23. See Thomas W. Simons, Jr., "The Peasant Revolt of 1846 in Galicia," *Slavic Review* (1971), 795–817; Wandycz, *The Lands*, 133–135. From 1815 to 1846, Cracow was administered by Austria in the name of the three partitioning powers.

24. Wandycz, *The Lands*, 145; Kieniewicz, *Emancipation*, 136–137.

25. Kieniewicz, *Emancipation,* 135. The peasants paid for much of the indemnification of the lords through taxes. Servitudes were retained; commissions dominated by the *szlachta* regulated claims on forests and formerly common lands in favor of the noble landowners.

26. On the 1848 revolution in Galicia, see the essays collected in *Galicja i jej dziedzictwo. Tom 12. Galicia w 1848 roku. Demografia, działalność politzczna i społeczna, gospodarka i kultura,* ed. Andrzej Bonusiak and Marian Stolarczyk (Rzeszów, 1999).

27. The German *Statthalter* is used in this book almost exclusively in order to allow for the use of a single designation for the equivalent government posts in other provinces of Cisleithania.

28. Bronisław Łoziński, an early biographer of Gołuchowski, praised this magnate as a realist who worked for the good of the Polish population. Wilhelm Feldman denounced Gołuchowski and other Galician pragmatists as "opportunists." Łoziński, *Agenor Hrabia Gołuchowski* (Lwów, 1901); Feldman, *Stronnictwa i programy polityczne w Galicyi 1846–1906* (Kraków, 1907), vol. 1, 49–51.

29. For an apologetic discussion of Grünne's career, see Marianne Gräfin Szapary, "Carl Graf Grünne. Generaladjutant des Kaisers Franz Joseph 1848–1859" (Ph.D. Diss., University of Vienna, 1935).

30. This interpretation is based on my reading of the relevant files of the Military Chancellery (MKSM) in Vienna's Kriegsarchiv (KA), the records of the Oberst-hofmeisteramt in the HHStA, and the archive of the Galician administration held in the Central State Historical Archives in L'viv (TSDIA-L).

31. The Austrian rank of field marshal lieutenant is the equivalent of major general in the United States Army. See Deák, *Beyond Nationalism,* 15.

32. KA, MKSM 6895/GA ex 1851, exped. 4 October 1851 and 6925/GA ex 1851; HHStA, OMeA, 1851/r. 65/II/6, ct. 606 [Z. 5846, Pr. 8 October 1851].

33. Because various chefs, guards, officers, and court officials accompanied Franz Joseph for particular stretches of the trips, it is difficult to provide an exact figure for the imperial suite at any one moment of the journey.

34. In 1851, the technology of travel differed little from that available to Joseph II during his visits in the late eighteenth century or to Franz I when he journeyed to Galicia in 1817. In June 1817, Franz and his wife departed with eighteen wagons drawn by one hundred horses on their trip to Galicia, Transylvania, and the Military Border. Some seventy-one officials and servants constituted Franz's suite, though some servants and bakers had been sent ahead to prepare for the arrival of the wagon train. HHStA, ZA SR, ct. 23 [Z. 873. Postreise-Wagen-Liste für die Reise Sr. Majestät des Kaisers und Ihrer Majestät der Kaiserin nach Galizien, Siebenbürgen und in die Bannater Militär-Grenze im Jahre 1817].

35. DALO, 350/1/252/3. At least twenty horses were held in ready at every post station along the route.

36. TSDIA-L, 146/4/3400/149 [Pr. 5675, 30 June 1851]. Many Polish magnates held titles of prince or count but could not qualify for *Hoffähigkeit* according to the strict rules of descent enforced by the Habsburg court. This same difficulty confronted the Hungrian and Lombardian nobilities.

37. Grünne's detailed orders to Gołuchowski included instructions to local officials

to provide foodstuffs along the emperor's route to serve as the raw material for the many cooks and bakers attending the emperor. To prepare breakfast, the imperial bakers required eight measures of "good" cream, twelve measures of cream of lesser quality, 150 to 180 croissants, milk-bread, other baked goods and many gallons of milk. Wherever *"souper dinatoire"* or a *"kleines Diner"* was scheduled, the court chef requested dozens of ducks and chickens to complement six pounds of bacon and six pounds of beef fat. Twelve pounds of bacon, ten pounds of beef fat, 500 eggs, sixteen pounds of salt, 120 pounds of beef, seventy pounds of veal, and four pieces of calves' liver were required to provide an evening meal of imperial quality. DALO, 350/1/252/7.

38. On the choice of *Hoflager,* see Promintzer, *Die Reisen,* 40–42.
39. DALO, 350/1/252/12–35 [Amtserinnerung wegen Verschärfung der Fremden Polizei aus Anlaß der Bevorstehenden Ankunft Sr. Maj nach Lemberg].
40. KA, MKSM-SR Reisen S. M., 53/1 [Rottenzettel und ausrückender Stand, 15 October 1851]; KA, MKSM, 6895/GA ex 1851.
41. TSDIA-L, 146/4/3402/3 [Nr. 9237, Gołuchowski to Kreisvorsteher, 7 October 1851]; 146/4/3400/1–19 [Pr. 5284. Grünne, 14 June and 19 June]; see also DALO, 350/1/252/3 [Gołuchowski to Kreisvorsteher, 18 June 1851].
42. In Venice, the aristocracy avoided the theater when Franz Joseph attended in March, and his reception in Milan in September was equally cold. Egon Caeser Corti, *Mensch und Herrscher: Wege und Schicksale Kaiser Franz Josephs I. Zwischen Thronbesteigung und Berliner Kongress* (Graz, 1952), 72, 80–82.
43. *GL,* 2 October 1851.
44. *GL,* 4 October 1851.
45. *WZ,* 14 October 1851; *GL,* 19 October 1851; KA, MKSM-SR Reisen S. M., 53/1 [Programm über die Feierlichkeiten bei der Anwesenheit Sr. Maj. zu Krakau].
46. TSDIA-L, 146/4/3401/5–7 [Pr. 5731; Pr. 5734, 2 July 1851. Ettmayer to Gołuchowski]. Jews were guaranteed equality before the law only in 1867.
47. *WZ,* 14 October 1851.
48. *GL,* 16 October 1851; *WZ,* 14 October 1851.
49. KA, MKSM-SR Reisen S.M., 53/1 [Program über die Feierlichkeiten bei der Anwesenheit Seiner Majestät zu Krakau]. In Lemberg, between 11 A.M. and 4 P.M. on 17 October Franz Joseph inspected several barracks, a military hospital, and fortifications. KA, MKSM-SR Reisen S.M., 53/1 [Zeiteintheilung des Aufenthaltes Sr. Majestät zu Lemberg am 17ten Oktober 1851].
50. *WZ,* 16 October 1851.
51. Jagiellonian University Library, manuscript 15029III [*Uniesienie wiernego ludu na przybycie do kraju Najjaśniejszego Cesarsza i Króla Franciszka Józefa I* (Lwów, 1851)].
52. *WZ,* 23 October 1851.
53. Himka, *Galician Villagers,* 32.
54. *Wjazd,* 38–40. The National Institute was built on the site of the former university library, destroyed during the bombardment of Lemberg in 1848. TSDIA-L, 146/4/3402/64.
55. *GL,* 21 October 1851; *GL,* 23 October 1851.
56. TSDIA-L, 146/4/3402/77.

57. Paweł Popiel, *Pamiętniki Pawła Popiela, 1807–1892* (Kraków, 1927), 124.
58. These petitions are discussed in Fras, "Podróże," 124–126. See also Łoziński, *Agenor Gołuchowski,* 252–257.
59. HHStA, Kab. Kanz., Geheime Akten, Nachlaß Schwarzenberg, ct. 9, Faszikel I, [N. 43, Gołuchowski to Schwarzenberg, 9 November 1851].
60. HHStA, Kab. Kanz., Geheime Akten, Nachlaß Schwarzenberg, ct. 9, Faszikel I, [N. 44, Schwarzenberg to Gołuchowski, 15 November 1851]. Schwarzenberg reminded Gołuchowski that everything had proceeded according to regulations, of which Gołuchowski was aware, and that his honor had in no way been undermined. In the spirit of the magnate petitions, Gołuchowski then pled for greater access for Polish nobles to positions in the Galician administration. HHStA, Kab. Kanz., Geheime Akten, Nachlaß Schwarzenberg, ct. 9, Faszikel I, [N. 45, Gołuchowski to Schwarzenberg, 30 November 1851].
61. *DP,* 12 September 1880, 2.
62. Alexander Nowolecki, *Pamiątka podróży cesarza Franciszka Józefa I po Galicji* (Kraków, 1881), xii–xiii. See also "Cesarz Franciszek Józef I w Krakowie w 1880 r." in *Kalendarz Krakowski,* 1880, 17. This same general narrative of the Polish relationship with Franz Joseph and with the Habsburg Monarchy as a whole is repeated in Polish-language commemorative books published during the 1908 imperial jubilee: Bronisław Sokalski, *O życiu i czynach najmiłosciwiej nam panującego, Najjaśnieszego Pana, Cesarza i Króla Franciszka Józefa I. w seśćdziesięcioletnią rocznicę wstąpienia na tron* (Lwów, 1908).
63. The Polish conservatives will be discussed in the next chapter.
64. HHStA, IB, ct. 23a (1849–1851) [Z. 8807/a, 20 October 1851. Allerunterthänigster Vortrag des Ministers des Innern Dr. Alexander Bach. Womit die Polizei-Wochen-Rapport für die Zeit vom 5. bis 11. October vorgelegt war].
65. TSDIA-L, 146/4/3402 [Prs. 9443]; TSDIA-L, 146/4/3402/90–100 include reports from Bochnia, Tarnów, and elsewhere attesting to the large crowds that came to see the emperor.
66. *WZ,* 4 October 1851.
67. The contents of the petitions are summarized in catalogue books in HHStA, Kab. Kanz. Varia, ct. 42/2, and TSDIA-L, 146/4/3399. ·
68. HHStA, OMeA 1851/r. 65/II/6, ct. 606 [Pr. 6044, 15 October 1851. Raymond to Liechtenstein, 12 October 1851].
69. HHStA, OMeA 1851/r. 65/II/6, ct. 606 [Pr. 6137, 21 October 1851. Raymond to Liechtenstein, 15 October 1851].
70. Franz Joseph to Sophie, 13 October 1851 in Dr. Franz Schnürer, ed., *Briefe Kaiser Franz Josephs I. an seine Mutter, 1838–1872* (Munich, 1930), 170.
71. *GL,* 23 October 1851.
72. Polish historians tend to agree with this interpretation. See Krzysztof Karol Daszyk, "Zanim Franciszek Józef stał się 'naszym dobrym cesarzem': Polacy z Galicji wobec Austrii I Habsburgów w latach 1848–1860," in *Galicja i jej dziedzictwo. Tom 12. Galicia w 1848 roku. Demografia, działalność polityczna i społeczna, gospodarka i kultura* (Rzeszów, 1999), 119–147; Fras, "Podróże," 124–126.

73. In Bach's view, only a few incidents marred the *Kaiserreise*. Informants reported that "the rural population has become disturbed by false rumors about the reinstitution of the *robot*." Police put those who spread these rumors before courts of law "so that the peasant population would be calmed and correctly informed about the intentions of the government." Unemployed Mathias Majewski was arrested during the entrance of the emperor into Lemberg "because, while in a strongly intoxicated state he said to those standing around him that one should not cheer such a young monarch so much, and beyond this, he was no genuine Polish king." The interior minister must have been pleased that two years after the suppression of revolution, the only counter-demonstration of note consisted of a few words uttered by one drunk unemployed man who must have been informed upon by those within earshot. HHStA, IB, ct. 23a (1849–51) [Die Polizei Rapport für den Zeitraum der Wochen vom 12. Bis 18. Oktober 1851]. Although not reported in the press, on the road from Tarnopol to Czernowitz three members of the imperial party were thrown from wagon eleven. One suffered a blow to the head, another broke his left arm, and the third received a mild head wound. The two more seriously injured men were left behind under care of military doctors. HHStA, OMeA 1851/r. 65/II/6, ct. 606 [Pr. 6271, Raymond to Liechtenstein, 21 October 1851].

74. Gołuchowski served as *Statthalter* of Galicia from 1849–1859, 1866–1868, and 1871–1875.

75. Wandycz, "The Poles in the Habsburg Monarchy," 82–83.

76. Wilhelm Feldman, *Dzieje polskiej myśli politycznej, 1864–1914* (Warsaw, 1933), 56.

77. On Ziemiałkowski and Polish politics in this period, see Zbigniew Fras, *Florian Ziemiałkowski (1817–1900)* (Wrocław, 1991).

78. Leon Biliński, *Wspomnienia i dokumenty 1846–1919* (Warsaw, 1924), vol. 1, 16.

79. AVA, Nachlaß Bach, ct. 15, Krakau/Zustand [Adam Potocki to Alexander Bach, 19 February 1850].

80. AVA, Nachlaß Bach, ct. 14 [Galizien: politisch Verdächtige].

81. *WZ*, 15 September 1868, 1. The Polish conservatives, backed by all Ruthenian and Polish peasant deputies, defeated a challenge to this expenditure from Smolka. This democratic leader had argued that a simpler reception would be more appropriate for such a poverty-stricken province. Since the emperor intended to see the real state of the crownland, Smolka noted, the harsh reality of Galician poverty should not be obscured by expensive festivities and receptions.

82. HHStA, NZA, r. XV, Hofreisen 1868, ct. 334, 1868/15/270 [Abschrift: Gołuchowski to KK. Kab. Direktor Adolf Ritter von Braun, 13 September 1868].

83. HHStA, NZA, r. XV, Hofreisen 1868, ct. 334, 1868/15/270 [Abschrift: Telegram from Hofmann to Gołuchowski, 15 September 1868].

84. In Cracow, the emperor and empress planned to stay from 26 September to 1 October in Adam Potocki's palace, *Pod Baranami*, the most impressive residence on the Market Square. They also planned to dine in Prince Sanguszko's palace outside of Tarnów and in Count Alfred Potocki's palace in Łancut (Alfred Po-

tocki, a cousin of Adam Potocki, was minister of agriculture in 1868, became minister president for a short time in 1870, and was later *Statthalter* of Galicia). HHStA, NZA, r. XV, Hofreisen 1868, ct. 334, 1868/15/270 [Tages-Eintheilung für die allerhöchste Reise in Galizien].

85. KA, GA 1868/172/185.

86. As in 1851, the number of officials and servants traveling with Franz Joseph can only be estimated. Many officials accompanied the emperor only for portions of the *Kaiserreise*. KA, GA 1868/172 [Personen Liste für die Reise Ihrer kk Majestäen nach Galizien im Jahre 1868].

87. For a brief discussion of the advantages of anachronism for the court, see David Cannadine, "The British Monarchy, c. 1820–1977," in Hobsbawm, ed., *The Invention*, 111–112.

88. KA, GA 1868/172 [Franz Joseph to General-Adjutant Bellegarde, 24 September 1868].

89. Sobiesław and Stanisław Mieroszewscy, *Wspomniena* (Kraków, 1964), 153.

90. HHStA, IB, 1868, ct. 7 [Nr. 1730, Notizen des Krakauer Polizei-Direktors].

91. *Czas*, 27 September 1868, 1.

92. *GN*, 26 September 1868, 1.

93. Leon Biliński, an official in the *Statthalterei* and later Austro-Hungarian finance minister, believed that Russian influence was decisive. Biliński, *Wspomnienia*, vol. 1, 16. Feldman, *Dzieje*, 73; Fras, "Podróże," p. 128; Jakub Forst-Battaglia, "Die polnischen Konservativen Galiziens und die Slawen (1866–1879)" (Ph. D. Diss., University of Vienna, 1975), 63; Kieniewicz, *Sapieha*, 204. For a convincing counter to this view, see Christoph Freiherr Marschall von Bieberstein, *Freiheit in der Unfreiheit: Die nationale Autonomie der Polen in Galizien nach dem österreich-ungarischen Ausgleich von 1867* (Wiesbaden, 1993), 84.

94. Bieberstein, *Freiheit*, 84–85.

95. Bieberstein, *Freiheit*, 69, 84–85.

96. HHStA, IB, 1868, ct. 7 [Nr. 1730, report 3, Kraków, 19 September 1868].

97. HHStA, IB, 1868, ct. 7 [Nr. 1730, report 6, Kraków, 24 September 1868]. Gołuchowski himself implied in private circles that Franz Joseph would accept the Polish crown. Stefan Kieniewicz, *Galicja w dobie autonomicznej (1850–1914)* (Wrocław, 1952), xxiii.

98. On 22 September, quartermaster Michael von Branko made final arrangements for court accommodations in Lemberg. KA, GA 1868/172 [Report from Branko, 22 September 1868]. On 23 September, the general-adjutant informed Gołuchowski that the emperor had agreed to receive Princess Czartoryska, even though this would require a relaxed interpretation of court etiquette. KA, GA/172/ad2 [General-Adjutant to Gołuchowski, 23 September 1868].

99. Smolka demanded a reorganization of the monarchy into four parts, transforming Austria-Hungary into Austria-Hungary-Bohemia-Galicia. The proposal would have required Galicia to join the Czech boycott of the Reichsrat had Franz Joseph rejected its provisions. Kazimierz Wyka quotes Smolka's speech in his classic study, *Teka Stanczyka na tle historii Galicji w latach 1849–1869* (Wrocław, 1951), 140. Smolka enjoyed some popularity outside of the Sejm; inside the Sejm, he was isolated. Bieberstein, *Freiheit*, 74.

100. *WZ,* 29 September 1868, 1. The Sejm debates were reported in *WZ,* 15–29 September 1868, especially 29 September 1868. For more detail, see Fras, *Florian Ziemialkowski,* 104–119.

101. Józef Szujski, *Der Antrag des galizischen Landtages gegenüber dem Interesse der österreich-ungarischen Monarchie* (Krakau, 1869), 7–15. Szujski sent this essay, written between 1–3 January 1869, to the Vienna parliament in an effort to explain the resolution, which, according to him, was meant only as an address.

102. Alice Freifeld discusses this moment and the success of "celebrity monarchy" in Hungary in her unpublished article manuscript "Empress Elisabeth as Hungarian Queen: The Uses of Celebrity Monarchism."

103. *Memoirs of Friedrich Ferdinand Count von Beust* (London, 1887), 98–99. A government representative repeatedly informed the Sejm that each and every clause of the resolution would be rejected in Vienna. *WZ,* 29 September 1868.

104. Schnürer, ed., *Briefe,* 368–369.

105. Freifeld, "Empress Elisabeth as Hungarian Queen."

106. This is discussed in Hugh Agnew's article in preparation "The Flyspecks on Palivec's Portrait: Francis Joseph, the Symbols of Monarchy, and Czech Popular Loyalty."

Chapter 3

1. The Polish "democrats" and "progressives" were only modestly more "democratic" than the Polish conservatives; however, the democrats did reject the absolute loyalism of the conservatives and oriented themselves more openly toward Poles in the other partitions. In 1880, the Polish democrats were weak, divided, and lacked a large and vibrant potential constituency—in this poor, agricultural province, members of the lower *szlachta,* younger sons of noble families, and Jews constituted the bulk of the urban professional classes. Maciej Janowski, *Inteligencja wobec wyzwań nowoczesność: Dylematy ideowe polskiej demokracji liberalnej w Galicji w latach 1889–1914* (Warsaw, 1996); Zbigniew Fras, *Democraci w życiu politycznym Galicji w latach 1848–1873* (Wrocław, 1997).

2. The 1880 inspection tour also included Bukovina. Franz Joseph's contemporary Tsar Alexander II sought expressions of popular dynastic loyalty during imperial visitations. Richard Wortman, "Rule by Sentiment: Alexander II's Journeys through the Russian Empire," *American Historical Review* 95 (1990): 745–71.

3. On literacy, see Adalbert Rom, "Der Bildungsgrad der Bevölkerung Österreichs und seine Entwicklung seit 1880 mit besonderer Berücksichtigung der Sudeten- und Karpatenländer," *Statistische Monatsschrift* 40 (n.s. 19) (1914). Harald Binder documents the growth of newspaper circulation in Galicia in "Die polnische Presse in der Habsburgermonarchie" and "Die ukrainische Presse in der Habsburgermonarchie" in *Die Habsburgermonarchie, 1848–1918,* vol. 8 (Vienna, Forthcoming).

4. The 1873 and 1879 celebrations are briefly discussed in chapter 4.

5. Taaffe believed that maintaining a liberal presence in the cabinet would enable him to preside over a government above parties. This proved elusive, however. William Jenks, *Austria under the Iron Ring, 1879–1893* (Charlottesville, 1965).

6. In June, Julian Dunajewski joined Florian Ziemiałkowski, minster for Galicia, in Taaffe's cabinet.

7. The Stańczyks worked for moderate reform of agricultural production and of the relations between landowners and peasants. The Stańczyks also sought some accommodation with the Ruthenians. The *podolacy* opposed these efforts. Stanisław Grodziski, *W królestwie Galicji i Lodomerii* (Kraków, 1976), 237–48 ; Jakub Forst-Battaglia, "Die polnischen Konservativen Galiziens und die Slawen (1866–1879)" (Ph.D. Diss., University of Vienna, 1975); Wyka, *Teka.* For Kieniewicz, "Stańczyk" denoted not only the Cracow conservative nobles, but also Habsburg loyalists, young careerists, autonomists, east Galician conservative magnates (*podolacy*), and Polish officials in the Galician administration (Mamelukes). Kieniewicz, *Sapieha,* 295.

8. The portfolio consisted of twenty letters allegedly penned by fictional historical figures.

9. Stanislaus Blejwas discusses organic work in *Realism in Polish Politics: Warsaw Positivism and National Survival in Nineteenth Century Poland* (New Haven, 1984). Feldman names the Stańczyks "the party of organic work *par excellence,*" Feldman, *Stronnictwa,* vol. 1, 177.

10. An excellent example of Stańczyk historical interpretation is Stanisław Koźmian's *Das Jahr 1863. Polen und die europäische Diplomatie,* Dr. S. R. Landau, trans. (Wien, 1896).

11. The Polonization of the Galician provincial administration begun by long-time Galician *Statthalter* Agenor Gołuchowski, and the appointment of Potocki, a west Galician conservative magnate, greatly diminished tensions between the Polish bureaucrats in the Galician administration and the Cracow conservatives. Feldman, *Dzieje,* 123; Kieniewicz, *Sapieha,* 220–25.

12. On this Greek Catholic by religion and Pole by conviction, see Irena Homola-Dzikowska, *Mikołaj Zyblikiewicz* (Wrocław, 1964).

13. *Czas,* 10 August 1880, 2; *DP,* 10 August 1880, 2; *DP,* 14 August 1880, 2–3. *DP,* 25 August 1880, 2.

14. *Stenograficzne Sprawozdania z trzeciej sesyi czwartego peryodu Sejmu Krajowego Królestwa Galicyi i Lodomeryi wraz z Wielkiem Księstwem Krakowskiem w roku 1880,* 421–22.

15. *GL,* 19 July 1880, 5. The central committee also included Dawid Abrahamowicz, Jerzy Ks. Czartoryski, Włodzimierz Dzieduszycki, Kazimierz Grocholski, and Artur Potocki (son of the late Adam Potocki).

16. *Czas,* 22 July 1880, 3; *DP,* 21 July 1880, 2; *GL,* 19 July 1880, 5; *DP,* 14 August 1880, 2.

17. *DP,* Special Edition (Dodatek) to 6 August 1880, 2. The Lemberg and Cracow committees sold space on tribunes set up along the streets to defray expenses. Tribune space in front of the arch near the train station in Lemberg ranged from ten gulden for a front-row spot reserved for the Kaiser's entire four-day stay, to

two gulden for a one-day pass on the upper level of the tribune. *DP,* 30 August 1880, 1.

18. TSDIA-L, 146/4/3465/13 [Pr. 8050, 5 August 1880. Badeni to the Presidium of the *Statthalterei*]. Military regulations required the full mobilization of garrisons, including infantry, artillery, and cavalry during a *Kaiserreise.* Troops would line all streets and squares. KA, GA 1880/82/24 [Telegram, Mondel to Potocki, 15 August 1880]. Issued on 23 August, Militär-Commando-Befehl No. 180 conformed to Potocki's wishes: KA, GA 1880/82/mixta/17.

19. AP, IT 872 [Regulamin strazy honorowej obywatelskie w czasie pobytu Najjaśniejszego Pana w Krakowie, dnia 1,2,3 i 4 Września 1880 r.].

20. The Lemberg committee could only raise 500 volunteers, and then only when the Galician administration pressured bureaucrats to sign on to the guard.

21. TSDIA-L, 146/4/3465–68. Galicia's district captains reported that representatives of rural communities elected delegations (mostly clergy and local notables) to greet the emperor in Cracow and Lemberg. The Jews of Łańcut and elsewhere planned to greet Franz Joseph with raised Torahs. District captains assured Potocki that Ruthenian peasant-mounted formations would receive funding and hospitality from local governments.

22. KA, GA 1880/82/15 [Potocki to Mondel, 18 August 1880].

23. Kazimierz Chlędowski, *Pamiętniki* (Kraków, 1957), vol. 1, 391–392. Chlędowski's account is confirmed in KA, GA 1880/82/37.

24. German translations of these speeches are collected in HHStA, Kab. Kanz. Varia, ct. 51.

25. *Czas,* 1 September 1880, 1. As discussed in chapter 2, the 1866 address from the Galician Sejm to Franz Joseph, denounced by many Polish democrats and nationalists and authored by Polish conservatives like Adam Potocki, was far from an obsequious acknowledgment of Austrian control of Galicia. The address offered Polish loyalty in return for Polish autonomy in Galicia.

26. For examples of this argument, see *WAZ* (morning edition), 29 July 1880, 1; *NFP* (morning edition), 20 August 1880, 3.

27. Polish democrats were stronger in Lemberg than in Cracow. Anti-Stańczyk Polish nationalists and progressives controlled *GN. Fremden-Blatt* termed *DP* the "main organ of the Lemberg liberals." *Fremden-Blatt* (evening edition), 7 September 1880, 1. On the Galician press, see Harald Binder's forthcoming "Die polnische Presse" and "Die ukrainische Presse"; and Józef Myśliński, "Prasa Polska w Galicji w dobie autonomicznej (1867–1918)," in *Prasa Polska w latach 1864–1918,* ed. Jerzy Lojka (Warsaw, 1976), 114–76.

28. *DP,* 22 July 1880, 1; *GL,* 10 August 1880, 4; *DP,* 13 August 1880, 2; *GN,* 20 August 1880. Some of these attacks responded specifically to the efforts by magnates to hold a *szlachta* ball for the emperor and to form a separate delegation of the "historic *szlachta.*"

29. *GN,* 31 August 1880, 1; *GN,* 1 September 1880, 1.

30. *GL,* 20 August 1880, 3; *DP,* 2 September 1880, 1; *Czas,* 30 July 1880, 5; *Czas,* 1 August 1880, 2.

31. *Czas,* 8 September 1880, 1–2. This chapter only discusses in detail three of the

five Stańczyk highlights. The emperor's return from a military school outside of Cracow accompanied by 600 peasant riders and the great ball in the Sukiennice were the other two "images" *Czas* designated as highlights.

32. *WAZ* (afternoon edition), 1 September 1880, 1; *GL,* 2 September 1880, 2. Even when Franz Joseph was in his eighties, official sources and panegyric publications continued to praise his "elastic steps" and youthful energy.

33. *Czas,* 2 September 1880, 2; *GL,* 2 September 1880, 1; TSDIA-L, 146/4/ 3468/125.

34. *Czas,* 2 September 1880, 1.

35. The Polish press repeatedly commented on Franz Joseph's alleged mastery of Polish, noting each time he signed his name *Franciszek Józef* in a school guest book (*Czas,* 4 September 1880, 1). The emperor's knowledge of Polish, however, appears to have been very limited. He received German translations of all speeches and, though crowds cheered his few words of Polish, Franz Joseph uttered only a few stock phrases similar to his usual public comment in German: "How lovely."

36. AP, JT 872/12 [Program uroczystego wjazdu do Krakowa Najjaśniejszego Pana Cesarza Franciszka Józefa Igo w dniu 1 września 1880 r. oraz pobytu w Krakowie]. The delegations included, among others, members of the Habsburg house orders, Catholic clergy, magnates greeting the emperor in the name of the "Polish *szlachta* of Galicia," Zyblikiewicz and the Cracow city council, Józef Majer as president of the Academy of Sciences, Józef Szujski as rector of the University, artist Jan Matejko as director of the Imperial-Royal School of Fine Arts, and Marshal Wodzicki as president of the Agricultural Society in Cracow. The first to receive an audience was the Russian governor of Warsaw. According to *DP,* as Governor Albedyński arrived at the Potocki Palace only one small boy had the courage to break the silence of the crowds and shout: "Poland Still Lives!" *DP,* 3 September 1880, 3.

37. Notables gathered at Franz Joseph's last stop in Galicia agreed to support this project. See Alexander Nowolecki's detailed commemorative book, *Pamiątka podróży cesarza Franciszka Józefa I.,* 216.

38. Jacek Purchla, *Krakau unter österreichischer Herrschaft, 1846–1918* (Wien, 1993), 56–57.

39. In order to present Polish culture to the emperor, the reception committees and some individual nobles had to order Polish decorations and Polish "national" clothes from theater companies and antique dealers in the imperial capital. *DP* and *GN* pointed to these facts as proof of the limited success of the conservatives in promoting Polish culture. *DP,* 15 August 1880, 1–2; *DP,* 22 August 1880, 2; *DP,* 26 August 1880, 2; *GN,* 14 August 1880, 2; *NFP* (morning edition), 20 August 1880, 3.

40. Zyblikiewicz initiated this resolution in July. *Sprawozdanie stenograficzne Sejmu Krajowego Królestwa Galicyi i Lodomeryi wraz z Wielkiem Księstwem Krakowskiem w roku 1880. 15. Posiedzenia z dnia 7 Lipca 1880,* 421–422. In fact, Austrian troops vacated Wawel only in 1905. David Crowley, "Castles, Cabarets and Cartoons: Claims on Polishness in Kraków around 1905," in

The City in Central Europe: Culture and Society from 1800 to the Present, ed. Malcolm Gee, Tim Kirk, and Jill Steward (Cambridge, 1999), 105.

41. *Czas,* 4 September 1880, 1. *DP*'s editors claimed that their paper, not the conservatives, had brought the issue to public notice two years before. *DP* noted that Galicians would be responsible for building a military post to replace the garrison on Wawel. *DP* was not enthusiastic about the Polish people financing a permanent home for imperial troops. *DP,* 4 September 1880, 1.

42. These "genuine" peasant celebrations featured costumes and floats designed by Polish artists and paid for by the city of Cracow and the district council.

43. *Czas,* 5 September 1880, 2.

44. *Czas,* 8 September 1880, 2; *Czas,* 5 September 1880, 2.

45. *Czas,* 7 September 1880, 1; *Czas,* 8 September 1880, 1; *Czas,* 14 September 1880, 1.

46. Military officers from Russia, France, Germany, and elsewhere observed the maneuvers.

47. *WZ,* 5 September 1880, 5.

48. *WAZ* (afternoon edition), 13 September 1880, 3.

49. Jacek Purchla, "Die Einflüsse Wiens auf die Architekture Lembergs 1772–1918," in Purchla, ed., *Architectura Lwowa XIX wieku* (Cracow, 1997), 30–53; Hans Bisanz, ed, *Lemberg-L'viv 1772–1918. Wiederbegegnung mit einer Landeshaupstadt der Donaumonarchie* (Wien, 1993), 36.

50. On the transformation of Lemberg into a Polish town, see above all Binder, "Making and Defending a Polish Town."

51. A minority of Greek Catholics, including Cracow's mayor, Zyblikiewicz, considered themselves Poles, and some Ruthenians were Roman Catholics. Himka, *Religion and Nationality;* Himka, *Socialism in Galicia: The Emergence of Polish Social Democracy and Ukrainian Radicalism (1860–1890)* (Cambridge, 1983).

52. Anna Veronika Wendland, *Die Russophilen in Galizien: Ukrainische Konservative zwischen Österreich und Russland, 1848–1915* (Wien, 2001); Wendland, "Die Rückkehr der Russophilen in die ukrainische Geschichte: Neue Aspekte der ukrainischen Nationsbildung in Galizien, 1848–1914," *Jahrbücher für Geschichte Osteuropas* 49 (2001): 178–99; Himka, "The Greek Catholic Church and the Ukrainian Nation in Galicia," in *Religious Compromise, Political Salvation: The Greek Catholic Church and Nation-Building in Eastern Europe,* ed. James Niessen (Pittsburgh, 1993). Paul Magosci sees a clear divide between Russophiles and Old Ruthenians (*starorusyny*), whom he defines as "first and foremost local Galician patriots who had a vague sense of cultural unity with other Rus' people . . . but whose national, political, and religious loyalties did not extend beyond the boundaries of the Austrian Empire." Magocsi, "Old Ruthenianism and Russophilism: A New Conceptual Framework for Analyzing National Ideologies in Late 19th Century Eastern Galicia" in *American Contributions to the Ninth International Congress of Slavists,* vol. 2: *Literature, Poetics, History,* ed. Paul Debreczeny (Columbus, 1983), 310.

53. The Kachkovs'kyi Society and rural newspapers founded by Naumovych and

other Russophiles "facilitated communication between the Ruthenian elite and the rural population," thereby serving as "an important basis for national mobilization." Wendland, "Die Rückkehr der Russophilen," 185. The Kachkovs'kyi Society was, with approximately 6,000 members, the largest Ruthenian cultural organization when the emperor came to Lemberg in 1880. Magocsi terms this association "an ideological child of the so-called Old Ruthenian (*starorusyny*) movement." Magocsi, "The Kachkovs'kyi Society and the National Revival in Nineteenth-Century East Galicia," *Harvard Ukrainian Studies* 15 (1991): 49–87.

54. Prosvita failed to spark much interest among the peasantry in its first years, due at least in part to its high fees and expensive publications. Prosvita surpassed the Kachkovs'kyi Society in membership only around 1900. On Prosvita, see Himka's *Galician Villagers.*

55. *WAZ* (afternoon edition), 13 September 1880, 2–3. The *WAZ* reported that 3,500 people arrived on the Karl-Ludwig rail 10 September alone; *WAZ*, 11 September 1880, 6. *NFP* counted more than 40,000 who traveled to Lemberg for the *Kaiserfest; NFP*, 17 September 1880, 7.

56. Each peasant received a commemorative medal. *DP*, 15 September 1880, 2.

57. Despite their constant attack on the conservatives' stewardship of the province, in 1880 the Polish democrats sat in the unified delegation and advocated a common policy toward the imperial center. Philip Pajakowski, "The Polish Club and Austrian Parliamentary Politics, 1873–1900" (Ph.D. Diss, Indiana University, 1989).

58. *GL*, 20 August 1880, 3.

59. According to the senior court official accompanying the emperor, the theater presented a "lovely image"; however, he added, "only the choice of the piece which was presented must be deemed highly unfortunate." HHStA, NZA, r. XV, Hofreisen 1880, ct. 367 [Loebenstein to the Office of the Grand Court Master, 17 September 1880]. Philipp Ther discusses this incident in his unpublished paper "Das polnische Theater in Lemberg 1842–1914. Trägerschichten und Repertoire," presented at "Eine multikulturelle Gesellschaft: Polen, Ukrainer und Juden in Galizien 1772–1918," conference at the University of Vienna's Institut für Osteuropäische Geschichte, 25–26 January 2002. Dobrzański returned to the directorship of the theater in 1883.

60. *NFP* (evening edition), 9 September 1880, 2; *DP*, 14 September 1880, 2. The court announced the addition of the second synagogue less than 24 hours prior to the visit, inspiring all-night preparations. *Der Israelit*, 8 October 1880, 1–2. Ruins and plaques are all that mark the locations of these two synagogues, both destroyed by the Nazis in 1941.

61. *WAZ* (afternoon edition), 13 September 1880, 4; *KVZ*, 14 September 1880, 4. According to the *KVZ*, liberal Rabbi Loewenstein spoke in German and orthodox Rabbi Ornstein in Hebrew.

62. *Der Israelit*, 8 October 1880, 2. These two events were not the only signs of imperial favor toward the Jews of Galicia. At a special audience, Jewish community leaders thanked the emperor for raising Jews to the status of equal

citizenship. On 12 September Rabbi Loewenstein joined Greek and Roman Catholic clergy, politicians, military officers, magnates, high bureaucrats and other prominent Galicians at the emperor's table. HHStA, NZA, r. XV, Hofreisen 1880, ct. 367.

63. *Czas*, 7 July 1880, 1.

64. *GN*, 15 September 1880, 3. *Czas* did not report on such incidents, but other papers did publicize them. *NFP* (morning edition), 19 September 1880, 7; *WAZ* (morning edition), 15 September 1880, 5; *NFP* (morning edition), 14 September 1880, 7; *NFP* (evening edition), 14 September 1880, 2.

65. HHStA, Kab. Archiv Direktionsakten 1880–1884, ct. 11, folders 5 and 11. The influx of petitions resulted in internal initiatives to regularize the evaluation process.

66. HHStA, Kab. Kanz., Korrespondenz-Akten, ct. 109 [Z. 1061, Kundrat to Franz Joseph, 2 September 1880; Z. 1064, ad. Z. 1064, Potocki to Kab. Kanz., 23 December 1880]. Petitioners were not all peasants. Widows of long-serving officials of the Galician administration (a result of the influx of sons of the Polish nobility and urban intelligentsia into government service after 1867) and wives of sick and debilitated government and train employees and military veterans also sought financial assistance. DALO, 350/1/2404–2407.

67. HHStA, Kab. Kanz., Korrespondenz-Akten, ct. 109 [Z. 1062, Kab. Kanz. to *Statthalterei*, exped. 8 September 1880].

68. *Nauka*, 1 September/1 October 1880, 333. This issue also includes a long editorial about the various grievances of the Ruthenians against the Polish Galician administration.

69. Each of the major Ruthenian associations and institutions sent two representatives. *Slovo*, 24 July 1880, 3 (dates cited from Ruthenian newspapers are given here according to the new style); *DP*, 23 July 1880, 2.

70. TSDIA-L, 196/1/112 [Politische Verein—(Ruska Rada): Program des Besuches S.M. in Halicka Rus']; *Dilo*, 21 August 1880, 1.

71. *NFP* (morning edition), 26 July 1880, 5; *Slovo*, 24 July 1880, 3. The Kachkovs'kyi Society and the Ruthenian Council called on their affiliates to send deputations to Lemberg for the reception. *Nauka*, 1 July 1880; *Nauka*, 1 August 1880; *Slovo*, 20 August 1880; *Slovo*, 21 August 1880; *Dilo*, 21 August 1880.

72. *Dilo*, 7 August 1880, 1.

73. *Slovo*, 12 August 1880, 1.

74. *Dilo*, 21 August 1880, 1–2. The Ruthenian committee did agree to convene a mass meeting after the departure of the emperor. This all-party Ruthenian meeting took place on 30 November in conjunction with the centennial anniversary of Joseph II's accession to the throne. The Ruthenians contrasted Joseph II's recognition of their rights with the suppression of these rights by the Poles in the era of Polish autonomy. The all-Ruthenian meeting and Joseph II celebrations coincided with festivities organized by Polish democrats for the fiftieth anniversary of the failed November uprising against Russian. The Polish conservatives opposed all of these events. DALO, 350/1/2378/56 [Pr. 969. Police Report to Ministry of the Interior, 24 August 1880]; DALO, 350/1/2378/59. German liberals also celebrated Joseph

II, rallying Austro-German support for the policies of centralization, supposedly initiated by Joseph II and, in 1880, threatened by the Taaffe system.

75. TSDIA-L, 146/4/3465/I [Z. 74=549, pr. 23 July 1880. Metropolitan Josyf Sembratovych to Potocki].

76. *Dilo*, 15 September 1880, 2; Nowolecki, *Pamiątka*, 164–66.

77. The Polish provincial administration feared that this event would become a "demonstration against the Poles, which would be unpleasant for us and for the emperor." The *Statthalterei* received reports that the Ruthenian committee was in fact agitating in the provinces to gather signatures on a petition of grievances to be handed to the emperor at the National Institute. TSDIA-L, 146/4/3468/85; Chlędowski, *Pamiętniki*, 1:392–93. Ruska Rada and the Kachkovs'kyi Society seemed to favor such action prior to 24 August. *Slovo*, 21 August 1880, 1. In the end, no attempt was made to pass such petitions to Franz Joseph at the National Institute. The event did, however, serve as an all-Ruthenian national reception for the emperor. Places were set aside in the hall for representatives of the Stauropegion Institute, National Institute, Ruska Rada, Halytsko-Ruska Matytsia, Prosvita, Shevchenko Society, Ruska Besida, Druzhnyi Lykhvar, Akademicheskii Kruzhok, and the Kachkovs'kyi Society. A. N. Shcherban', ed., *Eho ts. i k. Velychestvo Frants-Iosyf I v "Narodnom Domi" dnia 2. (14.) veresnia 1880 h.* (L'viv, 1880), 6–7; Nowolecki, *Pamiątka*, 184–88; TSDIA-L, 146/4/3486/118 and 146/4/3467/41.

78. *Dilo*, 15 September 1880, 2–3.

79. TSDIA-L, 146/4/3468/63 and 3468/95.

80. TSDIA-L, 146/4/3468/30; TSDIA-L 146/4/3468/144.

81. *Nauka*, 1 September 1/1 October, 324–33. *Nauka* reported that twenty-four local Ruthenian gatherings had approved a petition of grievances over servitude, Polish elections manipulation, lack of Ruthenian-language education, and a host of other issues. *Nauka* approved of the sentiments expressed, but complained that the petition was written in Polish: "Do these gatherings not know that Emperor Franz Joseph is emperor of the Ruthenians and so to him the Ruthenian language is no less worthy than the Polish?" Ruthenian peasants handed these petitions to court officials in Krysowice.

82. *GN*, 18 September 1880, 2.

83. *Slovo*, 23 September 1880, 1; *NFP* (morning edition), 24 September 1880, 5. The cooperation of all the Ruthenian institutions led the national populists to look forward optimistically to future all-Ruthenian cooperation for the enlightenment of the Ruthenian people. *Dilo*, 22 September 1880, 2–3.

84. *Przegląd Polski* 15(2) (1880): 6–38.

85. *Czas*, 21 September 1880, 1; *Czas*, 22 September 1880, 1.

86. *Fremden-Blatt* (morning edition), 21 September 1880, 1.

87. *WAZ* (morning), 18 September 1880, 1.

88. Loebenstein's reports are collected in HHStA, NZA, r. XV, Hofreisen 1880, ct. 367.

89. HHStA, NZA, r. XV, Hofreisen 1880, ct. 367 [Telegram no. 4335, 11 September 1880; No. 821, 15 September 1880; No. 4507, 18 September 1880; No. 853, 19 September 1880; Mondel to Obersthofmeister Hohenlohe-Schillingsfürst].

90. Franz Joseph attended military maneuvers in Galicia in 1886, 1900, 1903, and 1906; he visited Cracow for a few hours on his way through Galicia in 1896. Fras, "Podróże cesarza Franciszka Józefa," 121–122; *Program przyjęcia Najjaśniego Pana podczas pryejazdu przez Kraków w dniu 16 września 1896. r.*

91. *Fremden-Blatt,* 7 September 1894, 2. On the "new era," see Ihor Cornovol, *Pol's'ko-ukrajins'ka uhoda 1890–1894* (L'viv, 2000); Victor Hugo Lane IV, "Class Interest and the Shaping of a 'Non-Historical' Nation: Reassessing the Galician Ruthenian Path to Ukrainian Identity," in *Cultures and Nations of Central and Eastern Europe: Essays to Honor Roman Szporluk,* ed. Zvi Gitelman (Cambridge, 2000), 373–392.

92. Alfred Windischgrätz assigned Badeni this task already in December 1893. AVA, Ministerratsprasidium, Presseleitung, ct. 26, 1894 [Z. 33. Badeni to Windischgrätz, 13 January 1894; Z. 19. 1894. Referente-Erinnerung betreffend die galizische Landesausstellung in Lemberg].

93. TSDIA-L 146/4/3486/1; DALO 350/1/2375.

94. *DP,* 7 September (dodatek) 1894. Stops included a ten-minute halt in Cracow and seven minutes in Rzeszów.

95. TSDIA-L 146/4/3486/133 [Pr. 8624. 16 August 1894].

96. All of the major newspapers described these and other festivities. For one example, see *Głos Narodu,* 11 September 1894.

97. Kieniewicz, *Adam Sapieha,* 438. On the 1894 General Provincial Exhibition in Lemberg, see Jacek Purchla, "W stulecie Powszechnej Wystawy Krajowej we Lwowie 1894 roku" in the exhibition guide to *Lwowska Wystawa Krajowa 1894,* 15 March–4 April, 1994. Purchla, ed., *Architectura Lwowa XIX wieku* includes photographic reproductions of the exhibit pavillions. Albert Zipper, *Führer durch die Allgemeine Landes-Ausstellung sowie durch die Königl. Hauptstadt Lemberg* (Lemberg, 1894). The exhibition was not, however, a financial success. Kazimierz Chlędowski deemed it an "economic catastrophe." Chlędowski, *Pamiętniki,* 2:157.

98. *GL,* 8 September 1894, etc.

99. *Czas,* 14 September 1894, 1; *Czas,* 8 September 1894, 1.

100. *DP,* 7 September 1894; *DP,* 13 September 1894.

101. Walentyna Najdus, *Ignacy Daszyński* (Warszawa, 1988); Najdus, *Polska Partia Socjalno-Demokratyczna Galicji i Śląska, 1890–1919* (Warszawa, 1983). On Ukrainian socialism and nationalism, see Himka, *Socialism in Galicia.*

102. DALO 350/1/2514/64–65. The police were especially concerned about reports that individuals planned to set mourning flags on the Unionshügel, paint graffiti over the imperial eagle on post boxes, write subversive statements on the walls of houses, and hang flyers with illegal contents.

103. *Naprzód,* 15 September 1894, 1.

104. The Social Semocratic Party newspaper in Lemberg listed several instances of arrests for insulting the emperor as well as newspapers accused of the same offense during the emperor's visit. *Naprzód,* 1 October 1894, 1. Still, the few cases of direct verbal assaults on the emperor recorded in the files of the state prosecutor's office were not very threatening. Just prior to Franz Joseph's visit to the Galician Exhibition, for example, Jan Nytko, a Roman Catholic Pole living

in Lemberg, was heard by patrons in Abraham and Max Rothberg's tavern to have said: "Things will only be better if His Majesty is shot in the head." Nyta claimed he had been drunk and remembered little, but the Rothbergs testified that though Nytko had had a few, he was lucid and sober when he blurted out these words. After a short trial he was sentenced to one year in prison. TSDIA-L, 152/2/Spravy/16889 [No. 5210/94]. On 4 September, in another Lemberg tavern, 53-year-old Sabestyan Hermanski asked another drinker what he was writing. The fellow vodka consumer showed Hermanski a petition he intended to hand to the emperor. Witnesses, who had also consumed liberal quantities of vodka, immediately rushed out of the tavern to inform the police of Hermanski's reply. Hermanski was eventually acquitted of the charge of lèse-majesté. Because they had been inebriated at the time of the incident, the witnesses could not convince the judge that Hermanski had in fact said, "I shit on the emperor's head and neck" rather than "I shit on the whole show." TSDIA-L 152/2/16888.

105. Keely Stauter-Halsted, "Rural Myth and Modern Nation: Peasant Commemorations of Polish National Holidays, 1879–1910," in Bucur and Wingfield, eds., *Staging the Past,* 153–177; and Patrice M. Dabrowski, "Folk, Faith and Fatherland."

106. Krzystof Dunin Wąsowicz, *Jan Stapiński. Trybun ludu wiejskiego* (Warsaw, 1969); Dunin Wąsowicz, *Dzieje Stonnictwa Ludowego w Galicji* (Warsaw, 1956). On the early career of anti-Semitic priest Stanisław Stojałowski, see Fr. Kacki, *Ks. Stanisław Stojałowski i jego dzialalność polityczna* (Lwów, 1937). On the agricultural circles initiated by Stojałowski, see Antoni Gurnicz, *Kółka rolnicze w Galicji* (Warsaw, 1967). See also Andrzej Meissner, *Kultura i oświata wsi* (Rzeszów, 1996). The Potoczek brothers were the dominant force in the Peasant Union. Stanisław Potoczek was elected to the Sejm in 1889 and edited *Związek Chłopski.* Jan Potoczek was elected a peasant representative in the Reichsrat in 1891. Their relationship with Stojałowski fluctuated between antagonism and cooperation.

107. *Przyjaciel Ludu,* 1 January 1894, 5; *Przyjaciel Ludu,* 15 May 1894; *Przyjaciel Ludu,* 1 September 1894; *Kurjer Lwowski,* 27 August 1894.

108. Catherine Albrecht, "Pride in Protection: The Jubilee Exhibition of 1891 and Economic Competition between Czechs and Germans in Bohemia," *AHY* 24 (1993): 101–118; Alice Freifeld, "Marketing Industrialism and Dualism in Liberal Hungary: Expositions, 1842–1896," *AHY* 29(1) (1998): 63–92; Jiri Pernes, *Spiklenci proti jeho velicenstvu: Historie tzv. spiknutí Omladiny v cechách* (Prague, 1988).

Chapter 4

1. HHStA, Franz Ferdinand Nachlaß, ct. 1, Folder Kaiser Franz Joseph I. 1900–1907 [Franz Joseph to Franz Ferdinand, 7.2.03].

2. Carl Schorske describes this new style of politics as a reflection of the rejection of liberalism. Schorske, *Fin-de-siècle Vienna* (New York, 1981), 116–180.

3. Isabel Hull, "Prussian Dynastic Ritual and the End of Monarchy"; Elizabeth

Fehrenbach, "Images of Kaiserdom"; Röhl, *Kaiser, Hof und Staat;* Blessing, "The Cult of Monarchy."

4. Among many examples, see Anton Werner, *Die Festtage Wiens vom 22. bis 30. April 1854* (Wien, 1854). The most detailed newspaper accounts can be found in the *Wiener Allgemeine Theaterzeitung,* a leading revolutionary organ in 1848. By the early 1850s, this same paper welcomed the reestablishment of dynastic rule.

5. Alfred Ritter von Arneth, biographer of Maria Theresa and director of the Court and State Archives, chose scenes from the Habsburg past for the pageant. Crown Prince Rudolf and others portrayed Habsburg heroes before members of the imperial family and a few invited guests in the mansion of Franz Joseph's brother, Franz Carl. See *Hofdamen-Briefe. Sammlung von Briefen an und von Wiener Hofdamen a.d. 19 Jahrhundert* (1903). Arneth, a participant in the Frankfurt National Assembly in 1848–49, remained throughout his life, according to historian Adam Wandruszka, "at once truly devoted to the dynasty and German-liberal in disposition." Wandruszka, "Die Historiographie der theresianisch-josephinischen Reformzeit," in Anna Drabek, Richard G. Plaschka, and Wandruszka, eds., *Ungarn und Österreich unter Maria Theresia und Joseph II. Neue Aspekte im Verhältniss der beiden Länder* (Wien, 1982), 21.

6. In 1873 and 1879 Franz Joseph granted audiences to delegations from both houses of the Cisleithanian parliament, the liberal government of the city of Vienna, provincial capitals, Jewish communities, the Academy of Sciences, and various voluntary societies. HHStA, ZA, Prot. 88, vol. iv, Ceremonial Protocol 1873 [1 December entry, 128].

7. Hecher, *Hans Makart,* 66–82. The 24 April illumination of the Votive Church and the Ring was the first public use of electric lighting in Vienna. Elisabeth Springer, *Geschichte und Kulturleben der Wiener Ringstrasse* (Wiesbaden, 1979), 519.

8. HHStA, AR, 1888, F1, ct. 36, Folder 11 [Circular 28 September 1888]. This information was published in the official *Wiener Abendpost* on 20 October 1888.

9. While Schorske views the Ringstrasse as "an iconographic index to the mind of ascendant Austrian liberalism," Springer writes that "the Ringstrasse owes its origin to the representation ideas of Emperor Franz Joseph and his advisor on this matter, Interior Minister Alexander von Bach." *Fin-de-siècle Vienna* (New York, 1981), 27; Elisabeth Springer, *Geschichte und Kulturleben der Wiener Ringstrasse,* 1. On the museums and their place in the never completed imperial forum, see Peter Stachel, "An Austrian 'Place of Memory': The Heldenplatz in Vienna as a Historic Symbol and Political Metaphor," in *Collective Identities in Central Europe in Modern Times,* Moritz Csáky and Elena Mannová, eds. (Bratislava, 1999), 159–178.

10. Arneth determined which of Maria Theresa's advisors were depicted in the monument. See his two *Denkschriften* collected in HHStA, OMeA 1873/r. 90, ct. 921. The statue was designed to place a different kind of dynastic stamp on the modernizing city than had the equestrian figures of the Habsburg generals Eugene of Savoy and Archduke Charles initiated during neoabsolutist rule and

unveiled on the grounds of the imperial palace in the early years of Dualism. On monuments and identity in Austria, see the collection of essays in Stefan Riesenfellner, ed., *Steinernes Bewußtsein: Die öffentliche Repräsentation staatlicher und nationaler Identität Österreichs in seinen Denkmälern* (Wien, 1998).

11. The emperor sat in the center box and those holding the highest rank took places in the boxes on his left and right. The grand court master reserved the upper balconies for bureaucrats and officers and their wives and issued unnumbered entrance tickets (presumably for standing room) to military cadets. HHStA ZA Prot. 112, Ceremonial Protocol 1888 [Anhang zum Ceremoniel-Protokoll II].

12. Schönerer claimed that he and his colleagues only wanted to "express the opinions of German men" to the "press Jews." *Unverfälschte Deutsche Worte*, 16 March 1888 and 1 April 1888. The Pan-German press termed the charges against Schönerer a typical lie from the "Judenblätter." *Unverfälschte Deutsche Worte*, 16 May 1888, 121–122.

13. *Das Vaterland* denounced the Pan-German radicals for failing to realize that cries of "Up with Schönerer" did nothing to undermine the supposedly entrenched power of the Jews and would not benefit the Christian population. *Das Vaterland,* 18 May 1888, 1.

14. For a description of Vogelsang's relationship with Lueger and his role in the early Christian Social Movement, see Boyer, *Political Radicalism,* 166–183.

15. *Das Vaterland,* 4 December 1888, 1.

16. On the Iron Ring, see W. A. Jenks, *Austria Under the Iron Ring.* Steven Beller argues compellingly that Taaffe's policy of "muddling through" pushed many German liberals to move into the radical nationalist camp. Facing loss of status as the acknowledged "state people" and exclusion from the ruling coalition, some German politicians turned their energies to protecting perceived German national interests against the incursions of the Slavs. Beller, *Francis Joseph,* 126–127.

17. Judson, *Exclusive Revolutionaries,* 248–254.

18. Badeni's short tenure has been dubbed the "Polish government" of Austria. Badeni, a former Galician *Statthalter,* kept the portfolio for the Ministry of the Interior in addition to his position as minister president; Leon Biliński served as finance minister; Agenor Gołuchowski Jr. (son of the long-time *Statthalter* of Galicia) was common minister of foreign afairs; and Edward Rittner held the post of minister for Galicia. Waldemar Łazuga, *"Rządy polskie" w Austrii: Gabinet Kazimierza hr. Badeniego, 1895–1897* (Poznań, 1991).

19. The first four curias for Reichsrat elections were as follows: large estate owners, towns, chambers of commerce and trade, and rural communities. Only the 1907 election laws finally scrapped the curial system in favor of universal (manhood) suffrage. On the expansion of the suffrage, see Harald Binder, *Galizien in Wien. Parteien, Wahlen, Fraktionen und Abgeordnete im Übergang zur Massenpolitik* (Wien, 2005).

20. Bruce Garver, *The Young Czech Party, 1874–1901, and the Emergence of a Multi-Party System* (New Haven, 1978), 245–247; Berthold Sutter, *Die Badenischen Sprachen-Verordnungen von 1897,* 2 vols. (Graz and Cologne, 1965).

21. In 1908, for example, the party executive in Vienna rejected for "practical reasons" suggestions to officially discourage workers from allowing their children to participate in the children's jubilee event in Schönbrunn. Verein für die Geschichte der Arbeiterbewegung, Vorstands-Protokolle, 19.3.1906 bis 10.3.1910, Heft 5, entry for 5 May 1908.

22. *AZ* (morning edition), 1 January 1898, 5.

23. On Victoria's jubilees, see Thomas Richards, *The Commodity Culture of Victorian England;* W. Arnstein, "Queen Victoria's Diamond Jubilee," *American Scholar,* 66; David Cannadine, "The Context, Performance and Meaning of Ritual: The British Monarchy and the 'Invention of Tradition,' c. 1820–1977," in Hobsbawm and Ranger, eds., *The Invention of Tradition,* 100–164.

24. Robert Kann, *Erzherzog Franz Ferdinand Studien* (Wien, 1976).

25. In the 1890s, the court created a ceremonial department under the control of the ceremonial director in order to address the increasing specialization needed to produce imperial celebrations. On the early discussion surrounding the creation of this department, see OMeA, SR, ct. 373 [Memorandum from Eduard Wlassak, Court Secretary, 1 January 1870]; Dr. Egon Freiherr Loebenstein von Aigenhorst, "Das Zeremoniell unter Kaiser Franz Joseph," 399–400.

26. Official jubilee events also included a military gala dinner as well as family and state dinners. A number of events were later added to the official program: the unveiling of a monument dedicated to Archduke Albrecht (discussed below); official receptions of deputations from the provincial legislatures, the two capitals, and Bosnia and Herzegovina on 29 November; and an illumination of the city of Vienna on 2 December. HHStA, Neue Zeremonial Akten (NZA), 1898, ct. 143 [Protokoll der am 17. und 20. Dezember 1897 stattgehabten Sitzungen betreffend die Hoffestlichkeiten . . .].

27. The invitation list for the court mass in St. Stephen's Cathedral included 1,000 members of the armed forces and 1,400 civilians, including 180 from the provincial legislatures, 70 delegates from provincial capitals and the imperial and royal capitals of Vienna and Budapest, 500 from the Cis- and Transleithanian parliaments, and delegations from the universities, the Catholic, Orthodox, and Lutheran churches, representatives of the Jewish communities, and court dignitaries and holders of high imperial titles. See NZA, 1898, ct. 143 [Sitzungsprotokol 20/6 98].

28. HHStA, OMeA, 1898/r. 19/a/22, ct. 1369 [Protocol from 31 May 1898].

29. The Ministry of War and the Cisleithanian minister president each received half of the tickets to the second performance to distribute to government officials and army officers not invited to the first performance. HHStA, NZA, ct. 143 [Sitzung am 20/6 1898].

30. Local communities and voluntary associations often produced pageants and plays for imperial occasions. According to the *NFP,* for example, Sidonie Heindl-Purschke and Leonie Schwenger's *Hoch Österreich!* was performed "on many Austrian stages" and was provided free to amateur theaters and voluntary associations. *NFP* (morning edition), 26 July 1898, 7.

31. Robert Musil, *Der Mann ohne Eigenschaften* (Berlin, 1930–1943).

32. Carld Erdmann Edler, professor of literature and history, Martin Greif, German author of patriotic works like *Prince Eugen,* and Wilhelm von Wartenegg, a curator in the court museum of fine arts and an author of the prize-winning play *Mozart,* written for the Vienna Mozart festival in 1891, sent in proposals.

33. HHStA, GI, 1897, ct. 167 [Z. 1082]; HHStA, GI, 1897–1898, ct. 169 [Z. 48]; HHStA, OMeA 1898/r. 19/a/22, ct. 1369.

34. HHStA, GI, 1897, ct. 167 [Z. 1082].

35. Copies of the minutes and other materials related to this meeting are in HHStA, OMeA 1898/r. 19/a/22, ct. 1369 [Pr. 2773. Protocol from 22 March 1898]; HHStA, GI, 1898, ct. 169 [ad. Z. 48].

36. As undersecretary in the Ministry of Religion and Education from 1848–1861, Helfert had pushed the ministry to adopt educational materials that would use the Habsburg dynasty as a binding force in the state. Helfert was also president and a founding member of the *Österreichischer Volksschriften-Verein,* dedicated since 1848 to promoting "love of fatherland."

37. Thun-Salm's works included *"Was die Grossmutter erzählte." Märchen und Erzählungen* (Wien, 1906). She delivered her corrected manuscript to the director of the Court Theater on 6 May. He sent a copy to Franz Ferdinand. On 28 May Liechtenstein, Plappart, Gołuchowski, and Thun met and approved of Thun-Salm's work. HHStA, GI, 1897–1898, ct. 169 [Z. 48].

38. Thun-Salm, *Des Kaisers Traum,* 58–59.

39. HHStA, 1898/r. 19/a/22, ct. 1369 [Prot. 2773. Protocols from 22 March and 31 May 1898].

40. *NFP* (morning edition), 30 November 1898, p.5.

41. *Illustrirtes Wiener Extrablatt,* 3 December 1908, 13.

42. On Mayerling, see Brigitte Hamann, *Rudolf. Kronprinz und Rebell* (Wien, 1978).

43. Brigitte Hamann, *Elisabeth. Kaiserin wider Willen* (Wien, 1981), 290.

44. On Elisabeth's image in the Hungarian half of the monarchy, see Gerő, *Emperor Francis Joseph.*

45. Geertz, "Centers, Kings, and Charisma," 125.

46. Once news of the tragedy reached Vienna, Loebenstein and the ceremonial department quickly probed precedents and scripted the coming ceremonies. HHStA, ZA Prot. 122, Ceremonial Protocol 1898 [Anhang VII].

47. *NFP* (morning edition), 16 September 1898, 1; (evening edition), 17 September, 2.

48. HHStA, ZA Prot. 122, Ceremonial Protocol 1898 [Anhang VII].

49. AVA, MI, Präs., 1898, ct. 17 [Pr. 7247, 15 September 1898].

50. Churches held services in all the major cities and towns of Galicia. Cracow's Bell of Sigmund rang out the moment the funeral procession in Vienna commenced. Stores closed from 4–6 P.M. *Słowo Polskie,* 11 September–19 September 1898.

51. The *NFP* reported that the wagon bearing the sarcophagus weighed 9,000 kilograms and informed its readers in great detail about the wounds suffered by the empress. *NFP* (evening edition), 12 September 1898, 2; *NFP* (morning edition), 13 September 1898, 1.

52. *Związek Chłopski,* 21 September 1898, 209.
53. Among many examples, see *GN,* 11 September 1898, 1; *Vaterland,* 18 September (morning edition), 1898, 1.
54. *Gablonzer Zeitung,* 18 September 1898, 1; *NFP* (morning edition), 20 September 1898.
55. *Das Vaterland* (morning edition), 16 September, 1.
56. *ÖFZ,* 20 September 1898, 1.
57. The Social Democratic press noted the irony of this posthumous embrace of the empress by the Christian Socials. *Arbeiterinnen-Zeitung,* 15 September 1898, 6.
58. HHStA, NZA, 1898, ct. 57 [Expose über die Titulatur auf den Wappen weiland Ihrer Majestät der Kaiserin und Königin Elisabeth. Loebenstein, 27 February 1899; Pr. 8504, Prs. 6 October 1898; 8929, Pr. 19 October 1898; 1642, Pr. 20 February 1899].
59. The opposition had been pressing Bánffy for a more forceful statement in support of the Hungarian Revolution of 1848 and against celebrations of the military campaigns associated with Franz Joseph's accession—campaigns that cost the lives of thousands of Hungarians. Many Hungarian political leaders opposed any action that might confirm that Franz Joseph had ruled Hungary as king since 1848. He was, in their view, only king of Hungary since his crowning in 1867. See Peter Hanak, *Der Garten und die Werkstatt: Ein kulturgeschichtlicher Vergleich Wien und Budapest um 1900* (Wien, 1988), 101–16.
60. Loebenstein directed the party responsible for the original oversight of the empress's Hungarian title, a captain of the palace guard, to admit his error to the Hungarian minister president. Loebenstein also provided evidence that court documents invariably included the correct version of the empress's title.
61. HHStA, ZA Prot. 122, Ceremonial Protocol 1898.
62. An infuriated Loebenstein denounced Bánffy's call to convene a conference including representatives of the Hungarian government to determine the ceremony for all future Habsburg funerals as "self-serving." Such a conference should only be called when the grand court master believed such a meeting to be necessary. HHStA, ZA Prot. 122, Ceremonial Protocol 1898; HHStA, NZA, 1898, ct. 57 [Z. 9842, Pr. 17 November 1898. Kaiserin Elisabeth. Beschwerden seitens Ungarn anlässlich der Leichenfeierlichkeiten].
63. Gottfried Mayer, *Österreich als katholische Grossmacht;* C. A. Macartney, *The Habsburg Empire, 1790–1918* (London, 1968), 573–574.
64. HHStA, Franz Ferdinand Nachlaß, ct. 2, Albrecht Folder [Albrecht to Franz Ferdinand, 10 August 1881]. Brigitte Hamann argues persuasively that Albrecht's views on this subject reflected Franz Joseph's as well. Brigitte Hamann, "Erzherzog Albrecht," 62–77.
65. *Wiener Diöcesanblatt,* nr. 22, 1898. Many newspapers printed the letter, which was also distributed in pamphlet form. For comments on the letter, see *NFP* (morning edition), 16 November 1898, 1. The *Reichenberger Zeitung,* 17 November 1898, 1 rejected the Catholic hierarchy's vision of the monarchy as a "mosaic" of peoples and criticized the bishops for encouraging the Catholic political parties.

66. J. Schnitzer, ed., *Franz Joseph und seine Zeit. Cultur-Historischer Rückblick auf die Franco-Josephinische Epoche* (Wien, 1898), 8.
67. On Franz Joseph's attachment to military life, see István Deák, *Beyond Nationalism;* Bled, *Franz Joseph:* Egon Caesar Conte Corti, *Vom Kind zum Kaiser.*
68. Deák, *Beyond Nationalism,* 55–58.
69. Jaszi, *The Dissolution of the Habsburg Monarchy,* 141; Deák, *Beyond Nationalism,* 4; Cole, "Vom Glanz der Montur."
70. Stekl, "Der Wiener Hof," 32–34. Johann Christoph Allmayer-Beck, *Der stumme Reiter: Erzherzog Albrecht, der Feldherr "Gesamtösterreichs"* (Graz, 1997); Matthias Stickler, *Erzherzog Albrecht von Österreich: Selbstverständnis und Politik eines konservativen Habsburgers im Zeitalter Kaiser Franz Josephs* (Husum, 1997). On Albrecht's role in the Habsburg family, see Brigitte Hamann, "Erzherzog Albrecht—Die Graue Eminenz des Habsburgerhofes: Hinweise auf einen unterschätzten Politiker," in Isabella Ackerl, Walter Hummelberger, and Hans Mommsen, eds., *Politik und Gesellschaft im alten und neuen Österreich. Festschrift für Rudolf Neck zum 60. Geburtstag* (Wien, 1981), vol. 1, 62–77.
71. KA, 1895, ct. 934 contains the lists of contributions.
72. The monument was revealed in an elaborate ceremony on 21 May 1899. Events commemorating the unveiling included a theater production in the opera, a reception at court attended by almost 1,600 persons. HHStA ZA, Prot. 123, Ceremonial Protocol 1899 [Anhang IV].
73. KA, 1895, ct. 934 [Pr. 2600, 1896; 2845, 1896].
74. *NFP* (morning edition), 22 November 1898, 6.
75. WStLA, HA, KB, ct. 61-3, Mappe 11/1. The liberal Vienna city council distributed a few hundred of these medals to its own members, the imperial family, some court officials, city bureaucrats, and a number of those who worked on the Makart procession.
76. *WZ,* Separat-Abdruck, 18 August 1898.
77. Already in the first half of November, newspapers reported on the plans made by the Joint Army for 2 December. See *NFP* (morning edition), 10 November 1898, 5.
78. *Fremden-Blatt* (morning edition), 2 December 1898, 51. Kriegshammer sent copies of this pamphlet to the minister of religion and education. AVA, MCU, Präs., 1898, ct. 264 [Z. 3090, Pr. 31 December 1898. Kriegshammer to Arthur Bylandt Rheydt, minister of religion and education].
79. Deák, *Beyond Nationalism.*
80. *Gedenkschrift für die Soldaten anlässlich des 50 jährigen Regierungs-Jubiläums S. M. des Kaisers Franz Joseph I* (Wien, 1898), 4.
81. *Gedenkschrift für die Soldaten,* 12–13.
82. *GL,* 4 January 1898, 3. *GL* took many of its daily notices from those published in the official *WZ* and the organ of the ministry of foreign affairs, the *Fremden-Blatt.*
83. *GL,* 20 March 1898, 1.
84. HHStA, AR, 1898, F1, ct. 37 [Thun to Gołuchowski, 19 March 1898].
85. HHStA, OMeA, 1898, r. 133, ct. 1396 [Z. 9056, Pr. 22 October 1898].

86. The *NFP* estimated that three million medals were given to active and retired members of the armed forces and 40,000 to state bureaucrats. *NFP* (morning edition), 15 November 1898, 4–5. The *NFP* estimate was very conservative. Over 100,000 medals were distributed to government employees in the Hungarian half of the monarchy alone. HHStA, AR, F1, 1898, ct. 36, Kaiser Franz Josef 11 [Z. 1577, Pr., 9 January 1899. Bánffy to Gołuchowski, 4 January 1899].

87. HHStA, Nachlaß Braun, Varia VII, Private and official correspondence, 1849–1897 [From "A True Patriot," March 1898].

88. AVA, MCU, Präs., 1898, ct. 257 [Z. 1469. Pr. 31 May 1898]. After the death of the empress, festive events were canceled; however, all the monarchy's students were still required to listen to patriotic speeches delivered by teachers and school directors. For examples of these school celebrations, see *XXI. Jahresbericht des K.K. Rudolf-Gymnasiums I Brody* (Brody, 1899); *Jahres-Bericht des Gymnasiums der k.k. Theresianischen Akademie in Wien* (Wien, 1899). In Brody, Vienna, and elsewhere, school officials explained to the children that for the previous fifty years the emperor devoted himself "to advance the welfare of his subject peoples." Chapter 5 discusses publications directed toward enhancing the patriotic feelings of the monarchy's youth.

89. *Kaiser Jubiläums Festblatt der Wiener Zeitung,* 2 December 1898.

90. In what he certainly considered a great concession, Franz Joseph allowed Franz Ferdinand to retain his titles and to remain heir to the throne despite marrying Baroness Chotek, a daughter of an old aristocratic family not considered worthy of marrying into the House of Habsburg. Franz Ferdinand was required to sign a pledge acknowledging that the offspring from this marriage would have no claim to the Habsburg throne. Only after signing this pledge did Franz Joseph reaffirm Franz Ferdinand as next in line to the throne. At Franz Joseph's specific command, the *WZ* publicized Franz Ferdinand's pledge on 29 June 1900. HHStA, ZA Prot. 124, Ceremonial Protocol 1900 [Entry from 28 June 1900].

91. Franz Joseph reaffirmed his authority to approve or deny requests by members of the imperial family to serve as official protectors for publications, events, charities, and the like in 1901 after Franz Ferdinand agreed to lend his name to a Catholic School Association, part of the network of Christian Social–oriented civic associations. HHStA, Franz Ferdinand Nachlaß, ct. 1, Folder Kaiser Franz Joseph I 1900–1907 [XX, D 17. Franz Joseph to Franz Ferdinand, 18 April 1901; XX 11, 20 April 1901, Franz Joseph to Franz Ferdinand].

92. J. Schnitzer, ed., *Franz Joseph und seine Zeit;* Max Herzig, ed., *Viribus Unitis. Das Buch vom Kaiser* (Wien, Budapest, Leipzig, 1898). Herzig's elaborate commemorative book cost 200 fl for the "luxury" edition, and 50 fl for the "salon" version.

93. Rudolf Beer, *Zwei Prachtwerke zu dem Regierungs-Jubiläum des Kaisers Franz Joseph I.*

94. Herzig, *Viribus Unitis,* introduction.

95. Herzig, *Viribus Unitis,* 88.

96. *Huldigungs-Ausstellung: Unser Kaiser 1848–1898–1908* (Wien, 1908).

97. Schnitzer, *Franz Joseph,* 8. James Shedel reaches similar conclusions to those

presented above about the prominence of comparisons between Franz Joseph and Christ in publications appearing in the last months of the jubilee year in "Emperor, Church and People."

98. Schnitzer, *Franz Joseph,* 3.

99. Wagner contributed essays on art and architecture to many commemorative publications, including *Kaiserblatt* and *Zum Zweiten December 1848–1898,* both discussed in Chapter 5. On the architect's tenure as juror in 1898 see WStLA, HA, KB, ct. 63-3, Mappe 5 [St. Z. 7622]. On Wagner's patriotic activities in 1879, see WStLA, HA, KB, ct. 61-3, Mappe 9 and WStLA, HA, KB, ct. 61-4 [Programm für den Huldigung-Festzug in Wien zur Feier der silbernen Hochzeit Ihrer Majestäten des Kaisers und der Kaiserin (Wien, 1879).

100. Brigitte Hamann, "Die Wiener Hof," p. 66.

101. James Shedel, "Emperor, Church and People," p. 72.

Chapter Five

1. Piotr Babczyszyn, *Od Gniezny i Seretu po Łynę, Odrę i Nysę. Wspomnienia.* Part 1: *Łozniów – Trembowla (1890–1914).* Ossolineum manuscript 15336/II, 168–169. Babczyszyn attempted to convince Galician peasants to view themselves as members of a larger Polish nation divided between the three partitioning powers and to win them over for a program dedicated to rebuilding a Polish state. He encountered a great deal of indifference and even hostility to his message even in the last decades before World War I.

2. Thomas Richards, *The Commodity Culture of Victorian England.*

3. Beller, *Francis Joseph.*

4. Certainly, Franz Joseph's commitment to charitable giving stemmed from his sincerely held beliefs concerning his duties as Habsburg emperor. For insights into Franz Joseph's self-conception as ruler, see Brigitte Hamann, "Erzherzog Albrecht," 62–77.

5. Franz Joseph also granted freedom to hundreds convicted of anti-government activities and *lèse-majesté*. Franz Tschudy Freiherr von Clarus, *Illustrirtes Gedenkbuch zur immerwährende Erinnerung an die glorreiche Vermählungs-feier Sr. k.k. Apostolische Majestät Franz Joseph von Österreich mit ihrer köngl. Hoheit der Durchlauchtigsten Frau Herzogin Elisabeth in Baiern, vollzogen in Wien am 24 April 1854.* (Wien, 1854), 111. Tschudy's relatively expensive commemorative book (2 gulden) includes a listing of the amount of charity the emperor gave out to each capital city. Half of the profits from the sale of this book were to be distributed to the poor of the outlying communities of Vienna.

6. The mayor of Vienna made direct requests to the guilds and wealthy individuals. WStLA, HA, KB, ct. 61-1, Mappe 1/10 [Prs. 164. 16 March 1854]. In reality, many recipients were government employees or children of government officials. WStLA, HA, KB, ct. 61-1, Mappe 1/31 [Verzeichnis der 40 mit der Ausstattungsbeiträge 500fl betheilten Brautpaare].

7. Already in 1849 Franz Joseph made an appeal for the public to make charitable donations rather than hold costly festivities for his birthday. HHStA, NZA, 1849, ct. 85 [Prs. 2750, 9 August 1849].

8. The official *Wiener Abendpost* publicized the wishes of the emperor; government newspapers in the provinces, like Galicia's *GL,* quoted the emperor and encouraged readers to join local communities, institutions, and individuals already following the wishes of the emperor and working for the common good in a multitude of jubilee actions. See, among many others, *GL,* 20 March 1898, 1.

9. In 1888, public donations in honor of the emperor's fortieth anniversary amounted to some 8,849,000 gulden. Retired Colonel Alfred Sypniewski estimated that 143 humanitarian institutions received 2,566,000 gulden, 560 foundations (many founded for the jubilee) gained 3,194,000 gulden, and another 3,087,000 gulden in donations were offered in 970 other acts of charity in 1888. Sypniewski, *Fünfzig Jahre Kaiser* (Wien, 1898), 282.

10. The final listing can be found in HHStA, Kab., Kanz., Korrespondenz-Akten (Korr. A.), ct. 197 [ad. Corr. 47, 1899].

11. C. Henop, *Das Jubiläumsjahr 1898. Ein Gedenkbuch an die humanitären und festlichen Veranstaltungen aus Anlass des 50 jährigen Regierungs Jubiläums Sr. Majestät des Kaiser FJI. am 2. December 1898* (Wien, 1898). Though Henop planned to publish two volumes, the Austrian National library holds only the first volume, available for sale in the fall of 1898. See *NFP* (morning edition), 14 August 1898, 8.

12. AVA, MI, Präs. 1, 1898, ct. 16 [Nr. 6243, 25 July 1898; Nr. 4377, 13 May 1898; Nr. 5304, June 1898].

13. AVA, MI, Präs. 1, 1898, ct. 16 [Nr. 4974, 6 June 1898].

14. AVA, MI, Präs. 1, 1898, ct. 15 [Nr. 4197, 4 April 1897].

15. For a few examples: AVA, MI, Präs. 1, 1898, ct. 15 [Nr. 5345, 2 June 1897, Tetsche an der Elbe; Nr. 8893, Franz Ferdinand von Österreich Oeste Prager Mil. Vet. Vereine; Nr. 8491, Crown Prince Rudolf Teresianstadt Military Veterans' Association; Nr. 11227, Warriors' Association for Lipa and the Surrounding Area].

16. NöLA, 1898, ct. 973 [L8, z. 1063].

17. Henop, *Das Jubiläumsjahr 1898,* 19.

18. *NFP* (morning edition), 4 December 1898, 8.

19. Henop, *Das Jubiläumsjahr 1898,* 18.

20. AVA, Ministerratspräsidium, Presseleitung, ct. 26, 1894 [z. 240].

21. NöLA, 1898, ct. 974 [L8, z. 4073, 3 July 1898].

22. NöLA, 1898, ct. 975 [L8, z. 6748; L8, z. 7283].

23. Henop, *Das Jubiläumsjahr 1898,* 18.

24. See AVA, MI, Präs. 1, 1897/1898, cts. 15, 16, 17.

25. *GL,* 8 December 1898.

26. *NFP* (morning edition), 6 July 1898, 5.

27. NöLA, 1898, ct. 975 [L8, z. 6748; L8, z. 7283].

28. Typical of these festivities, the First Funeral and Support Association of the Employees of the Imperial-Royal Post and Telegraph Institute in Vienna sponsored a "Kaiser-Jubilee-Charity-Festival" and dedicated all proceeds to the supporting fund of the association. The Christian House Caretakers and Porters held their jubilee festival in Vienna's Fuchs Hotel, while the Vienna Christian Women's

Association received reluctant government approval to hold a Kaiser Jubilee and Second Founding Festival on 7 August in Waigl's Dreherpark. The Association of Styrians in Vienna held their celebration in the same venue. NöLA, 1898, ct. 974 [L8, z. 4171, 7 July 1898; z. 4450; z. 4763, 7 August 1898]. Waigl's was a favorite location for Kaiser Festivals in 1898 and 1908.

29. NöLA, 1898, ct. 974 [L8. z. 5332, 1 September 1898].

30. NöLA, 1898, ct. 974 [L8, z. 5280, 27 August 1898]. Franz Joseph wrote to his wife about the jubilee bicycle race. See Georg Nostitz-Rienek, ed., *Briefe Kaiser Franz Josephs an Kaiserin Elisabeth 1859–1898* (Wien, 1966), vol. 2, 424.

31. As long as proceeds were donated to charity, the ministry of the interior and the provincial governors gave permission to associations to dub theirs a "Kaiser-lottery." For one such request, from Stefanie Gräfin Wenckheim as president of "Mater Admirabilis" in Vienna, see NöLA, 1898, ct. 973 [L8. z. 1357, 18 ad. 516]. This association wished to use funds from the Kaiser-lottery in order to rent part of a Vienna cloister for a home for poor female workers.

32. On the Jewish handworkers' association Gwiazda and the jubilee, see TSDIA-L, 146/8/182/21.

33. *Das Strafgesetz vom 27. Mai 1852, Nr. 117 RGBl., samt den dasselbe ergänzenden und erläuternden Gesetzen und Verordnungen, unter Anführung einschlägiger Beschlüsse und Entscheidungen des Obersten Gerichts- und Kassationshofes.* (Wien, 1908). Elgin Drda, "Die Entwicklung der Majestätsbeleidigung in der österreichischen Rechtsgeschichte unter besonderer Berücksichtigung der Ära Kaiser Franz Josephs" (Ph.D. Diss., University of Linz, 1992), 103.

34. On imperial holidays, Franz Joseph regularly freed some of those arrested and imprisoned for lèse-majesté. Transgressions against this law appear to have been more common when Franz Joseph was in the vicinity and during the First World War when lèse-majesté was punishable by immediate execution.

35. *Reichsgesetzblatt für die im Reichsrathe vertretenen Konigreiche und Länder*, No. 40, 1886, 395 reprints the text of the 1858 imperial decree.

36. Evaluations of requests to use the imperial image for the 1898 and 1908 jubilees cite MI, Allgemein Zl. 39961/1897 and Zl.106/1898. Zl. 39961 is missing from the AVA. The examples cited here are among the few that still exist, and some of these are partially burned and difficult to read.

37. AVA, MI, Präs. 1, 1898, ct. 15 [z. 5245, 14 June 1898].

38. AVA, MI, Präs. 1/J, 1908, ct. 1210 [Prs. 4262, 1 May 1908].

39. *Amtsblatt der k.k. Polizei-Direktion in Wien,* 1898, 54.

40. AVA, MI, Präs. 1/J, 1908, ct. 1210 [Prs. 1846, 2 March 1908].

41. AVA, MI, Präs. 1/J, 1908, ct. 1210 [Prs. 5423, 16 June 1908]. This file refers to the regulations from 30 December 1897, z. 39961, and 22 January 1898, z. 106.

42. *NFP* (morning edition), 29 November 1898, 1. One carpet seller suggested that "carpets are the most beautiful and cheapest decorations" because they could be used both for furnishing and for hanging from the balcony as a symbol of patriotic devotion. *KVZ,* 15 August 1898, 7.

43. Minister President Thun encouraged provincial governors to persuade their underlings to purchase Pichl's creations. NöLA, 1898, ct. 974 [L8, z. 2718, Thun to Kielmansegg, 28 April 1898].

44. WStLA, HA, KB , ct. 63-2, Mappe 3 includes a copy of the Pichl brochure.
45. *NFP* (morning edition), 27 November 1898, 22. Wahliss offered Kaiser-Medallions also designed by Professor Benk as wall decorations. Wahliss's Kaiser busts ranged in price from 80 kreuzers to 2.80 gulden and from 22–75 centimeters high.
46. Some Ruthenian language schools handed out portraits of the emperor to pupils. *Ruslan,* 27 November, 1908, 4.
47. *NFP* (morning edition), 5 June 1898, 18.
48. Many schools received from five to fifty copies of Pietzner's photograph in several waves. Even after sending out these copies, at least 1,000 more remained in the archives of the Lower Austrian *Statthalterei.* NöLA, 1898, ct. 974 [L8, z. 4168, 7 July 1898].
49. The Galician administration bought fourteen Kaiser portraits with wood, two with mahogany, and sixteen with gold-plated frames from R. Lechner. The Galician administration also ordered forty-five copies of Pietzer's portrait of Franz Joseph and forty-five of Elisabeth. AP, Polizei-Direction Kraków, ct. 51 [Prs. 1154].
50. *NFP* (morning edition), 23 June 1898, 14.
51. *NFP* (morning edition), 5 June 1898, 27. A Bohemian silverware manufacturer offered several sizes of this jubilee item for sale. The knives were decorated with a portrait of the emperor with a laurel wreath, his initials, and the Austrian crown.
52. *NFP,* 27 June 1898, 19.
53. *NFP* (morning edition), 4 December 1898, 37.
54. *OR,* 27 November 1898.
55. Schönerer's paper railed against such publications, which "sprout up like mushrooms." *Unverfälschte Deutsche Worte,* 1898, Nr. 9, 113. Hundreds of commemorative books written for various imperial celebrations are collected in the Austrian National Library and the Vienna City and Provincial Library. The Austrian National Library possesses over 100 different titles of commemorative pamphlets for the imperial wedding of 1854, approximately the same number for the twenty-fifth wedding anniversary in 1879, and more than 150 each for the jubilee years of 1898 and 1908. The 1873 twenty-fifth jubilee of Franz Joseph's reign generated only a handful of commemorative books and pamphlets, most of which contained published sermons by rabbis and speeches by school directors.
56. For example, Antoni Tesseryk penned his commemorative account of the emperor's 1851 tour of Galicia after the 1853 assassination attempt and earmarked the proceeds for the fund to erect the Votive Church in Vienna as a monument to what Rabbi Moses Eisen from Tarnopol deemed the "miraculous rescue" of Franz Joseph. Tesseryk, *Wjazd najjaśniejszego Franciszka Józefa I;* Moses Eisen gave his sermon on Franz Joseph's survival at the home of Hirsch Fränkl before a group of Galician Jews, *Predigt zum Andenken der göttlichen Errettung Sr. k.k. ap. Majestät des Kaisers Franz Josef I.* (Vienna, 1853). Anastazy Rusinowsky published *Wspomnienie 18 Lutego 1853 i pożądanego wyzdrowienia Jego c.k. Apostolskiej Mości Cesarza Franciszka Józefa* (Tarnów, 1853). The proceeds from this tiny pamphlet, which cost only 20 kreuzer and included hymns and

prayers for Franz Joseph in Hebrew on the back, were to go to the building of a monument in the cathedral of Tarnów to commemorate the same event.

57. J. F. Boehringer, *Österreichs Jubeltage oder: Wien am 22 bis 30. April 1854* (Wien, 1854); Adolph Carl Naske, *Gedenkbuch über die Vermählungs-Feierlichkeiten Seiner k.k. apostolischen Majestät Franz Joseph I., Kaiser von Österreich, mit Elisabeth, Herzogin in Baiern* (Wien, 1854). Naske's book, which contains advertisements for Boehringer's and other 1854 commemorative books, claims that over 30,000 copies of Boehringer's book had been sold for thirty kreuzers per copy. Naske, *Gedenkbuch*, 157. Other commemorative publications produced in 1854 include *Versi del dottor Angelo Galletti. Ottave scritte fin d'allora che fu pubblicata la notizia del promesso matrimonio di Sua mesta J.R.A. Francesco Giuseppe I imperatore d'Austria etc.* (Verona, 1854); Johann Capistran Klemsch, *Epithalamion oder Huldigung Galiziens zur Feier des Allerhöchsten Belagers Sr. Kais. Kön. Apost. Majestät Franz Josef I . . . mit Elisabeth, Amalia, Eugenia* (Lemberg, 1854).

58. *NFP* (evening edition), 17 September 1898, 2.

59. Julius Laurencic, ed., *Jubiläums-Ausstellung Wien 1898* (Wien, 1898).

60. For example, see the *Verordnungsblatt für den Dienstbereich des Ministeriums für Cultus und Unterricht* (Wien, 1898), 174, 299, and 394.

61. Leon Smolle, *Kaiser Joseph II. Für das Volk und die Jugend Österreichs* (Wien, 1880). *KVZ*, 11 November 1898. An 1880 Joseph II commemorative book by Sigmund Berger, published in German in Moravia and including "folkloristic anecdotes from [the emperor's] life" was sold in bookstores as far away as Lemberg. *Der Israelit*, 22 October 1880, 7.

62. Smolle, *Das Buch von unserem Kaiser. 1848–1888*, 1.

63. Smolle updated this book in 1898 as *Fünf Jahrzehnte auf Habsburgs Throne* (Wien, 1898) and also produced a new edition of his more concise version of the same material, *Kaiser Franz Josef I*. In 1908, he again updated his patriotic book as *Unser Kaiser. Sein Leben und Wirken der Jugend erzählt*.

64. Some, like Knight of the Franz Joseph Order Wenzel Wächtler, scarcely lagged behind Smolle in tapping into the youth market for patriotic publications. Among Wächtler's publications "for youth and adult": *Edelsteine aus der Krone S.M. Franz Joseph I.* (Wien, 1888); *Österreichs Kaiser Franz Josef I.* (Wien, 1890); *Das goldene Jubiläum Franz Josephs I. Ein Gedenkbuch seiner fünfzigjährigen Regierung, seines Lebens und Strebens für Jugend und Erwachsene* (Wien, 1898). Ferdinand Zöhrer dedicated his 1890 *Das Kaiser-Buch. Erzählungen aus dem Leben des Kaisers Franz Josef I* to "Austria-Hungary's youth" and his 1898 *Hoch Habsburg!* to "Austria's people and youth." Hermine (Camilla) Proschko subtitled both her 1898 *Unseres Kaisers diamantenes Jubelfest* and *Unseres Kaisers goldenes Jubelfest 1908* "a commemorative booklet for Austria's youth."

65. Smolle, *Das Buch von unserem Kaiser* (Wien, 1888). The Pedagogic Society in Lemberg published a Polish translation of the book: *Czterdziesci lat panowania Cesarza Franciszka Józefa I. 1848–1898* (Lwów, 1898).

66. *Głos Narodu*, critical toward anything that could be interpreted as encroaching

on or challenging Polish national interests, recommended this book to its readers due to its high-quality pictures and text. *Głos Narodu,* 13 April 1898, 4.

67. To list just a few examples: in Slovenian: Tomo Zupan, *Nas Cesar Fran Josip I. 1848–1898* (Ljubljana, 1898); *Nas Cesar Fran Josip. 1848–1908* (Ljubljana, 1908); in Polish: Dr. Albert Zipper, *Cesarz i Król Franciszek Józef I. Dzieje jego żywota i rządów* (Zwołchów, 1888), Bronisław Sokalski's small and inexpensive *O życiu i czynach najmiłościwej nam panującego, Najjaśniejszego Pana, Cesarza i Króla Franciszka Józefa I* (1898 and 1908) covered material similar to Smolle; Jan Tiray, Karel Tichy, Mactous Vaclavek, Carl Weide and many other authors published commemorative books for children in 1898 and 1908 in Czech.

68. *Głos Narodu,* 28 November 1898, 7.

69. Thun-Salm was concerned that the similarities in her play and Berger's could raise questions of plagiarism. HHStA, GI, 1897–1898, ct. 169 [4 May 1898. Thun-Salm to Gen. Intendanz].

70. *NFP* (morning edition), 9 March 1898, 9–10.

71. Among numerous such works: Bela Kuderna, *Kaiser-Sonette, 1848–1898* (Wien und Leipzig, 1898). On page 229, the book announces that the Ministry of Religion and Education has recommended this volume to teachers. Franz Karl Grafen von Marenzi, *Jubelhymne zum fünfzigjährigen Regierungs-Jubiläum Seiner Majestät des Kaisers Franz Joseph des Ersten. Melodie: Volkshymn.* Many of these song books were advertised or reviewed in the daily press. *NFP* (morning edition), 26 July 1898, 7 reviewed Sidonie Heindl-Purschke and Leonie Schwenger's *Hoch Österreich!* According to the *NFP,* this play was performed "on many Austrian stages" and was provided free to amateur theaters and voluntary associations.

72. *FLS,* 10 July 1898, 250.

73. *Głos Narodu,* 11 May 1898, 1.

74. Helfert, ed., *Zum Zweiten Dezember 1848–1898* (Wien, 1898), introduction.

75. Helfert, *Zum Zweiten,* 3–4.

76. *Das Vaterland* (morning edition), 3 May 1898.

77. Ernst Bruckmüller, "Die österreichische Revolution von 1848 und der Habsburgermythos des 19. Jahrhunderts."

78. Helfert, *Zum Zweiten,* 21.

79. F. Albert Bacciocco, "Ein Charakterbild," in *Zum Zweiten December,* 28–31.

80. *Das Vaterland* (morning edition), 3 May 1898.

81. Hans Maria Truxa, ed., *Kaiser-Jubiläums-Dichterbuch. 50 Jahre Österreich. Literatur. Huldigungsgabe* (Wien, 1898).

82. Truxa, "Die Huldigung der Mitarbeiter des österreichisch Kaiser-Jubiläums-Dichterbuches," in *Kaiser-Jubiläums-Dichterbuch.*

83. *ÖV,* 20 May 1898.

84. Peter Eppel, *"Concordia soll Ihr Name sein." 125 Jahre Journalisten- und Schriftstellerverein* (Wien, 1984); WStLA, Magistratsabteilung 119, Vereinsakt 12226/27.

85. *Kaiserblatt: Festschrift des Wiener Journalisten- und Schriftstellervereines Concordia* (Wien, 1898), 3.

86. *Kaiserblatt*, 4.
87. *Kaiserblatt*, 10.
88. Julius Laurencic, *Unser Monarchie. Die Österreichische Calendar zur Zeit des fünfzigjährigen Regierungs-Jubiläums Sr. k.u.k. Apostol. Majestät Franz Josef I* (Wien, 1898), introduction.
89. The building was opened to the public following the jubilee religious services planned for the morning of 2 December. *Kurjer Lwowski,* 28 October 1898, 6. In Lemberg, as elsewhere, Jews were prominent among those donating and organizing charitable actions in honor of the jubilee. This same issue of *Kurjer Lwowski* informed its readership of these donations: 30,000 gulden from the Jewish community for its home for old and disabled women; 150,000 from M. Lazarus, director of the Bank-Hipoteczny, for the Jewish hospital; 50,000 for a fund to provide no-interest loans for poor Jewish handworkers from Sam Horowitz; 6,000 from Dr. S. Schaff for a stipend to support orphans; property from Aron Philipp for poor girls; 5,000 from Hersch Horowitz to fund two stipends for pupils of a Jewish high school; 5,000 from the heirs of Jakob Klarfeld to fund the construction of a home for invalids; 2,800 from the heirs of Abr. Buber for the same purpose.
90. *GL,* 3 December 1898, 3–6.
91. *DP,* 4 December 1898. On illuminations in Galicia, see also *Slowo Polskie,* 3 December 1898.
92. *Linzer Volksblatt,* 4 December 1898. On Vienna's decorations and illuminations see, among many others, *Das Vaterland* (evening edition), 1 December 1898; *Neues Wiener Abendblatt,* 1 December 1898; *The Times,* 3 December 1898.
93. *DP,* special edition to 3 December 1898; *GL,* 4 December 1898.
94. *GL,* 4 December 1898, 3. The city of Cracow donated 150,000 for humanitarian actions, 50,000 for a new Kaiser hospital, 100,000 for a new trade school, and also named a new pipeline after the emperor. *Glos Narodu,* 1 December 1898, 4.
95. In 1854, for example, the Jewish community in Vienna decorated the front of the Seitenstettengasse synagogue with a huge illuminated imperial crown, imperial eagle, and laurel wreath constructed by a Cracow glass maker. The decorations were lit with hundreds of lamps. Tschudy, *Illustrirtes Gedenkbuch,* 67.
96. Ch. L. Horowitz, *Festrede anläßlich des Dankgottesdienstes am fünfzigjährigen Jubiläumstage Sr. Majestät des Kaisers Franz Josephs am 2. Dezember 1898. gehalten in der alten Synagoga zu Krakau vom Rabiner-Stellvertreter Horowitz* (Krakau, 1899).
97. Rudolf Schickler, *Festprolog. Kaiser Jubiläums Huldigungs-Feier. Mai 30, 1898. Verein zur Ausspeisung armer Israel. Schulkinder des XVI und XVII Bezirkes* (Wien, 1898). Numerous published sermons, editorials in Jewish newspapers, and speeches by directors of Jewish schools contain similar sentiments. Among others, see Simon Schreiber, ed., Alexander Schreiber, *Zwei Kaiserreden und ein hebräischer Dank-Psalm* (Czernowitz, 1908); W. Reich, *Patriotische Reden* [2d ed.] (Baden, 1900); Majer Balaban, *Żydzi w Austryi na panowania cesarza Franciszka Józefa I* (Lwów, 1909).
98. Dr. Joseph Schneider, ed., *Anonymous. Kaiser Franz Joseph I. und sein Hof. Erinnerungen und Schilderungen aus den nachgelassenen Papieren eines persönlichen Ratgebers* (Wien, 1919), 111–112.

99. A few well-publicized incidents were used by anti-Semitic politicians to expand their political influence: the Hilsner blood libel in Bohemia, the Tisza-Eszlar blood libel in Hungary, the Röhling-Bloch Talmud controversy. On several occasions Franz Joseph uttered his distaste for anti-Semitism. His public demonstrations of favor toward Jews, and his reluctance to confirm Lueger as mayor of Vienna, earned him the title of "Judenkaiser." Wistrich, *The Jews of Vienna,* 179.

100. On Jewish identification with the emperor, see Wistrich, *The Jews of Vienna,* 164–202. Marsha Rozenblit argues that many Jews in the Habsburg Monarchy developed "tripartite" identities as Jews; as Germans, Czechs, Poles, etc; and as "Austrians." Rozenblit, *Reconstructing a National Identity.*

101. Even many Jews who had emigrated to Palestine or the United States retained some semblance of Austro-Hungarian identity. The Edl. v. Laemel School in Jerusalem, standing under the official protection of Austria-Hungary, held a celebratory gathering on 2 December, including speeches, music, prayer for the emperor, and the distribution of charity. HHStA, Administrativ Registratur (AR), 1898, F1, ct. 45 [Pr. 65728, 24/12, 1898]. A similar program was carried out by the Austrian-Hungarian-Bohemian-Moravian Israelite community of Jerusalem in 1908: AR, 1908, F1, ct. 51, [Pr. 5201, 18 January 1909].

102. On associations, see Thomas Nipperdey's classic article, "Die Organisation der bürgerlichen Parteien in Deutschland vor 1918," in Nipperdey, *Gesellschaft, Kultur, Theorie* (Göttingen, 1976).

103. *Ruslan,* 25 November 1908, 3; *Dilo,* 30 November 1908, 2; *GL,* 13 November 1908, 3; *GL,* 19 November 1908, 3; *GN,* 19 November 1908, 2; *GL,* 24 November 1908, 3 notes that ten days after the announcement, 137,000 illumination cards had already been sold to cities and institutions.

104. Among many examples, see *Ruslan,* 25 November 1908, 3; *Dilo,* 30 November 1908, 2.

Chapter 6

1. Marsha Rozenblit, *The Jews of Vienna, 1867–1914: Acculturation and Identity* (Albany, 1983), 71; Steven Beller, *Vienna and the Jews, 1867–1938* (Cambridge, 1989), 43–44; William McCagg, Jr., *A History of Habsburg Jews;* see also Robert S. Wistrich, *The Jews of Vienna.*

2. John Boyer demonstrates that the lower artisans "were the first social group to embrace political antisemitism." Boyer, *Political Radicalism,* 41; Peter Pulzer, *The Rise of Political Anti-Semitism in Germany and Austria* (Cambridge, 1988).

3. On the rise of the Christian Social Party, see above all John Boyer's two-volume study of the Christian Social Party: *Political Radicalism* and *Culture and Political Crisis in Vienna: Christian Socialism in Power, 1897–1918* (Chicago, 1995). See also Brinkmann Brown, *Karl Lueger, the Liberal Years: Democracy, Municipal Reform, and the Struggle for Power in the Vienna City Council, 1875–1882* (New York and London, 1987); Richard S. Geehr, *Karl Lueger: Mayor of fin de siecle Vienna* (Detroit, 1990); Wistrich, *The Jews of Vienna,* 205–237.

4. Though the liberals had lost their Cisleithanian parliamentary majority in 1879, they retained a majority on the Vienna city council for almost two more decades. Pieter M. Judson, *Exclusive Revolutionaries.*

5. Lueger personally looked over materials relating to the 1860s *Volksfeste* and the 1880 birthday celebration when preparing for 1898. WStLA, HA, KB, ct. 62-1, Mappe 1 [GRZ. 4240 ex 1880].

6. WStLA, HA, KB, ct. 62-1, Mappe 1 [Zum 18. August 1863]. The 1863 Kaiserfest took place just as Franz Joseph traveled to Frankfurt to confront the Prussian challenge to Austrian leadership in the German Confederation.

7. WStLA, HA, KB, ct. 62-1, Mappe 1 [GRZ. 4240 ex 1880].

8. Some members of the city council were reluctant to institutionalize a celebration of the constitution on the emperor's 18 August birthday rather than on the date of the promulgation of the February Patent of 1861. Others objected that money spent on beer and various entertainments would line the pockets of entrepreneurs and bring only meager benefits for charity. WStLA, HA, KB, ct. 62-1, Mappe 2 and Mappe 1 [GRZ. 4240 ex 1880]; WStLA, HA, KB, ct. 10-7, Mappe 12 [Protokol der 297. Sitzung des Gemeinderats der Reichshaupt- und Residenzstadt Wien am 17. Juni 1864].

9. Martin Hecher, "Hans Makart und der Wiener Festzug von 1879" (Ph.D. Diss., University of Vienna, 1986), 93–100. Franz Joseph initially rejected the idea that Vienna should spend large sums of money to produce this event. He gave his approval only in late January 1879.

10. On the Ringstrasse and historicism, see Schorske, *Fin-de-siècle Vienna*, 24–115; Elisabeth Springer, *Geschichte und Kulturleben.*

11. *Wien 1848. Denkschrift zum 2 Dezember 1888* (Wien, 1888), vi.

12. *Wien 1848*, viii; WStLA, HA, KB, ct. 62-1, Mappe 1 WStLA, HA, KB, ct. 10-7, Mappe 12. Although some members of the city council subcommittee overseeing the publication of the book desired to "make [the book] available to all sectors of society," the city council printed only 2,000 of the originally projected run of 5,000 copies. In 1892, more than 200 copies still remained in the warehouse of the booksellers authorized to market the book.

13. The majority on the council rejected motions to construct subsidized housing and a public building to house reading rooms, theaters, and space for voluntary societies to meet in order to raise "the sense and tastes" of workers and craftsmen. The sponsors of this project had hoped that such a "People's Palace," modeled on those built in London to commemorate Victoria's 1887 jubilee, would save the lower classes from the *"Trinkzwang"* of the taverns and encourage the "blessing of self-cultivation." WStLA, HA, KB, ct. 63-1, Mappe 2 [M.Z. 82782, ex 1894]. See *Amtsblatt der k.k. Reichshaupt- und Residenzstadt Wien,* 17 May 1895, 1211; 2 April 1895, 1069; 28 May 1895, 1281–1282. WStLA, HA, KB, ct. 63-1, Mappe 2 [Mag. Z. 108157, prs. 12 June 1895].

14. *NFP* (morning edition), 4 February 1894, 4–5; *DZ* (morning edition), 9 February 1894, 4. The museum was to be built using 500,000 gulden of city funds.

15. WStLA, HA, KB, ct. 63-1, Mappe 2 [ad. St. Z. 1143 ex 1894]. Lueger's city council revived this project several times. Disagreements over location and style complicated the issue. Wagner's plans for a truly modern museum were set aside

and the box-like building next to the Karlskirche was erected after World War II. *Otto Wagner und der Kaiser Franz Joseph Stadtmuseum: Das Scheitern der Moderne in Wien* (Wien, 1988).

16. Franz Joseph heeded the advice of Ernst von Plener, the leading liberal minister in the Cisleithanian coalition of Liberals, Clericals, and Poles in power from 1893–1895. Wistrich suggests that Hungarian pressure led to Franz Joseph's refusal to confirm Lueger. Wistrich, *The Jews of Vienna,* 179.

17. Boyer provides a gripping account of the electoral advance of the Christian Social Party in *Political Radicalism,* 316–385.

18. Mandl was Lueger's early mentor and ally. Boyer, *Political Radicalism,* 198.

19. WStLA, HA, KB, ct. 62-1, Mappe 1 [Z. 4240, Pr. 14/9, 1880].

20. *Reichspost,* 4 January 1898, 2.

21. *ÖFZ,* 23 January 1898, 1.

22. *NFP* (morning edition), 14 March 1898, 1.

23. *Amtsblatt der k.k. Reichshaupt- und Residenzstadt Wien,* 18 January 1898, 214: City council sitting 14 January 1898. WStLA, HA, KB, ct. 61-4 [Programm für den Huldigung-Festzug in Wien zur Feier der silbernen Hochzeit Ihrer Majestäten des Kaisers und der Kaiserin (Wien, 1897)].

24. On Fischhof, see Ian Reifowitz, *Imagining an Austrian Nation: Joseph Samuel Bloch and the Search for a Multiethnic Austrian Identity, 1846–1919* (New York, 2003); Judson, *Exclusive Revolutionaries,* 31.

25. On the 13 March events, see: *Reichspost,* 15 March 1898, 3; *NFP* (morning edition), 14 March 1898, 1; *AZ* (afternoon edition), 1–2; Archiv der Bundes-Polizeidirektion Wien, ct. 6 [z. 1213 and addendums, 1898]. The police estimated that 50,000 workers and family members took part in the march to the cemetery, while the Social Democrats estimated their numbers at closer to 200,000. All were agreed that it was the largest such demonstration by the Social Democrats in commemoration of 13 March.

26. On Gessmann's role in the early organization of Lueger's coalition, see Boyer, *Political Radicalism,* 207–208, 366–367.

27. *Amtsblatt der k.k. Reichshaupt- und Residenzstadt Wien,* 11 March 1898, 730–747. *Reichspost,* 10 March 1898, 9–10; *Reichspost,* 11 March 1898, 1–2; *DV* goes further in emphasizing the victory of the Jews and is more sympathetic to the martyrs of 1848, 13 March, 10–12; *DZ* (morning edition), 9 March 1898, 1.

28. *Reichspost,* 23 March 1898, 1.

29. This list is paraphrased from WStLA, HA, KB, ct. 63-2, Mappe 4 [St. Z. 1348 ex 1898, Beschluß vom 8. Februar 1898]. All of Vienna's major newspapers reported Lueger's speech and this jubilee program.

30. Only 80 city council members participated in the voting, and each of the original 36 elected members received 74 or more votes. WStLA, HA, KB, ct. 63-2, Mappe 4 [St. Z. 2268, Prs. 8/3, 1898]; WStLA, HA, KB, ct. 63-2, Mappe 4 [Verzeichnis der Mitglieder der Commission zur Durchführung des Gemeinderaths Beschluß vom 11. Feburar 1898].

31. This is a summary of WStLA, HA, KB, ct. 63-2, Mappe 4 [Protokoll vom 15. März 1898].

32. School teacher Leopold Tomola proved his dedication to the anti-Semitic program of the Christian Social Party in late November. Before a gathering of the Währing district club of the Vienna Christian Women's Association, Tomola called for the separation of Jewish and Christian children in the school system. *Reichspost,* 30 November 1898, 4. The *FLS* noted with bitterness that teachers, unlike other government workers and military officers, did not receive jubilee medals from the state, though Tomola, a lackey of Lueger, did: *FLS,* 11 December 1898, 436, 441.

33. On Schuh, see Boyer, *Political Radicalism,* 390. The liberal Progressive Party (*Fortschrittliche Partei*) club of Vienna's ninth district bitterly regretted its previous backing of Klotzberg, elected as a promoter of the "progressive program" and now a devotee of Lueger. *NFP* (morning edition), 9 April 1898, 6.

34. WStLA, HA, KB, ct. 63-1, Mappe 2 [Mag. Z. 108157, Pr. 12 June 1895]. Lueger's conversion to the cause of social welfare—like his attempt to claim credit for the expansion of Vienna, which began under the liberals and was pushed forward by Lower Austrian *Statthalter* Kielmansegg, often in the face of Lueger's opposition—angered Kielmansegg. According to the *Statthalter,* Lueger funded the hospital, finally completed several years after the 1898 jubilee, by selling land at an exorbitant price to the state. Kielmansegg argued that Lueger then used this money to appear generous and concerned for the common good by building the hospital, forcing the state to cover its operating costs, and excoriating the state for its alleged failures in the field of social welfare. According to Kielmansegg, Lueger took advantage of Cisleithanian minister president Ernst von Koeber's need for Christian Social parliamentary support. Erich Graf Kielmansegg, *Kaiserhaus, Staatsmänner und Politiker* (Wien, 1966), 74–75.

35. *Reichspost,* 13 February 1898, 2.

36. Boyer comments on this insurance fund and Lueger's yearly 2 December ceremony to distribute funds in *Culture,* 16–17.

37. See Rozenblit, *The Jews of Vienna.*

38. WStLA, HA, KB, ct. 63-1, Mappe 2 [Heinrich Apfelthaler to Lueger, undated]. The Catholic hierarchy defined the building of the Jubilee Church as an act of patriotism: *Wiener Diöcesanblatt,* 1898, nr. 6, 61. On the building of the Jubilee Church, see Inge Scheidl, "Die Kaiser Franz Josef-Jubiläumskirche in Wien von Viktor Lunt: Der Wettbewerbsverlauf, die Konkurrenzentwürfe und die Baugeschichte" (MA Thesis, University of Vienna, 1991); Kielmansegg, *Kaiserhaus,* 107–109; *Reichspost,* 20 March 1898.

39. *Reichspost,* 14 January 1898, 1. The drive to build a theater dedicated to "German Christian culture" began in Vienna's eighteenth district in 1896. Eventually, the city of Vienna under Lueger rescued the foundering fund drive, offering the Kaiser-Jubilee-City Theater Association monetary support and city land. The executive committee of the Association included many prominent supporters of the Christian Social Party, like Christian Social city council members Karl Constenoble and Dr. Theodor Wähner. *Reichspost,* 14 January 1898, 1–2. Though eventually constructed, the jubilee theater was a failure, and by 1904 dropped its dedication to German Christian culture in an effort to avoid financial disaster.

See AVA, MI, Präs. 1, 1898, ct. 16 [Nr. 5636, 29/30 June 1898]; Boyer, *Culture,* 63; Geehr, *Karl Lueger,* 192–197.

40. *Reichspost,* 13 February 1898, 2.
41. "Das walte Gott!"*ÖFZ,* 16 February 1898, 1–2.
42. Geehr, *Karl Lueger,* 155.
43. Ironically, as the Social Democratic press pointed out, the London Children's Festival, the model for Lueger's procession of the children, was organized by a group of mainly Jewish journalists. WStLA, HA, KB, ct. 63-2, Mappe 3 [Jub. Comm. IV. z. 10, Lueger to Lord Mayor of London, 21 March 1898; ad. Z. 10, Prs. 18/4 1898]. Months before the announcement of the city jubilee program, two voluntary associations, the Maria Troster Spatzen Verein, and the Bauerngesellschaft Hainbach took steps to arrange a historical procession of 6,000–10,000 Vienna schoolchildren, ages 8–16. The proceeds of this procession were to establish and maintain a Kaiser Franz Joseph jubilee vacation colony for poor sick Viennese schoolchildren. The city council, while wishing the associations well, refused a request to merge this event with that proposed by the city's jubilee commission. The mayor did not want to dampen the effect of his singular procession of the children, KB, ct. 63-2, Mappe 4 [Jubiläums Festlichkeiten/Com IV. Sitzung vom 4/4 1898]. The Ministry of the Interior cited the plans of the city of Vienna, the reliability of the organizers of the event, and the stress it would cause on the children in its recommendation against approving this event to the grand court master. This last objection was not made in relation to the city of Vienna's procession of the children. AVA, MI, Präs, 1898, ct. 15 [Nr. 2946, Prs. 30 March 1898].
44. WStLA, HA, KB, ct. 63-2, Mappe 3 [Johann Strasser to jubilee commission, 11 May 1898]. Strasser wrote that many parents would not want their children to march for hours in conditions that would be trying even for members of the armed forces. In April and May, school officials wrote to the jubilee commission requesting a change to Schönbrunn, where the children would at least have some shade and not have to march for as many hours. See WStLA, HA, KB, ct. 63-2, Mappe 3 [z 79, Jub. Com. IV, Prs. 14/5, 1898].
45. WStLA, HA, KB, ct. 63-2, Mappe 4 [10 April 1898. Tomola: Referat über die Veranstaltung des Huldigungs-Festzuges der Wiener Schulkinder].
46. WStLA, HA, KB, ct. 63-2, Mappe 4 [Protokol über die am 28. März 1898 . . . Sitzung der Comite I].
47. WStLA, HA, KB, ct. 63-2, Mappe 4 [Comite IV. Besprechung von 18/5 1898]. The jubilee commission confirmed all its decisions with school officials. WStLA, HA, KB, ct. 63-2, Mappe 4 [Schulleiterconferenz am 18/5 1898].
48. WStLA, HA, KB, ct. 63-2, Mappe 4 [Comite IV. Sitzung vom 23/3 1898; WStLA, HA, KB, ct. 63-2, Mappe 4 [Protokoll über die Sitzung der Subcomites für den Huldigungszug der Wiener Schuljugend vom 26. April 1898].
49. WStLA, HA, KB, ct. 63-2, Mappe 3 [Jub. Comm IV. z. 99, Prs. 24/5 1898].
50. WStLA, HA, KB, ct. 63-2, Mappe 3 [Jub. Comm. Z. 134 ex 1898].
51. *OR,* 17 June 1898, 4.
52. *OR,* 8 June 1898, 2; *OR,* 12 June 1898, p.7.

53. *AZ* (morning edition), 15 June 1898, 5; *AZ* (morning edition), 16 June 1898, 5; *AZ* (morning edition), 18 June, 5.
54. *Volkstribune,* 16 June 1898, 1.
55. *AZ* (morning edition), 21 June 1898, 4. The Christian Social Party attempted to counter what they viewed as the anti-Christian influence of the socialist-leaning provisional teachers (*Unterlehrer*), known as the *Jungen.* The *FLS* was the mouthpiece of the *Jungen* movement. See Boyer, *Culture,* 46–57.
56. *NFP* (evening edition), 24 June 1898, 1.
57. Kielmansegg commented bitterly on Lueger's cultivation of his own almost imperial ceremonial style; Lueger would arrive to events late with a train of officials in special uniforms in tow. On such occasions, after a series of speeches in which Lueger would express his satisfaction with the execution of his will, the mayor would leave with fanfare. Kielmansegg, *Kaiserhaus,* 389–390. Already during the procession of the children, Lueger appeared in public surrounded by this new ceremonial pomp.
58. *AZ* (morning edition), 25 June 1898, 5.
59. *FLS,* 26 June 1898, 228.
60. *OR,* 7 June 1898.
61. *Reichspost,* 25 June 1898, 5.
62. *NFP* (evening edition), 14 June 1898, 1–3.
63. See, for example, *NFP* (evening edition), 24 June 1898, 1. The Czech press, of course, took the opposite view, interpreting the emperor's emotional statement as proof of the destructive effect of German obstructionism in parliament and German national chauvinism in general. Whereas the German-language press attacked Taaffe and Badeni as the instigators of the crisis, Czech journalists praised Taaffe and Badeni for their understanding of the interests of the Slavic peoples. *Politik,* 25 June 1898.
64. *Amtsblatt der k.k. Reichshaupt- und Residenzstadt Wien,* 28 June 1898, 1673: 24 June sitting of the city council.
65. *DV* (morning edition), 25 June 1898, 1–2.
66. *Reichspost,* 28 June 1898, 6.
67. *ÖV,* 28 June 1898, 2.
68. *Wiener Abendpost,* 24 June 1898, 1.
69. *Neuigkeits-Weltblatt.* This quotation is taken from the collection of hundreds of clippings of newspaper articles concerning the 1898 jubilee held in Vienna's Stadt- und Landesbibliothek: *Observer* 56334a, Box 9, Nr. 68.
70. *Die Vedette. Beilage zur Reichswehr,* 3 July 1898, 2–3.
71. *NFP,* 26 June 1898. WStLA, *Observer,* 56334A, Box 10.
72. Bled discusses Franz Joseph's love of hunting as a retreat from his public duties. Bled estimates Franz Joseph's kills at 55,000. Bled, *Franz Joseph,* 208–209.
73. *DZ* (morning edition), 18 August 1898, 1.
74. *DZ* (morning edition), 2 December 1898, 1.
75. Lueger informed committee IV of his decision to hold such a festivity: WStLA, HA, KB, ct. 63-2, Mappe 4 [Protokoll vom 20. April 1898].
76. On 22 November, at a meeting of committee I, Lueger instructed all district chairmen to organize local committees. These district committees were to decorate

the streets and building facades as well as to encourage people to participate in the illuminations on 2 December. Lueger directed local officials that the committees were to have a "private character." WStLA, HA, KB, ct. 63-2, Mappe 4 [Jubil. Comm. Comite I. Protokoll über die Sitzung der Jubiläums-Commission vom 22. Nov. 1898].

77. In 1900, to mark the emperor's seventieth birthday, Lueger installed a plaque in the Rathaus memorializing the words of the speeches given by Franz Joseph and Lueger on the occasion of the procession of the children, which had been published in the 1898 pamphlet. This was typical of Lueger's eagerness to have his name inscribed on new buildings all over the city, allowing him to take credit for the modernization of Vienna.

78. Alfred Freiherr von Berger, *Habsburg* (Wien, 1898). Vienna had contracted with another writer to produce a commemorative publication for Vienna's schoolchildren. When this writer acknowledged that he could not complete the task in the allotted time, the director of the City Library, Dr. Glossy, suggested to committee I that Berger's work, with a few changes, would be ideal. WStLA, HA, KB, ct. 63-2, Mappe 4 [Jub. Comm. Comite I. Protokolle über die Sitzung des Comite I. vom 21. Juli, 1898]. Almost 200,000 copies of Berger's play were passed out to Vienna's schoolchildren. *Schluß-Bericht der gemeinderäthlichen Comission zur Durchführung der Feier des 50jährigen Regierungs-Jubiläums Sr Majestät des Kaisers* (Wien, 1899), 7. Berger's play had been performed earlier in the year at the German Volkstheater, in other forums in Vienna, and throughout the monarchy. WStLA, *Observer,* 56334 A, Box 7 [*Wiener Tagblatt* 30/4 1898].

79. WStLA, Magistratsabteilung 119 [Vereinsakt 5195/21: Wiener Christlicher Frauenbund Österreichs 1898]. The Vienna Christian Women's Association had 26 local sections in 1898. In August 1938, as part of the program of *Gleichschaltung* following the *Anschluß,* the entire organization was merged into the NS *Frauenschaft.* See Fritz Steinkellner, "Emanzipatorische Tendenzen im christlichen Wiener Frauen-Bund und in der Katholischen Reichsfrauenorganisation Österreichs," in Rudolf G. Ardelt, Wolfgang J.A. Huber, and Anton Staudinger, eds., *Unterdrückung und Emanzipation. Festschrift für Erika Weinzierl zum 60. Geburtstag* (Wien and Salzburg, 1985), 55–67. On the "Lueger Gretl," see Geehr, *Karl Lueger,* 209–232.

80. For example, after a group of Jewish women wrote a letter of support to Emile Zola, the *Frauenbund* rallied 4,000 women to protest the use by the Jewish women of the shield and symbols of the city of Vienna. The *Frauenbund* leadership declared that their group, which opposed Zola and Dreyfuss, and not the Jewish women, represented the women of Vienna. *Reichspost,* 19 February 1898, 2; see also *Vaterland* (morning edition), 18 February 1898, 6, and any issue of the *ÖFZ.*

81. The Police Direction and the Lower Austrian *Statthalterei* were hesitant to approve the *Frauenbund*'s request to sponsor a Kaiser-jubilee and Second Founding Festival of the Vienna Christian *Frauenbund.* Since the proceeds from the event were earmarked for orphans, the police eventually approved, and the *Frauenbund* held the event on 7 August. NöLA, 1898, ct. 974 [L8, z. 4450, Prs. 20 August 1898].

82. *NFP* (morning edition), 2 July 1898, 7.

83. Lueger intimate Marianne Beskiba wrote about the willingness of the *Frauen-bund* members to brave the worst weather for a chance to hear "der schöne Karl" speak, and it seems clear from newspaper reports that Lueger returned the favor by appearing whenever possible at *Frauenbund* functions. Marianne Beskiba, *Aus Meinen Erinnerungen an Dr. Karl Lueger* (Wien, n.d.), 31–32.

84. *Reichspost,* 30 November 1898, 4; *DV* (evening edition), 29 November 1898, 4.

85. *DZ* (evening edition), 5 December 1898, 2.

86. The anti-Semitic rhetoric was less evident at the *Frauenbund*'s official jubilee celebration, postponed until 15 December by Lueger. Members from all the district sections gathered in the Hall of the People in the Rathaus; a bust of the emperor surrounded by plants took center stage at this dynastic festival. *DZ,* 16 December 1898, 7. Accounts of the festivities suggest that Platter muted her usual anti-Semitic rhetoric for this event.

87. Geehr, *Karl Lueger,* 157.

88. *DZ* (evening edition), 28 November 1898, 2; *DV* (evening edition), 28 November 1898, 3.

89. Dominik Hardegg, "The Jubilee Exhibition," in Schnitzer, ed., *Franz Joseph und seine Zeit,* 408. Hardegg estimated that 2.5 million had visited the exhibition by the time this commemorative book was published.

90. Hardegg, "The Jubilee Exhibition," in Schnitzer, ed., *Franz Joseph und seine Zeit,* 409.

91. On the 1851 exhibition in London, see Richards, *The Commodity Culture of Victorian England,* 17–72.

92. In 1873, the Vienna World Exhibition drew many foreign dignitaries to Vienna. Though displaying admirably the industrial and artistic achievements of the decade of liberal domination of the Cisleithanian government, including the formal opening of the new, if as yet incomplete, Ringstrasse, which had replaced the once formidable city defenses, the exhibition did not meet attendance expectations. Eight days after poor weather marred the opening of the exhibition, the stock market crashed, ushering in an extended economic slump in much of Central Europe. A cholera epidemic in Vienna discouraged many who might have traveled to Vienna for the spectacle. The failed Vienna World Exhibition and the collapse of the economy contributed to the less-than-enthusiastic celebrations of the 1873 jubilee.

93. Chapter 3 includes a brief discussion of the 1894 Galician Exhibition.

94. *NFP* (morning edition), 17 April 1898, 5.

95. TSDIA-L, 146/6/1235/156 [Geheime L70/g]; AVA, Ministerrats-Präsidium, PL, 1894, ct. 26 [240/PL].

96. In April 1894, the press department of the ministerial council sent letters to all provincial governors informing them that Cisleithanian minister president Windischgrätz supported the exhibition and calling on them to promote the exhibition in official newspapers and in private circles to ensure its success. Members of the Lower Austrian parliament's executive committee, delegates

to the Reichsrat, prominent liberals in the Vienna government, estate owners from the Imperial-Royal Agricultural Society, the leadership of the Central Association of Austrian Industrialists, the Industrial Club, the Austrian-Hungarian Bank, the Association for Mountain, Iron, and Machine Industrialists in Austria, and other prominent business and industrial institutions joined the committee. AVA, PL, 1894, ct. 26 [240].

97. AVA, PL, 1894, ct. 26 [240].
98. *Neues Wiener Abendblatt,* 26 April 1894.
99. *NFP* (morning edition), 30 October 1898, 6.
100. *DZ* (morning edition), 30 October 1896, 4.
101. The city program dedicated 50,000 gulden to constructing the pavilion. *Amtsblatt der k.k. Reichshaupt- und Residenzstadt Wien,* 11 June 1897. Otto Wagner participated in judging the architecture plans to choose a design. WStLA, HA, KB, ct. 63-3, Mappe 5 [7622 EX 1897].
102. *Reichspost,* 8 May 1898, 17.
103. NöLA, 1898, ct. 973 [L8, z. 2324, 1897]; for a description of the Welfare Exhibition, see *NFP* (morning edition), 1 May 1898, 6.
104. *NFP* (morning edition), 7 May 1898, 7.
105. *NFP* (evening edition), 9 May 1898, 6; 9 May (evening edition), 6.
106. *Reichspost,* 8 May 1898, 17.
107. *Jubiläums-Ausstellung Wien, 1898* (Wien, 1898).
108. *NFP* (morning edition), 5 June 1898, 7.
109. *NFP* (morning edition), 14 May 1898, 5. According to this report, "death is getting cheaper." "The flame" burned a body in 1.25 hours at 1,000 degrees Celsius for just 9 marks.
110. *NFP* (morning edition), 13 May 1898, 7.
111. *NFP* (morning edition), 13 August 1898, 5.
112. *NFP* (morning edition), 12 June 1898, 12; 8 June (morning edition), 7; 12 June (morning edition), 12.
113. *DV,* 1 May 1898, 7. Even after Lueger decided to support the exhibition, some ambivalence remained in the Christian Social camp. This article also complained about the great profits Jewish entrepreneurs would make from their food concessions in the Jubilee Exhibition.
114. *NFP* (morning edition), 8 May 1898, 1.
115. *OR,* 8 May 1898, 5.
116. *Słowo Polskie* (morning edition), 9 May 1898, 1; 12 May (morning edition), 3.
117. *Głos Narodu,* 8 May 1898, 7.
118. *Kurjer Lwowski,* 13 May 1898, 2–3.
119. At many of these events, busts and portraits of Lueger occupied the place of honor in the front of the room—similar to the almost ubiquitous Kaiser busts found at hundreds of small-scale celebrations throughout the monarchy. For discussions of some of the meetings, see: *DZ* (evening edition), 25 November 1898, 2; *DV,* 29 November 1898; *Reichspost,* 7 December 1898, 4.

Conclusion

1. This account of Grand Court Master Montenuovo speaking for the dead emperor and the Capuchin abbot answering from behind the door of the Capuchin crypt, the last resting place of the Habsburgs, is taken from Bled, *Franz Joseph,* 323. Christian Dickinger argues convincingly that this dramatic scene, copied from one biographer and historian to another, never actually took place. Christian Dickinger, *Franz Joseph I: Die Entmythisierung* (Vienna, 2002), 192–193.

2. AVA, MI, Präs. 1, 1897, 1898, ct. 15 [Nr. 6124, 21 July 1897]; AVA, MI, Präs., 1897, 1898, ct. 15 [Nr. 10832, 27 October 1897].

3. AVA, MI, Präs. 22 Boh., ct. 857 [Nr. 6797, 19–21 August 1898].

4. *Alldeutsches Tagblatt,* nr. 24, 1898; *Unverfälschte Deutsche Worte,* nr. 11, 1898.

5. The Social Democrats did not protest the jubilees nor did the central committee of the party recommend that party members distance themselves from imperial celebrations. In fact, the central committee of the party voted 7 to 3 in favor of participation in the official mourning session of the Reichsrat after the murder of the empress. Social Democratic Archives, Sozdem. Verband (Klubprotokolle) 25.3.1897 bis 25.9.1903. Heft 1 [Sitting on 24 September 1898]. In 1908, the party executive voted against advising Social Democrats to keep their children from participating in Lueger's homage of the children in Shönbrunn. SDA, Parteivertretung, Handprotokolle 19.3.1906 bis 10.3.1910, Heft 5 [4 May 1908].

6. Social Democrats and conservative Polish nobles blamed the anti-Semitic radical priest, newspaper editor, and peasant organizer Stanisław Stojałowski, his new Christian People's Party, and the United Peasant Party for the riots. Dunin-Wąsowicz, *Dzieje Stonnictwa Ludowego w Galicji;* Dunin-Wąsowicz, *Jan Stapiński.* For an example of anti-Semitic rhetoric printed in peasant-oriented newspapers at the time of the outbreak of these riots, see *Związek Chłopski,* 11 May 1898.

7. *Związek Chłopski,* 1 July 1898.

8. *Związek Chłopski,* 21 August 1898.

9. On this effort designed to create a single great charitable patriotic action, see AVA, Ministerrats-Präsidium, 1908, ct. 77a [Z. 526]. From the beginning some voices warned that competing national movements would raise the fear that contributions made by members of one ethnic group would benefit charities designed to help members of other nationalities.

10. HHStA, Kab. Kanz, 1908 [Z. 3660, Prs. 1 December 1908].

11. Wilhelm Müller, editor, *Der Kaiser-Huldigungs-Festzug Wien. 12. Juni 1908* (Wien, 1908), xxvii. On the crowd's reception of the Galician group, see *Nowa Reforma* (afternoon edition), 13 June 1908, 2.

12. Grossegger, *Der Kaiser-Huldigungs-Festzug,* 89.

13. This message, echoing that of the 1898 jubilee play, also paralleled the main themes of the multivolume *Die österreichisch-ungarische Monarchie in Wort und Bild.* This series of books on the provinces and their peoples, begun in 1884 and completed in 1902, originated under the protection of Crown Prince Rudolf and was often termed the *Kronprinzenwerk.* Count Hans Wilczek, a close

friend and advisor to Rudolf, was a coeditor of the *Kronprinzenwerk* and, in 1908, the chair of the committee that organized the *Festzug*. Peter Urbanitsch also makes this observation in "Pluralist Myth and Nationalist Realities." On the *Kronprinzenwerk,* see James Shedel, "The Elusive Fatherland: Dynasty, State, Identity and the Kronprinzenwerk," in Moritz Csáky and Klaus Zeyringer, eds., *Inszenierungen des kollektiven Gedächtnisses* (Innsbruck, 2002); Christiane Zintzen, "Das Kronprinzenwerk. Die österreichische-ungarische Monarchie in Wort und Bild. Ein deliberater Rund- und Umgang mit einem enzyklopäischen Textkosmos," in *Literarisches Leben in Österreich 1848–1890,* ed. Klaus Mann, Hubert Lengauer, and Karl Wagner (Vienna, 2000); Zintzen, *Die Österreichische-ungarische Monarchie in Wort und Bild. Aus dem "Kronprinzenwerk" des Erzherzog Rudolf* (Vienna, 1999).

14. HHStA, ZA Prot. 132, Ceremonial Protocol 1908 [Anhang V].
15. On controversies surrounding the Galician delegations to the 1908 *Festzug,* see: *Nowa Reforma* (morning edition), 7 June 1908, 1; *Nowa Reforma* (morning and afternoon editions, 12 June 1908; *GL,* 10 June 1908, 2.
16. Relying on the *NFP* and the satirical pen of Karl Kraus, Steven Beller argues that the 1908 procession was a colossal symbolic failure: Beller, "Kraus's Firework: State Consciousness Raising in the 1908 Jubilee Parade in Vienna and the Problem of Austrian Identity," in Wingfield and Bucur, eds., *Staging the Past.*
17. The 6 September unveiling of a three-meter-high marble image of Franz Joseph in Dittersbach in northern Bohemia was typical of such events. Veterans' associations, firefighters, German singing and exercise societies donated the funds. AVA, MI, Präs, 1908, ct. 1211 [Nr. 18828]. In November, the Ministry of the Interior received Franz Joseph's approval for several dozen requests by German majority towns in Bohemia to place monuments to the emperor in public spaces. AVA, MI, Präs, 1908, ct. 1212 [1/J, Nr. 11938].
18. Dr. Franz Bayer, mayor of the Bohemian city of Reichenberg, declared that "[Kaiser Franz Joseph] stands especially close to us Germans, he is after all of our tribe and blood." *Amtsblatt der Stadt Reichenberg,* 15 December 1908.
19. See T. Mills Kelly, "Taking It to the Streets"; Nancy Wingfield's work in progress, "Pitched Battles in Public Places," will include a chapter concerning German-Czech violence and the 1908 jubilee.
20. HHStA, Ceremonial Protocol, 1908, ZA 132 [Anhang XV].
21. Maureen Healy, *Vienna and the Fall of the Habsburg Empire: Total War and Everyday Life in World War I* (Cambridge, 2004).
22. Clifford Geertz, "Centers, Kings, and Charisma: Reflections on the Symbolics of Power," in *Local Knowledge: Further Essays in Interpretive Anthropology* (New York, 1983), 124.
23. Benedict Anderson, *Imagined Communities.*

ABBREVIATIONS

AHY	*Austrian History Yearbook*
AP	Archivum Panstwowe (State Archive of Cracow)
AR	Administrativ-Registratur
AZ	*Arbeiter-Zeitung*
DA	Erzbischöfliches Diözesanarchiv
DALO	Derzhavnyi Arkhiv L'vivs'koi Oblasti (State Archive of L'viv Oblast)
DP	*Dziennik Polski*
DV	*Deutsches Volksblatt*
DZ	*Deutsche Zeitung*
FLS	*Freie Lehrerstimme*
GA	General-Adjutantur
GI	General-Intendanz
GL	*Gazeta Lwowska*
GN	*Gazeta Narodowa*
HA, KB	Hand-Akten, Kleine Bestände
HHStA	Haus-, Hof- und Staatsarchiv (House, Court, and State Archives, Vienna)
IB	Informations-Büro (Bureau of Information, Vienna)
KA	Kriegsarchiv (War Archives, Vienna)
Kab. Kanz.	Kabinettskanzlei (Cabinet Chancellery)
KVZ	*Konstitutionelle Vorstadt-Zeitung*
MCU	Ministerium für Cultus und Unterricht
MI	Ministerium des Innern (Ministry of the Interior)
MKSM	Militär-Kanzlei Seiner Majestät des Kaisers (Military Chancellery of His Majesty the Emperor)
NFP	*Neue Freie Presse*
NöLA	Niederösterreichisches Landesarchiv (Lower Austrian State Archive)
NZA	Neue Zeremonial Akten (New Ceremonial Files)
ÖFZ	*Österreichische Frauen-Zeitung*
OMeA	Obersthofmeisteramt (Office of the Grand Court Master)
OR	*Ostdeutsche Rundschau*
ÖV	*Österreichische Volkszeitung*
PL	Presse-Leitung (Press Department)
SR	Sonderreihe
TSDIA-L	Tsentral'nyi derzhavnyi istorychnyi arkhiv Ukrainy, L'viv (Central State Historical Archive, L'viv)
WAZ	*Wiener Allgemeine Zeitung*
WStLA	Wiener Stadt- und Landesarchiv (Vienna City and Provincial Archives)
WZ	*Wiener Zeitung*
ZA	Zeremonial Akten (Ceremonial Files)

BIBLIOGRAPHY

Archival Sources

1. Haus-, Hof- und Staatsarchiv, Vienna
   A. Private Papers
      Nachlaß Alfred von Arneth
      Nachlaß Adolf von Braun
      Nachlaß Erzherzog Franz Ferdinand
   B. Obersthofmeisteramt
      OMeA, 1848–1916: Rubrics 19, 30, 31, 33, 65, 90, 121, 133, 134, 136
      Neue Zeremonial Akten, 1847–1916
      Varia, 1848–1895
      Zeremonial Akten, Sonderreihe
      Zeremonial Protokolle, 1849–1916
   C. General-Intendanz, 1897–1909
   D. Ministerium des Äussern
      Administrativ-Registratur, 1888, 1898, 1908
   E. Informations-Büro, 1851–1898
   F. Kabinettskanzlei
      Geheimakten, Nachlaß Schwarzenberg
      Kabinetts-Archiv, Direktionsakten, 1880–1884
      Korrespondenz-Akten, 1880–1909
      Varia, ct. 51.
2. Österreichisches Staatsarchiv, Vienna
   A. Allgemeines Verwaltungsarchiv, Vienna
      Ministerium des Innern, Präsidialakten, 1880–1910
      Ministerratspräsidium
      Presse-Leitung, 1879–1898
      Ministerratsprotokolle, 1880–1898
      Ministerium für Kultus und Unterricht, Präsidialakten, 1880–1908
      Nachlaß Alexander Bach
   B. Kriegsarchiv, Vienna
      Militär-Kanzlei Seiner Majestät des Kaisers, Sonderreihe, 1851
      General-Adjutantur, 1868, 1880, 1894
4. Wiener Stadt- und Landesarchiv, Vienna
   Hand-Akten Kleine Bestände
   Magistratsabteilung 119, Vereinsakt 12226; Vereinsakt 5195
5. Handschriftensammlung, Stadtbibliothek, Vienna
   Nachlaß Karl Lueger
6. Erzbischöfliches Diözesanarchiv, Vienna
   Bischofs-Konferenz, ct. 1, 1836–1849

7. Niederösterreichisches Landesarchiv
   Präsidiale, Regierungs-Jubiläum, 1898–1908
8. Verein für die Geschichte der Arbeiterbewegung, Vienna
   Vorstands-Protokolle, Social Democratic Party, 1898–1908
9. Bundes-Polizeidirektion, 1880–1910, Vienna
10. Archiwum Panstwowe, Cracow
    A. Inventarz Tymczasowe
    B. Polizei-Direction
10. Biblioteka Ossolineum, Wrocław
    Piotr Babczyszyn: Od Gniezny i Seretu po Łynę, Odrę i Nysę. Wspomnienia.
    Part 1: Loszniów – Trembowla (1890–1914).Ossolineum maniuscript 15336/II.
11. Derzhavnyi arkhiv L'vivs'koi oblasti
    Lemberg Police-Direction, 1851–1894
12. Tsentral'nyi derzhavnyi istorychnyi arkhiv Ukrainy, L'viv
    Archive of the Galician Administration

Newspapers and Journals

Alldeutsches Tagblatt
Allgemeine Theaterzeitung
Amtsblatt der k.k. Polizei-Direktion in Wien
Amtsblatt der k.k. Reichshaupt- und Residenzstadt Wien
Arbeiter-Zeitung
Arbeiterinnen-Zeitung
Correspondenzblatt für den katholischen Clerus Österreichs
Czas
Deutsches Volksblatt
Deutsche Zeitung
Dilo
Dziennik Polski
Freie Lehrerstimme
Fremdenblatt
Gazeta Lwowska
Gazeta Narodowa
Głos Narodu
Halyczanin
Illustrirtes Wiener Extrablatt
Illustrierte Zeitung
Der Israelit
Konstitutionelle Vorstadt-Zeitung
Kalendarz Krakowski
Kurjer Lwowski
Linzer Volksblatt
Naprzód
Nauka
Neuigkeits-Weltblatt

Neue Freie Presse
Neues Wiener Abendblatt
Neues Wiener Tagblatt
Österreichische Frauen-Zeitung
Österreichische Volks-Zeitung
Österreichisches Volksblatt
Österreichischer Volksfreund
Ostdeutsche Rundschau
Przegląd Polski
Przyjaciel Ludu
Pszczółka
Reichenberger Zeitung
Reichsgesetzblatt für die im Reichsrathe vertretenen Konigreiche und Länder
Reichspost
Ruslan
Slovo
Slowo Polskie
Unverfälschte Deutsche Worte
Das Vaterland
Die Vedette. Beilage zur Reichswehr
Volksfreund. Zeitschrift für Aufklärung und Erheiterung des Volkes
Volksstimme
Währinger Bezirks Nachrichten
Die Welt
Wiener Allgemeine Theaterzeitung
Wiener Allgemeine Zeitung
Wiener Diöcesanblatt
Wiener Kirchenzeitung
Wiener Zeitung
Wiener Abendzeitung
Wieniec
Związek Chłopski

Selected Published Primary Materials

Berger, Alfred Freiherr von. *Habsburg.* Wien, 1898.

Beskiba, Marianne. *Aus meinen Erinnerungen an Dr. Karl Lueger.* Wien, n.d.

Beust, Friedrich Count von. *Memoirs of Friedrich Ferdinand Count von Beust.* London, 1887.

Biliński, Leon. *Wspomnienia i dokumenty 1846–1919.* Warsaw, 1924.

Bobrzyński, Michał. *Z moich pamiętników.* Wrocław, 1957.

Boehringer, J. F. *Österreichs Jubeltage oder: Wien am 22 bis 30. April 1854.* Wien, 1854.

Brentano, Hanny. *Kaiser Franz Joseph I. 1848–1908. Sein Leben—Seine Zeit.* Wien, 1908.

Chłędowski, Kazimierz. *Pamiętniki Galicja.* Kraków, 1957.

Daszyński, Ignaz. *Pamiętniki.* Warsaw, 1957.

Directiven für das Einschreiten um die allergnädigste Verleihung der k. und k. Kämmererswürde. Wien, 1898.

Eisenmenger, Victor. *Erzherzog Franz Ferdinand. Seinem Andenken gewidmet von seinem Leibarzt.* Zürich, Leipzig, and Wien, 1930.

Emmer, Johannes. *Kaiser Franz Joseph I. Fünfzig Jahre österreichische Geschichte.* Wien, 1898.

Emmer, Johannes. *60 Jahre auf Habsburgs Throne. Festgabe zum 60-jährigen Regierungs-Jubiläum Sr. Majestät Kaiser Franz Joseph I.* Wien, 1908.

Feldman, Wilhelm. *Stronnictwa i programy polityczne w Galicyi 1846–1906.* Kraków, 1907.

Fugger, Nora Fürstin. *Im Glanz der Kaiserzeit.* Zurich, 1932.

Funder, Friedrich. *Vom Gestern ins Heute. Aus dem Kaiserreich in die Republik.* Vienna, 1952.

Gedenkschrift für die Soldaten anläßlich des 50 jährigen Regierungs-Jubiläum S. M. des Kaisers Franz Joseph I. Wien, 1898.

Gerstenberger von Reichsegg, Karl Ritter. *Liebe des Volkes.* Wien, 1908.

Goebl, Nelly, and Risan Bernt. *Unser Franzi. Wahre Geschichten aus der Kinderzeit unser lieben Kaisers Franz Joseph I.* Wien, 1908.

Helfert, Joseph Alexander, ed. *Zum Zweiten Dezember 1848–1898.* Wien, 1898.

Henop, C. *Das Jubiläumsjahr 1898. Ein Gedenkbuch an die Humanitären und festlichen Veranstaltungen aus Anlaß des 50 jährigen Regierungs Jubiläums Sr. Majestät des Kaiser FJI. am 2. December 1898.* Wien, 1898.

Herzig, Max, ed. *Viribus Unitis. Das Buch vom Kaiser.* Wien, Budapest, Leipzig, 1898.

Hofdamen-Briefe. Sammlung von Briefen an und von Wiener Hofdamen a.d. 19 Jahrhundert (1903).

Hofschematismus/Hofkalender. Wien, 1845–1916.

Holzer, Dr. Wilhelm. *W 70-ta rocznice urodziń cesarza Franciszka Józefa I.* Lwów, 1900.

Horowitz, Ch. L. *Festrede anlässlich des Dankgottesdienste am fünfzigjährigen Jubiläumstage Sr. Majestät des Kaisers Franz Josephs am 2. Dezember 1898. gehalten in der alten Synagoga zu Krakau vom Rabiner-Stellvertreter Horowitz.* Krakau, 1899.

Huldigungs-Ausstellung unser Kaiser 1830–1848–1908. Wien, 1908.

Jahres-Bericht des Gymnasiums der k.k. Theresianischen Akademie in Wien. Wien, 1899.

XXI. Jahresbericht des K.K. Rudolf-Gymnasiums I Brody. Brody, 1899.

Jubiläums-Ausstellung Wien, 1898. Wien, 1898.

Kaiserblatt. Festschrift des Wiener Journalisten- und Schriftstellervereines Concordia. Wien, 1898.

Der Kaisertage von Reichenberg und Gablonz zur Erinnerung an den Besuch der Deutschböhmisch Ausstellung Reichenberg 1906 durch seine Majestät der Kaiser. Reichenberg, 1906.

Kaindl, Raimond Friedrich. *Geschichte von Czernowitz von der ältesten Zeite bis zur Gegenwart.* Czernowitz, 1908.

Ketterl, Eugen. *Der alte Kaiser wie nur Einer Ihn sah. Der wahrheitsgetreue Bericht des Leibkammerdieners Kaiser Franz Josephs I.* Wien, 1929.

Kaiser-Huldigungs-Festzug Wien Juni 1908. Eine Schilderung und Erklärung seiner Gruppen. Wien, 1908.

Kielmansegg, Erich Graf. *Kaiserhaus, Staatsmänner und Politiker.* Wien, 1966.

Klopfer, Carl, ed. *Unser Kaiser. Ein Gedenkbuch der fünfzigjährigen Regierung, zugleich ein Lebens- und Characterbild Kaiser Franz Josef I.* Wien, 1898.

Koźmian, Stanisław. Dr. S. R. Landau, trans. *Das Jahr 1863. Polen und die europäische Diplomatie.* Wien, 1896.

Kupelwieser, Paul. *Aus den Erinnerungen eines alten Österreichers.* Wien, 1918.

Laurencic, Julius, ed. *Jubiläums-Ausstellung Wien 1898.* Wien, 1898.

———. *Unser Monarchie. Die Österreichische Calendar zur Zeit des fünfzig jährigen Regierungs-Jubiläums Sr. k.u.k. Apostol. Majestät Franz Josef I.* Wien, 1898.

Lieber Rudolf. Briefe von Kaiser Franz Joseph und Elisabeth an ihren Sohn. Introduced by Friedrich Weissensteiner. Wien, 1991.

Lowy, Dr, and Ehrenfeld, Oberrabbiner in Prague. *Jubelworte. Eine Sammlung patriotischen Casualreden.* Prague, 1898.

Madejczyk, Jan. *Wspomnienia.* Warsaw, 1965.

Maciołowski, Julian. *Pamiatka jubileauszowa dla polskich dzieci.* Kraków, 1908.

Michejda, Jerzy. *Nasz Cesarz. 1848–1898. Obrazek jubileuszowy.* Cieszyn, 1898.

Mieroszewscy, Sobiesław and Stanisław. *Wspomniena.* Cracow, 1964.

Musil, Robert. *Der Mann ohne Eigenschaften.* Berlin, 1930–1943.

Naske, Adolph Carl. *Gedenkbuch über die Vermählungs-Feierlichkeiten Seiner k.k. apostolischen Majestät Franz Joseph I., Kaiser von Österreich, mit Elisabeth, Herzogin in Baiern.* Wien, 1854.

Nostitz-Rienek, Georg, ed. *Briefe Kaiser Franz Josephs an Kaiserin Elisabeth 1859–1898.* Wien, 1966.

Nowolecki, Aleksander. *Pamiątka podróży cesarza Franciszka Józefa I. po Galicyi.* Kraków, 1881.

Petermann, Reinhard. *Wien im Zeitalter Kaiser Franz Josephs I.* Wien, 1908.

Popiel, Paweł. *Pamiętniki Pawła Popiela, 1807–1892.* Kraków, 1927.

Poppera, Franciszka. *Trzydziesci lat panowania cesarza Franciszka Jozefa I.* Kraków, 1879.

Proschko, Hermine (Camilla). *Unseres Kaisers diamantenes Jubelfest.* Wien, 1898.

———. *Unseres Kaisers goldenes Jubelfest 1908.* Wien, 1908.

Rauch, Josef. *Erinnerungen eines Offiziers aus Altösterreich.* Munich, 1918.

Reich, Rabbiner W. *Patriotischen Reden.* Baden, 1900.

Rene, Carl. *Kaiser Frans Joseph I. Ein Wort zu seiner 60 jährigen Regierungs-Jubiläum.* Berlin, 1908.

Renglovics, Joseph von. *Lebenserinnerugen eines ehemaligen Hofbeamten der Kaiser- und-Königlichen Hofhaushaltung.* Vienna, 1938.

Rostok, Robert. *Die Regierungszeit seiner Majestät des Kaisers und Königs Frany Josef I.* Graz, 1898.

Rusinowsky, Anastazy. *Wspomnienie 18 Lutego 1853 i pożądanego wyzdrowienia Jego c.k. apostolskiej mości cesarza Franciszka Józefa.* Tarnów, 1853.

Schickler, Rudolf. *Festprolog. Kaiser Jubiläums Huldigungs-Feier. Mai 30, 1898. Verein zur Ausspeissung armer Israel. Schulkinder des XVI und XVII Bezirkes.* Wien, 1898.

Schluß-Bericht der gemeinderäthlichen Comission zur Durchführung der Feier des 50jährigen Regierungs-Jubiläums Sr Majestät des Kaisers. Wien, 1899.

Schmid, Norbert. *Des Thrones Jubelfest.* Wien, 1879.

Schneider, Dr. Joseph, ed. *Anonymous. Kaiser Franz Joseph I. und sein Hof. Erinnerungen und Schilderungen aus den nachgelassenen Papieren eines persönlichen Ratgebers.* Wien, 1919.

Schnitzer, J., ed. *Franz Joseph und seine Zeit. Cultur-Historischer Ruckblick auf die Franco-Josephinische Epoche.* Wien, 1898.

Schnürer, Dr. Franz, ed. *Briefe Kaiser Franz Josephs I. an seine Mutter, 1838–1872.* Munich, 1930.

Schreiber, Alexander Salomon. Simon Schreiber, ed. *Zwei Kaiserreden und ein hebräischer Dank-Psalm.* Czernowitz, 1908.

Shcherban', A. N., ed. *Eho ts. i k. Velychestvo Frants-Iosyf I v "Narodnom Domi"dnia 2. (14.) veresnia 1880 h.* L'viv, 1880.

Skedl, Arthur, ed. *Der politische Nachlaß des Grafen Eduard Taaffe.* Vienna, 1922.

Slomka, Jan. *From Serfdom to Self-Government. Memoirs of a Polish Village Mayor 1842–1927.* Trans. by Illia John Rose. London, 1941.

Smolle, Leo. *Das Buch von unserem Kaiser. 1848–1888.* Wien, 1888.

———. *Czterdziesci lat panowania Cesarza Franciszka Józefa I. 1848–1898.* Opracowania polskie na podstawie dziela Dr. Leona Smollego „Das Buch von unserem Kaiser." Lwów, 1898.

———. *Fünf Jahrzehnte auf Habsburgs Throne, 1848–1898.* Wien, 1898.

———. *Kaiser Franz Josef I.* Wien, 1888, 1898.

———. *Unser Kaiser. Sein Leben und Wirken der Jugend erzählt.* Wien, 1908.

Sokalski, Bronisław. *O życiu i czynach najmiłościwej nam panującego, najjaśniejszego pana, Cesarza i Króla Franciszka Józefa I.* Lwów, 1898, 1908.

Spitzer, S. *Najjaśniejszy Pan Cesarz i Król Franciszek Józef I. w siędmdziesiąta rocznicę urodziń.* Kraków, 1900.

Stapiński, Jan. *Pamiętniki.* Warszawa, 1958.

Stenograficzne Sprawozdania z trzeciej sesyi czwartego peryodu Sejmu Krajowego Królestwa Galicyi i Lodomeryi wraz z Wielkiem Księstwem Krakowskiem. Lwów, 1880.

Das Strafgesetz vom 27. Mai 1852, Nr.117 RGBl., samt den daselbe eränzenden und erläuternden Gesetzen und Verordnungen, unter Anführung einschlägiger Beschlüsse und Entscheidungen des Obersten Gerichts- und Kassationshofes. Wien, 1908.

Sypniewski, Alfred. *Fünfzig Jahre Kaiser.* Wien, 1898.

Szujski, Józef. *Der Antrag des galizischen Landtages gegenüber dem Interesse der österreich-ungarischen Monarchie.* Krakau, 1869.

Szczepański, Stanisław. *Nędzy Galicji w cyfrach i program energicznego rozwoju gospodarstwa krajowego.* 2nd ed. Lwów, 1888.

Tesseryk, Antoni. *Wjazd najjaśniejszego Franciszka Józefa I. Cesarza Austryi do*

Krakowa, tudzież podróz J. Ces. Król. Apost. Mości po Galicyi i Bukowinie. Kraków, 1853.

Truxa, Hans Maria, ed. *Kaiser-Jubiläums-Dichterbuch. 50 Jahre Österreich. Literatur. Huldigungsgabe.* Wien, 1898.

Tschudy, Franz Freiherr von Clarus. *Illustrirtes Gedenkbuch zur immerwährende Errinerungen an die glorreiche Vermählungsfeier Sr. k.k. Apostolische Majestät Franz Joseph von Österreich mit ihrer köngl. Hoheit der Durchlauchtigsten Frau Herzogin Elisabeth in Baiern, vollzogen in Wien am 24 April 1854.* Wien, 1854.

Thun-Salm, Christiane Gräfin. *Des Kaisers Traum.* Wien, 1898.

Uhl, Friedrich. *Aus meinem Leben.* Stuttgart and Berlin, 1908.

Uniesienie wiernego ludu na przybycie do kraju Najjaśniejszego Cesarsza I Króla Franciszka Józefa I. Lwów, 1851. Jagiellonian University Library, Manuscript 15029III.

Verordnungsblatt für den Dienstbereich des Ministeriums für Cultus und Unterricht. Wien, 1898.

Wächtler, Wenzel. *Edelsteine aus der Krone S.M. Franz Joseph I.* Wien, 1888.

———. *Österreichs Kaiser Franz Josef I.* Wien, 1890.

———. *Das goldene Jubiläums Franz Josephs I. Ein Gedenkbuch seiner fünfzigjährigen Regierung, seines Lebens und Strebens für Jugend und Erwachsene.* Wien, 1898.

Wajda, Stanisław. *Na Pamiatke 60-cioletniego jubileuszu panowania Jego Cesarskiej i Królewskiej, Apostolskiej Mości Cesarza Franciszka Józefa I. w Austryi. 1848–1908.* Kraków, 1908.

Wien 1848. Denkschrift zum 2 Dezember 1888. Wien, 1888.

Witos, Wincenty. *Moje Wspomnienia.* Warsaw, 1981.

Die Widmungen und Veranstaltungen der Gemeinde Wien zum 60 jährigen Regierungs-Jubiläum seiner Majestät des Kaisers Franz Joseph I. im Jahre 1908. Wien, 1908.

Wilczek, Hanz. *Hanz Wilczek erzählt seinem Enkeln Erinnerungen aus seinem Leben.* Elisabeth Kinsky-Wilczek, ed. Graz, 1935.

Zipper, Albert. *Cesarz i Król Franciszek Józef I. Dzieje Jego żywota i rządów.* Zwolchów, 1888.

———. *Führer durch die Allgemeine Landes-Ausstellung sowie durch die Königl. Hauptstadt Lemberg.* Lemberg, 1894.

Zöhrer, Ferdinand. *Das Kaiser-Buch. Erzählungen aus dem Leben des Kaisers Franz Josef I.* Wien, 1890.

———. *Hoch Habsburg.* Wien, 1898.

Zupan, Tomo. *Nas Cesar Fran Josip I. 1848–1898.* Ljubljana, 1898.

———. *Nas Cesar Fran Josip. 1848–1908.* Ljubljana, 1908.

Secondary Works

Adamson, John, ed. *The Princely Courts of Europe: Ritual, Politics, and Culture under the Ancien Regime 1500–1700.* London, 1999.

Albrecht, Catherine. "Pride in Production: The Jubilee Exhibition of 1891 and Economic Competition between Czechs and Germans in Bohemia." *Austrian History Yearbook* 24 (1993): 101–118.

Allmayer-Beck, Johann Christoph. *Der stumme Reiter: Erzherzog Albrecht, der Feldherr "Gesamtösterreichs".* Graz, 1997.

Alter, Peter. *Nationalism.* 2nd ed. London and New York, 1994.

Anderson, Benedict. *Imagined Communities: Reflections on the Origin and Spread of Nationalism.* London, 1983.

Andics, Hellmuth. *Luegerzeit. Das schwarze Wien bis 1918.* Wien, 1984.

Arnstein, W. "Queen Victoria's Diamond Jubilee." *The American Scholar* 66 (1997): 591–597.

Baidins, Valdins. "Franz Joseph, Kaisertreue and Loyalty in the Late Habsburg Empire." Ph.D. Diss., University of Washington, 1999.

Bałaban, Mayer. "Herz Homberg in Galizien." *Jahrbuch für jüdische Geschichte und Literatur* 19 (1916).

———. *Żydzi w Austryi na panowania cesarza Franciszka Józefa I.* Lwów, 1909.

Barkey, Karen, and Mark von Hagen, eds. *After Empire: Multiethnic Societies and Nation-Building: The Soviet Union and the Russian, Ottoman and Habsburg Empires.* Boulder, 1997.

Bartal, Israel, and Antony Polonsky, eds. *Focusing on Galicia: Jews, Poles, and Ukrainians, 1772–1918.* Portland, 1999.

Beales, Derek. *Joseph II.* Cambridge, 1987.

Beck, Leopold. "Das Bild und der Mythos der Habsburger in den Schulgeschichtsbücher und im "vaterländischen Schriften" der franzisko-josephinischen Ära, 1848–1918." MA Thesis, University of Vienna, 1991.

Beller, Steven. *Francis Joseph.* London and New York, 1996.

———. *Vienna and the Jews, 1867–1938.* Cambridge, 1989.

———. "Kraus's Firework: State Consciousness Raising in the 1908 Jubilee Parade in Vienna and the Problem of Austrian Identity." In Maria Bucur and Nancy Wingfield, eds., *Staging the Past: Commemorations in Habsburg Central Europe.* West Lafayette, 2000: 46–71.

Berner, Peter, Emil Brix, and Wolfgang Mantl, eds. *Wien um 1900. Aufbruch in die Moderne.* Munich, 1986.

von Bieberstein, Christoph Freiherr Marschall. *Freiheit in der Unfreiheit. Die nationale Autonomie der Polen in Galizien nach dem österreich-ungarischen Ausgleich von 1867.* Wiesbaden, 1993.

Binder, Harald. *Galizien in Wien: Parteien, Wahlen, Fraktionen und Abgeordnete im Übergang zur Massenpolitik.* Wien, 2004.

———. "Polen, Ruthenen, Juden. Politik und Politiker in Galizien 1897–1918." Ph.D. Diss., University of Bern, 1997.

———. "Making and Defending a Polish Town: 'Lwów' (Lemberg) 1848–1914." *Austrian History Yearbook* 34 (2003): 57–81.

———. "Die polnische Presse in der Habsburgermonarchie." In *Die Habsburgermonarchie, 1848–1918,* vol. 8. Vienna, Forthcoming.

———. "Die ukrainische Presse in der Habsburgermonarchie." In *Die Habsburgermonarchie, 1848–1918,* vol. 8. Vienna, Forthcoming.

Bisanz, Hanz, ed. *Lemberg/L'viv, 1772–1918. Wiederbegegnung mit einer Landeshauptstadt der Donaumonarchie.* Wien, 1993.

Blanning, T. C. W. *Joseph II.* London and New York, 1994.

Bled, Jean-Paul. *Franz Joseph,* trans. T. Bridgeman. Oxford, 1987.

Blessing, Werner. "The Cult of Monarchy, Political Loyalty and the Workers' Movement in Imperial Germany." *Journal of Contemporary History* 13/2 (1978): 357–375.

———. *Staat und Kirche in der Gesellschaft. Institutionelle Autorität und mentaler Wandel in Bayern während des 19. Jahrhunderts.* Göttingen, 1982.

Blackbourn, David, and Geoff Eley. *The Peculiarities of German History: Bourgeois Society and Politics in Nineteenth-Century Germany.* Oxford, 1984.

Blejwas, Stanislaus. *Realism in Polish Politics: Warsaw Positivism and the National Survival in Nineteenth Century Poland.* New Haven, 1984.

Bloch, Marc. *The Royal Touch.* Paris, 1924.

Blöchl, Andrea. "Die Kaisergedenktage. Die Feste und Feiern zu den Regierungsjubiläen und runden Geburtstagen Kaiser Franz Josephs." In Emil Brix and Hannes Stekl, eds., *Der Kampf um das Gedächtnis. Öffentliche Gedenktage in Mitteleuropa.* Wien, 1997.

Blum, Jerome. *Noble Landowners and Agriculture in Austria, 1815–1848.* Baltimore, 1948.

Boyer, John W. *Political Radicalism in Late Imperial Vienna: Origins of the Christian Social Movement 1848–1897.* Chicago, 1981.

———. *Christian Socialism in Power: Culture and Political Crisis in Vienna, 1898–1918.* Chicago, 1995.

———. "Religion and Political Development in Central Europe around 1900: A View from Vienna." *Austrian History Yearbook* 25 (1994): 13–57.

Brandt, Harm-Hinrich. *Der österreichische Neoabsolutismus: Staatsfinanzen und Politik 1848–1860.* 2 vols. Göttingen, 1978.

Brock, Peter. "The Early Years of the Polish Peasant Party, 1895–1907." *Journal of Central European Affairs* 14/3 (1954): 219–235.

Brown, Karin Brinkmann. *Karl Lueger, the Liberal Years: Democracy, Municipal Reform, and the Struggle for Power in the Vienna City Council, 1875–1882.* New York and London, 1987.

Brubaker, Rogers. *Nationalism Reframed: Nationhood and the National Question in the New Europe.* Cambridge, 1996.

Bruckmüller, Ernst. "Die österreichische Revolution von 1848 und der Habsburgermythos des 19. Jahrhunderts." In Hubert Lengauer and Primus Heinz Kucher, eds., *Bewegung im Reich der Immobilität.* Wien, 2001: 1–33.

———. "Österreich: An Ehren und an Siegen reich." In Monika Flacke, ed., *Mythen der Nationen. Ein europäisches Panorama* (Berlin, 1998): 269–294.

Buck, August, and Georg Kauffmann, eds. *Europäische Hofkultur im 16. und 17. Jahrhundert.* Hamburg, 1981.

Bucur, Maria, and Nancy M. Wingfield. *Staging the Past: The Politics of Commemoration in Habsburg Central Europe, 1848 to the Present.* West Lafayette, 2001.

Burke, Peter. *The Fabrication of Louis XIV.* New Haven, 1992.

Buszko, Józef. *Polacy w parlamencie wiedeńskim, 1848–1918.* Warszawa, 1996.

Cannadine, David. "The Context, Performance and Meaning of Ritual: The British Monarchy and the 'Invention of Tradition', c. 1820–1977." In Eric Hobsbawm and Terrance Ranger, eds., *The Invention of Tradition.* Cambridge, 1983: 101–164.

Cohen, Gary B. *Education and Middle-Class Society in Imperial Austria, 1848–1918.* West Lafayette, 1996.

———. "Neither Absolutism nor Anarchy: New Narratives on Society and Government in Late Imperial Austria." *Austrian History Yearbook* 29/1 (1998): 37–61.

———. *The Politics of Ethnic Survival: Germans in Prague.* Princeton, 1981.

Cole, Laurence. *"Für Gott, Kaiser und Vaterland": Nationale Identität der deutschsprachigen Bevölkerung Tirols 1860–1914.* Frankfurt, 2000.

———. "Patriotic Celebrations in Late Nineteenth Century Tirol." In Maria Bucur and Nancy Wingfield, eds., *Staging the Past: Commemorations in Habsburg Central Europe.* West Lafayette, 2001.

———. "Province and Patriotism: German National Identity in Tirol in the Years 1850–1914." Ph.D. Diss., European University Institute, Florence, 1995.

———. "Vom Glanz der Montur. Zum dynastischen Kult der Habsburger und seiner Vermittlung durch militärische Vorbilder im 19. Jahrhundert." *Österreichische Zeitschrift für Geschichtswissenschaften* 7 (1996): 577–591.

Confino, Alon. *The Nation as a Local Metaphor: Württemberg, Imperial Germany and National Memory, 1871–1918.* Chapel Hill and London, 1997.

Coreth, Anna. *Pietas Austriaca. Österreichische Frömmigkeit im Barock.* Wien, 1982.

Cornovol, Ihor. *Pol's'ko-ukrajins'ka uhoda 1890–1894.* L'viv, 2000.

Corti, Egon Caesar Conte. *Vom Kind zum Kaiser: Kindheit und erste Jugend Kaiser Franz Josephs I. und seiner Geschwister.* Graz, 1950.

———. *Mensch und Herrscher. Wege und Schicksale Kaiser Franz Josephs I. Zwischen Thronbesteigung und Berliner Kongress.* Graz, 1952.

Crowley, David. "Castles, Cabarets and Cartoons: Claims on Polishness in Kraków around 1905." In *The City in Central Europe: Culture and Society from 1800 to the Present,* ed. Malcolm Gee, Tim Kirk, and Jill Steward, 101–122. Cambridge, 1999.

Csáky, Moritz, and Peter Stachel, eds. *Speicher des Gedächtnisses.* 2 vols. Wien, 2000, 2001.

Csáky, Moritz, and Klaus Zeyringer, eds. *Inzenierungen des kollektiven Gedächtnisses.* Innsbruck, 2002.

———. *Pluralitäten, Religionen und kulturelle Codes.* Innsbruck, 2001.

———. *Ambivalenz des kulturellen Erbes: Vielfachcodierung des historischen Gedächtnisses.* Innsbruck, 2000.

Dabrowski, Patrice M. *Commemorations and the Shaping of Modern Poland.* Bloomington, 2004.

———. "Folk, Faith and Fatherland: Defining the Polish Nation in 1883." *Nationalities Papers* 28/3 (2000): 397–416.

Danner, Daniela. "Das Regierungsjubiläum 1898 im Spiegel der Presse." MA Thesis, University of Vienna, 1994.

Daszyk, Krzystof Karol. "Między Polska racja stanu a Habsburskim mitem." *Galicia i jej dziedzictwo* 1 (1994).

———. "Zanim Franciszek Józef stał się 'naszym dobrym cesarzem': Polacy z Galicji wobec Austrii I Habsburgów w latach 1848–1860." *Galicja i jej dziedzictwo* 12 (1999): 119–147.

Davies, Norman. *God's Playground: A History of Poland.* New York, 1982.

Deák, István. *Beyond Nationalism: A Social & Political History of the Habsburg Officer Corps, 1848–1918.* New York, 1990.

———. *The Lawful Revolution: Louis Kossuth and the Hungarians, 1848–1849.* New York, 1979.

Decloedt, Leopold R. G., ed. *An meine Völker: Die Literarisierung Franz Joseph I.* Bern, 1998.

Dickinger, Christian. *Franz Joseph I: Die Entmythisierung.* Vienna, 2002.

Dickens, A. G., ed. *The Courts of Europe: Politics, Patronage and Royalty, 1400–1800.* London, 1977.

Dickson, P. G. M. *Finance and Government under Maria Theresia, 1740–1780.* Oxford, 1987.

Dirnberger, Franz. "Das Wiener Hofzeremoniell bis in die Zeit Franz Josephs. Überlegungen über Probleme, Entstehung und Bedeutung." In *Das Zeitalter Kaiser Franz Josephs.* Part 1: *Von der Revolution zur Gründerzeit 1848–1880.* Wien, 1984.

Dollinger, Heinz. "Das Leitbild des Bürgerkönigtums in der europäischen Monarchie des 19. Jahrhunderts." In Karl Ferdinand Werner, ed., *Hof, Kultur, und Politik im 19. Jahrhundert,* 325–362. Bonn, 1985.

Dohrn, Verena. *Reise nach Galizien. Grenzlandschaften des alten Europa.* Frankfurt am Main, 1991.

Drda, Elgin. "Die Entwicklung der Majestätsbeleidigung in der österreichischen Rechtsgeschichte unter besonderer Berücksichtigung der Ära Kaiser Franz Josephs." Diss., University of Linz, 1992.

Dubin, Lois. *The Port Jews of Habsburg Trieste: Absolutist Politics and Enlightenment Culture.* Stanford, 1999.

Duindam, Jeroen. *Vienna and Versailles: The Courts of Europe's Dynastic Rivals, 1550–1780.* Cambridge, 2003.

———. "Ceremonial Staffs and Paperwork at Two Courts: France and the Habsburg Monarchy ca. 1550–1720." In Klaus Malettke and Chantel Grell (eds.), *Hofgesellschaft und Höflinge an europäischen Fürstenhöfen in der Frühen Neuzeit (15.–18. Jh.),* 369–388. Marburg, 2000.

Dunin-Wąsowicz, Krzystof. *Czasopismiennictwo ludowe w Galicji.* Wrocław, 1952.

———. *Dzieje Stonnictwa Ludowego w Galicji.* Warsaw, 1956.

———. *Jan Stapiński Trybun ludu wiejskiego.* Warsaw, 1969.

Durkheim, Emile. *On the Elementary Forms of the Religious Life.* trans. J. W. Swain. London, 1915.

Ehalt, Hubert Ch. *Ausdrucksformen absolutistischer Herrschaft. Der Wiener Hof im 17. und 18. Jahrhundert.* Wien, 1980.

Elias, Norbert. *Die höfische Gesellschaft. Untersuchungen zur Soziologie des Königtums und der höfischen Aristokratie mit einer Einleitung: Soziologie und Geschichtswissenschaft.* Berlin, 1969.

Eppel, Peter. *"Concordia soll Ihr Name sein."* *125 Jahre Journalisten- und Schrift- stellerverein "Concordia."* Wien, 1984.

Evans, R. J. W. *The Making of the Habsburg Monarchy, 1550–1700.* Oxford, 1979.

Fassler, Peter, Thomas Held, and Dirk Sawitzki, eds. *Lemberg—Lwów—L'viv. Eine Stadt im Schnittpunkt europäischer Kulturen.* Köln, 1993.

Fehrenbach, Elizabeth. "Images of Kaiserdom." In John C. G. Röhl, ed., *Kaiser Wilhelm II: New Interpretations,* 269–285. Cambridge, 1982.

Feldman, Wilhelm. *Stronnictwa i programy polityczne w Galicyi 1846–1906.* Kraków, 1907.

———. *Dzieje Polskiej myśli politycznej, 1864–1914.* Warszawa, 1933.

Fink, Carole, Isabel V. Hull, and MacGregor Knox, eds. *German Nationalism and the European Response, 1890–1945.* Norman, 1985.

Firth, Raymond. *Symbols Public and Private.* Ithaca, 1973.

Forst-Battaglia, Jakub. "Die polnischen Konservativen Galiziens und die Slawen (1866–1879)." Ph.D. Diss., University of Vienna, 1975.

Fras, Zbigniew. *Florian Ziemiałkowski (1817–1900).* Wrocław, 1991.

———. "Mit dobrego Cesarza." *Polskie mity polityczne XIX I XX Wieku.* Wrocław, 1988.

———. "Podróże cesarza Franciszka Józefa I do Galicji." In Mark Czapliński, Romualda Gelles, and Krystyna Matwijowski, eds., *Z dziejów Galicji, Śląska, Polski i Niemiec. Prace ofiarowane profesorowi drowi Adamowi Galosowi w siedemdziesiątą rocznicę urodzin. Wrocław, 1994.*

Freifeld, Alice. *Nationalism and the Crowd in Liberal Hungary, 1848–1918.* Baltimore, 2000.

———. "Marketing Industrialism and Dualism in Liberal Hungary: Expositions, 1842–1896." *Austrian History Yearbook* 29/1 (1998): 63–92.

Fritsche, Victor von. *Bilder aus dem österreichischen Hof- und Gesellschaftsleben.* Wien, 1914.

Garver, Bruce. *The Young Czech Party, 1874–1901, and the Emergence of a Multi-Party System.* New Haven, 1978.

Geehr, Richard S. *Karl Lueger: Mayor of fin de siècle Vienna.* Detroit, 1990.

Geertz, Clifford. "Centers, Kings, and Charisma: Reflections on the Symbolics of Power." In Geertz, *Local Knowledge: Further Essays in Interpretive Anthropology.* New York, 1983.

———. *The Interpretation of Cultures.* New York, 1973.

Gellner, Ernest. *Nations and Nationalism.* Ithaca, 1983.

Gerő, Andras. *Francis Joseph, King of the Hungarians.* New York, 2001.

Gillis, John, ed. *Commemorations: The Politics of National Identity.* Princeton, 1994.

Godsey, William D., Jr. *Aristocratic Redoubt: The Austro-Hungarian Foreign Office on the Eve of the First World War.* West Lafayette, 1999.

———. "'La societé était au fond légitimiste': Émigrés, Aristocracy, and the Court at Vienna, 1749–1848." *European History Quarterly* 35 (2005): 63–95.

———. "Oberstkämmerer Rudolph Graf Czernin (1757–1845) und die 'Adelsrestaura-tion' nach 1815 in Österreich." *Études danubiennes* 19(1/2) (2003), 59–74.

———. "Quarterings and Kinship: The Social Composition of the Habsburg Aristocracy in the Dualist Era." *Journal of Modern History* 71/1 (1999): 56–104.

Good, David. *The Economic Rise of the Habsburg Empire, 1750–1914.* Berkeley, 1984.

Greenfeld, Liah. *Nationalism: Five Roads to Modernity.* Cambridge, 1992.

Grodziski, Stanisław. *Franciszek Józef I.* Wrocław, 1990.

———. *W królestwie Galicji i Lodomerii.* Kraków, 1976.

Grossegger, Elisabeth. *Der Kaiser-Huldigungs-Festzug Wien 1908.* Wien, 1992.

Gurnicz, Antoni. *Kółka rolnicze w Galicji.* Warszawa, 1967.

Haiko, Peter, and Renata Kassal-Mikula. *Otto Wagner und das Kaiser Franz Josef-Stadtmuseum: Das Scheitern der Moderne in Wien.* Wien, 1988.

Halbwachs, Maurice. *On Collective Memory.* Chicago, 1992.

Hamann, Brigitte. *Elisabeth. Kaiserin wider Willen.* Wien, 1981.

———. "Erzherzog Albrecht—Die Graue Eminenz des Habsburgerhofes. Hinweise auf einen unterschätzten Politiker." In Isabella Ackerl, Walter Hummelberger, and Hans Mommsen, eds., *Politik und Gesellschaft im alten und neuen Österreich. Festschrift für Rudolf Neck zum 60. Geburtstag.* Wien, 1981.

———. *Rudolf. Kronprinz und Rebell.* Wien, 1978.

———. "Der Wiener Hof und die Hofgesellschaft in der zweiten Hälfte des 19. Jahrhunderts." In Karl Möckl, ed., *Hof und Hofgesellschaft in den deutschen Staaten im 19 und beginnenden 20. Jahrhundert.* Boppard am Rhein, 1990.

Hanak, Peter. *Der Garten und die Werkstatt. Ein kulturgeschichtlicher Vergleich Wien und Budapest um 1900.* Wien, 1988.

Hartmann, Eleonore. "Die Hofreisen Kaiser Franz I." Ph.D. Diss., University of Vienna, 1968.

Hartmann, Wolfgang. *Der historische Festzug. Seine Entstehung und Entwicklung im 19. und 20. Jh.* Munich, 1976.

Healy, Maureen. *Vienna and the Fall of the Habsburg Empire: Total War and Everyday Life in World War I.* Cambridge, 2004.

Hecher, Martin. "Hans Makart und der Wiener Festzug von 1879." Ph.D. Diss., University of Vienna, 1986.

Heindl, Waltraud. *Gehorsame Rebellen: Bürokratie und Beamte in Österreich 1780 bis 1848.* Wien, 1991.

Herrsche, Peter. *Der Spätjansenismus in Österreich.* Wien, 1977.

Heydte, Friedrich August von der. *Die Monarchie. Eine europäische Idee. Österreich vom Wiener Kongress bis St. Germain.* Wien, 1993.

Himka, John-Paul. *Galician Villagers and the Ukrainian National Movement in the Nineteenth Century.* Edmonton, 1988.

———. "The Greek Catholic Church and the Ukrainian Nation in Galicia." In Jim Niessen, ed., *Religious Compromise, Political Salvation: The Greek Catholic Church and Nation-Building in Eastern Europe.* Pittsburgh, 1993.

———. *Religion and Nationality in Western Ukraine: The Greek Catholic Church and the Ruthenian National Movement in Galicia, 1867–1900.* Montreal, 1999.

———. *Socialism in Galicia: The Emergence of Polish Democracy and Ukrainian Radicalism (1860–1890).* Cambridge, 1983.

Höbelt, Lothar. *Kornblume und Kaiseradler. Die deutschfreiheitlichen Parteien Alt-österreichs 1882–1918.* Wien, 1993.

Hobsbaum, Eric. ed. *The Invention of Tradition.* Cambridge, 1983.

———. *Nations and Nationalism since 1780: Programme, Myth, Reality.* Cambridge, 1990.

Hofmann, Christina. *Das spanische Hofzeremoniell von 1500–1700.* Frankfurt, 1985.

Homola-Dzikowska, Irena. *Mikołaj Zyblikiewicz.* Wrocław, 1964.

Hroch, Miroslav. *Social Preconditions of National Revival in Europe.* Cambridge, 1985.

Hull, Isabel. "Prussian Dynastic Ritual and the end of Monarchy." In Carole Fink, Isabel Hull, and Macgregor Knoz, eds., *German Nationalism and the European Response, 1890–1945,* 13–41. Norman, 1985.

Hunt, Lynn. *Politics, Culture and Class in the French Revolution.* Berkeley, 1984.

Janowski, Maciej. *Inteligencja wobec wyzwań nowoczesności. Dylematy ideowe polskiej demokracji liberalnej w Galicji w latach 1889–1914.* Warsaw, 1996.

Jaszi, Oscar. *The Dissolution of the Habsburg Monarchy.* Chicago, 1929.

Judson, Pieter. *Exclusive Revolutionaries: Liberal Politics, Social Experience, and National Identity in the Austrian Empire, 1848–1914.* Ann Arbor, 1996.

———. "Whether Race or Conviction Should Be the Standard: National Identity and Liberal Politics in Nineteenth-Century Austria." *Austrian History Yearbook* 22 (1991): 76–95.

Ingrao, Charles. *The Habsburg Monarchy, 1618–1815.* Cambridge, 1994.

Jenks, William. *Austria under the Iron Ring, 1879–1893.* Charlottesville, 1965.

Kacki, Fr. *Ks. Stanisław Stojałowski i jego działalność polityczna.* Lwów, 1937.

Kantorowicz, Ernst. *The King's Two Bodies: A Study in Medieval Political Theology.* Princeton, 1957.

Kann, Robert. *Erzherzog Franz Ferdinand Studien.* Wien, 1976.

———. *A History of the Habsburg Empire, 1526–1918.* Berkeley, 1974.

———. *The Multinational Empire: Nationalism and National Reform in the Habsburg Monarchy, 1848–1918.* 2. vols. New York, 1950.

Kelly, T. Mills. "Taking It to the Streets: Czech National Socialists in 1908." *Austrian History Yearbook* 29/1 (1998): 93–112.

Kieniewicz, Stefan. *Adam Sapieha.* Lwów, 1939.

———. *The Emancipation of the Polish Peasantry.* Chicago, 1969.

———. *Galicja w dobie autonomicznej (1850–1914).* Wrocław, 1952.

King, Jeremy. *Budweisers into Czechs and Germans: A Local History of Bohemian Politics, 1848–1948.* Princeton, 2002.

Kiszling, Rudolf. *Fürst Felix Schwarzenberg.* Graz, 1952.

Klanska, Maria. *Daleko od Wiednia.* Kraków, 1991.

Kolmer, Gustav. *Parlament und Verfassung in Österreich.* Wien/Leipzig, 1902–1914.

Komlos, John. *Economic Development in the Habsburg Monarchy and in the Successor States.* Boulder, 1990.

Komlos, John. *The Habsburg Monarchy as a Customs Union: Economic Development in Austria-Hungary in the Nineteenth Century.* Princeton, 1983.

Kovacs, Elisabeth. "Kirchliches Zeremoniell am Wiener Hof des 18. Jahrhunderts im Wandel von Mentalitat und Gesellschaft." *Mitteilungen des Österreichischen Staatsarchives* 32 (1979): 109–142.

Kozik, Jan. *Ukraiński ruch narodowy w Galicji w latach, 1830–1948.* Kraków, 1973.

Kulak, Teresa. "Między austriacka lojalnościa a polska narodowoscia." *Galicia u jej dziedzictwo* 1 (1994).

Kugler,Georg. *Des Kaisers Rock.* Wien, 1989.

———. *Uniform und Mode am Kaiserhof.* Wien, 1983.

Lane, Victor Hugo, IV. "Class Interest and the Shaping of a 'Non-Historical' Nation: Reassessing the Galician Ruthenian Path to Ukrainian Identity." In Zvi Gitelman, ed., *Cultures and Nations of Central and Eastern Europe: Essays to Honor Roman Szporluk,* 373–392. Cambridge, 2000.

———. "State Culture and National Identity in a Multi-Ethnic Context: Lemberg, 1772–1914." Ph.D. Diss., University of Michigan, 1999.

Łazuga, Waldemar. *"Rządy polskie w Austrii": Gabinet Kazimierza hr. Badeniego, 1895–1897.* Poznań, 1991.

Loebenstein von Aigenhorst, Egon. "Das Zeremoniell unter Kaiser Franz Joseph." In Eduard Ritter von Steinitz, ed., *Erinnerungen an Franz Joseph I Kaiser von Österreich Apostolischer König von Ungarn.* Berlin, 1930.

Łoziński, Bronisław. *Agenor Hrabia Gołuchowski.* Lwów, 1901.

Lukes, Stephen. *Essays in Social Theory.* London, 1977.

Link, Edith Murr. *The Emancipation of the Austrian Peasant, 1740–1798.* New York, 1949.

Macartney, C. A. *The Habsburg Empire, 1790–1918.* London, 1968.

Magocsi, Paul R. *A History of Ukraine.* Toronto, 1996.

———. "The Kachkovs'kyi Society and the National Revival in Nineteenth-Century East Galicia." *Harvard Ukrainian Studies* 15 (1991): 49–87.

———. "Old Ruthenianism and Russophilism: A New Conceptual Framework for Analyzing National Ideologies in Late 19th Century Eastern Galicia." In Paul Debreczeny, ed., *American Contributions to the Ninth International Congress of Slavists,* Vol. 2: *Literature, Poetics, History.* Columbus, 1983.

Magris, Claudio. *Der Habsburgische Mythos in der österreichischen Literatur.* Salzburg, 1966.

Mark, Rudolf A. *Galizien unter österreichischer Herrschaft. Verwaltung—Kirche—Bevölkerung.* Marburg, 1994.

Markovits, Andrei, and Frank E. Sysyn, eds. *Nationbuilding and the Politics of Nationalism: Essays on Austrian Galicia.* Cambridge, 1982.

Marcus, George, ed. *Rereading Cultural Anthropology.* Durham, 1992.

May, Arthur J. *The Hapsburg Monarchy, 1867–1918.* Cambridge, Mass., 1951.

Mayer, Gottfried. *Österreich als katholische Grossmacht. Ein Traum zwischen Revolution und Liberaler Ära.* Wien, 1989.

McCagg, William O., Jr. *A History of Habsburg Jews, 1670–1918.* Bloomington, 1992.

MacHardy, Karin J. *War, Religion and Court Patronage in Habsburg Austria: The Social and Cultural Dimensions of Political Interaction, 1521–1622.* New York, 2003.

Meissner, Andrzej, ed. *Kultura i oświata wsi.* Rzeszów, 1996.

Melton, James Van Horn. *Absolutism and the Eighteenth-Century Origins of Compulsory Schooling in Prussia and Austria.* Cambridge, 1988.

Motyl, Alexander. "From Imperial Decay to Imperial Collapse: The Fall of the Soviet Empire in Comparative Perspective." In Richard Rudolph and David Good, eds., *Nationalism and Empire: The Habsburg Empire and the Soviet Union,* 15–43. New York, 1992.

Myśliński, Józef. "Prasa polska w Galicji w dobie autonomicznej (1867–1918)." In Jerzy Lojka, ed., *Prasa polska w latach 1864–1918,* 114–176. Warsaw, 1976.

Najdus, Walentyna, *Ignacy Daszyński.* Warszawa, 1988.

———. *Polska Partia Socjalno-Demokratyczna Galicji i Śląska, 1890–1919.* Warszawa, 1983.

———. "The Relation of the Polish Social Democrats in Galicia to the Habsburg Empire and the Austrian Social Democratic Workers Party." In Keith Hitchins, ed., *Studies in East European Social History,* vol. 1. Leiden, 1977.

Narkiewicz, Olga. *The Green Flag: Polish Populist Politics, 1867–1970.* London, 1976.

Nemes, Robert. "The Politics of the Dance Floor: Culture and Civil Society in Nineteenth-Century Hungary." *Slavic Review* 60/4 (2001): 802–823.

Nolte, Claire. "Every Czech a Sokol: Feminism and Nationalism in the Czech Sokol Movement." *Austrian History Yearbook* 24 (1993): 79–100.

Nora, Pierre. *Realms of Memory: The Construction of the French Past.* English-language edition edited by Lawrence Kritzman. New York, 1996–1998.

Niederle, Helmuth A. *"Es war sehr schön, es hat mich sehr gefreut." Kaiser Franz Joseph und seine Untertanen.* Wien, 1987.

Nipperdey, Thomas, *Gesellschaft, Kultur, Theorie.* Göttingen, 1976.

Ozouf, Mona. *Festivals and the French Revolution.* Cambridge, 1988.

Pajakowski, Philip. "The Polish Club and Austrian Parliamentary Politics, 1873–1900." Ph.D. Diss, Indiana University, 1989.

Palairet, Michael. "The Habsburg Industrial Achievement in Bosnia-Hercogovina, 1878–1914: An Economic Spurt That Succeeded?" *Austrian History Yearbook* 24 (1993): 133–152.

Palmer, Alan. *Twilight of the Habsburgs: The Life and Times of Emperor Francis Joseph.* London, 1994.

Pannenkowa, Irena. *Walka Galicji z centralizmem wiedeńskim. Dzieja rezolucji Sejmu galicyjskiego z 24 IX 1868.* Wrocław, 1951.

Partacz, Czesław. *Od Badeniego do Potockiego. Stosunki polsko-ukraińskie w Galicji w latach 1888–1908.* Toruń, 1996.

Pernes, Jiri. *Spiklenci proti jeho velicenstvu: historie tzv. Spiknutí Omladiny v cechách.* Prague, 1988.

Pfandl, Ludwig. "Philipp II. und die Einführung des burgundischen Hofzeremoniells in Spanien." *Historisches Jahrbuch* 58 (1938): 1–33.

Plunkett, John. *Queen Victoria: First Media Monarch.* Oxford, 2003.

Polek, Johann. *Joseph's II Reisen nach Galizien und der Bukowina und ihre Bedeutung für letztere Provinz.* Czernowitz, 1895.

Pollak, Martin. *Nach Galizien. Von Chassiden, Huzulen, Polen und Ruthenen.* Wien and München, 1984.

Press, Volker. "The Habsburg Court as Center of Imperial Government." *Journal of Modern History* 58, Supplement (1986): 23–45.

Promintzer, Petra. "Die Reisen Kaiser Franz Josephs (1848–1867)." Ph.D. Diss., University of Vienna, 1967.

Pulzer, Peter. *The Rise of Political Anti-Semitism in Germany and Austria.* Cambridge, 1988.

Purchla, Jacek. *Krakau unter österreichischer Herrschaft, 1846–1918.* Wien, 1993.

———. "Die Einflüsse Wiens auf die Architekture Lembergs 1772–1918." In Purchla, ed., *Architectura Lwowa XIX wieku.* Cracow, 1997.

Rath, John R. *The Viennese Revolution of 1848.* Austin, 1957.

Redlich, Joseph. *Emperor Francis Joseph of Austria: A Biography.* New York, 1929.

Reifowitz, Ian. *Imagining an Austrian Nation: Joseph Samuel Bloch and the Search for a Multiethnic Austrian Identity, 1846–1919.* New York, 2003.

Representation. Spring, 1989 no. 6. Special Issue on Memory and Counter-Memory. ed. Natalie Zeman Davis and Randof Tarn.

Richards, Thomas. *The Commodity Culture of Victorian England: Advertising and Spectacle, 1851–1914.* Stanford, 1990.

Riesenfellner, Stefan, ed. *Steinernes Bewußtsein. Die öffentliche Repräsentation staatlicher und nationaler Identität Österreichs in seinen Denkmälern.* Wien, 1998.

Robertson, Ritchie, and Edward Timms, eds. *The Habsburg Legacy: National Identity in Historical Perspective.* Edinburgh, 1994.

Röhl, John, ed. *Kaiser, Hof und Staat: Wilhelm II und die deutsche Politik.* Munich, 1987.

———. ed. *Kaiser Wilhelm II: New Interpretations.* New York, 1982.

Rom, Adalbert. "Der Bildungsgrad der Bevölkerung Österreichs und seine Entwicklung seit 1880 mit besonderer Berücksichtigung der Sudeten- und Karpatenländer." *Statistische Monatsschrift* 40 (n.s. 19) (1914).

Rosdolsky, Roman. *Untertan und Staat in Galizien: Die Reformen von Maria Theresia und Joseph II.* Mainz am Rhein, 1992.

Rozenblit, Marsha. *Reconstructing a National Identity: The Jews of Habsburg Austria during World War I.* Oxford and New York, 2001.

———. "The Dilemma of Identity: The Impact of the First World War on Habsburg Jewry." In Ritchie Robertson and Edward Timms, eds. *The Habsburg Legacy: National Identity in Historical Perspective,* 144–157. Edinburgh, 1994.

———. *The Jews of Vienna, 1867–1914: Acculturation and Identity.* Albany, 1983.

Schacter, Daniel, ed. *Memory Distortion: How Minds, Brains and Societies Reconstruct the Past.* Cambridge, 1995.

Scheidl, Inge. "Die Kaiser Franz Josef-Jubiläumskirche in Wien von Viktor Lunt: Der Wettbewerbsverlauf, die Konkurrenzentwürfe und die Baugeschichte." MA Thesis, University of Vienna, 1991.

Schorske, Carl. *Fin-de-siècle Vienna.* New York, 1981.

Schultz, Uwe, ed. *Das Fest.* Munich, 1988.

Shedel, James. "Austria and Its Polish Subjects, 1866–1914: A Relationship of Interests." *Austrian History Yearbook* 19–20/2 (1983–84): 23–41.

———. "The Elusive Fatherland: Dynasty, State, Identity and the Kronprinzenwerk." In Moritz Csáky and Klaus Zeyringer, eds., *Inszenierungen des kollektiven Gedächtnisses.* Innsbruck, 2002.

———. "Emperor, Church, and People: Religion and Dynastic Loyalty during the Golden Jubilee of Franz Joseph." *Catholic Historical Review* 76 (1990): 71–92.

———. "Fin de Siècle or Jahrhundertwende: The Question of an Austrian *Sonderweg.*" In Steven Beller, ed., *Rethinking Vienna 1900.* New York, 2001.

Silber, Margit. "Obersthofmeister Alfred Fürst von Montenuovo. Höfische Geschichte in den beiden letzten Jahrzehnten der österreichisch-ungarischen Monarchie (1897–1916)." Ph.D. Diss., University of Vienna, 1987.

Simons, Thomas W., Jr. "The Peasant Revolt of 1846 in Galicia." *Slavic Review* 30/4 (1971): 795–817.

Sked, Alan. *The Decline and Fall of the Habsburg Empire 1815–1918.* London, 1989.

———. *Historians, the Nationality Question, and the Downfall of the Habsburg Empire.* London, 1981.

Smith, Anthony. *The Ethnic Origins of Nations.* Oxford, 1986.

Sperber, Jonathan. *The European Revolutions, 1848–1851.* Cambridge, 1994.

Springer, Elisabeth. *Geschichte und Kulturleben der Wiener Ringstrasse.* Wiesbaden, 1979.

Stachel, Peter. "An Austrian 'Place of Memory': The Heldenplatz in Vienna as a Historic Symbol and Political Metaphor." In Moritz Csáky and Elena Mannová, eds., *Collective Identities in Central Europe in Modern Times,* 159–178. Bratislava, 1999.

Stauter-Halsted, Keely. *Nation in the Village: The Genesis of National Identity in Austrian Poland, 1848–1914.* Ithaca, 2001.

———. "Patriotic Celebrations in Austrian Poland: The Kosciuszko Centennial and the Formation of Peasant Nationalism." *Austrian History Yearbook* 25 (1994): 79–95.

Steinkellner, Fritz. "Emanzipatorische Tendenzen im christlichen Wiener Frauen-Bund und in der Katholischen Reichsfrauenorganisation Österreichs." In Rudolf G. Ardelt, Wolfgang J.A. Huber, and Anton Staudinger, eds., *Unterdrückung und Emanzipation. Festschrift fur Erika Weinzierl zum 60. Geburtstag,* 55–67. Wien, 1985.

Stekl, Hannes. "Der Wiener Hof in der ersten Hälfte des 19. Jahrhunderts." In Karl Möckl, ed., *Hof und Hofgesellschaft in den deutschen Staaten im 19. und beginnenden 20. Jahrhundert.* Boppard am Rhein, 1990.page numbers

Stickler, Matthias. *Erzherzog Albrecht von Österreich: Selbstverständnis und Politik eines konservativen Habsburgers im Zeitalter Kaiser Franz Josephs.* Husum, 1997.

Stourzh, Gerald. "Ethnic Attribution in Late Imperial Austria: Good Intentions, Evil Consequences." In Ritchie Robertson and Edward Timms, eds. *The Habsburg Legacy: National Identity in Historical Perspective,* 67–83. Edinburgh, 1994.

Strong, George V. "The Austrian Idea: An Idea of Nationhood in the Kingdom and Realms of the Emperor Franz Joseph I." *History of European Ideas* 5/3 (1984).

Subtelny, Orest. "The Habsburg and Russian Empires: Some Comparisons and Contrasts." In Teruyuki Hara and Kimitaka Matsuzato, eds., *Empire and Society: New Approaches to Russian History.* Sapporo, 1997.

———. *Ukraine: A History.* Toronto, 1988.

Sutter, Berthold. *Die Badenischen Sprachen-Verordnungen von 1897.* Graz and Cologne, 1965.

Szapary, Marianne Gräfin. "Carl Graf Grünne Generaladjutant des Kaisers Franz Joseph 1848–1859." Ph.D. Diss., University of Vienna, 1935.

Taborski, Roman. *Polacy w Wiedniu.* Wrocław, 1992.

Tanner, Marie. *The Last Descendant of Aeneas: The Habsburgs and the Mythic Image of the Emperor.* New Haven, 1993.

Taylor, A. J. P. *The Habsburg Monarchy, 1809–1918.* London, 1948.

Telesko, Werner. "Die Wiener historischen Festzüge von 1879 und 1908. Zum Problem der dynastischen Identitätsfindung des Hauses Österreich." *Wiener Geschichtsblätter* 51/3: 133–146.

Thomas, Christiane. "Die Wiener Weltliche Schatzkammer. Verwaltung und Funktion, 1800–1870." Ph.D. Diss., University of Vienna, 1963.

Tinti, Baron Hermann. *Hoffähigkeit. Eine Studie.* 2nd ed. Wien, 1904.

Urbanitsch, Peter. "Pluralist Myth and Nationalist Realities: The Dynastic Myth of the Habsburg Monarchy—a Futile Exercise in the Creation of Identity?" *Austrian History Yearbook* 35 (2004): 101–141.

Vocelka, Karl. *Glanz und Untergang der höfischen Welt. Repräsentation, Reform, und Reaktion im habsburgischen Vielvölkerstaat.* Wien, 2001.

Vogel, Juliane. *Elisabeth von Österreich. Momente aus dem Leben einer Kunstfigur.* Wien, 1992.

Wandruszka, Adam, and Peter Urbanitsch, eds. *Die Habsburgermonarchie 1848–1918,* vol. 3, *Die Völker des Reiches.* Wien, 1980.

———. "Die Historiographie der theresianisch-josephinischen Reformzeit." In Anna Drabek, Richard G. Plaschka, and Wandruszka, eds., *Ungarn und Österreich unter Maria Theresia und Joseph II. Neue Aspekte im Verhältniss der beiden Länder.* Wien, 1982.

Wandycz, Piotr S. *The Lands of Partitioned Poland.* Seattle, 1974.

Wangermann, Ernst. *From Joseph II to the Jacobin Trials.* Westport, Conn., 1969.

Wank, Solomon. "The Disintegration of the Habsburg and Ottoman Empires: A Comparative Analysis." In Karen Dawisha and Bruce Parrott, eds., *The End of Empire? The Transformation fo the USSR in Comparative Perspective,* 94–120. Armonk, 1997.

———. "Some Reflections on the Habsburg Empire and Its Legacy in the Nationalities Question." *Austrian History Yearbook* 28 (1997): 131–146.

Weber, Max. *On Charisma and Institution Building.* Edited by S. N. Eisenstadt. Chicago, 1968.

Wendland, Anna Veronika. *Die Russophilen in Galizien. Ukrainische Konservative zwischen Österreich und Russland, 1848–1915.* Wien, 2001.

————."Die Rückkehr der Russophilen in die ukrainische Geschichte: Neue Aspekte der ukrainischen Nationsbildung in Galizien, 1848–1914." *Jahrbücher für Geschichte Osteuropas* 49 (2001): 178–99.

Wereszycki, Henryk. *Pod berłem Habsburgów.* Kraków, 1975.

————. *Historia Austrii.* Wrocław, 1986.

Werner, Karl Ferdinand, ed. *Hof, Kultur, und Politik im 19. Jahrhundert.* Bonn, 1985.

Wheatcroft, Andrew. *The Habsburgs: Embodying Empire.* London, 1995.

Wilenz, Sean, ed. *Rites of Power: Symbolism, Ritual and Politics since the Middle Ages.* Philadelphia, 1985.

Wingfield, Nancy. "Pitched Battles in Public Places: How the Bohemian Lands Became Czech, 1880–1948." Unpublished manuscript.

Wistrich, Robert. *The Jews of Vienna in the Age of Franz Joseph.* New York, 1989.

Wortman, Richard S. *Scenarios of Power: Myth and Ceremony in Russian Monarchy.* vols. 1 and 2. Princeton, 1995, 2000.

————. "Rule by Sentiment: Alexander II's Journeys through the Russian Empire." *American Historical Review* 95 (1990): 745–71.

Wróbel, Piotr. "The Jews of Galicia under Austrian-Polish Rule, 1869–1918." *Austrian History Yearbook* 25 (1994): 97–138.

Wyka, Kazimierz. *Teka Stańczyka na tle historii Galicji w latach 1849–1869.* Wrocław, 1951.

Żbikowski, Andrzej. *Zydzi krakowscy i ich gmina w latach 1869–1919.* Warszawa, 1994.

Zeller, Ingrid. "Die Tagebücher der Flugeladjutante Kaiser Franz Josephs I." Ph.D. Diss., University of Vienna, 1969.

Zintzen, Christiane. "Das Kronprinzenwerk. Die östreichische-ungarische Monarchie in Wort und Bild. Ein deliberater Rund- und Umgang mit einem enzyklopädischen Textkosmos." In Klaus Amann, Hubert Lengauer, and Karl Wagner, eds. *Literarisches Leben in Österreich 1848–1890,* 843–858. Vienna, 2000.

————. *Die Österreichische-ungarische Monarchie in Wort und Bild. Aus dem "Kronprinzenwerk" des Erzherzog Rudolf.* Vienna, 1999.

Żolger, Ivan. *Der Hofstaat des Hauses Österreich.* Wien, 1917.

INDEX

Page numbers in italics refer to illustrations.

1851 Inspection tour: 1880 inspection tour, compared to, 43; accommodation for emperor, 38–39; armed forces, role of, 39; authority over planning, 37–38; court etiquette, adherence to, 38; evaluation of, 42–46; newspapers used to promote, 39–40, 45; procession during, 40–42

1854 Wedding celebrations, 54, 79, 116, 121

1868 Inspection tour, abandoned, 46–51

1873 World Exhibition in Vienna, 54, 89, 146, 165, 168, 172

1879 Silver Wedding Celebrations, 29, 54, 67–68, 79, 99, 116, 121, 131; the Makart Procession, 6, 85, 111, 147–148, 156, 161

1880 Inspection tour, 8–9; 1851 inspection tour, compared to, 43; Cracow, celebrations in, 60–64; Lemberg, celebrations in, 65–70; planning for, 55–57; press coverage, 58–60, 71; public interest, reasons for, 53–54; security for, 56–57

1888 Jubilee celebrations, 147–148; Kaiser Jubilee Exhibition in Vienna, 166

1894 Galician Provincial Exhibition (Lemberg), 72–76

1896 Millennium Exhibition, 75

1898 Jubilee celebrations, 83–88; architectural monuments, *92*, 118–119; armed forces, role of, 97–101, *101*; Catholic hierarchy, message from, 94–97; charitable contributions, 101–102, 116–118; of Christian Social Party, 152–155; of Vienna Christian Women's Association, 162–163; of Christian Social Workers' Association, 162–163; festival of the peoples, 162; focus on the emperor, 9; by Jews, 141–142; Lueger, Karl, role of, 168–169, *169;* partisan advantage, used for, 9;

planning for, 148; press coverage of, 157–159, 160–161; publications of commemoration, 105–111; Reichsrat session, boycott of, 177; religious services, 140–142; schoolchildren in, 103, 155, 156–158, 159, *159;* theatrical plays, 132, 133; town programs, 138–144. *See also* 1898 Kaiser Jubilee Exhibition in Vienna

1898 Kaiser Jubilee Exhibition in Vienna, 164–165, *165*, *169*; all-Austrian exhibition, abandoned plans for, 166–167; Bosnian Pavilion, 170, *171;* opening ceremonies, 169–170, *169*, *170;* press coverage of, *172–173;* Vienna Pavilion, 167, *168. See also* 1898 Jubilee celebrations

1908 Jubilee celebrations, 177

1908 *Kaiser-Huldigungs-Festzug* in Vienna, 179–180, *179*

Abrahamowicz, Dawid, 66

Accommodations for emperor, during 1851 inspection tour, 38–39

Advertisements for jubilee celebrations, 120, *120*, 125, *125*

Agricultural Society, 66

Ahnenprobenexaminator. See Imperial court, structure of, under Franz Joseph

Albrecht, Archduke 95, 98, 150; monument to, 98–99

Alcohol monopoly (*propinacya*), 35

Alexander II, tsar of Russia, 49

Allegemeine Theaterzeitung, 27

Anti-Semitism: of Christian Social Party, 146, 153, 154–155; of Christian Social Vienna Women's Association, 162, 163; of Christian Social Workers' Association, 163–164; Galicia, riots in, 177; on Vienna city council, 153, 154–155

Apfelthaler, Heinrich, 154

Architectural monuments: for 1898 Jubilee celebrations, 92, 118–119; for Victoria (Queen of England), 119. *See also* Portrait busts of the imperial couple

Armed forces: during 1851 inspection tour, role of, 39; during 1898 jubilee celebrations, 97–101, *100*

Arndt, Ernst Moritz, 147

Assassination attempt on Franz Joseph, 54

Association of Women Writers and Artists, 136

Auersperg, Karl von, 49, 94

Ausgleich (Compromise) (1867), 3

Austrian People's Publications Association (ÖVV), publications of, 133–135

Austro-German liberals, and erosion of church privileges, 94

Authors, patriotic, 129–138, *132*

Bach, Alexander (Interior Minister), 37, 46

Badeni, Kazimierz: as Galician *Statthalter*, 72; on suffrage expranison, 81–82; and the confirmation of Karl Lueger, 148; language ordinances of 81–82, 149, 177; and the jubilee exhibition, 167–168

Bánffy, Baron Dezsö, 92

Baroque altar in Vienna, 13, *14*

Berger, Alfred Freiherr von, 132, 133

Birthday celebrations: for emperors, 24; for Franz Joseph, 24–25, 181–182

Bobrzyński, Michael, 55

Boehringer, J. F., 128

Bohemia: 1891 exhibition, 75; nationalist conflicts, 7; and the burial of Elisabeth

Boyer, John, 4

Catholicism: in Galicia, 34; Habsburg court, importance in, 12–13; hierarchy, message from, 94–97; Joseph II, and erosion of church privileges, 16–17; reform movement of Jansenism, 16; rituals of, 13, 15, 26–32; Habsburg expressions of. *See also* Piety

Charisma, of Franz Joseph, 182–183

Charitable contributions: 1888 jubilee commemoration, 147–148; 1898 jubilee commemoration, 101–102, 116–118; by Franz Joseph, 116, 131; by Jewish communities, 141; by the public, 116–118

Charles V, 15

Charles VI, 13, 15

Charles VII, 15

Chlędowski, Kazimierz, 57–58

Christian Social Party, 4; anti-Semitism in, 146, 153, 154–155; Empress Elisabeth as martyr, 91; loyalty, as a political weapon, 149, 150, 151–152; partisan advantage of jubilee celebrations, 9; schoolchildren in orchestrated popular patriotism, 155, 156–158, 159

Christian Social Workers' Association, anti-Semitism in, 162–164

Cisleithania, 2, 7; re-formation of government, 54. *See also* Vienna

Cohen, Gary, 3

Cole, Laurence, 7

Commemorative Pamphlet for the Soldiers on the Occasion of the Fiftieth Jubilee of His Majesty Franz Joseph I, 99–101

Compromise (1867), 3

Concordia (literary association), 135–137

Constitution: legal oversight of commercial use of imperial images, 120–124, 129; reforms to, 46–51

Constitutional power of European rulers, 5

Constructivist theories, social, 4

Consumer products, jubilee-related: legal oversight of commercial use of imperial images, 120–124, 129; marketing channels, criticism of, 125–126; publications, criticism of, 127; types of (*see individual items*); Victoria (Queen of England), popularity and, 114

Corpus Christi procession, 6, 8, 13, 26–32, *31*, 54, 78, 94, 97, 115, 141

Court etiquette, adherence to, 38

Cracow: 1851 inspection tour, 40–41; 1880 inspection tour, 60–64; 1898 jubilee program, 140; Stańczyks' program, and historical school, 55

Croatia, and Franz Joseph, 7

Crowning of Franz Joseph in 1867 in Budapest, 50–51

Czas (newspaper): 1868 (abandoned) tour, conspiracy theory on, 49; 1880 inspection tour, 53, 58–59, 60, 64; 1894

Galician Provincial Exhibition, 73;
  Franz Joseph as Polish king, 62
Czech-German street violence, 7

Death and internment of Franz Joseph,
  175–176, *176*
Diet, devolution of power to, 47
Dilo (The Deed), 65, 68; confiscation of
  paper in 1894, 74
District captains, reporting of inspection
  tours, 39, 42, 44
Dobrzański, Jan, 67
Dual monarchy of Austria-Hungary, 7,
  50, 180
Dynastic celebrations: in Austia, 6; in
  European states, 5, 6; in Habsburg,
  3; inspection tours (*see under year of
  celebration*); jubilee celebrations (*see
  under year of celebration*); popular
  support for, 113–115; World War I and
  demise of, 182
Dynastic patriotism of the Austrians, 1–2,
  3; schooling in, 53–54
Dziennik Polski, 43, 59

Easter week foot-washing. *See* Foot wash-
  ing ceremony
Edicts of Toleration of Joseph II, 17, 36
Elisabeth (Empress of Austria), 54, *93, 128*;
  assassination of, 88–89, 119, 128–129,
  162; mourning ceremonies for, 89–94;
  rejection of designated roles, 89
The Emperor's Dream (Thun-Salm),
  86–87, 132, 134, 181
Faltin, Kamil, 122
February Patent (1861), 46
Ferdinand (emperor), 11, 19; orchestrated
  abdication of, 27
Ferdinand II (emperor), 12
Ferdinand III (emperor), 12
Ferdinand, Archduke of Toscana, 134
Fifth Austrian United Shooting Festival
  (*Bundesschiessen*), 161
First Arciere Body-Guard, 20
Fischhof, Adolf, 151
Foot washing ceremony, 13, 15, 29–30, *30*
Francisco-Josephine era, 143
Frankel, Hubert, 169–170
Franz Ferdinand, 77, 83–84, 95, 96, 105,
  161

Franz I, 17, 19; imperial accommodation
  for, 39
Franz Joseph (emperor): ascent to throne,
  11; Catholic piety of, 78, 86, 104, 112,
  116, 133, 182; crowning of, 50–51;
  death and internment of, 175–176,
  176; Edicts of Toleration, 17, 36; Germanness of, 180–181; imperial court,
  structure of, 19–24, 25; Jewish community, identification with, 141–142;
  marriage celebrations, 79; personal
  communications by, 45; poetry on,
  135, 137; Polish king, portrayal as, 62;
  wedding celebrations, 79, 147
*Franz Joseph and His Times: A Cultural-
  Historical Look at the Francisco-Josephine Epoch*, 105, 106–108, *107,
  108, 110*
Franz Karl, 27
Franz Stephen of Lorraine, 15, 16, *18*
Frederick II, 15
Fremden-Blatt, 101; on reconciling Ruthenians and Poles, 72

Galicia: anti-Semitic riots, 177; constitutional reform (1868), 49–50; devolution of power to diet (Sejm), 47; diets,
  provincial, 46; ethnic diversity of, 34;
  Franz Joseph, personal communications on, 45; governors of, 36, 37; imperial celebrations in, 8; imperial suite
  (1851), 37–38; inspection tours of (*see
  under year of celebration*); newspapers, official (*see Gazeta Lwowska*);
  peasant reforms in, 35, 36; Polish
  uprising (1846 and 1848), 36–37. *See
  also* 1851 Inspection tour
Galicia (*continued*)
Gartenberg, Moses, 117
Gazeta Lwowska (newspaper), 39–40, 57,
  101; 1894 Galician Provincial Exhibition, 73
Gazeta Narodowa (newspaper): on 1868
  abandoned tour, 49; on 1880 tour,
  59–60, 67; theatrical presentation in
  the Lemberg theatre, 67
Geertz, Clifford, 3, 33, 182
Geheime Räte. See Imperial court, structure of, under Franz Joseph
German-Czech street violence, 7

Germanness of Franz Joseph, 180–181
Gessmann, Alberg, 151–152, 163
Goluchowski, Agenor (Governor of
Galicia), 37, 39; and 1868, 46–50; and
Mamelukes, 54; and October Diploma,
46; and Polinization of Galician ad-
ministration, 59; resignation of (1851),
43, 48
Goluchowski, Agenor (the Younger),
85–86, 88, 93, 102
Good Emperor, legend of the, 35, 37, 44
Greek Catholics in Galicia, 34, 35, 36, 42,
56, 65, 68, 69, 70, 73, 139
Grocholski, Kazimierz, 47
Grünne, Carl (Graf), 37, 46; reorganiza-
tion of court, 19–21

Habsburg Monarchy, 2
Habsburg *Sonderweg*, 3–7
Halyczanin, confiscation of newspaper
(1894), 74
Hamann, Brigitte, 111–112
Hardegg, Dominik, 165
Helfert, Joseph Alexander von, 134–135
Henop, C., 117
Herrengasse, commemoration of failed
revolution (of 1848–49), 150–152
Hirsch, Baroness Clara, 117
Hoeger, Karl, 151
Hofburgwache. See Imperial court, struc-
ture of, under Franz Joseph
Hofchargen. See Imperial court, structure
of, under Franz Joseph
Hofdienste. See Imperial court, structure
of, under Franz Joseph
Hoffmann, Josef, 108, 110, *110*, 111
Hoflager. See Accommodations for
emperor
Hofstäbe. See Imperial court, structure of,
under Franz Joseph
Hohenzollern emperors, 5
Horowitz, C., 141
Hungary: constitutional reform in,
46–47, 50; crowning as Hungarian
king, 50–51; and dispute over burial
of Elisabeth, 90–93, 180; and Franz
Joseph, 7; Millennium Exhibition
(1896), 75; nobles in imperial guard,
20; revolution of 1848, 11. *See also*
Dual Monarchy

Illumination cards, 143
Illuminations 1880: 53; 1894: 73; 1898 in
Vienna: 124, 153, 154, 164, 172; 1898
local illuminations: 138, 140, 142; 1908
in Galicia: 143; 1908 in Vienna: 178
Imperial court: absolutist, 15; of Maria
Theresa, 15–16; structure of, under
Franz Joseph, 19–24, 25
Inspection tours. *See* under year of cel-
ebration
Insurance funds as jubilee charities,
117–118
Iron Ring coalition, 51, 54, 76

Jansenism, 16
Jaszi, Oscar, 6
Jewish community: 1898 Jubilee celebrations, 141–142; and anti-Semitic riots,
177; citizenship, recognition of, 36,
67; Franz Joseph, identification with,
141–142; in Galicia, 34; tavern owners
and alcohol monopoly, 35; in Vienna,
145–146
Joint Army. *See* Armed forces
Joseph II, *18*, 26; court etiquette, position
of Church in state, reform of, 16–17;
Edicts of Toleration, 17, 36; Galicia,
inspection tours of, 34; peasant and
Church reforms in Galicia, 36; military
attire of, 39, 97; image among Ruthe-
nians of, 70; and the 1898 jubilee play,
85–86
Jubilee celebrations. *See under year of
celebration*
Kachkovs'kyi Society, 65, 69, 70
Kaiser Jubilee and Fifth Austrian United
Shooting Festival (*Bundesschiessen*),
161
Kaiser Jubilee Church, 92
Kaiserblatt, 135–138
Kaiser-Jubilee-Poetry-Book, 135
Kelly, T. Mills, 7
Kempen-Fichtenstamm, Johann (police
minister), 46
Kieniewicz, Stefan, 35
Kitsch industry. *See* Consumer products,
jubilee-related
Klobukowski, Ánton, 58–60, 71
Klotzberg, Emerich, 153
Kohler, Julius, 123

Kossak, Juliusz, 61
Kovals'kyi, Vasyl, 69
Koźmian, Stanisław, 55
Kronawetter, Ferdinand, 151
Krupp, Arthur, 118, 143
Kübeck, Karl Friedrich von, 12
Kundrat, Joseph von, distribution of funds
   to petitioners, 68
Kurjer Lwowski (newspaper): confiscation
   of paper (1894), 74; peasant political
   movement, role in, 75

Lands and Kingdoms Represented in the
   Reichsrat. *See* Cisleithania
Laurencic, Julius (patriotic writer), 135,
   137–138
Lefler, Heinrich, 110, *110*, 136, *136*
Lemberg Temple, visit by Franz Joseph,
   67
Lemberg: 1851 inspection tour, 41–42;
   1880 inspection tour, 65–70; 1894
   Galician Provincial Exhibition, 72–76;
   1898 jubilee program, 139–140; di-
   versity of population, 65; newspapers
   of, 65; Polish autonomy, transition
   during, 65
Leopold I (emperor), 12, 13, 15
Leopold II (emperor), 26
Liechtenstein, Karl Fürst von und zu, 21,
   22, 24
Liechtenstein, Rudolf Fürst von und zu,
   84–85.
Literacy rates, and growth in commemo-
   rative publications, 128
Lobkowitz, Georg, 92
Lodomeria, 34
Loebenstein von Aigenhorst, Heinrich, 71,
   83; and the burial of Elisabeth, 92–93
Loewenstein, Rabbi Bernard, 56
Lower Austrian Trade Association (*Nieder-
   österreichischer Gewerbe-Verein*), 166
Łoziński, Władysław, 57, 58
Luccheni, Luigi, 88
Lueger, Karl: 1898 Kaiser Jubilee Ex-
   hibition, role in, 168–169, *169*; and
   the assassination of Elisabeth, 91;
   Christian Social Party and anti-Semi-
   tism, 145–146; festival of the peoples,
   162; Franz Joseph hesitant to confirm,
   142, 148; and 1880 imperial birthday,

149; and March Martyrs, 150–152; opposition to other political parties, 164;
   partisan advantage, use of the jubilee
   celebrations for, 9; schoolchildren in
   orchestrated popular patriotism, 155,
   156–158, 159; Vienna, mayor of,
   148–149

Mahler, Gustav, 84
Majer, Józef, 55
Makart, Hans (The Makart Procession), 6,
   85, 111, 147–148, 156, 161
Mamelukes, 47, 54
Mandl, Ignaz, 149
The Man Without Qualities (Musil), 84
Maria Theresa (empress) 15–16, *18*, 20;
   unveiling of monument for, 79–80,
   80, 81
Maria Valerie, 89, 105
Medals, commemorative, 99, *100*,
   102–103
Military. *See* Armed forces
Modernization process, 4
Monarchial celebrations. *See* Dynastic
   celebrations
Mondel, Friedrich von, 56, 67, 71
Montenuovo, Alfred Fürst von, 84–85,
   175
Moscophiles. *See* Russophiles in Lemberg
Moser, Koloman, 108, 109, 111, 126
Mucha, Alphonse, 110, 111
Musil, Robert, 84

Naprzód, confiscation of paper (1894), 74
Naske, Adolph Cark, 128
Naske, Adolph Cark, 128
National Populists, 65; 68
National Populists, 65; 68
National-Democratic Society, 47
Nationalism, 4
Nauka, 65
Naumovych, Ivan, 65, 68
Naumovych, Ivan, 65, 68
Neoabsolutism: centralized bureaucracy
   of, 12; imperial court under, 37; news-
   papers used to promote, 39–40, 45
Newspapers. *See individual papers*
Nobility, hereditary: during 1851 inspec-
   tion tour, 38; and constitutional reform,
   46–47; homage to the hunters, 161;

Nobility (*continued*)
Poland-Lithuania, privileges in, 34–35; subordination of, 45
Nowa Reforma, confiscation of paper (1894), 74

Oberstallmeister. See Imperial court, structure of, under Franz Joseph
Obersthofchargen. See Imperial court, structure of, under Franz Joseph
Obersthofmarschall. See Imperial court, structure of, under Franz Joseph
Obersthofmeister. See Imperial court, structure of, under Franz Joseph
Oberstkämmerer. See Imperial court, structure of, under Franz Joseph
October Diploma (1860), 46
On the Second of December (ÖVV), 134
Order of the Star-Cross, 23
Orders of the House of Habsburg, 23–24
Ossolineum, the Polish library, 42
Österreichischer Volksfreund (newspaper), 28–29
Our Monarchy (Laurencic), 137–138
ÖVV. See Austrian People's Publications Association

Pan-Germans, and the Maria Theresa Monument, 79–81; and parliamentary obstruction, 82; criticism of the jubilee, 125, 127, 157–158; and anti-Semitism, 136, 149, 160, 163, 172; and the commemoration of the 1848 revolutions, 151, 152
Partisan advantage, use of jubilee celebrations for, 9
Patriotism. See Dynastic patriotism of the Austrians
Peasant culture, portrayal in 1880 inspection tour, 62–63, 66, 69–70
Peasant reforms, in Galicia, 35, 36
Peasants: in Galicia, 35; political organization of, 74–75; taxation of, 35
Personal communications of Franz Joseph, 45; 1868 abandoned inspection tour, 50; on national separatism, 77
Petitions submitted to Franz Joseph, 43, 44, 67–68, 69; during World War I, 182
Pietas Austriaca, 12–13, 16, 27, 30
Piety, Catholic expressions of, 12–19, 78,
86, 116, 182; and Franz Joseph, *see* Franz Joseph, Catholic piety of
Plappart von Leenheer, August Freiherr, 84–86
Podhalicz, Władysław, chocolate Kaiser as patriotic gift, 1, *1*
Poetry acclaiming Franz Joseph, 135, 137
Poland, partition of, 34
Poles: autonomy in Galicia, 47–48, 54; conservatives, manipulation by, 8–9; uprising in Galicia (1846 and 1848), 36–37
Popiel, Paweł, evaluation of 1851 inspection tour, 42–43
Portrait busts of the imperial couple, *111*, 121, 122–124, *122*, *123*, 125, 127, *127*, 130, *130*; by Wahliss, Ernst, 124
Postcards, jubilee, *126*
Potocki, Adam: and 1880 inspection tour, 56–57; devolution of power, address on, 47; imprisonment of, 43; Polish autonomy in Galicia, 47–48
Potocki, Alfred, 55, 56, 57, 60, 66, 67, 69, 71
Press censorship, 39; during 1880 inspection tours, 57–58; during 1894 Galician Provincial Exhibition, 73
Press coverage: of 1894 Galician Provincial Exhibition, 72, 73; of 1898 jubilee celebrations, 101, 102, 157–159, 160–161; 1898 Kaiser Jubilee Exhibition in Vienna, 172–173; Empress Elisabeth, funeral of, 90–91
Prix, Johann, 148
Prosvita (Enlightenment), 65, 69
Protests against creation of Austria-Hungary, 47
Przeglad Polski (newspaper), 55; relationship between Galicia and the monarchy, 71
Przyjaciel Ludu (newspaper), and peasant political movement, 75
Pszczółka (newspaper), and peasant political movement, 75
Publications, commemorative: at 1898 jubilee celebrations, 105–111; by armed forces, 99–101; by Austrian People's Publications Association (ÖVV), 133–135; Concordia (literary association), 135–137, *136*, *138*; criticism of,

127, 133; literacy rates and growth of
audience, 128

Rail system used in imperial tours, 38, 48,
57, 73
Raymond, Franz von (court official), 44
Reichsrat, 46–47, 50; Austro-German
liberals in, 54; boycott of 1898 jubilee
session, 164, 177; Polish democrats
in, 59; Polish conservatives in, 73, 76;
suffrage to, 53
Religion: Catholicism in Habsburg Court,
12–13; of Galicians, 34, 35
Revolutions of 1848–49, 3, 11
Ringstrasse, 147, 155–156, ??
Roman Catholics: in Galicia, 34; in
Lemberg, 65
Romanov tsars, 5
Rudolf I (emperor), 13
Rudolf, Crown Prince, 61, 89, 90, 94, 98,
177, 179
Russophiles in Lemberg, 65
Ruthenian Council, 68
Ruthenian National Institute, 42, 69, 70
Ruthenians: 1880 tour, national culture
during, 68–70; in Galicia, 34, 35; in
Lemberg, 65; loyalty of, 41–42

Sapieha, Adam, 66, 73, *74*
Schönerer, Georg von, 79–80, 82, 95, 157,
160, 177, 183
School system: 1898 jubilee celebrations,
use of schoolchildren in, 103; 1908
jubilee celebrations, use of schoolchil-
dren in, 178; patriotic publications,
distribution of, 125, 129–130, 131,
162; popular patriotism, orchestration
of, 155, 156–158, 159, *159*; theatrical
plays during jubilee celebrations, 132
Schuh, Karl, 153
Schwarzenberg, Felix von, 11, 12, 43
Security: for 1851 inspection tour, 39; for
1880 inspection tour, 56–57
Sejm. *See* Diet
Separatism and lack of civic education in
patriotism, 6
Serfdom in Galicia, 35
Shedel, James, 3
Slovo (*The Word*), 65, 68
Smith, Anthony, 4

Smolka, Franciszek, 47
Smolle, Leon (patriotic writer), 129–131
Social constructivist theories of nations, 4
Social Democracy, 82; in Galicia: 73–74,
76; in Vienna: 82, 91, 143, 146, 149,
150–152, 156–158, 160, 164, 173, 177
Solferino, and failure of neoabsolutism,
46
Sonderweg. See Habsburg *Sonderweg*
Souvenirs, monarchical. *See* Consumer
products, jubilee-related
Stadion, Franz, 11; as Governor of Galicia
and peasant reforms, 36
Stamps, jubilee, *126*
Stańczyk political grouping, 54–55; dur-
ing 1880 inspection tour of Galicia,
61, 70–72
Stelzl, Alois, use of imperial name in
products, 121–122
Stojałowski, Stanisław, 74–75
Strobach, Joseph, 148
Supreme Ruthenian Council, 36, 41–42
Szlachta. See Nobility, hereditary
Szujski, Józef, 55

Taaffe, Eduard, 49; Iron Ring coali-
tion, 51, 54, 59, 76, 81; and the 1880
inspection tour, 57, 183
Tarnowski, Stanisław, 55; Galicia and the
monarchy, relationship between, 71
Taxation of peasants, 35
Theatrical plays at 1898 jubilee celebra-
tions, 83–88, 132, 133
Thun und Hohenstein, Count Franz
Anton von, 82, 85–86, 88, 93, 118,
124, 167
Thun-Salm, Christiane (Gräfin), 86, 87,
132, 134, 181
Toleration, Joseph II's Edicts of, 17, 36
Tomola, Leopold, 153, 163
Transport facilities for imperial tours: in
1851, 38; in 1861, 48; in 1880, 57; in
1894, 73
Trinity Monument in Vienna's Graben,
13, *14*
Turkish siege of Vienna, 13
Tyrol, 7

Ukrainians. *See* Ruthenians
United Left, 149

Victoria (Queen of England), 5; architectural monuments for, 119; children, role in celebrations, 155, 157; jubilee products and popularity, 114; and jubilees, 82–82, 114, 120, 122, 142–143

Vienna Christian Women's Association (*Christlicher Wiener Frauenbund*): 1898 jubilee celebrations, 149–150, 162–163; Empress Elisabeth as martyr, 91

Vienna: 1873 World Exhibition, 54; 1888 Jubilee celebrations, 147–148, 166; 1898 Christian Social jubilee, 152–155; 1898 Kaiser Jubilee Exhibition, 164–165, *165, 169;* 1908 Kaiser-Huldigungs-Festzug, 179–180, *179*; anti-Semitism in, 146, 153, 154–155; architecture and imperial celebrations, 8, 13, *14*, 92; Jews in, 145–146; *Konditorei* Demel, 1; partisan advantage, use of the jubilee celebrations for, 9; transformation during reign of Franz Joseph, 137; Turkish siege of, 13; wedding anniversary celebrations for Franz Joseph, 147. *See* Ringstrasse

Viribus Unitis: The Book about the Kaiser, 105–106, *109–110*

Vogelsang, Karl von, 81

Vogler, Ludwig, 150, 153

Wagner, Otto, 111, *111*, 137, 147

Wähner, Theodor, 153

Wawel Castle, 41, 43, 61–62

Wedding celebrations of Franz Joseph and Elisabeth of Bavaria: in 1854, 79; 1879 anniversary, 147

Wiener Allgemeine Zeitung (newspaper), success of 1880 inspection tour, 71

Wiener Zeitung (newspaper), 39; 1880 inspection tour, details of, 64; 1898 jubilee celebrations, 101, 102–103, *103*

Wieniec (newspaper), and peasant political movement, 75

Wilczek, Graf Hans, 179

Windischgrätz, Alfred, 72

Wingfield, Nancy, 7

Wodzicki, Ludwik, 55

Wolf, Karl Hermann, 151, 157

World Exhibition in Vienna (1873), 54, 89, 146, 165, 168, 172

World War I, demise of imperial celebrations, 182

Ziemialkowski, Florian, 47

Żolger, Ivan, 19

Zwiazek Chłopski (newspaper), peasant political movement, 75

Zwiazek Stronnictwa Chopskiego. See Peasants, political organization of

Zyblikiewicz, Mikołaj, 55, 61